NO SWORD TO BURY

JAPANESE AMERICANS IN HAWAI'I DURING WORLD WAR II

In the series

Asian American History and Culture

edited by Sucheng Chan, David Palumbo-Liu, and Michael Omi

NO SWORD TO BURY

JAPANESE AMERICANS

IN HAWAI`I

DURING WORLD WAR II

Franklin Odo

 Temple University Press

PHILADELPHIA

Temple University Press, Philadelphia 19122
Copyright © 2004 by Temple University
All rights reserved
Published 2004
Printed in the United States of America

⊗ The paper used in this publication meets the requirements of
the American National Standard for Information Sciences—Permanence
of Paper for Printed Library Materials, ANSI Z39.48-1984

Library of Congress Cataloging-in-Publication Data
Odo, Franklin.
   No sword to bury : Japanese Americans in Hawai`i during World War II /
Franklin Odo.
      p. cm. — (Asian American history and culture)
   Includes bibliographical references and index.
   ISBN 1-59213-207-3 (cloth : alk. paper) — ISBN 1-59213-270-7 (pbk. : alk. paper)
    1. Japanese Americans—Hawaii. 2. Hawaii—Ethnic relations. 3. Pearl Harbor
(Hawaii), Attack on, 1941. 4. World War, 1939–1945—Participation, Japanese
American. I. Title.
D753.8.O36 2003
305.895′60969′09041—dc21
                                         2003053948

2 4 6 8 9 7 5 3 1

This book
is dedicated to
Enid

Contents

Introduction
The Making of a Model Minority

Very early on the morning of December 7, 1941, Akira Otani was helping prepare the banners, flowers, and food for the gala reopening of his family's fish market in downtown Honolulu. But the festivities would have to wait—for years, it turned out—because the Japanese Imperial Navy had just bombed the United States into World War II. "I was scared. You know, I didn't know what to do. Of course, the radio announcer was very excited and we looked toward Pearl Harbor, where there was nothing but black smoke; . . . you finally realize that it was war and we were being attacked. I started driving home, but I couldn't drive because I shook so much. I was nervous and scared and—but I made it back home. . . . I wasn't thinking about anything, just trying to get home."[1]

Soon after eight o'clock in the morning, radio announcers issued an urgent call for all members of the University of Hawai`i Reserved Officers' Training Corps (ROTC) to report for duty. Akira Otani was one of several hundred undergraduates, many of them second-generation Japanese Americans, who donned uniforms and made their way to the armory on the campus in Manoa valley overlooking Honolulu. Amid frantic rumors that Japanese paratroopers had landed on St. Louis Heights, adjacent to the campus, Sergeant Bob Hogan issued each youngster an old Springfield

.30-06 rifle and a single clip with five rounds. The boys assembled in formation and marched off anticipating combat.

Few of these undergraduates had ever fired a weapon, and they clung to their rifles with excitement and terror. At 4:30 on that Sunday afternoon, when Governor Joseph B. Poindexter turned the territorial government over to General Walter Short, martial law was declared and the army assumed control. The ROTC was called in from the hills to form the Hawaii Territorial Guard (HTG) and was augmented by volunteers; by nightfall its thirty-five officers and 370 men were armed and dispatched to guard reservoirs, power plants, hospitals, and other critical areas, freeing regular army troops to defend against a possible invasion.

No one seemed concerned about the large numbers of Japanese Americans in the ROTC or the HTG. The fear of invasion was widespread; anyone willing to fight was embraced. The large community of Japanese Americans, including the immigrants (*issei*), their children (*nisei*), and a growing number of the third-generation (*sansei*), totaled about 160,000, the largest single ethnic group in the islands, comprising nearly 40 percent of the total population of Hawai`i.

Within two weeks of the attack, General Walter Short and Admiral Husband Kimmel, held responsible for the disaster at Pearl, were replaced by General Delos Emmons and Admiral Chester Nimitz. Emmons, who became commander of the army's Hawaiian Department and military governor of the territory, had serious reservations about the presence of so many armed nisei. And although they had been defending vital installations for a full month, presumably against sabotage from their own ethnic kind, the absence of incidents generated suspicion rather than trust or confidence. Worse, mounting anti-Japanese paranoia in the continental United States made it increasingly difficult to maintain racial peace in the Hawaiian Islands.

This book tells the story of Japanese Americans rejected by the U.S. government as unfit for war service who responded by volunteering to perform manual labor for one year. Most of the 169 members of the Varsity Victory Volunteers, also called the Triple V or the V-V-V, later went on to combat in the famed 442d Regimental Combat Team in Europe or as Japanese-language experts in the Military Intelligence Service.

The VVV was the leading wedge of a strategy that culminated in two related but distinct transformations in post–World War II America. The first was the establishment of a radically new multicultural democracy in Hawai`i, liberated from the stranglehold of an entrenched white oligarchy. The second was the incorporation of Japanese American "success" into what has since become widely known as the "model minority" thesis.

The United States had centered its collective animus on Japan from the earliest years of the twentieth century until shortly after the end of World War II—a hostility returned from the western rim of the Pacific. In the decades leading up to World War II, the United States and Japan each made clear its determination to exclude, marginalize, and demonize the other as an enemy "race."[2] Japanese immigrants and their children in the United States were subjected to numerous acts of racism directed against them because of their ancestry.

Partly as a result of this history and their relative numbers in Hawaii's population, Japanese Americans played a central role in the prosecution of the war and the creation of post–World War II Hawai`i. On the west coast of the United States, however, Japanese Americans numbered only about 120,000, much less than one percent of the population and easily scapegoated. Mass evictions and forced removal to inland concentration camps were the result.

Such draconian measures were not practicable in Hawai`i, where the Japanese community was older, much larger, and more solidly entrenched in the local society. Perhaps more to the point, Japanese Americans comprised more than one-half of the skilled labor force and so were indispensable to the general economic well-being of the territory, as well as to the successful prosecution of the war. Further, this was a relatively well educated work force.

Because Hawai`i was the command post of the Pacific war, it would have been disastrous to implement repressive policies that could have imprisoned the large Japanese American community. The effort to do so would have consumed enormous amounts of precious resources and labor precisely when Japanese troops were advancing rapidly across the Pacific. Worst of all, this strategy might well have turned one-third of the population into disgruntled residents or enemy sympathizers. Resolving the "Japanese question," then, soon became the single most important issue for wartime Hawai`i.[3]

This resolution was to be no mean feat; there was pressure from President Franklin Roosevelt and his aides to lock up all Japanese Americans, and Hawaii's military governor sometimes had to circumvent orders to avoid doing just that. At the same time, the army and civilian leaders had to maintain enough discipline over the Japanese American population to placate the rising tide of anti-Japanese hostility, not only from the white, or haole, community but from the Chinese, Filipinos, and Koreans, whose ancestral homelands were being ravaged by Japanese invaders.

It was clear to both military and civilian leaders in Hawai`i that a workable system of racial justice was required and that careful consideration had to be given to the nature of race relations and the "place" Japanese Americans would occupy after the end of hostilities. Thus, the VVV became a crucial weapon in the strategy to reposition the Japanese American community into the Hawai`i body politic. The heroics of the war veterans became the next phase in the rehabilitation of this ethnic group.

I HAD FOUR main reasons for writing this book. First, the VVV men offer uncommon stories of seemingly ordinary lives. I began with oral history interviews of the former VVV men, focusing on their year of voluntary labor, but soon delved into their experiences of childhood in the 1920s and adolescence in the 1930s that provided the context for their actions during World War II and their postwar lives. Much of this book is based upon these oral histories.[4]

Second, this work examines the context in which nisei males lived and the ways in which they thought, felt, and acted in the several decades before and during World War II. These young men elected to take an unusual initiative in the face of hostile action from their own society. In this sense, the book is a case study of cultures in conflict and will help, I hope, to call into question simplistic notions of ethnic culture, identity, and acculturation. The issue of identity is an important one that has been enriched by critical research even as it has been confused by oversimplified generalizing; I hope to help ground this discussion with more attention to historical detail.[5]

Third, through a detailed examination of the formation of the VVV, I wish to challenge a number of commonly held assumptions about the nature of and reasons for the upward mobility of the nisei, particularly in Hawai`i. Every important commentary on modern Hawai`i and the role of Japanese Americans in its formation highlights the racism directed against this group before World War II, their leadership in developing a radically new and "democratic" postwar society, their seemingly unexpected and explosive mobility in the 1950s, and their rise to prominence—some suggest control—in contemporary Hawai`i.

Fourth, I want, through the VVV, to suggest that World War II was the incubation period for the contemporary model-minority myth. Born in the 1950s and popularized in subsequent decades, this myth pointed to Asian Americans in general and Japanese Americans in particular as oppressed minorities that had successfully transcended racism in U.S. society. The message, usually unstated, was that other minorities still mired in poverty had only themselves or their own cultures to blame.

A version of this success-story mythology operated in Hawaiʻi through the last half of the twentieth century. The local interpretation highlighted nisei success and added the bright promise of a "new" society in which racial harmony would prevail in an economy of plenty and an egalitarian milieu. Since the 1970s, however, there have been powerful protests for group rights, especially from Native Hawaiians and Filipinos, whose numbers and demands have increased over the years. In this context, a more thorough review of the making of postwar race relations is an important agenda item.

We need periodic reminding that our core beliefs about our own history and culture play important roles in contemporary discussions of politics, race relations, gender, and class. As Christopher Lasch has suggested:

> The political culture of modern societies consists largely of an implicit argument about the past, and it is the job of historical criticism to make that argument explicit and to point out the political consequences that follow from any given reading of the past. For a variety of reasons—professional caution, political indifference or despair, doubts about their ability to make themselves understood by a broader public, the embarrassment of taking ideas seriously—historians have retreated from their role as social critics.[6]

With Lasch, I believe that historians must address the contemporary political consequences of their interpretations of the past. To accomplish this task, I wish to examine the ways in which the nisei past has been used.

The extraordinary ethnic success story of the nisei is usually explained as the result, primarily, of a confluence of strong cultural values, including hard work, education, patience, dedication, and sacrifice, along with the nisei's military accomplishments in World War II and the rise of a Democratic Party.[7] But there were other important forces at work, including nisei emigration from an already modernizing nation, the mixed class backgrounds of their immigrant parents, the complex nature of the ethnic community in the 1920s and 1930s, the significant roles of the International Longshoremens and Warehousemens Union in organizing agricultural labor, and the ways in which the larger society developed a "place" for the nisei during and after World War II. Just as important was the long-term postwar economic boom in the United States; Japan's dramatic transition from despised enemy to client ally had an enormous impact on nisei mobility. I also want to demonstrate the need for more careful thinking about inherited or transmitted cultural values. Thus, the book examines the issei and vague notions of "cultural baggage" brought with them from Japan.[8]

By the 1950s, the Japanese Americans' success in Hawai`i and on the mainland had become a topic for social scientists pondering America's prolonged failure to integrate its people of color, especially African Americans, who were leading a revitalized civil rights drive. Thus, the nisei became a key component of a collective metaphor for the U.S. success story. In such accounts, the Japanese American experience was reconfigured into a larger Asian American framework and revisioned as the American dream of an oppressed minority group's transcending hardship to achieve middle-class status through its own efforts (without disturbing the status quo, not coincidentally).

The essential argument for the Hawai`i case begins with an immigrant issei generation beset by "overt racial oppression, imposed poverty, and social rejection," followed by a nisei generation that "not only inherited a world of limited opportunity, but had to confront the catastrophe of a war which seemed to spell doom for their way of life." In the end, however, "rather than succumbing to fatalism or racial bitterness," Japanese Americans poured their energies into positive futures for their children, believing that "if one worked hard, then material, social, and spiritual well-being would be possible for the coming generation."[9]

Since so much of this model-minority argument rests upon a particular interpretation of history—especially on the crucial role of the nisei—my hope is that this book extends previous efforts to provide an alternative interpretation.[10] It may be ironic, however, that the VVV should serve as a vehicle for a challenge to the model-minority thesis, since so many of the men did, in fact, return to occupy important positions and to do well.

The VVV is assuredly not a typical group of Japanese Americans, if any ever existed; the men of the VVV are a fascinating collection of individuals whose accounts tell of considerable diversity within a single ethnic group. Their stories encourage us to question our assumptions about assimilation—especially the notion that it is a linear process proceeding from ignorant or stubborn retention of ethnic culture to enlightened or inevitable assimilation into "mainstream America." To explore the possibility that there may be a variety of ways of "becoming American" and considerable diversity in preserving ethnic culture, we need to look to interpretations more nuanced and capable of reflecting the multiple ways in which ethnic groups were treated and struggled to get ahead.[11]

At this book's core are oral histories, documentary materials, and a historical analysis that relies on the concept of hegemony to illuminate the mechanisms that drew Japanese Americans into the existing civil society and class structure in Hawai`i from the 1920s into the 1940s.[12] Robert Cox has noted that hegemony may be defined, broadly, as "a structure of values and understandings about the nature of order that permeates a whole system of state and non-state entities."[13]

The concept of hegemony is important here because pre–World War II Hawai`i is often miscast, at one extreme, as an incipient melting-pot democracy working out its flaws or, at the other, as a semi-feudal kingdom or neocolonial dependency in the grip of an all-powerful white oligarchy. Interestingly, both interpretations encourage us to see World War II as a major historical divide between a repressive past and a democratic present.[14] In fact, the political and cultural contexts were more fluid and accessible to influence and manipulation from various avenues than previously assumed, and the history of the VVV helps illustrate this point.

It is certainly true that several dozen haole males controlled the forces of production and the direct apparatuses of state power in pre–World War II Hawai`i, such as the legislature, courts, and police systems. But they were also keenly involved in establishing a broad structure, including schools, financial institutions, and the various media, directed toward an integrated system of beliefs and codes that would sustain their power.

In Hawaii's form of capitalist democracy, where the haole elite was numerically small and sharply demarcated from the rest of society, it was particularly important to have the large majority of indigenous Native Hawaiians and immigrant Asian laborers accept the "values and understandings" that made up the "order" in that society. Otherwise, the social cost of maintaining stability through state power, largely in police and military form, would have been prohibitive, as well as run counter to standard beliefs about American democracy. As a result, pre–World

War II Hawai`i was beset with many struggles among groups contending for hegemonic supremacy or counterhegemonic influence.

Beginning in the late nineteenth century, the major corporate holding companies, collectively designated the "Big Five" or "Merchant Street," dominated among competing forces. The U.S. military, by the 1920s, rapidly became a powerful and influential collaborator-rival. By the late 1930s, a fledgling multiracial/multiethnic labor union, the International Longshoremens and Warehousemens Union, became a third force. From the 1890s and throughout the twentieth century, the large and increasingly important Japanese community was the fourth. The subjects of this particular study were not aware of the crucial roles allotted them in this period, but, as the first generation of American-born Japanese, they were widely appreciated as critical to the perpetuation of haole, Big Five hegemony or to its challenge.

These Japanese American stories will be of interest to those concerned with questions of immigration, ethnicity, acculturation, and the many facets of becoming and being an "American," particularly those interested in the experiences of Asian Americans. In at least one arena, there is now considerable information—the World War II exploits of Japanese American GIs. In general, however, there is not a great deal of critical work on the nisei.[15]

We have heard much too little from within the Japanese American community. We do not know much about their family histories, their educational backgrounds, their cultural perceptions, their religious sentiments, their reflections on triumphs or failures, or their dreams and aspirations as children. As I have already indicated, our major works on the Japanese experience in Hawai`i are informed by a persistent justification of the status quo and hence are ill-equipped to deal with problematic areas. Indeed, the best sources for some sense of nisei men's lives are to be found in short stories, novels, and plays.[16]

I started this project by doing what I thought would be simple oral histories of perhaps one dozen men who had participated in an unusual patriotic endeavor in 1942. By the end, I had conducted some fifty interviews and spent considerable time with the men of the VVV at meetings and reunions in the 1980s and 1990s. And while we did not become especially close, I have learned to respect them for the lives they have fashioned, and I hope that the following chapters do some justice to their lifetimes of effort.

1

Immigrant Parents

Most of the Japanese immigrants in Hawai`i left their homeland during the Meiji Era (1868–1912), a period of enormous change. In this period, Japan was transformed from a semi-feudal collection of several hundred domains into the mightiest empire in Asia, poised to do battle with European and American nations that had become industrial and political powers long before. In the process of modernizing, more than one million Japanese left to became part of a diaspora that stretched from Korea and the Sakhalin Islands in Northeast Asia south into the Pacific and eastward across both Americas. Well over 100,000 settled in North America, while approximately 200,000 went to Hawai`i. The issei parents of the 169 nisei who became members of the Varsity Victory Volunteers in 1942 were part of this large population movement.

THE IMMIGRANT PARENTS of the VVV men were a diverse lot. A few were Christians, converted in Japan or shortly after arrival in Hawai`i. Most were Buddhists, including two Buddhist priests who traced their lineages back many generations in that calling. The parents came from families that included merchants, farmers, and fishermen. Like other issei, most came from prefectures like Yamaguchi and Hiroshima in southwest Honshu or Fukuoka and Kumamoto in northern Kyushu.

Most of the VVV parents arrived in Hawai`i as young men and women, although a few had accompanied their own parents as very young children. Except in a few instances, VVV members knew little about their parents. Many lamented that lack, feeling that they should have acquired more family history before it was too late.[1]

This discussion of the issei families of the VVV begins with an overview of Meiji Japan's culture and politics, not only to contextualize individual histories but also to challenge some of the prevailing assumptions that undergird academic and popular accounts of Japanese American history. Indeed, it will be useful, for this purpose, to go back even further to take brief stock of the Tokugawa period (1600–1868). Contemporary Japanese American success stories—versions of model-minority myths—depend principally upon notions of cultural values purportedly rooted in traditional Japan. These invariably include hard work, patience, education, fatalism, passivity, honesty, and willingness to sacrifice for the family. However, as recent research on the Meiji Era discloses and stories about the VVV parents suggest, these values were by no means universally respected or upheld in Japan.

This chapter also suggests that the issei began life in Hawai`i with advantages not shared by other immigrants and that they enjoyed some social mobility from the very earliest years of settlement. Unlike other groups, such as the Chinese and Filipinos, they arrived with families or the means and mechanisms to establish families and communities. Their numbers included professionals and entrepreneurs with sufficient capital to create new businesses and to hire other Japanese, thus creating their own community economies. Even under Tokugawa feudalism, Japan had a fairly advanced system of education for commoners, and Meiji reforms included steadily increasing levels of compulsory schooling. As a result, many issei arrived with more formal education than even their European counterparts of the same era. The issei came from a nation rapidly modernizing and seeking a place among the international powers. Japan's relative position in the world thus assured the issei of a homeland able and sometimes willing to stand up for the rights of its subjects.

Finally, it will be useful to provide a conceptual framework by dealing directly with notions of specific values, the cultural baggage brought from Japan. These values are often presumed to have been transmitted from the issei to the nisei. They include *enryo* (restraint), *gaman* (enduring adversity), *shikata ga nai* (fatalism), an emphasis on education (*kyoiku*), spiritual values (*shushin*), for the sake of the children (*kodomo no tame ni*), and national chauvinism (*yamato damashi*). These were indeed values espoused by many Japanese and Japanese Americans. They have, however, become stereotypically associated with this ethnic group and imbued with nearly mystical powers to explain the ability of Japanese Americans to "make it" in American society.[2]

This particular constellation of values explicitly celebrates a strategy of ethnocentric pride, patience, and passivity on the part of an entire ethnic group. Unfortunately, the use of these values to explain Japanese American upward mobility obscures more than it illuminates. Worse, this variant of the model-minority myth is sometimes invoked to indict racial and ethnic minority groups such as African Americans or Latinos or Native Americans who have been less successful in socioeconomic terms.[3] Linking the success of Japanese Americans to their cultural values creates a context in which an ethnic group finds pride in its cultural heritage, usually by asserting common ties with the culture into which it worked to assimilate. This line of thinking validates the essential fairness of the status quo. Meanwhile, by implication, the "less successful" groups have only themselves or their cultural values to blame for their lack of achievement. The dangers of the model-minority myth have been apparent for decades. As Amy Tachiki noted in "The Emergence of Yellow Power in America":

> Asian Americans are perpetuating racism in the United States as they allow white Americans to hold up the "successful" Oriental image before other minority groups as the model to emulate. White America justifies the blacks' position by showing that other non-whites—yellow people—have been able to 'adapt' to the system. . . . Unfortunately, the yellow power movement is fighting a well-developed racism in Asian Americans who project their own frustrated attempts to gain white acceptance onto the black people. They nurse their own feelings of inferiority and insecurity by holding themselves as superior to the blacks. (11–12)

In Hawai`i, "blacks" today include not only African Americans but Native Hawaiians, other Pacific Islander peoples, Puerto Ricans, and Filipinos—most of the "brown" populations.

Meiji society was especially volatile, and recent research makes it clear that no simple set of cultural values could explain the experiences of the Japanese people, even in Japan itself. Translating simplistic notions di-

rectly to the overseas issei experience is even more problematic. Some
of these interpretations have been appropriated from the historic and social scientific arenas into social policy and psychotherapeutic fields, and
the potential for mischief is considerable.[4]

During the Tokugawa period, "Japan" was comprised of several hundred feudal domains. There was a central Tokugawa Shogunate to which
individuals and groups owed varying degrees of allegiance. But there
was only a minimal, albeit growing, sense of a national entity. In 1868,
the Tokugawa regime was dismantled and a new nation-state formed. By
the end of the Meiji emperor's reign in 1912, Japan had become one of
the great powers of the world. Its major goal was embodied in the slogan *fukoku kyohei*, wealthy nation and powerful military.

This process of "modernization" generated countervailing forces that
ranged from former samurai on the Right to newly empowered commoners and disgruntled former samurai on the Left. The result, as Carol
Gluck has demonstrated, was a society in which nearly every important
value was deeply contested. In such a setting the establishment of an effective ideological or cultural orthodoxy was hardly a foregone conclusion, even late in the Meiji period.[5] The immigrants, then, could not
have left Japan with a set of rigid orthodoxies. Instead, they bore a variety of perspectives and complex sets of values as they set out for new
worlds and new homes.

Themselves cut off from familiar terrain—geographic, familial, cultural, and political—the issei were hard-pressed to transmit significant elements of their heritages to their children. How, for example,
were they to inculcate respect for ancestors or the *ie*, the family itself,
in the absence of temples, landmarks, or even gravesites? In the late
nineteenth and early twentieth centuries, news from Japan arrived in
Hawai'i slowly and intermittently; letters from relatives were rare. There
was the occasional appearance of recent immigrants who brought
news from the region, but these newcomers were not always from the
same villages or even the same prefectures; the community turned to
newspapers as a primary means of communication. As a result, Japanese-
language newspapers quickly assumed considerable importance. They
contained reports from Japan, as well as information about and advocacy
of immigrant issues in Hawai'i, advertisements, and general social
news.[6]

The young nation the issei left behind has become the object of intense scrutiny both in Japan and in the West, especially among U.S.

scholars. Research on the Meiji period in the last few decades has produced a wealth of information and insights. The literature on Japanese Americans, including the Japanese in Hawai`i, however, ignores this scholarship and too often assumes an "orientalist" view, depicting Meiji Japan as an exoticized and timeless society.[7]

One widely used text on the Japanese in Hawai`i, for example, asserts that "the stabilization of the Issei community also meant a perpetuation of the more fundamental cultural values and beliefs of the immigrant. Many of these values were the formal tenets of Buddhism and the extensive *Bushido* ethic—self-sacrifice, hard work, getting an education, and the attitude of *shikata ga nai* (it cannot be helped)."[8] These values are not, in fact, intrinsic to either Buddhism or Bushido (code of the samurai); more important, there is no reason to privilege them over other values in the complex and shifting cultural baggage the issei brought to America.[9]

Similarly, there is the assertion that Japanese immigrants arrived in America and Hawai`i with "a presumption of inequality," naturally accepting social conformity and a lowly place in the plantation economy and in the general society.[10]

Yet while Japanese tradition did emphasize hierarchy, Japan has a venerable history of social protest and mavericks, including many willing to be imprisoned or executed for their actions. The issei left a country with a rich heritage of rebellion—a fact widely acknowledged among students of Japanese history.[11] Numerous commoner revolts and protests in Japan, especially during the Tokugawa and Meiji periods—five to six thousand separate incidents between 1600 and 1912, or as many as twenty per year—suggest that the regard for hierarchical status and "knowing one's place" did not always govern behavior. Individuals, villages, or entire regions joined illegal demonstrations and protests against samurai or official abuse.[12]

The Meiji Era, the culture in which the issei were reared, blended elements derived from the preceding Tokugawa period with new ideas from the West. Some of these Western ideas were distinctly modern, including the concept of human rights in the form of democratic self-awareness, an awakening individualism, and self-consciousness—especially among those who had direct contact with the West or with Christianity. Finally, and perhaps most significant, was the new system of capitalism—materialism, utilitarianism, and a market economy—that developed to contest older feudal values. Irokawa Daikichi suggests, therefore, that the transition between old and new could "be found in the decline of Confucian ethics and of the ideals of bushido."[13]

The *kanyaku imin* were government-contract laborers whose arrival (1885-93) preceded that of the VVV parents by about a decade. These laborers established the foundations of the Japanese community in Hawai`i. Many were in their thirties when they arrived, born in the last decades of the Tokugawas, which were characterized by dynamic changes, some propelled by internal stresses and others created by the intrusion of the Western powers, especially the arrival of Commodore Matthew Perry from the United States in 1853-54.

Many future issei were in their teens in the 1870s when their villages were disrupted by the official change and social turbulence that followed the Meiji Restoration in 1868. Among the most important of the new regulations were the imposition of universal conscription and education, as well as a revolutionary land tax. The new government degraded traditional respect for Buddhism and installed a new state Shinto system with a powerful emperor symbol. Committed to modern forms of political and economic development, the Meiji oligarchy pursued an aggressive foreign policy to compete with Western imperialist nations. The end result was a destabilized society for which relatively large-scale emigration became, after initial reluctance, an important safety valve for political and social pressures. This, then, was the society into which most issei had been socialized before emigration.[14]

In their headlong rush to join the Western powers, the Meiji oligarchs set in motion a wide variety of new dynamics. One of the most important was to promote nationalism and draw upon the productive forces of commoners, especially merchants, who had been dominated by the samurai during the previous millennium. The oligarchs used a combination of education, reform, and repression aimed at maintaining control of the society even as they deliberately destroyed barriers. For example, they extended voting rights to commoners but only to males with substantial means. And they financed modernization by extracting more taxes from the farming population while simultaneously abolishing the samurai class. Further, the new "right" to participate in universal conscription reflected the diminished power of the samurai but cost many peasant families the labor and earning power of their young males. These policies elicited a growing number of serious popular movements to expand the franchise and protect the interests of rural areas in the national arena.[15]

Among the traditional practices that encouraged the Japanese to leave for Hawaiʻi was that of seeking wage employment beyond the village; the practice, termed *dekasegi*, evolved during the Tokugawa period and flourished during the early years of the Meiji Era. As natural disasters, famines, and the collapse of traditional industries created large-scale unemployment, this search for cash took workers to the next village, the nearest city, or a distant nation. But long-term structural changes also eroded traditional practices that had enabled peasants to survive difficult times. Perhaps the most drastic was the imposition of the land tax on which the new government relied for its income: 80.5 percent of total revenues in 1875–79 and 85.6 percent in 1882–92.[16] The combination of structural change and short-term catastrophe created significant incentives for emigration. But the assumption that poverty drove emigration does not suffice.

Many areas of Japan suffered as much as or more than the southwestern prefectures from which the Hawaiʻi immigrants had come, rendering any direct correlation between poverty levels and emigration problematic. It appears more likely that the principal labor recruiter for the Hawaiian kingdom, Robert Walker Irwin, influenced Meiji leaders to favor the southwestern regional areas, including Yamaguchi-Hiroshima and Fukuoka in the initial period.[17]

Hiroshima became the most generous of the prefectures in the export of *dekaseginin*, who hoped to return with capital to begin a better life, often by buying back land they had been forced to sell. When researchers tabulated figures for *kanyaku imin* who left Hiroshima for Hawaiʻi between 1885 and 1892, they discovered a total of 8,325 individuals, including 6,771 males and 1,554 females (just about 19 percent, or the one in five mandated by the Japanese government). The total number of *kanyaku imin* from Japan was 29,069. Hiroshima had provided 28.6 percent of that group.[18]

Among the more enticing cultural values is *kodomo no tame ni*—for the sake of the children. It is asserted that the issei were unusually devoted to their children, that they were selfless in their dedication to the next generation. That value, it is claimed, provided the collective ethnic fuel that eventually propelled the group to success. Not all agree.

In a panel discussion among third-generation sansei, Michael Yoshii recalled that, in the 1970s, "we were idealizing Issei and putting them up on a pedestal. We were creating this myth of who they were and what they struggled through."[19] It is important to keep this issue in balance;

I am not suggesting that the issei did not care for their children or were not concerned for the future of the group, simply that they ought not be romanticized. In addition, values like effort, patriarchy, diligence, honesty and fear of bringing shame (*haji*) to the family, community, and race, all reportedly informed nisei lives in that California community.

Another defining characteristic of most depictions of issei society is intense patriarchy. As Eileen Tamura put it: "The patriarch controlled the family's property and the lives of its members; his word was law." [20] Indeed, the term "Meiji man" is sometimes invoked as shorthand to suggest the domineering, stubborn, noncommunicative, and self-indulgent husband and father. These characteristics are attributed to "traditional" Japanese culture. But research on women in Japanese history, and especially during the Meiji years, suggests a rich variety of conditions that should caution us against oversimplification.

In Japan itself, well into the 1920s and 1930s, considerable economic production took place in relatively small units, including the household, especially in rural, small-town, or suburban areas. There, merchants and artisans shared child-rearing responsibilities and girls were valued for their real economic contributions. It seems, in fact, that the petite bourgeoisie and peasant classes from which the immigrants came were far more egalitarian toward women than were former samurai or aristocratic circles in Japan.

It seems clear, then, that a syndrome of pride, passivity, patience, patriarchy, and far-sighted reliance on education could not have reigned uncontested among the issei. There was little pride in the fact that the immigrant society suffered major social ills—including alcohol, prostitution, and gambling—which were hardly eradicated. There was a broad pattern of activist reform and resistance to real and imagined problems or affronts, from individual acts of spontaneous revenge or lonely despair to carefully planned labor strikes against formidable obstacles. In all of this, the issei were following a durable peasant tradition that dates far back in Japanese history.

The imposition of compulsory schooling in 1872 is often touted as one of the Meiji government's outstanding success stories and evidence of the traditionally high value placed on education. There is little debate about the impressive gains in schooling—indeed, the Japanese were among the most educated of any immigrant group in the United States in the early twentieth century. As one study of high school education on the island of Maui in the 1920s and 1930s revealed: "Most of the children brought from Japan (*yobiyose*) have completed elementary school or better so have the confidence to do well in spite of the language difference in Hawai`i."[21]

But the new Meiji policy was complex and certainly not monolithic. The issei schooled from the 1860s to the 1890s did not emerge from a single mold. As Mark Lincicome has pointed out, there were fierce debates over the very goals of education and the methods to pursue them.[22] And beyond this disagreement over ends and means, compulsory education itself was not always welcome—suggesting, for one thing, that there never was a traditional, uncontested value on education in the abstract. For example, parents in numerous localities in the early Meiji period resisted schooling by refusing to enroll their children, by keeping them out of the classrooms on certain days or in certain periods critical to household production, or by burning and razing elementary schools when they were seen as inimical to peasant interests.[23]

In Hawai`i, the issei were regularly criticized for keeping their children home to celebrate important Japanese holidays, such as *tenchosetsu*, the emperor's birthday. In the most compelling example, the school system was forced to accommodate coffee farmers, most of whom were Japanese. In the district of Kona on the Big Island, Hawai`i, harvesting the ripe bright-red coffee beans called "cherries" took place in the fall, after summer vacation had ended and while school was in session. But harvesting the beans was extremely labor intensive, and the nisei children were required to help as soon as they could walk. During the weeks of intensive work, not a single family member could be spared, and the issei consistently rejected official demands to release their children to their schools. The school system eventually gave in and, as a result, for many years all Kona school children enjoyed their "summer" vacation in late fall, during the harvest season.

Many nisei, especially women, were forced to take jobs after completing the eighth grade. That they lamented this necessity provides evidence, according to Eileen Tamura, of the value Japanese placed on education. In 1918, nisei boys were six times more likely than nisei girls to attend high school. By the mid 1920s, boys were twice as likely. It was only in 1941 that girls achieved parity. This suggests strongly that Japanese families forced their female children into the job market when their wages, however meager, were deemed necessary for the family unit. When conditions permitted, when clerical jobs became available to the Japanese, and when there was sufficient societal pressure exerted, the girls continued their education into high school.[24] Both boys and girls stayed in school longer after the Japanese American community's economic base became more stable. Girls stayed in school longer, that is, even as older Japanese values weakened.[25]

Discussions of the cultural baggage maintained and transmitted by the issei is often obscured by lack of reference to the national mission that lies behind and beneath the seemingly benign "values." In Meiji Japan, the oligarchs had a clear mission—to unify a feudal and fragmented set of peoples into a modern nation-state. In the United States, some issei attempted to manipulate these same values to remain part of the "Japanese world order." This immigrant impulse should not, however, be identified with the thrust from Tokyo that sought to capitalize on the issei presence in order to move the national Japanese agenda forward. Anti-Japanese forces in the United States seized on the confluence of these separate but related streams and constructed a seamless and sinister web of a "yellow peril" for domestic consumption. At the same time, Japanese immigrants understood that Tokyo was using them and complained, in a characteristically Japanese play on words, that they were more *kimin* (abandoned people) than *imin* (immigrants) in the eyes of their own government. Yuji Ichioka, in his *Issei*, has pointed out that this sense of rejection by both Japan and the Unites States forced the issei to place their destinies in the hands of the nisei, who were U.S. citizens by birth. The difference between the generations, then, became pivotal.

While a diverse lot, the issei who arrived in Hawai`i during the last years of the nineteenth century and the early years of the twentieth might be characterized in the following ways: Most of the men and many women were at least minimally literate as a result of widespread basic schooling by the end of the Tokugawa era and universal primary education in the early Meiji period;[26] they were pressed to provide remittances to families beset by debt and growing tenancy; they were being indoctrinated into a radical movement of emperor worship and national chauvinism that emphasized racial superiority, especially to other Asians and peoples of color; the majority, sugar workers, lived monotonous and often brutish lives; gambling, alcohol, and prostitution were common; they turned to religion for comfort and meaning, especially in Jodo Shinshu Buddhism, which had been severely repressed in their home areas in the early 1870s, and in Christianity, which proclaimed an entirely new vision of ultimate loyalty; and they had some experience in, and a long tradition of, resistance to authority, whether local or regional, samurai or bureaucrat.

Japanese Americans had long been the only ethnic group in the world to count membership in terms of generational distance from the geographic homeland. In recent years, more immigrants from Asia have been employing versions of this concept. (Asian immigrants who arrived as young children, after liberalization of anti-Asian immigration laws in 1965, are sometimes referred to as the "1.5" generation to distinguish them from their immigrant parents and the generation born in the United States.)[27] But it was the Japanese American community that invented and maintained this model, and in this sense Japanese Americans claim a unique position in the looming discourse on Asian diasporas and the specific question of the meaning of emigrant societies to national identity issues within Asia.[28]

The meanings imputed to geogenerational categories are important in Japanese American historiography. Much of the literature relies on this paradigm, and most Japanese Americans assume the categories to be transparently meaningful. This may not be the case. Thus, for one example, the issei are usually described as the first generation of Japanese who settled in America—the immigrants. But they may also be interpreted as the first generation *away* from their homeland, Japan. The nisei then become the second-generation removed, and so forth.

To date, the Japanese American community, historically stereotyped and victimized like other Asian immigrants as incorrigibly "alien," has argued that the issei be viewed as immigrants making a fundamental break away from Japan and into the United States. Hence, recent literature downplays the sojourner mentality taken for granted by earlier generations of scholars. For the issei themselves, the concept may also have affirmed their ongoing relationship with Japan. The notion of immigrants as the first generation removed from but still bound to Japan enables us to appreciate the close ties they maintained with the homeland through language, culture, and politics. Examining issei political activity from this perspective allows us to see, for example, elements of their national chauvinism directed against other Asians in the United States, an issue which has not yet received the attention it deserves; finally, their grandchildren, the acculturated third generation, reflect on family and community experiences and the significance of their immigrant grandparents and their ethnic culture.[29]

To understand why the Japanese so carefully crafted this geogenerational schema, we need to look beyond traditional values or the formation of Japanese American identity. The Japanese immigrant experience was unique. European immigrants, even the southern and eastern Europeans who were targeted for immigration restrictions in 1924, arrived over a much longer period of time. Some families arrived in stages as circumstances and finances allowed. The long duration of a group's and even a family's immigration resists the historian's attempt to organize these immigrants' experiences in terms of discrete generations.

Immigrants from Asian countries, notably China and the Philippines, were subject to restrictions and conditions that severely inhibited family formation. Chinese laborers suffered intolerable gender imbalances into the mid–twentieth century, and Filipinos recruited after the Spanish-American War of 1898 were overwhelmingly male.[30]

Predominantly male societies of all nationalities were characterized by cheap labor, prostitution, substance abuse, and gambling. Meiji leaders were acutely aware of the racism directed against earlier Chinese immigrants and the propensity of the U.S. press and leadership to justify ill treatment as the consequence of social deviance on the part of the newcomers. The Japanese government, since its earliest contacts with the modern West in the mid–nineteenth century, had spent several decades modifying Japanese behavior to convince European and U.S. leaders that Japan belonged among the world's powers. It soon employed the same strategy with its issei communities. One immediate result was a policy that encouraged or required the inclusion of wives among the immigrants to ensure the development of relatively stable communities. (In the first boat that bore contract laborers to Hawai`i, the *City of Tokio*, for example, of 944 Japanese immigrants, 199—nearly 20 percent—were women. Perhaps more impressive, nearly one-half of the group belonged to a nuclear family, as couples, as children, or, in the case of seven individuals, as siblings of one of the spouses.)[31]

In the Immigration Convention of 1886 between Hawai`i and Japan, articles 6 and 7 guaranteed Japanese interpreters and physicians for the immigrant laborers. Equally important, there was a separate agreement that approximately 30 percent of the immigrants be women.[32] In spite of these precautions, by the early 1890s both official and unofficial reports noted widespread gambling and prostitution among the Japanese in Hawai`i and on the West Coast, where none of the Hawai`i agreements applied.[33] But the Meiji government, much more powerful than the disintegrating Qing Dynasty, was able to institute reforms that helped stabilize the Japanese immigrant community from its inception in a way no other pre–World War II Asian group could replicate.

Immigration patterns that led to family and community development were clearly delineated. Most immigrants arrived between 1890 and 1920. Anti-Japanese agitation quickly led to treaties and legislation that reduced immigration from Japan. The Gentlemen's Agreement of 1907–8 was the first major turning point: Japan ceased issuing passports to laborers. Others, like merchants, students, and family members, continued to be eligible, but their numbers were small, except for wives of the issei.

The next decisive historical phenomenon was the ethnic community's use of the "picture bride" process. In the first two decades of the twentieth century, and particularly after the Gentlemen's Agreement, immigrant bachelors often secured wives from Japan through a system of formally arranged marriages. The *shashin hanayome*—picture brides—were partners in *shashin kekkon*, or, literally, photo marriages. These women constituted one element in a general migration pattern the Japanese called *yobiyose*—to summon or "bring over"—to describe the process of building or completing their families and communities. Approximately twenty thousand women entered Hawai`i before the Immigration Act of 1924 finally and firmly closed the doors.[34]

Because one major purpose of these marriages was the perpetuation of the *ie*, or household, there was a sizable baby boom in the 1910s and 1920s, the decades immediately following the arrival of the picture brides. It made sense, then, to establish a category for this new, large, and important generation and to provide it a distinctive label.

Finally, there was another reason to label this generation. From the point of view of the immigrants, the 1922 U.S. Supreme Court decision that rejected issei Takao Ozawa's bid to become a naturalized citizen, as well as the 1924 Immigration Act had consigned them to political impotence. In the future, it was understood, the ethnic community's fortunes would rest with their American-born children, who enjoyed citizenship rights. The existence of a significant nisei generation, then, distinguished the Japanese from other Asian immigrants and enabled them to envision a social and political role for their families that would be beyond the reach of Chinese and Filipinos.

Hawai`i at the turn of the century, when most of the parents of the VVV arrived, was an extraordinary place. It had witnessed, in the course of the last decade of the nineteenth century, the illegal overthrow of the last reigning monarch of the Hawaiian kingdom, installation of an "independent republic," and annexation by the United States. The men responsible, overwhelmingly U.S. businessmen, predicated the removal of Queen Liliuokalani on the willingness of the United States to annex Hawai'i. This action was supported by U.S. Marines in 1893. For the next five years, as the U.S. government vacillated, Hawai'i remained under the rule of a provisional government and then became a self-proclaimed republic. Eventually, the inexorable march of U.S. imperialism led to the 1898 annexation of the islands—along with the acquisition of Puerto Rico, Guam, and the Philippines as a result of the Spanish-American War. In 1900, the Organic Act, the governing framework for the Territory of Hawai'i, took effect. It would be replaced only when statehood was granted in 1959.

By 1900, there were more than sixty thousand Japanese in Hawai'i, about 40 percent of the total population, and there was already serious talk about a Japanese "takeover" of the islands. The predictable result was a U.S. military buildup—with Pearl Harbor as the centerpiece—which began to escalate at about the same time as, but especially immediately after, the Japanese defeat of Russia in 1905.

By 1900, it was clear that the large Japanese population was becoming a permanent settlement. Japanese labor dominated the sugar-plantation workforce, while many other Japanese were moving into urban areas. In 1900, more than half of the more than seven thousand souls in Honolulu's "Chinatown" were Japanese. Hilo, on the Big Island of Hawai'i, was rapidly becoming a Japanese enclave. Planters therefore sought workers from Puerto Rico, Europe, the Philippines, and California to diversify the labor pool and discourage proletarian solidarity. There were Japanese wholesalers and retailers, newspapers, theaters, hotels, and historians. Several identifiable Japanese gangs in Honolulu oversaw highly profitable gambling and prostitution activities; one even printed and circulated its own newsletter.[35]

What, then, might we say about the Japan-based background of the VVV parents specifically? The forty-five VVV participants who responded for this book to a written questionnaire about their parents reported that most arrived around the turn of the century. I originally assumed that there would be significant differences between the lives and experiences of VVV members born to issei parents and the eight who had at least one nisei parent; I expected there would be even greater differences for the four reared by two nisei parents, who were thus third-generation sansei. This was not the case, and here, at least, is some evidence that the geogenerational schema needs to be used with care.

In general, the VVV members knew little about their families' backgrounds in Japan. Of the forty-five men who responded, the majority (60 percent) did not know the name of a single grandparent. They had, with a few exceptions, little interest in or knowledge of their families beyond their parents' immediate experiences. Their attitudes probably reflect the context of the 1920s and 1930s (described in chapters 2 and 3) and their determined attempts to assimilate into Hawaii's highly stratified society.

The men of the VVV knew much more about their own largely immigrant parents. Three-quarters of the men described fairly well educated parents (Table 1).[36] Nearly half (46 percent) had at least one parent who had gone beyond eight years of school. (The Meiji system included eight grades at the elementary level; those who completed *shogakko*, elementary school, had attained the level of today's junior high schools.) Fathers of two of the men had college degrees.

Of the one-fourth who did not know or list their parents' level of education, some might have been embarrassed, but my sense is that they did not recall or know how far their parents had gone in school. Perhaps parents with little schooling avoided discussing the subject with their children. It is also possible that education, as an abstract cultural value, was not as critical in these families.

All but two of the VVV respondents knew something about their fathers' employment (Table 2). The standard image of the Japanese before World War II, powerfully associated with manual labor, especially in the sugar and pineapple industries, can be misleading, as the 39 per-

Table 1 Schooling of VVV Parents

Level	Number	Percent
None	2	6
Elementary	17	48
Intermediate	9	26
High School	4	14
College	2	6
Totals	35	100

Table 2 Occupations of VVV Fathers

Occupation	Number	Percent
Laborer	5	12
Supervisor (e.g., foreman, postmaster)	5	12
Skilled craftsman (e.g., mason, carpenter)	10	23
White-collar worker (e.g., salesman, clerk)	4	9
Small business owner (e.g., jeweler, farmer)	17	39
Professional (clergy, dentist)	2	5
Totals	43	100

cent of business owners among the VVV fathers suggests. The VVV fathers, an unusual but not extraordinary group of issei in the 1920s, add complexity and texture to the standard image.

All major public institutions in 1920s Hawai`i, including the school system and government agencies, were controlled by whites or Native Hawaiians. Downtown Merchant Street, with its core of several dozen white males, dominated the private sector. But while the racism directed against Hawaii's Japanese American community before World War II was palpable, the group was large enough to provide a critical mass for employment at many levels, including skilled workers, professionals, and entrepreneurs.

The ethnic community supported a large number of educators in the Japanese-language schools; there were cultural workers who taught the arts as well as a vast range of entrepreneurs who produced food, purveyed goods, and provided services from midwifery to mortuaries—from birth to death.[37] In some areas, such as law, big business, media, finance, transportation, insurance, public office, and engineering, substantial progress would have to wait until after World War II, but there was a solid core of petite bourgeoisie within the Japanese community, and most of the VVV families were securely within that tradition.

Many of the issei arrived in Hawai`i as children—unlike the North American experience—a fact that helps to explain the trajectory and mobility of the Japanese in Hawai`i. Their children, although technically nisei, were beneficiaries of parents who had grown up in Hawai`i and who knew the basic rules of the society. These included language, sometimes Hawaiian but usually Hawaiian Creole English (pidgin English), and familiarity with the major institutions such as the school system.

Unlike issei who arrived as adults, they understood holiday customs such as Thanksgiving, Easter, and Christmas and had grown up in multiethnic communities with a healthy regard for the power of the white elite. These generalizations largely held true for most of the men I interviewed. Their early adjustment to school and society was, as a result, reasonably smooth and successful.

The relatively close relationship between the the VVV men and their issei parents was not the case in the general population. Perhaps the more broad-minded nature of the families helps explain the men's ability to contemplate forming and joining the VVV; these young men assumed, for the most part, that their parents would support their actions. The generation gap between many other issei and nisei was often wide and difficult to bridge. Many nisei had regular and vigorous disagreements with their parents, as clearly depicted in Milton Murayama's fictional Oyama family in *All I Asking for Is My Body*.

THE MEN OF THE VVV, born in 1920 or thereabouts, were contemporaries of the fictional boys in Murayama's novel. Their stories, at least the twenty detailed ones I collected, include few of the dramatic clashes portrayed in this and other fictional accounts. Barney Ono is perhaps the only one to relate serious conflict; he defied his parents as a youth and moved out of his home on at least two occasions.[38]

A few of the men vividly recalled stories about their family backgrounds in Japan, but most knew very little. Many had no sense of any family existence prior to their own direct experiences in Hawai`i. The ones who had learned about their family backgrounds tended to come from families with some social standing, those of merchants or Buddhist priests, for example. This was not true, however, for Ralph Yempuku:

> My father was a Buddhist minister and I don't know too much about what they did before because, amongst the Japanese anyway, amongst our kind, there wasn't too much of that communication between the parents and their children. My father used to talk to me about "Don't do this, don't do that," but nothing about "Look, when I was young I was in Japan; I did this, I did that." (1)[39]

Yempuku's father had immigrated about a decade before Ralph's birth in 1914. Reverend Yempuku was the second of five boys in the family. He first ministered to the Japanese community in Papaikou on the Big Island of Hawai`i. Both he and Ralph's mother taught in the Japanese-language schools to supplement the meager income provided by the Higashi Hongwanji—Eastern Temple—division of Jodo Shinshu Buddhism. The Yempukus eventually moved to Kahuku, on the north shore of Oahu, where Reverend Yempuku maintained a temple and both parents continued to teach in a Japanese-language school.

The family lived on sugar-plantation property and was obligated to the plantation for temple land and support. During the massive 1920 sugar strike, Ralph said, his father was forced to oppose the Japanese strikers:

> They called him an *inu* [literally, "dog"; stool pigeon or traitor]. A dog, eh. . . . You see, because we were given a home. . . . You know, there was a plantation camp; . . . our home was away from them and we were mostly in the haole district. . . . We were about the only Japanese living in this district.
>
> And I think the plantation treated my father more as an executive than as a laborer. So when the strike came, . . . I remember my father being criticized because he was for the plantation; . . . [the children] ostracized us but not to the extent that we got hurt or anything like that. (6–7)

Masato Doi "never even heard my grandparents mentioned." Masato knew that his father had arrived from Yamaguchi prefecture in 1889 and worked on the Paauhau sugar plantation on the Big Island of Hawai`i as a government-contract laborer. The family branched out on its own, cultivating cane on marginal land the plantation was willing to lease to the workers. As for his mother: "I have absolutely no knowledge of any of her background. . . . All I know is that I was born when she was forty and my father was fifty-two. That's all I know about her" (2).

Shiro Amioka knew that his father's family might have been fishermen in Japan, but, like Doi, he knew little of his mother's background. He did recall that she was born on the Island of Kaua`i and had been sent to the village of Jigozen in Hiroshima to receive an education. Jigozen was famous as a site that sent many of its inhabitants to Hawai`i. She later returned to Hawai`i as a picture bride: "I don't know why they came and all that sort of thing; . . . in my mother's case, she was born in Eleele and I don't even know their names. I was meaning to do some kind of genealogy record but I never got around to doing it" (3–4).

Most of his close friends call Ryoji Namba "Bull." The nickname stuck primarily because he was so stubborn, a quality that served him well in securing a Ph.D. in entomology and then fighting for a position at the University of Hawai'i in the 1950s, when hiring faculty of color was exceedingly rare. His parents were Christians, unusual for issei in general, especially in the years before World War II, when conversion required courage. Namba was not aware, however, of any problems the family had with their religion. No one discussed the reason for the conversion; no one in the family told him much about life in Japan, either. His father worked for Union Trading Company, a sizable firm that dealt with imports from Japan. His mother "never worked. The old style, eh."

> I really don't know too much about their home background but they are both from Okayama-ken; . . . my father came to Hawai'i when he was . . . only about sixteen or seventeen. . . . All I know is that he was a salesman, always in sales right from the time he lived in Kaua'i in the early years. He was pretty fluent in Hawaiian—one of the few old Japanese who could speak Hawaiian.
>
> Then, my mother, I don't know when she came. I didn't ask her. She was the more educated one. I think she was a Japanese schoolteacher for a while. She's the one that's always stressing that we should get educated. My father was too busy working. (1, 3)

Yugo Okubo became a leftist radical, an advocate of social justice and labor rights. Like Namba, Doi, and Amioka, he knew little about his father and virtually nothing about his mother's background. Both his parents emigrated from Ehime prefecture on the small island of Shikoku in Japan's Inland Sea. They were also Christian, probably not baptized, but with a strong sense of social mission. Yugo knew that his father had arrived to work in a sugar plantation, although in a white-collar position and not as a laborer. His father left the village in order to earn some money, joining thousands in the *dekasegi* process, after an older brother had failed to keep the family business afloat. Yugo had powerful memories of his father helping other immigrants write letters home and of ensuring that the Okubo children were involved with an ethnically diverse group of children through his contacts and the schools they attended (1–2).

Edward Nakamura, an outstanding labor lawyer and a state supreme court justice, knew only that his parents were born in Mie prefecture, from which only a handful of other immigrants came. "I presume they must have come here in 1910 or so, because my father told me that he was a veteran of World War I . . . drafted," [he laughed]. And he served at Schofield Barracks as a member of the First Hawaiian Infantry, whatever it was called at that time. I recall that when the veterans of World War I received a bonus, he got a check, which I thought" [he laughed] "was sizeable, at that time" (3).[40]

Akira Otani has detailed knowledge of his father, Matsujiro, from his father's autobiography, *Waga hito to narishi ashiato—hachijunen no kaiko* (Becoming a man—memoirs of my eighty years).[41] Like his father, Akira sold fish, a family business which grew into a thriving wholesale market. As Akira related, Matsujiro started from humble beginnings that included daily rounds as a fish peddler:

> He came from a little fishing village in Okikamuro on an Inland Sea Island of Yamaguchi-ken [prefecture]. . . . He somehow felt, as I gathered from what he used to tell us, as well as what I gathered from reading his book, that . . . there was no future for him on the little island; . . . he also wanted to be . . . recruited to Hawai`i, but he never made it. Therefore, he made a second choice, which was to go to Korea. . . . However, just before the time when he was supposed to go to Korea he found out that there was somebody who had canceled, . . . and he asked to be the replacement for that particular party . . . [but] they rejected him [because] the agent . . . wanted two fares, rather than one fare; . . . my dad said, well, he would pay the commission to cover two persons' fare and therefore he was able to come. . . .
>
> My dad didn't have very much education, I think somewhere along grade school; the schools on the little island were very limited—very, very limited. . . . He could read and write, yes. In fact, I think one of the pictures we have around shows him studying in his kimono and whatnot, but, yeah . . . he is more or less self-educated, really.
>
> My mom was born on the Big Island. She's really a nisei. So we, her children, would be, well, two and one-half [generation]; . . . after getting married to my dad, she worked in the fish cannery. She also worked in the pineapple cannery for a long time. (1–2)

There are interesting differences between Akira's recollections and Matsujiro's autobiography. While Akira describes his father as largely "self-educated," Matsujiro claims considerable schooling, at least for those times. He completed four years of primary school in Okikamuro and, in order to continue, went to another school some distance away at the age of eleven. It was so far, in fact, that he became a boarder in the principal's home. He had to leave school after two more years because his family needed his labor; still, he recalled one teacher encouraging him to "go on for a doctorate and become a great man" (1).

Matsujiro Otani goes on to write that he initially had wanted to go to Korea but reconsidered after a family friend told of the money to be made simply peddling fish in Hilo, Hawaiʻi. Interestingly, another friend urged him to go to Korea, where "the Japanese exploit the Koreans; in Hawaiʻi, the barbarians (*keto*, "hairy" Caucasians) exploit the Japanese. Give up the idea of Hawaiʻi and go to Korea instead" (2).

Father Matsujiro and son Akira also have different versions of Matsujiro's arrangements for passage from Yamaguchi to Honolulu. Matsujiro describes his first attempt, which ended in failure when the young clerk in the office of the Bocho Emigration Company told him that they did not process applications from individuals, that only married couples were eligible. Dejected, Matsujiro returned to his little island village on the next boat. There he would not let the matter rest and wrote to Shimanuki Hyotayu, who wrote on emigration matters for the influential magazine *Shonen Sekai* (World of youth). Shimanuki wrote back, explaining that the company was simply seeking more profits, since it received twenty yen as a handling charge for a couple and only ten yen for an individual.

The next morning, Matsujiro writes, he booked passage back to the Bocho office and took a room at a Japanese inn. He ordered tea, and his spontaneous and substantial tip for the maid produced a surprising amount of sweets. Armed with this new knowledge about the power of cash, Matsujiro set off for the office. This time he demanded to see the manager, who reiterated the company policy. When Matsujiro replied that he was willing to pay the twenty yen, the man simply said that was, of course, assumed but would make no difference. So Matsujiro offered thirty yen and suggested that the manager could simply produce a receipt for ten yen. This offer was more than acceptable; indeed, the manager simply crossed one couple's name off the ship's list for the December trip and added Otani's. Later, on the train ride to Kobe, the port of debarkation, Matsujiro read in a newspaper headline that the United States and Japan had agreed to halt further labor migration. The Gentlemen's Agreement of 1908 would take effect, and it was only timeliness and his wit that allowed the young man to reach Hawaiʻi.[42]

Are the differences between the son's and the father's story significant? If so, how do we account for them? I would suggest that they provide subtle but important nuances to the meanings constructed by issei and nisei regarding their heritages. By his own account, Matsujiro Otani was fairly well educated; had a reasonable amount of capital to "invest" in the emigration process; and was quite prepared to exploit the greed of the emigration-company official to achieve his goal. He did not bow to authority; he did not wait patiently for any next opportunity; and he was assertive in that context. It is possible, of course, that the written autobiographical account was embellished or that the elder Otani was involved in his own selective recreation of a family heritage. For him, the image of a brash sixteen-year-old with education and means in his family might fit better than a version conjured up for him, however well intentioned, by the next generation.

For nisei like Akira, however, it may have made more sense to reconstruct an image more in tune with the prevailing one: the poor, hard-working, honest, law-abiding, relatively uneducated youngster who succeeds not through luck or chicanery but with a thoroughgoing work ethic. That is to say, the Otani family succeeded by dint of struggle and hard work and correct values. And, while the nisei Akira might prefer this interpretation, his issei father, Matsujiro, felt no such need. Much of this interpretive difference has to do, I will suggest, with the generalized evolution of a myth that purports to explain and justify the upward mobility of Japanese Americans after World War II.

Richard Zukemura recalls next to nothing about his mother but knows that his father's family had considerable property in Yonabaru, Okinawa. In fact, they owned a ship that transported lumber from distant forests to their town. But beyond that: "Grandparents—I don't know anything about my grandparents" (1).

The family was quite prosperous when Zukemura's father left Okinawa "as soon as he graduated high school, because he was afraid of the conscription going on; he volunteered to come as an immigrant to Hawai'i" (1). Zukemura's father was not unique. There were numbers of issei who left Japan to evade the draft, especially as Japan increasingly widened its colonial base and imperial adventures in the early twentieth century. It must have been especially difficult for Okinawans, themselves victims of Japanese expansion, to be conscripted and forced to participate in further overseas imperialism.

As Meiji Japan expanded into an empire in the 1870s, the Japanese differentiated between the *naichi* (the "inner lands" of the archipelago) and the *gaichi* (the "outer lands" of inferior folk appended to the growing nation). And while the knowledge or memory of this history is at best opaque, these rifts remain salient in the Japanese American community.[43]

Another of the VVV, Yoshiaki Fujitani, became a bishop in the Nishi Hongwanji sect of Jodo Shinshu Buddhism. The Fujitani family had been priests for generations in Shimane prefecture, north of Hiroshima, fronting the Japan Sea. Yoshiaki's father, a second son who would not inherit the family temple, was nevertheless committed to the ministry, traveled to India, and did missionary work in Okinawa before moving on to Hawai'i. Yoshiaki's mother had arrived from Toyama and was the only child of an issei masseur on Kauai who eventually returned to Japan:

> My dad was Kodo Fujitani and he first came to Hawai'i in 1920; . . . we just assumed that he was rather adventurous and he didn't want to be tied down to any place. . . . [He had] the equivalent of a university education.
>
> And he came out here when he was about thirty-two or thirty-three, and he was single. My mother, who had come earlier, when she was four years old, to Hawai'i, just happened to be at the main temple on Pali Highway at the dormitory as the "dormitory mother," as the position was called. And somebody decided that they should get married; . . . I guess it was arranged.
>
> So we had the benefit of a Japanese-speaking father and an English-speaking mother; . . . she was bilingual. We, of course, preferred English so we spoke English more at home.
>
> She was one of the earlier young people to go into teaching. She was a graduate of the normal school here. . . . But, being born in Japan, she was considered an alien, and she couldn't teach. . . . I think she went to Philips Commercial school to learn secretarial work. (1–3)

Ted Tsukiyama was one of the few VVV members who knew a great deal about both parents and their families. His parents were unusually well educated, and Ted became a well-known attorney and an even better known labor arbitrator. His father graduated from prestigious Keio University in Tokyo and arrived in Hawai'i in 1911; his mother was from the Kagawa family, related to the prominent Isoshima merchants in Honolulu. Perhaps this background helps explain Ted's youthful sense that the VVV experience was worth documenting; he used a camera systematically and diligently and also kept his letters and documents from the 1942 VVV and wartime experiences. (Most of the photographs in this volume come from a set of negatives he had tucked away for decades in an old Best Pal candy box.) Ted understood that his family background was unusual.

My father is a Tokyo-born person and those are kind of rare in Hawaiʻi; ... we always thought he should have been a college professor or something rather than a businessman. ... My mother happened to be born in Japan when my grandmother happened to be visiting the old village in Kagawa ken [prefecture], which is on a little island [Shikoku] on the Inland Sea. She's technically issei but soon after birth she was brought back here. And then when she was of school age they sent her back to Japan to a school called Ferris ... the missionary schools. So she is bilingual. She could be considered an older nisei. She speaks English quite fluently. (1–2)

Unlike most of the VVV interviewees, Herb Isonaga, an unusually thoughtful man, had reflected seriously about his family experiences and understood that he had been told much more about his mother than his father because of the social-class difference between their families. Herb's father was educated only through the elementary grades in Yamaguchi prefecture, but his mother completed *chugakko*, the equivalent perhaps of high school today. His mother was the storyteller in his family, and Isonaga remembers that she recounted many tales of a more comfortable life in Japan:

See, my mother came from a merchant family—a fairly wealthy family ... my mother loved to talk about it. My dad, on the other hand, came from a poor family so he never said much about his side. ...

My parents directed their business solely to the Filipino trade, whereas the other Japanese merchants, naturally, ... geared mostly for the Japanese trade. My parents, my father, felt that he wanted to do business with the Filipinos; ... he said because they were a clean people to deal with. No static. ... He didn't want to deal with them [the Japanese]. ... My dad to his dying day said that dealing with the Filipinos— he thought that the Filipinos were the most wonderful people in the world. (2–4)

Herb's parents were unusual; on New Year's Day, when Japanese families visited one another, the Isonagas made it a point to invite some of their best Filipino customers and friends: "The single ones. ... Not everybody, but the ones that the family knew very well" (13). His mother regularly read the *Reader's Digest* in Japanese translation, perhaps the single best magazine at the time through which the stories and values of "middle America" might be absorbed. His father, on the other hand, read voraciously but concentrated on business and other commercial magazines (5). The Isonaga parents were curious about the world around them and transmitted this value to their children. It is not surprising, then, to learn that Herb's sister was one of a few dozen women from Hawai'i to volunteer for the Women's Army Corps during World War II.

Former VVV George Yamamoto, a sociology professor, also learned considerably more about his mother. In Yamamoto's case, this was largely due to his father's early death, but he also researched her family background.

Yamamoto's father died in a fishing accident in 1928 when George was only ten years old. As a result, "like many other nisei, I regret very much not having talked with my mother more about my father's background, especially about his early years in Hawai'i, . . . while she was still living."

> My father was from Hiroshima, Takata-gun. . . . He was a plantation hand on the Big Island when he first came. I don't know whether he actually committed some kind of crime, but he and two others moved to Oahu and changed their names.
>
> See, it wasn't like escaping during the government-contract period kind of thing. But he may have decided he wasn't going to take any more of the stuff. . . . So I went to school with the name of Yamaoka, the new name. In fact, we were known as the Yamaoka family. . . .
>
> I learned that we were really Yamamotos when I was in the sixth grade. When I went to Central Intermediate, on my own just registered as Yamamoto. (1–2)

Yamamoto's musings about his father's escaping from a Big Island plantation contract are entirely plausible. In the government-contract period (*kanyaku imin jidai*), 1885–1894, as well as in the period of private contracts (*shiyaku*), 1894–1900, many immigrant workers simply deserted when faced with pay or conditions that disappointed. The search for such men became a cottage industry that involved, among others, plantation personnel, Hawai'i sheriffs, bounty hunters, and detectives hired from Japan. Desertion was a common and major form of resistance by sugar-contract laborers. It was generally known that many Japanese immigrants fled to places like Waimanalo on Oahu or Kona on the Big Island, where their ethnic communities sheltered and hid workers from the authorities. As Jiro Nakano put it: "They ran through the dense koa or kiawe forests at the foothills of Mauna Kea and Mauna Loa and walked across the vast lava desert. Some of them were chased relentlessly by horse-riding *lunas* and sent back to the plantation when caught. If the escapees resisted their command or fought against the *lunas*, these escapees were shot to death by police officers. After long, dangerous journeys on foot the fortunate escaped Japanese laborers who reached the Japanese villages in Kona changed their names to avoid being identified and prosecuted."[44]

The end of government-enforced labor contracts in 1900 meant that Yamamoto's father could not have been prosecuted by the territory, but there certainly were extrajudicial means of retaliation. Plantation managers regularly exchanged "blacklists" to exclude troublemakers from employment, and, since both public and private sectors were effectively controlled by the same small oligarchy, resistance was difficult except by changing one's name and burrowing into the ethnic community.

IT IS ENTIRELY reasonable that Japanese Americans want and need to find reasons to be proud of their heritage. In the stories of the VVV families, as with the larger Japanese American communities, there is much of value, but their accomplishments and "contributions" need to be carefully contextualized. The issei were a hardy and very human people who lived through extraordinary times and brought forth an energetic new generation, the nisei. In the past, the Chinese are said to have favored the expression, when wishing ill will upon others: "May you live in interesting times!" Since the social ideal was tranquility and stability, "interesting times" were best avoided. For better or worse, both issei and nisei were fated to live through some of the most fascinating decades in U.S. history.

2

Generation on Trial

The 1920s

orn about the year 1920, the men of the VVV entered a world of conflicting political and economic ideologies. The success of the 1917 Bolshevik revolution had triggered a global war between socialism and capitalism. U.S. chauvinism was expressed in bigotry and racism against eastern Europeans, Jews, Catholics, and all peoples of color. The Ku Klux Klan and other nativist groups were gaining power across the country. Anti-Asian, especially anti-Japanese, movements proliferated in California and on the rest of the West Coast.[1] In Hawai`i, the brunt of this nativist reaction was turned against the Japanese American community, the largest and most militant of the several minority groups imported to work on the sugar plantations.

The decade began with two critical issues facing Hawai`i and its Japanese community: a growing conviction among the haole elite that Japanese-language schools had to be eliminated, and the escalating class war between sugar planters and their Japanese workers. In an intensified version of the 1909 strike, the 1920 version was the most devastating in Hawaii's history. The Big Five oligarchy successfully portrayed the Japanese as an enemy race scheming to take over the islands through their control of sugar-plantation labor. In the end, sugar planters succeeded in breaking the costly strike by isolating the Japanese from other strikers, principally Filipinos.[2]

The decade ended with the swift execution, on November 19, 1929, of Myles Yutaka Fukunaga, a nisei teenager, who confessed to kidnaping and murdering the young son of a Big Five executive. This execution may be interpreted as a "racial project," as opposed to a single or several loosely related racial incidents, designed to maintain haole supremacy in the face of a rapidly growing nisei population.[3]

Before the 1920s ended, the United States had declared that Japanese could not enter the country, could not own land in many states, could not marry whites, and could not become naturalized citizens. Further, the issei were urged to direct their U.S.-born children to assimilate completely, to the point of divesting themselves of dual citizenship and any remaining elements of Japanese culture, including their language and traditional religious beliefs. In this tumultuous decade, the nisei became the center of their community's ambitions and the target of Big Five concerns for preserving a stable social order and haole hegemony.

THE 1922 SUPREME COURT decision in the case of Takao Ozawa, whose protracted attempt to become naturalized began in Hawai`i, effectively terminated any possibility of Japanese immigrants becoming U.S. citizens, a state of affairs that last until 1952. Also in 1922, Congress passed the Cable Act, mandating the loss of U.S. citizenship for women who married aliens ineligible for naturalization, legislation that clearly targeted the Japanese. (The act was amended in 1931 and finally repealed in 1936.) The consequences were especially unhappy for nisei women who married issei men. The Immigration Act of 1924 finally prohibited all Japanese immigration into the country. Yuji Ichioka argues that this event marked the end of all hope that the issei held for the U.S. system. Adding final insult to injury, the U.S. Supreme Court confirmed in 1925 that Toyota Hidemitsu, although a World War I veteran, could not be naturalized.[4]

Some 454 Hawai`i issei who had served in the U.S. military during World War I were naturalized by Judge Harold Vaughn, but their citizenship was revoked in 1927.[5] Unlike on the mainland, anti-alien land laws were unnecessary in Hawai`i because well over 90 percent of the land was already firmly in the hands of the federal, territorial, and local governments and a handful of corporations, including the Big Five. When an anti-alien land law was proposed, Riley Allen, editor of the Honolulu *Star-Bulletin*, warned in 1921 that it would serve "only to increase friction among the races and retard the progress of Americanization. . . . The legislature did not pursue the issue."[6]

Both the sugar-strike and language-school issues revealed the extent to which the haole elite was willing to manipulate race. Big Five control of the sugar industry also ensured control of major sectors of the economy, as well as state power in the territorial government. But a democratic form of government required a variety of sophisticated institutions beyond the obvious and crude sanctions of economic and police powers. Moreover, it was clear that, as Stephen Gill has put it, "the achievement of hegemony within a particular social formation is a complex and contradictory process, since counter-hegemonic forces will come to challenge the prevailing institutional and political arrangements."[7]

In Hawai`i before World War II, extremely diverse elements of the Japanese community, all working to advance the ethnic community, were using vastly different perspectives in their counterhegemonic efforts. They included communist and socialist labor leaders on the left, reform leaders in the center, and accommodationists on the right.

The Big Five, largely through the print media, effectively created and encouraged the specter of a Japanese American community expanding to engulf the entire territory. In fact, the Japanese American community was growing exactly in proportion to the total population, at slightly less than 40 percent of the total, where it had remained relatively fixed since the turn of the century.

The nature of that community, however, was changing. Immigration from Japan had ended in 1924, but birth rates among the issei were high—not surprising, since so many picture brides had joined their husbands in the decade before 1920. The VVV nisei, for example, typically came from families in which there were four to eight children. In 1900, the nisei comprised a mere 8 percent of the Japanese population. By 1910 they were 25 percent. In 1920, the year some of the VVV members were born, the figure had jumped to 44.5 percent.[8]

By 1924, there were 25,858 students of Japanese ancestry in the public school system, just over half of the total student population.[9] For the foreseeable future, the percentage of nisei students would be substantial. In 1925, for example, there were 4,286 Japanese American second graders of a total 8,878 in Hawaii's public and private schools.[10]

These young nisei would eventually become voters. A negligible influence in 1920, nisei voters became increasingly visible with each election. In 1930 two nisei were even elected on the Republican Party ticket to the territory's house of representatives. If, as the haole elite feared, this group voted as a bloc and maintained Japan as a cultural and political reference point, the entire structure of Hawaiian society would be jeopardized. The stakes were enormous.[11]

Big Five interests saw Japanese-language schools as the primary institution through which the issei and Japan's leaders would indoctrinate the nisei. The first Japanese-language school was built on Maui in 1895, exactly one decade after the arrival of the *kanyaku imin*, the government-contract laborers.[12] Growth was impressive: 1,552 students in 11 schools in 1900; 4,966 in 120 schools in 1907; 17,541 in 143 schools in 1920; peaking in 1933 with 43,606 in 190 schools.[13] There was minor opposition to Japanese-language schools from the very beginning, but serious attacks followed indications, as early as 1900, that the Japanese community was in Hawai`i to stay.

The Japanese undertook several preemptive moves to defuse this growing hostility, most notably in a 1915 conference called largely to revise standard textbooks from Japan. The new texts replaced, for example, stories of the heroic exploits of the great feudal shogun, Tokugawa Ieyasu, with the virtues of George Washington and the cherry-tree incident; peasant philosopher Ninomiya Sontoku's admonitions for living the virtuous life disappeared to make room for tales of Abraham Lincoln's freeing the slaves.[14] These moves were not nearly enough to satisfy the schools' critics.

In 1917, the territorial legislature began drafting laws that restricted Japanese schools, at the same time that the national mood was reflecting anti-immigrant sentiment under the slogan "One nation, one language." In particular, Act 30, passed in a special session of the legislature in November 1920, required foreign-language-school administrators and teachers to obtain permits from the Department of Public Instruction. Within a year, the department followed with regulations that gradually eliminated the language schools entirely. These attacks precipitated a complex set of responses within the Japanese community that led to a lawsuit which was finally resolved in 1927 by the U.S. Supreme Court.[15]

In the 1920s, three prominent community leaders, Takie Okumura, Yasutaro Soga, and Frederick Kinzaburo Makino, took distinctly different approaches to permanent settlement in Hawai`i. Reverend Takie Okumura, head of Makiki Christian Church and founder of the first Japanese-language school in Honolulu, urged the community to comply with the wishes of the haole elite and abandon the language schools as anachronistic and antagonistic. When some of the issei leaders planned a lawsuit to force the territory to withdraw its most restrictive actions, Okumura was quoted as saying the action would be "foolhardy." "Even if we win on legal points, we would only increase their [the Americans'] suspicion, and would endanger the future of our children in Hawaii."[16]

Yasutaro Soga, editor of the *Nippu Jiji*, was less eager for thorough assimilation into U.S. society but saw cooperation as acknowledging political reality. In one editorial, he urged his community to accept the demise of the language schools and "weep into silence" (*naki neiri*): "when I think about the future of the Japanese people, how delicate the situation is, I must take this attitude. The fact that I must do so is sad."[17]

Frederick Kinzaburo Makino was convinced that compromise was folly. Born in Yokohama, Makino was the son of a British silk merchant and a Japanese woman; he took his mother's maiden name and went to Hawai`i in 1899. He began publishing the *Hawaii Hochi* in 1912, using it to help establish a long record of championing equal rights campaigns on behalf of the Japanese in the territory.[18] His basic approach was that good Americans fought aggressively for their rights and respected others who did the same.

When the Supreme Court's 1927 verdict vindicated the long and arduous campaign he had led on the language-school issue, Makino spoke to a group of more than five thousand supporters on March 29, 1927: "The Americans are only too well cognizant of the fact that it is the right of the people living in a free democracy to advocate their rights guaranteed under the Constitution and to seek legal clarification of doubtful points in the enforcement of laws. . . . We ask that the Japanese schools cooperate with the Territorial government officials to strive to raise good American citizens capable of understanding both the English and Japanese languages."[19]

The territory lost this particular battle, but it had several other fronts to open. Of critical importance was the public school system, whose task it was to assimilate the nisei in ways that would promote loyalty both to the United States and the status quo in Hawai`i. The two most influential journalists of the period, Lorrin Thurston, publisher of the *Pacific Commercial Advertiser*, and Riley Allen, editor of the *Honolulu Star-Bulletin*, agreed that the public schools were crucial. In a 1919 address to Japanese-language-school teachers, Thurston definitively stated that public schools were the only hope to Americanize the nisei; Allen wrote that public schools would be the "chief agency" to develop citizenship because they reached "impressionable children, quick to grasp a new language and new ideas."[20]

Like many others across the country, Hawaii's public schools were charged with the task of assimilating large numbers of immigrants and their children in the 1920s. Japanese Americans were, however, a "minority" group of color and, moreover, relatively cohesive and educated. They were also conscious of a homeland that was rapidly developing into an international military power; the issei were relatively nationalistic and their children were taught to respect Japan's national stature. Further, the Japanese had begun to be assimilated not only into an abstract "American society" but also into a local culture that included other nonhaole ethnic groups. That culture was largely defined by its working-class, sugar-plantation context, and was in direct contradistinction to the Big Five, Republican, haole power structure. This local culture had evolved its own language: pidgin English or, as linguistics scholars like Charlene Sato have suggested, Hawaiian Creole English (HCE).[21] Almost to a man, the VVV members grew up in the 1920s speaking HCE as their first language.

That the multiethnic working class spoke pidgin was an issue often raised by Big Five families, who traditionally sent their children to private schools, thus shielding them from relationships which might dangerously blur class and race distinctions. Big Five children attended elite Punahou Academy, which maintained a rigid quota, restricting students of Asian descent to less than 10 percent of enrollment, a practice continued well into the post–World War II period. Punahou's 1920 graduating class of thirty-eight, for example, included twenty-six haoles, eight part-Hawaiians, three Chinese, and one Japanese.[22]

In 1920, the U.S. Bureau of Education conducted a major study of education in Hawai`i. It noted that only 2–3 percent of children entering public schools at ages six or seven could speak Standard English. This study set the stage for the creation, in 1924, of a separate set of schools to protect the minority white children from HCE contamination.

The end result was a successful effort to set aside a few schools (never more than half a dozen in the entire territory) to serve white children in a separate track. The first site, established in 1924, was Lincoln Elementary School on Oahu. Roosevelt Junior High was established when these students advanced to the seventh grade, and in 1929 Roosevelt High School was created.[23] The *Hawaii Hochi*, Makino's paper, criticized the English Standard Schools as a "Nordic caste system" "utterly at variance with the ideals for which America stands."[24] Makino's journalistic hyperbole had a point. The new system upheld the status quo and gave the small but growing white middle class an education superior to that provided for "local others" and validated, in highly visible fashion, the supremacy of Anglo-American culture. In a more general way, the English Standard School system served as a powerful metaphor for the race and class divide between haole and nonhaole, with Native Hawaiians occupying a peculiar and precarious middle ground.

This was, then, an extraordinary decade in which to spend the first years of life, especially for Japanese American boys in Hawai`i. It was also an important period for several adults who would become important to the VVV: John Young, Richard Lum, Shigeo Yoshida, and Hung Wai Ching. These individuals helped create a climate in which the VVV became a political project in the face of extraordinary anti-Japanese hostility. Their experiences illuminate important forces affecting Hawai`i in the 1920s and describe the context in which the VVV men spent their early, formative years.

John Young, haole director of the Nuuanu branch of the YMCA in 1942, helped serve as midwife to the birth of the VVV. He had been recruited from college in Springfield, Ohio, in 1924 to head the Nuuanu YMCA branch, where he remained until he was sent to Japan in 1928. After four months, he was despatched to establish a religious education program in Nanking, China, and stayed until "the Chinese, the communists," ordered him to leave in 1934. He returned to complete his seminary work and then went to Maui for two years, 1936–38, before resuming his post at the Nuuanu YMCA, where he worked with the urban working-class Japanese and Chinese American youth until mid-1942 (2–3).

Young's initiation into Hawaii's social and racial dynamics was swift. He learned quickly that the "Central YMCA catered to the haoles, the Hawaiians, and the Portuguese," who at the time occupied the higher reaches of the social hierarchy. As for the Japanese or Chinese kids: "Well, if you came and said, 'May I join the YMCA?' they would take you, but quite reluctantly, yeah. Now it wasn't the fault of the YMCA secretaries. It was the fault of the board of directors of the YMCA, who were the plantation people" (17).

At the Nuuanu YMCA, Young found 2,500 boys vying for attention in a facility originally planned for 125 youngsters. And since he was occasionally required to discipline troublemakers, he had to live with youthful retaliation: "It was not unusual to find at least three or four nails in one of my tires." Young felt that "the Japanese kids had a degree of devilish in them. The same with the Chinese kids. But it was mostly—it wasn't malicious" (26). These relationships instilled in him a deep and abiding trust in the youngsters and a willingness to become a staunch advocate during the war. As a sympathetic nonlocal haole, he provided valuable cover for the nisei when times were especially bad.

The second figure who would be important to the VVV's success, Shigeo Yoshida, was a fascinating anomaly, a Japanese American with unusual influence among key military and civilian decision makers during World War II. Along with Chinese American Hung Wai Ching and haole Charles Loomis, Yoshida would join the critically important Morale Section, which advised and led civilian work for the military government.

Yoshida graduated in 1930 from the University of Hawaii, where he had developed a keen interest in debate. Fortunately for him, influential businessperson Charles Hemenway then headed the university's Board of Regents. Hemenway, whose only son had died in an accident, took a particular interest in undergraduates—especially those active in debate and athletics. Yoshida and the debate team met periodically at the Hemenway home to practice, a highly unusual situation because the only Asian Americans at that time allowed into most Big Five homes were domestics and other service personnel. It was Hemenway, ultimately, who was responsible for the participation of Ching and Yoshida in race-relations policymaking.

Yoshida had thought seriously about "racial matters from the time I was a high school kid when I had grave reservations . . . about us designating ourselves as 'Japanese-Americans,' as hyphenated Americans." By the 1920s there was a Japanese American Civic Association led by young nisei, including Jack Wakayama and Clifton Yamamoto, but Shigeo "didn't particularly like their approach. I objected even that early . . . to people in Hawai`i associating themselves or categorizing themselves as Japanese Americans or Chinese Americans." Later, as a direct result of the war with Japan, Yoshida would change his thinking because of having been singled out as enemy aliens and the children of enemy aliens, but in the 1920s, "Basically, my idea was that people in Hawai`i, made up of many races, should be amalgamated into one. That idea is not popular today. Today they emphasize the ethnic qualities—but basically we're all Americans" (20).[25]

Yoshida felt that the 1928 Fukunaga case had "brought out definitely the need for a greater voice on the part of Japanese Americans in what took place over here" (12). For him, issues like Japanese-language schools became part of the movement to secure that greater voice, although he was never a supporter of the schools. Yoshida's parents, like most issei, insisted that young Shigeo attend Japanese-language school, but he complied "only up to the fifth grade." He was aware that the schools were highly controversial, "even among the Japanese," but the primary reason for his resistance was the inconvenience of attending either before or after "regular" school hours. "So, while I was registered, I guess I spent more time playing hookey," he laughed, "than . . ." (14–15).

Shigeo Yoshida was one of a handful of nisei who in the pre–World War II years managed to negotiate the difficult haole/local boundaries in Hawai`i. Success depended on a thoroughgoing assimilationist stance, including the rejection of ethnic-based associations and of languages other than Standard English. Most individuals would not or could not manage the required degree of skill and alienation from their own ethnic groups. Yoshida cultivated a calm and deliberate bearing, a dignity and adroitness that would, in some measure, force his social superiors to confront the contradictions built into their ideology. In their own way, as a result, Yoshida and other assimilationists managed to push back the parameters of haole hegemony. Yoshida's colleague in the Morale Section, Hung Wai Ching, did this with a different set of strengths and a very different personality.

Hung Wai Ching is recalled as the "father" of the VVV—the man who engineered the formation of the group, who mentored its young leaders, and who insisted that its legacy be acknowledged. In a period marked by Chinese American rage against Japan and, sometimes, Japanese Americans because of Japan's atrocities in China, he worked aggressively for tolerance. When Ching graduated from McKinley High School in 1924, it was "the only [public] high school here, you know. . . . You must remember, Hawai`i, University of Hawai`i, was controlled. Everything—our education was absolutely controlled during that period" (22). At the University of Hawai`i he was an outstanding athlete, playing on the basketball team and selected captain of the track team. He was also class president for three years and active with Shigeo Yoshida in debate activity in spite of his heavy pidgin: "Number-one pidgin English. And I'll never forget the time when I ran for student-body president and I had to make a speech. Oh, boy, was I ashamed.

Lydgate beat me. You know, big haole family, Punahou. Oh, shamed, bo-oy!" (20).

Hung Wai had no reason to be ashamed. He was developing a personal style that was aggressively "local." He was brash, loud, explosive. He spoke his mind and let his passions show. Ching was not a debater but assisted the team and recalled meeting at Charles Hemenway's home, or that of another corporate lawyer "who took a liking of our local kids. We'd meet once or twice a month to debate issues in tournament" (20).

Ching also remembered going to language school—in his case, to study Chinese—although it was not all study, especially toward the end of the 1920s when Japan's increasingly virulent militarism targeted China. "I used to go look for Japanese kids to lick." [He laughed.] "Oh, my father was a Nationalist—there was a Japanese invasion. . . . At the language school, the Chinese teacher said, 'Let's go get some—lick some Japanese kid. Only pick on the little ones.' I wasn't a damn fool. I've stepped on Japanese kids' heads." [More laughter.] (31–32).

For the VVV members themselves in the 1920s, family, neighborhood, and elementary schools, both public and Japanese-language versions, were of primary importance. These years helped shape their values and attitudes and socialized them into prewar Hawai`i. Although a few were reared in homes where some English was spoken, most had issei parents who spoke only Japanese. Of forty-five VVV members queried in 1984, only nine included a nisei among their parents. It may be recalled that some of their parents were relatively well educated.

The VVV men grew up, by and large, apart from the material hardships of plantation families or of the urban poor usually associated with Hawaii's Asian American or Native Hawaiian population in the pre–World War II period. For one thing, the Japanese American community was much more stable than other Asian immigrant groups. In comparison, Filipinos, the most recent arrivals, were overwhelmingly bachelors. By 1920, only 50 percent of Chinese men over twenty-five were married, and only 38 percent of Korean men. Of Japanese men over twenty-five, however, fully 72 percent were married, and the fact that many spouses were employed helped family finances. In 1910, an astonishing 44 percent of Japanese females over the age of ten were gainfully employed outside the home; by 1920, the percentage had dropped to 30 but was still the highest among all ethnic groups.[26]

Most of the fathers of the VVV members worked as shopkeepers, supervisors, skilled craftsmen, or in white-collar jobs. At the ends of the spectrum, only four were described as laborers and two as professionals—one a dentist and the other, Yoshiaki Fujitani's father, a high-ranking Buddhist priest. Thus, most of the VVV came from a cohort of relatively well educated and well positioned families. Most (64 percent) of the forty-five men who responded to the survey grew up in rural areas; the others lived in Honolulu. Their families were, generally, fairly large—thirty-four included four to eight children, and at least two families had ten children.

Former VVV member Ralph Yempuku became a well-known promoter in post–World War II Hawai`i, bringing in entertainment shows from the mainland, as well as from Japan. Hung Wai Ching arranged his appointment as civilian supervisor of the VVV.

As a child, Ralph helped by cleaning his father's Buddhist temple and polishing "the ornaments" (3). He retains distinct impressions of the different ethnic groups in and around Kahuku Plantation, on Oahu's North Shore. He had little contact with the haole children, even though he lived closer to them than to the immigrant workers' camps. This social segregation was even more marked after he moved into Honolulu to attend Central Intermediate and McKinley High Schools. At Kahuku, the haole homes "had a tennis court. But they wouldn't let us play there, the Japanese kids. I mean, only the haole kids could play there. It was a plantation court, . . . you had to know your place; . . . you resented it, but not to the extent where you are going to do something about it. . . . Haoles own the plantation, you know." Because he did not participate in any organized sports, Yempuku felt the only way to express his feelings was to "compete with them [haoles] in the classroom. It encourages you to make better grades than them" (13). Regarding the other groups:

> Well, I liked the Hawaiians; . . . they didn't work too hard so you not only liked, you envied them. . . . I liked them much, much more than I liked the haoles; . . . maybe I felt closer to them. . . .
>
> There weren't too many Filipinos there at that time. . . . I didn't like the Filipinos. . . . My father used to say "*yabanjin*," . . . barbarians. . . . And they used cane knives and all that which the Japanese would never think of doing.
>
> Okinawans—I think if I had dated an Okinawan girl and my father found out, he'd kick my ass. . . . Yeah, they looked down on the Okinawans. . . . And Okinawans, usually, at that time they all had tattoos. They had that on their hands; . . . when my father and mother came

over here, they already had that feeling about looking down on the Okinawan. (14–15)

Yempuku is here describing attitudes held by him and his family in the 1920s; I suspect that many, probably most, of the Japanese families shared these prejudices. In the course of the interviews, I encouraged Yempuku and others to be candid about issues of race and racism; Ralph was more forthcoming, I believe, than many others in describing these prejudices.

His fellow VVV member Shiro Amioka grew up in the urban Kakaako district, part of a sizable Japanese community that had established a thriving fishing industry. Shiro's father was "a captain of a ship, so he was a kind of an entrepreneur in a way. So they were not too bad off. . . . Except my dad got sick and that changed the whole picture; . . . when I was growing up we were not well off. We were from the other side of the tracks" (4).

The Amioka family had ten children, although two died in infancy. Amioka could not remember the home they lived in while his father was healthy, but the second was a duplex:

> If you go in the first floor, the ground is just ground [packed earth]. . . .
> A portion of it then is elevated with *goza* [straw mat]. So I would say about three-fourths of the house may be on *tatami* [padded, straw mat]. The rest is just dirt. . . . No partition or anything; and then when you go up the steps—second floor—that's where we used to sleep. There were two rooms with a toilet upstairs. . . . Oh, no toilet downstairs, one toilet upstairs. . . . Of course *ofuro* [Japanese bath]—we used a barrel and funnel in the hot water from the outside. We used wood to heat it up and it comes in and you take the water and put it in the tub.
>
> My sisters and my parents used to sleep in one bedroom and all the boys slept in the other room. . . . I would use the dining table to study; . . . whoever wants to study would use that.
>
> If you look back and you want to put labels of contemporary sociology, well, we were disadvantaged, but when we were growing up, at least, I never felt that. (4–6)

Amioka was especially insistent that his home conditions be understood—that there was no sense of being "poor." A solidly packed dirt floor, he noted, can be kept nearly immaculate, its surface swept almost to a sheen. Amioka's home was typical of working-class families' circumstances. It was not simply that there was little disposable income but that houses were rented or leased—and it was extravagant to invest in anything the family would never own. I recall this reasoning in my own family, which moved from an urban grocery store with living quarters above to a small truck crop farm in 1943. Our house was not much better, for many years, than that commonly associated with southern sharecroppers' homes in the same time frame. Any income generated had to be plowed back into the farm, and there was precious little left for comforts in the home.

Communication within the Amioka family was not easy, even though Shiro was slightly better off than many of his peers, since his mother was a nisei, born on Kauai. Like his father, however, she had received her schooling in Japan, returning as a picture bride in an arranged marriage. His parents related to one another in "typical Hawai`i Japanese, but it was more Japanese than English." Shiro noted, however, that the language itself was not the major factor that inhibited free communication: "Well, it's not a question so much of the language in our case, because, you know, you could communicate. It may not be the best Japanese but you could sit down and talk. . . . So language—in my case, it's not the language so much that's a barrier, just making time to sit down and talk, which we did not do so much of. . . . You know, while you eating, Japanese style, you don't talk, just eat. Nowadays you make conversation, at least in our family" (7).

Kakaako developed a reputation as a tough district, with gangs of youths ready to fight over turf or "girls" or almost anything.[27] But Amioka was quick to point out that, in the pre–World War II period, the sense of community made a tremendous difference in preventing the social dislocation associated with contemporary urban-ghetto conditions:

> It was rough but unlike the so-called rough kids of today, we were growing up in a real community; . . . there were rules and regs, the community mores. So, within that framework, you had better behave, because the peers and your superiors around you will let you have it. Now they'll protect you against outside forces, but within it, if you don't behave, they'll let you have it . . . oh, give you a good licking, physically keep you in line. So there is this kind of community pressure, community ethics morality which, amidst this reputation of being rough, had organized discipline, and I think that had a lot to do with how we behaved in school. In regular school you dealt with the principal; in Japanese school you dealt with the teachers. (9)

Nearly every VVV member recalled this "sense of community" within which youngsters could negotiate the 1920s. No one locked doors; kids ate at each other's homes; it was difficult to avoid the close and compelling sense of belonging—some of which may have contributed to the young men's ability to form the VVV in 1942.

One of them, Masato Doi, later became one of the legendary nisei voted into office in the 1954 elections that brought the Democratic Party to power for the first time in Hawaiian history. Born in 1921, Doi grew up in a small sugar-plantation community in Paauhau on the Big Island with "mostly Japanese; second largest group would've been the Filipino. I remember one Chinese person. He was the cook, you know." Of course, there were "very few haoles, but they would be the managers and the supervisors. Very few Portuguese persons. They too would hold, let's say, the better jobs. You know, maybe mechanics, field supervisors [luna]." (3)

Doi recalled the pleasures of the countryside: "We kids did have a lot of fun together playing baseball, but baseball with tennis balls, now, not the regular hard balls because we wouldn't be able to get hold of real hard balls. . . . We called them 'skin-balls.'" They spent a lot of time "hiking into the mountains and going into the gulches, swimming in the pond and picking all kinds of fruits—guava, *ohia* [mountain apples], and things like that" (6). Masato remembered clear ethnic and racial stratification: "The Japanese would be looked at slightly above the Filipino group, and within the Japanese communities, the Okinawa group would be looked down on as not being on par with the rest of the Japanese groups, but the haoles and Hawaiians were above the Japanese. . . . I never experienced any kind of overt, you know, overt discrimination. . . . [The Portuguese were]—oh, in between the haoles and the Japanese." [He laughed.] (6–7)

The nature of the relations between the Okinawans and naichi (those from the "inner lands" of the archipelago) has always been difficult for the Japanese. Until very recent times, there have been numerous anecdotal versions of families who objected to dating or marriage between the groups; I recall prejudice among fellow naichi as I was growing up in the forties and fifties. When I asked Masato about his prewar experience with Okinawans, he thought for a moment and replied:

> I went to school with Okinawan kids and nothing ever showed as far as being discriminatory or class conscious. . . . But, you know, there's

something I have to tell you. I don't know for a fact, but I think that maybe my oldest sister married an Okinawan. The more I think about it now, the more I think so. I never thought about it, not once; never crossed my mind until about, well, until after he died when he was about seventy, when something about Okinawans came out between my wife and me. Her sister on the mainland is married to one. (7–8)

This is a very telling statement. In more contemporary times, when a powerful surge of ethnic consciousness emerged, it would have been difficult to imagine such unresolved confusion. But it was not until the 1970s that a more positive Okinawan "identity" became manifest in cultural, political, community-organizing, and history-making activities. Until then, sympathetic naichi sometimes denied the distinction or its significance. Official Meiji ideology disparaged Okinawan people and culture, a reflection of Japan's colonization of Okinawa in 1874.[28]

Former VVV member Herbert Isonaga, whose storekeeper parents preferred Filipino customers to Japanese, was born in 1921. His family's diet was

Fifty-fifty, Japanese and local, like chop suey and meat loaf and stuff like that. . . . Special occasions, we killed a rooster. Chicken was a must. Maybe a ham, sausages. Of course, I am not mentioning the typical Japanese stuff like *kamaboko* [Japanese fishcake] and salad. Potato salad and macaroni salad was a special treat (16). Life was comfortable and fun.Well, we went hiking. We went camping. We went fishing. We went swimming. We made a boat out of tin roofing . . . *totan* boat. And we went sledding with those palm—not the leaves, the semi-circular . . . stem from which the leaves come out, and we used to go up in the hills and slide down the grass slopes . . . better than ti leaf, we used to wax the bottom. . . . [We'd] ride horses and go out and cut grass . . . go for mangoes and mountain apples and bananas and things out in the wild. . . . It seemed like we had endless things to do. (8–9)

Isonaga's reference to "sledding" on palm or ti leaves is a particularly Hawaiian form of downhill sport. With ample leaves or stems and a steep and slicked grassy slope, riders achieved exhilarating and indeed dangerous speeds.

Herbert Isonaga's comments on the cultural and racial context of the 1920s were frank and interesting: "Somehow I never grew up with any strong feelings about racial discord. . . . And I hope that my feeling is not one of acceptance, you know . . . in the plantation community, the white bosses are the boss. No ifs and buts. You don't challenge it. So I guess some of that kind of rubs off" (8–15).

Since Hawai'i was comprised of a number of ethnic groups, it was through the attitudes of the parents that the children of the 1920s adopted and adapted the patterns of interaction. The Isonaga family's relationship with Filipinos was "excellent." Fortunately for the family, the rest of the Japanese community, which was notoriously contemptuous of Filipinos, did not react against the Isonagas "because we did business with the Filipinos," Herb said.

> Our family, in terms of its business, had very little to do with the Portuguese. Of course, I should say that my parents, and I guess most of the parents, they looked down on the Portuguese. . . . I don't know why, but they said, "*Portogee no ko to asobuna!* [Don't play with the Portuguese children]." . . . Going back, talking about the Filipinos, I don't know how my parents would have reacted if we associated with the Filipinos on a social level. . . . Business was one thing. But there were very few Filipino families. They were mostly single guys, bachelors. . . .
>
> Hawaiians were the same like Portuguese. Now I'm talking about my parents here. Their attitude, well, they looked down on the Hawaiians. . . . Oh, yeah. Yeah. There were [Hawaiian] landowners. I guess it's their *yaban* attitude. Barbarian. . . . My dad's evaluation of an individual—and this is why, I guess, one of the reasons he was crushed when Japan lost—was your worth as an individual representing a certain race depends on the strength of your country. . . . If your country is weak, you're nothing.
>
> Oh, he, during that period Korea was occupied by Japan. . . . Oh, well. You're nobody. Your country is nobody. . . . [China, too,] that's the same thing, see. Okinawans—really no country. (12–14)

Like most issei, Isonaga's parents were not especially religious or were typical Buddhists in tolerating other religious beliefs and the absence of church attendance. Indeed, they "encouraged us to go to the Christian church; . . . I wasn't an exception." "Looking back, it seemed that our parents were pretty smart in steering us to the Christian church, because the Christian church had a program, Sunday school, which is learning. Whereas the Buddhist church offered very little in that educational phase. . . . There wasn't any feeling of being forced to go, but we knew we had to go. Just like going to school" (15).

Former VVV member George Yamamoto was born in 1917 in Maunawili—across the Koolau mountain range from Honolulu (4). Yamamoto's father had completed at least eight years of schooling in Hiroshima prefecture before arriving in Hawai`i about 1905. After leaving the Big Island, he worked at Schofield Barracks as a stable boy. George's mother arrived from Yamaguchi prefecture in 1916 as a picture bride, and she and his father were employees of a pineapple plantation in Maunawili. After the plantation failed, George recalls the family's moving to Kaneohe, several miles from Maunawili, to work at a pineapple cannery (6–8):

> I remember some evenings, my father had access into the cannery. You know those crude kind of coolers, pineapple-can coolers, after the cans had been cooked and capped and then covered and then the cans would be, I guess, run through a low tank of water, which was just like a *furo* [bath]. Wooden, you know. I remember going with my father to take a bath. There was more or less heat left from a continued stream of cans, hot cans being cooled, during the day. (6–8)

George recalled, in careful detail, his youth in the 1920s. When he was about five years old, he saw a succession of Hollywood westerns that featured Tom Mix and Hoot Gibson, as well as Japanese silent films "accompanied by live actors. They would show the movie and after a certain portion of the film had been projected, then the projector would stop and then the lights in the stage would go up and the actors would take the place of the characters in the film and then do *shibai* [play, theater], regular *shibai*.

The cannery soon closed, however, and Yamamoto's father turned to fishing, as part of a team of Japanese *hikiami*, fishing from the shore with nets:

> You go out in the evening; it's always night work in the shallows, to catch mullet, but *weke* [a type of reef fish] and all kinds of other fish would—and crabs, a lot of them—would fall into the net. I learned that sometimes because of the quiet—"Don't make any noise" kind of thing—there must have been some poaching on this old *konohiki* [traditional Native Hawaiian land rights]. . . . One summer when I was thirteen—and nearly killed by the work—after my father died, to use up my summers profitably, I was the net boy. You got to pull the leaded bottom. (8)

George's father had a second job—brewing *okolehao*, the potent Hawaiian version of bootleg liquor distilled from the roots of the ti plant.

The Japanese in Hawai'i had been making varieties of beer, wine, and sake ever since their arrival and indeed had pioneered some innovations that eventually found their way back to the sake-brewing industry in Japan.[29] And, whether during the Prohibition Era (1920–34) when all alcohol was banned, or at other times when they were distilling it illegally, the issei were active as entrepreneurs and consumers. George's father, then, was part of a well-established tradition.

> His main job, it turned out, was to work at night for the *oyabun* [boss] there; . . . that guy was running a still. He had the car and he would transport not fish, but *okolehao*. . . . Once, it was daytime and some revenue agents or the police, they came down and they got all these five-gallon jugs of *okolehao*; line them up; . . . they got sledge hammers and right there, bust them up. Bang. Bang. Bang.
>
> But one time it was a night raid and my father was working; . . . he got nabbed, . . . he was actually operating the damn thing . . . [and] he was put into Honolulu jail. . . . How old was I? Seven or eight, maybe.
>
> Then my father decided that while he was over there that he might as well try to become an independent fisherman like most of them. So he started out with small boat with an outboard motor and he used to go fishing; . . . he drowned in an accident. . . . This was 1928. I was ten and half. (8–11)

By 1928, there were two younger sisters and a younger brother in addition to George and his mother.

> I became the man of the house. . . . And then we were on welfare; this [issei] minister had arranged for this kind of thing.
>
> My mother had to take in washing. To continue with the minister's influence, he finally was going to be the minister of a new church; . . . the idea was that she would do all kinds of things around there. He had a small little cottage set up for us. And I would do weekend raking of mango leaves and that kind of thing. It was 1929, I guess. (12–13)

Like fellow VVV member Edward Nakamura, Yoshimi Hayashi became a state supreme court justice. But where Nakamura was viewed as the quintessential intellectual, a serious judicial scholar, Hayashi was noted for his wit and informality—at least as soon as he removed the black robes of office. His "local boy" style was a lifelong trait; he was mischievous as a child, and his VVV colleagues took obvious delight in explaining how astonishing it was to see the ne'er-do-well of VVV days turn out such a distinguished success. Hayashi himself would agree that his youthful experiences would not have suggested a career on the state's highest court. Of his childhood activities, Hayashi recalls[30]:

> I was raised by my grandparents, and those days, in Manoa valley, . . . we didn't have any lights, there was only one road go all the way into the valley. . . . As kids, we used to climb up the guava tree and pick the ripe guavas and wait for cars to pass; then we would throw the guavas. . . .
>
> And on weekends . . . [we would] mark certain homes for their chickens, and we used to go at night and try to catch the chicken. Of course, they would make lot of noise, so the guys would just have to grab one fast and just run, . . . put 'em in a bag and go by the riverside, . . . climb the tree, tie the chicken in the bag to the tree overnight. Then, the next day, . . . clean the chicken by the riverside and cook the chicken. (2)

Ryoji "Bull" Namba was born in 1922 in Honolulu, the middle child among five siblings. Namba's parents were financially successful. His father was a salesman for Union Trading Company, which imported goods from Japan. With a wide variety of clients, Namba's father became fairly fluent in Hawaiian and English in addition to his native Japanese. "Surprisingly my parents were Christians," although Ryoji had no idea when or why they converted (1–4). "You know in the old days you never found Japanese Christians. . . . They used to have Bible classes and we used to go to those. . . . And my father, he wasn't a religious guy, eh. . . . The only time I've ever been to any Buddhist ceremony was for funerals." His family never discussed religion (4–8).

Namba is, like George Yamamoto, an emeritus professor at the University of Hawai`i at Manoa, having earned a Ph.D. in entomology from the University of Minnesota. Did the family suffer as a result of being Christian in a largely Buddhist environment? "I don't think so. Not in those days. The community as a whole wasn't too religious." And race, like religion, was not an issue for discussion.

> Maybe it's because they [my parents] never worked in the plantation system. . . . As far as I was concerned, they [haoles] didn't make any difference. Only thing was that English Standard School. Although I thought that maybe it was funny or unjustifiable, it didn't bother us.
>
> The only Hawaiian family that we really got to know well while we were growing up . . . was this Namaka family; . . . [David Namaka] is a lawyer. And that guy, the reason why we knew him real well, he went to Japanese school with us.
>
> In the old days Okinawans were considered a little lower grade. I don't think [my family] mentioned anything like that to us. But I re-

member in school, Japanese school, the kids themselves would talk . . . :
"Ah, you know him. He's Okinawan." Just by the tone—although some
of my best friends were Okinawans; . . . like we would say, "Oh, he's a
Portagee." There's an underlying feeling I would get—derogatory or
putting them in a lower class.

You know, I can just dismiss this thing, but I'm just trying to be very
open about it. . . . I think that, for my age, there was, to me, a significant
amount of prejudice, but I notice that when [you get to] the third generation, it gets less, and the fourth gets less and less, definitely. But my
time, yeah. You know, like they say that, "Oh, you going with an Okinawan girl?" They were some of the prettiest ones. . . . I tell you frankly,
before, if you were Okinawan, you try to hide the fact. (8–12)

Namba's candor is important to our understanding of some of the
subtle yet powerful ways in which stereotypes and prejudice were transmitted from generation to generation in Hawai`i. He correctly noted the
declining naichi prejudice against Okinawans, although it survives in an
insensitivity to an independent heritage trampled by more than a century of Japanese and Japanese American chauvinism.[31]

Namba was also helpful in discussing the elusive nature of the powerful "cultural values" assumed to be transmitted through the generations. For one thing, like other issei, his parents used Native Hawaiian
vocabulary that he took to be reflective of Japanese culture. Some words,
like *ohia* (mountain apple), were everyday items. Others, like *hana hana*
(to work) or *pau hana* (quitting time), related to work. "I grew up with
the idea that certain words were Japanese because my parents always
used those words. Then, later on in life, I found out they were Hawaiian words." His parents did tell their children to "study hard, work hard,
and all that kind of stuff," but they never used Japanese terms to moti-
vate them (14).

Former VVV member Akira Otani, whose father established a successful fishing enterprise, was born in 1921, the fifth in a family of nine
children. Like the Amiokas, the Otanis lived in Kakaako, where many
Japanese worked as fishermen or in the fish cannery. Akira's childhood
was filled with activities that cost little or nothing. Fishing for the kids,
for example, would require a short bamboo pole, would cost maybe three
cents, or five cents.

Then you'd buy some line costing another two cents and you'd look
around for some hooks; maybe we'd pay one cent for five hooks. Then
you'd go around catching bait—small shrimps around. And then you'd

go out fishing. . . . We played football, baseball, basketball—right out in
the streets, . . . you'd play skin-ball [hard ball]. Somebody would hit it
real bad and broke some windows and everybody would scatter," [Akira
laughed]. (10)

Of course, there was more to life than games and recreation in
Kakaako. It was a tightly knit community and, like Shiro Amioka, Akira
recalled a strong sense of solidarity. He noted the way in which Japanese
families were able to accommodate a variety of religions in the neighborhood:

> Our parents were primarily Buddhist. But we only went to Buddhist
> churches on certain occasions. Obon [Japanese festival for ancestral
> spirits]. . . . But my dad is also very strong in Shintoism. In fact, he was
> one of the founders of this Shinto shrine over there on River Street; . . .
> it wasn't a case of either-or, you know.
>   In the old days they used to have Christian missionaries—they used
> to bring slide shows. . . . And all the neighborhood, not only kids but
> the adults as well, would all assemble and they'd show pictures of Jesus
> and we'd sing hymns, every Sunday night, I think, . . . no charge or
> nothing; no offerings or nothing, . . . entertainment. We thought that
> was great. (7–11)

Ted Tsukiyama's parents, like Ryoji Namba's, were Christian, as well
as highly educated. Ted was born in 1920, the fourth of five children, and
was one of the few nisei accepted into the English Standard system. Unlike Ryoji's, his parents participated actively in the small Japanese Christian community. Because his father was a businessman and their neighborhood and ethnic community primarily working class, the Tsukiyama
family did not socialize much in the neighborhood. But they did not be-
long to the Japanese petite bourgeoisie either: "They didn't consider
themselves as part of the upper crust of Japanese society; . . . socially we
didn't mingle with them" (7), Ted's father was especially "active in the
church."

> My father was . . . baptized in Tokyo. . . . He just lived the life of, I got
> to say this, he didn't wear it on his sleeve or show it off, he was just
> very gentle or very kind; . . . he went to night school to learn English
> and the night school happened to be at this missionary or church re-
> lated, so that's how they got Bible training at the same time and he
> became a Christian. But here in Hawai`i, a lot of people were non-
> Christian. They had no church affiliations and we had very little con-
> tact with practicing or devout Buddhist types.

I credit my parents for an upbringing that has left all of us children free of any feelings of racial distinction or superiority or, while we didn't have great feelings of inferiority, . . . maybe the church background, the Protestant background, could also have been a factor, a life of racial acceptance and tolerance. . . . We never had much contact with Okinawans but unlike the stories I hear about naichi people saying don't go near, don't date, or don't marry Okinawans, . . . at that time I wasn't aware or sensitive of distinctions between naichi and Okinawans. (7–9)

Yugo Okubo, who became the VVV's leftist radical, was born in 1924 in Waikiki. Yugo was the seventh of eight children in the family; his brother Yoshio would also become a member of the VVV. By Yugo's early childhood years, in the late 1920s, the family had moved to Palolo, not far from fellow VVV member Edward Nakamura's home. He recalls a fairly isolated life as a child.

Okubo's mother was a Japanese-language schoolteacher in Reverend Takie Okumura's Makiki Christian Church. But none of the Okubo children was ever required to learn Japanese—a rare phenomenon in that community. His father "was kind of a middle-class Oriental." He took his children, including Yugo, on the streetcar to Castle Memorial Kindergarten in Honolulu—"right where the city hall building is"—instead of to the neighborhood school.

And if you talk to my oldest brother, my father used to take him around to visit his friends, and very few were Japanese friends. Most of them were Hawaiian, Chinese, haole. That's one reason why my oldest brother, instead of going to the Nuuanu Y, which was the 'Japanese' YMCA, went to the Central Y . . . sort of a non-Japanese sort of a relationship, . . . although he was active in all the Japanese societies. . . . He spent a lot of time at the newspaper offices, the *Nippu Jiji* and *Hawaii Hochi*. . . . He was a good friend of Fred Makino. (4–7)

That Yugo's father insisted on membership in the Central Branch of the YMCA—which John Young has described as overwhelmingly haole or part-Hawaiian—suggests that he was aware of the race and class stratification in the YMCA and that he was determined either to push the system to its limits or to secure the best for his own children through exposure to other ethnic groups and classes. In addition, regular communication with leaders like Soga, Okumura, and Makino assured the family of constant interaction with issues of the day.

Okubo's parents never openly disparaged other racial or ethnic groups, but he sensed that there was prejudice. Still, when his older brother was at the University of Hawaii, haole friends would visit the home and be welcomed by his parents. Yugo could not remember whether his parents had become Christians, but they "went along with the Okumura side in almost anything. . . . My parents never went to church but we went to Sunday school, and for a little while I went to Makiki Church. . . . They weren't baptized Christians, I don't think." Sunday School was taught by Reverend Takie Okumura's son, Umetaro, who had, for Yugo, only one memorable story. "The only story I remember is this: 'One time, I did a bad thing.' So he said that there was a guy who used to drink all the time; so one day he grabbed the beer bottle and peed in the beer bottle and the guy didn't know it and drank the pee." Yugo laughed. "He repeated that story every year" (11).

That so many individuals who became VVV members were significantly influenced by Christianity suggests that the relationship was not coincidental. Ted Tsukiyama's family life in the 1920s was comfortable and relatively unproblematic. Shiro Amioka and Yutaka Nakahata joined Christian churches as adolescents. Herb Isonaga's parents sent him to Sunday school for the educational exposure, and Ryoji Namba attended as well. Even Akira Otani, whose father was active in Buddhist and Shinto circles, joined the Kakaako neighborhood for Christian slide shows on Sunday nights.

There were at least two important facts about being Japanese American Christians in the 1920s: On one hand, being in the minority in a relatively cohesive ethnic community, part of a diaspora linked to a growing imperial power, required a degree of self-conscious reflection and willingness to risk comfort for principle; on the other hand, Japanese Christians shared religion with the haole elite and the larger American society. While this relationship did not necessarily assure access to status or position, it did suggest more successful acculturation or assimilation and approbation from the society at large.[32]

Language schools were a fundamental part of life for nearly every young Japanese American in the 1920s. Of all the VVV interviewees, only Yugo Okubo was entirely spared the regimen of Japanese school. Yoshiaki Fujitani recalled the ethnic mix of playmates at his father's Buddhist services and in Japanese school on Maui:

I guess I didn't know too many Caucasians, but there were many Filipinos and I got to know them very well. We were on such friendly terms that we could call each other all kinds of names, names that we can't use nowadays. . . . That was nice, you know. . . . Chinese, haoles [who attended Japanese school], . . . I guess some of the parents wanted their kids to be watched by the teachers. You know, language school was not only language learning, but it was like baby-sitting. (6–7)

Several of the men clearly recalled Japanese-language school as a negative experience. Edward Nakamura simply did not believe he should have to attend and found his eight years in such a school very trying.[33] Resisting his parents on this issue was the only form of rebellion he could safely express in his family, and "from about the seventh year, I was skipping language school for the most part."

Whereas parents didn't bother you so far as the public schools were concerned, as far as Japanese language was concerned, I think they felt that they had a right to push you. . . . It wasn't so much [being American]. Maybe it was. . . . But looking back, I think it was more the only form of rebellion you could engage in.

I remember the kids in the neighborhood would make fun about the Japanese school principal. It was a great sport not to respect the guy. (10–11)

Yoshimi Hayashi treated his principal with even less respect. He gleefully recalled taking a blueing agent used to whiten laundry, like modern-day bleach, and mixing the "blue with vinegar" at the Manoa *gakuin* (academy).

It has a powerful smell, and we used to take that into the Japanese classroom and pour 'em all around and the teacher would look around and get mad but we just act innocent. . . . We used to have Japanese movies —once a month if I recall. . . . We had what is known as *benshi*—the person that stays on the side when the movies been [sic] run, and he would interpret and give his version of what the [silent] movie is all about. And the principal used to sit somewhere in the back—you know, Manoa is a rainy area, so we used to make and throw mud balls on the principal's head. I'm just telling you, it was a lot of fun in those days.[34]

Ted Tsukiyama never understood why he had to attend Japanese school, especially since both his parents spoke English so well. His school record was spotty, good in some years, terrible in others. Tsukiyama "didn't apply myself." But he never tried to quit, even though he wanted to play high school baseball and language school conflicted with practice. "I resented it but I didn't rebel. . . . And there was always homework. So I used to resent the fact that I had to—that my afternoon plans were wiped out and then at night we had to study for both schools. . . . But in those days going to Japanese schools was the norm" (5).

On the other hand, there were boys who genuinely enjoyed Japanese-language school. Yutaka Nakahata attended Palama Gakuen for six years and the Buddhist Hongwanji school for another six (9). Ryoji Namba, whose father always seemed to be working but whose mother devoted her life to her children's well-being, said one of her concerns was inspiring them to study hard. "I did very well in Japanese school; . . . they always give you grades and prizes when you've been top students. I was always one of those guys. My whole family, in fact. I guess that's part of the so-called home discipline or whatever you want to call it. . . . Yeah, at times, you know, everybody else is playing but you have to go" (2, 5–6).

Shiro Amioka had extravagantly fond memories of Japanese-language school—he had clearly given considerable thought to his educational experiences.

> Language school for me was very pleasant, . . . because our class was very unusual in the sense that in Japanese school, by in [sic] large, the wahines excelled and the boys are the troublemakers. But in our class, for some quirk, the boys excelled.
>
> But more than that, what was unusual about our class was that there was a friendly sense of rivalry when it came to class work, but a tremendous amount of cooperation as a class. When a test is announced, a week before that, we said that we were going to study. . . . We'd play as a group and so we'd study as a group. When we play, everybody play. You better not go off and study by yourself—otherwise . . . (11–13)

The VVV, like so many of their peers in the 1920s, responded variously to the Japanese-language schools. Most, it seemed, would have been happier without this burden. However, all but a few accepted it as normal and found little reason to rebel. Still, it is important to note that a number did, in fact, enjoy the experience and learn a good deal from the schools. Part of the post–World War II mythology enveloping the nisei is that they were successfully and unalterably acculturated as good Americans in the pre–World War II period—and that they greatly resented these schools. As a result, according to this narrative, they remained relatively untouched by their years of language schooling. The logic of this myth is that the nisei transcended unfounded prejudice by consciously abandoning their linguistic heritage in the face of parental objection. This "Americanism" then manifested itself through their

World War II heroism and earned them the right to post–World War II political hegemony in Hawaiʻi and, by extension, model-minority status in the United States. The same myth also, not coincidentally, heightened the sense of injustice that accompanied the internment of so many assimilated citizens who had clearly abandoned their Japanese culture.

In fact, enough of the nisei learned the Japanese language sufficiently well to enter many areas of business requiring its reasonable mastery in the commercial world of their ethnic community during the 1920s and 1930s. Moreover, some six thousand eventually were recruited into the World War II Military Intelligence Service. The Japanese language is, especially in its written form, exceedingly difficult to master. A few months of intensive study in the military could not have prepared the nisei for effective service without the years of training they had received in the Japanese-language schools.[35]

In addition to the language schools, the nisei were busy making their way in their "English" or public schools, which had become the principal terrain on which the battle for nisei loyalties would be fought. This was a struggle to determine the nature and direction of compulsory education—to train workers who would sustain the agricultural industries in Hawaiʻi or to educate citizens who could participate in, and perhaps seize control of, the reins of democratic government in the territory.[36] The public schools, then, became critical and pivotal institutions.

Ralph Yempuku started elementary school at the age of six in 1920, soon after his Buddhist priest father moved the family to Kahuku, on the north shore of Oahu. Family life then was "not as liberal as today. You know what I mean? . . . six, seven, eight [years old]—you can't do anything that would disgrace the family. The face. So everything was very strict." His situation was particularly demanding, since his family ran the temple, "but it was much more so in the Japanese family than it was in the Hawaiian family or Filipino family or Portuguese family." His teachers, he remembered, included some Japanese, "some nisei, but had Hawaiians, Hawaiian-haole. . . . Not too many Japanese" (5).

On Kauai, Herbert Isonaga entered elementary school in the late 1920s and found it:

> not that competitive . . . except for the few that really innately chose to excel, but I was not one of those. When it came to the eighth grade, you started worrying, because in those days you didn't automatically get into high school.

We had part-Hawaiian teachers and, in the upper grades, we started running into Japanese male teachers in elementary school. . . . I don't recall any pure haole teachers, but there were part-Hawaiian teachers. . . . Then, of course, when we went to high school, I would say in the high school level, 95 percent were haole teachers. (9–10)

His most powerful memories of elementary school were of his first-grade teacher, Aiko Tokimasa. It was unusual, in the first place, for a nisei, especially a female, to be in the system in the 1920s. More important, she was "a fine teacher." But "I think she did me a grave dis-service" by having him skip a grade; "when you're young, one year difference makes a lot of difference, you know, when you're competing." He acknowledged that the young teacher had seen promise in him and was trying to encourage him to move ahead. Isonaga remembered her better, however, as Aiko Reinecke, when she and her husband, John Reinecke, were fired by the state school system in 1948, the first victims in the post–World War II move to eliminate communists and leftist-radicals from positions of leadership in labor, politics, and education. (They would much later be reinstated and receive both an official apology and compensation for the injury.)[37]

Teruo Himoto was born in 1923, almost a decade after Ralph Yem-puku, but he attended elementary school in the same Kahuku sugar plantation district. He recalled school and his working-class neighborhood as free from the racial prejudices that might be assumed, given the racial and class hierarchies of the times:

My dad used to be foreman for the camp, which had three to five hundred people, primarily . . . Japanese and Filipinos. So you don't see the racial prejudice, you know. When I went to school, we went to Kahuku, which is a plantation town—sugar plantation—and the people that attend the schools are primarily plantation workers' children. . . . The only area, I think, that you come down to is the superintendents and the bosses, I believe—both pineapple and sugar plantations. The haoles, you know, naturally they send the school kids to private schools. They don't want their kids to mix with lower-class plantation workers. So in school and growing up in the pineapple community, you don't see the actual racial prejudice.[38]

In Himoto's world, the Japanese were both more populous than other minorities and more politically empowered. Teruo's father was, after all, a camp foreman. From that perspective, it was easier to see the universe as relatively benign. (The Filipinos would no doubt have had a different view.)

In the small plantation village of Paauhau, Masato Doi's early education took place in something resembling a one-room schoolhouse; each teacher took several grades and taught all the subjects. "So from kindergarten through 6th grade, we had about three or four teachers running the whole school." Doi remembered that one teacher was "a plantation supervisor's wife; a second was the plantation manager's wife. One was a man who was strictly a teacher." All were haole except one part-Hawaiian woman (4). Doi's family thought teaching careers would be splendid for their children; they sent Doi's older sister to Normal School in Honolulu, and she taught in the 1930s for "about $90 a month." Later, Masato would aspire to a teaching career—before the war, before law school, before politics, and before becoming a judge.

In Kakaako's fishing community, Shiro Amioka faced tough going for a while. One of the problems was the social distance between his tight, ethnically cohesive neighborhood and the radically different world of haole, Standard English–speaking mores. The culturally different application of discipline became an issue, as did speaking up in class in a language second to his native pidgin:

> I remember elementary school—one is the discipline of the principal, Miss Agnes. She was a strict disciplinarian, . . . tough woman. The second—fifth and sixth grades, Chinese Hawaiian, I think, Mrs. Tyau. . . . She forced me to participate in the school assembly; . . . what she did for me was to make me overcome stage fright. . . . Tremendous thing, you know, for me. Because from then on, I was never afraid of speaking before people.
>
> Well, as I got older I got better, but according to what my mother tells me, the first three grades, I hardly talked. . . . I don't know what I did at school but I hardly talked. So she was afraid I was dumb, you know. Actually dumb. (7–9)

Amioka here pointed to two of the most important elements in the schooling of Japanese Americans in the 1920s, language and discipline. The full weight of a deliberately crafted system was brought to bear on this generation, largely through the medium of language; the nisei were socialized into a class-determined and race-bound hegemony by constant reference to the norm, Standard English. In return, and in defiance/defense, they turned to discipline—family and self—to transcend the boundaries established for them by the haole oligarchy.[39]

Finally, two VVV members, Ted Tsukiyama and Yugo Okubo, went through the English Standard system, where, as Eileen Tamura has shown, Japanese American pupils were dramatically underrepresented. Where 1.0 reflects equilibrium with regard to "ethnic occupancy," the proportion of Japanese Americans in English Standard schools in 1925 was 0.03; for part-Hawaiians, 1.53; for Portuguese, 0.91; for haoles, a whopping 53.49. To compare the raw figures for 1929, for example, there were 119 Japanese Americans in English Standard schools versus 38,700 in other public schools, while there were 1,662 haoles in English Standard schools versus only 2,767 in other public schools.[40]

Yugo Okubo recalled being trained to take the English Standard school entrance examination by his older sister, Setsu, who told him, "If you don't pronounce it right, you are going to get rejected." Setsu was bright enough to recognize the set-up; she prompted Yugo and had him memorize answers to questions likely to be posed.

Although an English Standard school was within a few blocks of the Okubo home in Palolo, the neighborhood kids walked a mile up the valley to the regular public school. Yugo felt keenly the sense of being an outsider in his own neighborhood. The other youngsters must have thought: "I really don't know what the guy's like. He looks kind of strange." English Standard School was never much fun for the young Yugo:

> Very few Japanese; . . . the kids in this school, . . . they really give me a hard time. . . . Oh, they call you "Jap" and all that kind of stuff. . . . Why, you can't do anything because you are a minority. . . . You are in a class with maybe thirty and there's maybe only two of you.
>
>   When we got out of elementary school, . . . my mother thought it was better if I went to McKinley. But all the brothers and sisters said, "No. No. No. You got to go to English Standard School. Go to Roosevelt." So I was in the minority again. It was really a miserable period in my life. (5–7)

These experiences helped sensitize Okubo to the tribulations of underdogs in all situations. His image among his VVV colleagues after their return from World War II was of someone who "marches to a different drummer," whom they, publicly at least, felt obliged to respect in spite of his open criticism of their own mainstream values.

Ted Tsukiyama, four years older than Yugo, evidently had a smoother voyage through the English Standard system. He attended Aliiolani Elementary through the sixth grade before going on to Stevenson Intermediate and Roosevelt High Schools. He had little to say about his elementary years: "Well, in those days, the Oriental, the Japanese, were still quite a minority. In those days, it was just 1 percent or 2 percent because it was sort of like a haole school. But there was no racial tensions or prejudice that I can recall" (3–4).

The difference between Okubo's and Tsukiyama's experience is dramatic enough to warrant some exploration. In many ways, the families were similar. Both families were Christian and the boys attended Sunday schools. Both fathers were unusually well educated. Yugo recalled his father writing many letters for illiterate issei; Ted's father had graduated from Keio University. Both fathers worked in white-collar positions in the business world. Both appeared equally at ease in the issei world of newspaper giants like Frederick Makino and Yasutaro Soga, in the circles inhabited by Reverend Takie Okumura of Makiki Christian Church, and in the broader society beyond the ethnic borders. Okubo's father, in particular, took special pains to provide a multiethnic environment for his children, beginning with a multiclass and multiethnic kindergarten, as well as YMCA.

Perhaps the different treatment at school accorded Ted and Yugo was simply coincidental, related to complex personal and social factors. But timing may have made a difference, since Yugo was several years younger and entered the system in the late 1930s when anti-Japanese sentiment was rapidly intensifying.

Neither Okubo nor Tsukiyama spoke much of their mothers, both evidently strong women. Tsukiyama's mother was born in Japan, but her father had already traveled to Hawai`i; she was educated at a school established by Christian missionaries in Japan and was thoroughly bilingual—more of an older nisei than an issei, according to Ted. Yugo's mother was a Japanese schoolteacher who did not send her own children to learn the language. Yugo recalled that she was angry at being treated with disrespect: "Metropolitan Market—they catered to the haoles. My mother used to go there because it was right around the corner. . . . Well, she used to go there and pick up vegetables, and the manager used to always watch her and tell her, 'Don't touch the vegetables.' And she used to get pissed off. He never said that to anybody else" (9).

Ted Tsukiyama and Yugo Okubo eventually went in very different directions. That their paths crossed as VVV members was due to their determination to make their lives count in a period when the nation was telling Japanese Americans that they were worse than useless in the war-driven crisis—that they were excess baggage weighing down the war effort and the best they could do was to step aside and let "real" Americans get on with it. One of the reasons the Varsity Victory Volunteers could even exist, however—as it could not have existed on the U.S. mainland—was the complex legacy of the 1920s and 1930s in Hawai`i. Part of that legacy was the fact that, although a tiny minority, nisei like Ted and Yugo were admitted into the English Standard system.

The decade that had begun with a massive sugar strike and a concerted attack on the Japanese-language schools ended with the execution, on November 19, 1929, of a nineteen-year-old nisei, Myles Yutaka Fukunaga.[41] Fukunaga had murdered Gill Jamieson, the young son of the vice-president of the Hawaiian Trust Company. At the time, the Fukunaga family was being evicted from their home by Hawaiian Trust because of back rent that totaled twenty dollars. Abandoning all hope of a decent life for his family in Hawai`i, Myles planned to kidnap the young Jamieson and use the ransom money to send his own parents back to Japan.

The eldest of six children, Myles enjoyed school. He graduated at the head of his class from elementary school but left because his family desperately needed him to find a job. He worked for some years, increasingly frustrated by low wages and promises of raises that never materialized. Finally, in desperation, Fukunaga kidnapped Jamieson from Punahou Academy, demanded $10,000 in ransom, but inexplicably killed the boy. He received only part of the money—in marked bills—and was soon captured, but not before considerable shock was registered by the haole community; Japanese parents warned their sons to stay off the streets.

Myles Fukunaga was quickly tried, convicted, and executed. The case assumed monumental proportions precisely because it so clearly symbolized the dangers inherent in the racial status quo. For the Asian immigrant and Native Hawaiian communities, this execution highlighted the oppressive conditions under which they lived and the dual standard of justice imposed. For the haole elite, the murder revealed a personal vulnerability, given the rage and potential for violence deeply embedded in the society. Such a dramatic and direct challenge to the status quo required a swift and clear response. Fukunaga's execution was, as a result, a foregone conclusion. The recollections of several of the men who became crucial to the VVV are helpful in interpreting the event.

Hung Wai Ching, who helped organize the VVV in 1942, remembered the highly charged racial climate of the time, including the threat of a lynching:

> Oh, hell, I was in charge of a platoon, with bayonets, of the National Guard—surround the police station. They were going to hang the guy, Fukunaga, the kid. . . . I was so scared, I pissed in my pants. I couldn't even load my .45. I had high school kids with fixed bayonets and rifles. . . . To keep them from, supposed to be a riot . . . Go free him, bring him out and hang him. Lynch . . . I was second lieutenant, Company C, Chinese company. [He laughed.] [The mob was a] mixture—haoles, maybe *pake* [Chinese], *kanakas* [Hawaiians]. It was, after all, a *buddahead* [Japanese] killed a haole boy. Big Five boy, too. Who the hell do you think you bastards are? You goddamn coolies, you dare? [More laughter]. (62–63)

Like Hung Wai Ching, Richard Lum was in the university ROTC program and was mobilized in the face of the threatened lynching. Lum was the Chinese American regular army officer in direct charge of the VVV at Schofield Barracks. His grandfather had arrived in Hawai`i in the 1860s and raised taro in Manoa valley. Lum was the eighth of fourteen children and "the only one privileged to attend the University of Hawai`i"(2). "We were fixed with bayonets but didn't have ammunition," he recalled. He noted the general tenor of the times: "Well, more and more, those days, the feeling, very racial conscious, you know. I mean there was a great feeling against the Orientals. I must say that" (3–5).

Ralph Yempuku, in the eighth grade at the time, said of the Fukunaga tragedy: "We're too young, I suppose, and [it] didn't bother me about how it would affect the Japanese or whatever; . . . you form your opinion by what you read in the newspapers. . . . And the newspapers were all against Fukunaga" (10).

But most who were aware of the case recalled being very concerned. Ted Tsukiyama vividly remembered the murder and execution, which occurred when he was in the fourth grade:

> I remember . . . the whole Japanese community was in a state of tension and anxiety. And that was reflected by my parents and the admonition to come straight home from school, because they were afraid of community reaction. There was a feeling of community shame among Japanese that a Japanese person would have done something so terrible as this.

There was *haji* [shame], great *haji*, that this happened and, of course, rather unthinkable that someone from this lowly social status, ethnic status, would dare to pull off an act such as demand ransom and then go and kill a scion of a Big Five family. (6–7)

Herb Isonaga was another VVV member who recalled the incident, even though he was growing up on the island of Kaua'i: "My reaction at that time, my parents' reaction, was for Japanese to be involved or committing such a horrible [crime] was unacceptable. I think I felt the same way. Even to this day, when I go through a newspaper column where they list all the criminal actions and when I see a Japanese name, I feel that he shouldn't be on that list. I don't know why, but I feel that" (10–11).

Japanese Americans now routinely deny any sense of collective guilt over "shameful" acts committed by anyone of Japanese descent. I recall this feeling of collective responsibility and, conversely, of feeling pleased by news of Japanese or Japanese American success; this seemed normal to me as a sansei growing up in the 1940s and 1950s. That most of us associate individual actions with ethnic or racial group characteristics is, I suggest, both intuited and learned. Ted Tsukiyama and Herb Isonaga are simply more forthcoming in this regard; it may be that many Japanese Americans feel that acknowledging a sense of collective guilt would reinforce racist notions that we are indeed bound by blood ties. Hence, we are especially careful around anniversaries of the attack on Pearl Harbor.

THE 1920S COMPRISED a decade of racism and resistance. The great sugar strike of 1920, begun with such high hopes by Filipino and Japanese workers trying to forge an interethnic labor alliance, ended in racial scapegoating and scabbing. Another quarter century would pass before a real interracial union could emerge. One message was clear: Class solidarity would be a difficult means by which to achieve ethnic mobility. The decade ended with the near lynching and hasty execution of Myles Fukunaga, the message of which, it seems, was for ambitious individual Japanese Americans to acknowledge their "place" in Hawaii's racial hierarchy and to limit their aspirations.

But the decade also became a crucible in which some battles for greater empowerment could be won, including the 1927 Supreme Court victory for Japanese-language schools. For the lads destined to become part of the VVV after Pearl Harbor, the 1920s found most of their families intact, most neighborhoods secure, most childhoods reasonably untroubled. Life was reasonably benign; they were unaware of the growing drama as Hawai`i grappled with the inevitable shock wave that would surely accompany the coming of age of the nisei. Not since the 1890s had the haole elite faced such a serious challenge to its hegemony in the islands. In this setting, the emergence of community leaders like John Young, Charles Hemenway, Hung Wai Ching, and Shigeo Yoshida was a critical element for the drama of the 1940s. In the meantime, however, the boys who eventually formed the VVV would need to weather the gathering storm of the 1930s.

3

Before the Fire

The 1930s

The 1930s opened with two events that would shape the context of adolescent life for the men of the VVV. In September 1931, the Japanese Army seized Mukden (now Shenyang); in what would be called the "Manchurian incident," the army served notice on the West, especially the United States, that Japan was moving decisively toward open competition for territory and resources in Asia.

In that same month, Hawaii's notorious Massie-Kahahawai case gained national attention. After a trial failed to convict five local youths of color for the rape of a white woman, the wife of a naval officer, her family, and a few sailors kidnapped and murdered one of the suspects. They were caught with the body, and even a defense mounted by famed attorney Clarence Darrow could not prevent their conviction. The territorial governor immediately commuted the sentences, however, and the defendants were free to leave the Islands.

The Manchurian incident foreshadowed the attack on Pearl Harbor a decade later but seemed too distant an event to be of much concern for the youngsters who would become the VVV. Similarly, the Massie cases made little lasting impression on most of the boys, although they proved apt metaphors for the racism in Hawai'i of those times. By the end of the decade, nearly everything else was overshadowed by the threat of war.

IN THE 1930S, the major challenge for the boys who were to volunteer for service with the Varsity Victory Volunteers, then graduating from McKinley and Farrington High Schools and Mid-Pacific Institute, was moving on to the University of Hawai`i. In this, they were not typical of the vast majority of Japanese Americans, especially the women, who had little opportunity to attend college anywhere before World War II.[1]

The United States had been preparing for an eventual military confrontation with Japan as early as the first decade of the twentieth century. As Michael Slackman and Gary Okihiro point out, the U.S. government, from President Franklin Roosevelt to the military stationed in Hawai`i, was involved in serious preparation for a war by the early 1930s, following decades of anti-Japanese actions and policies in Hawai`i and the mainland.[2] One result was a formidable military buildup in Hawai`i—including additional troops, acquisition of land for training, construction of fuel storage tanks, and, especially, increased attention to Pearl Harbor.

Even at the beginning of the decade, given the threatening international context, that there were 139,631 people of Japanese descent, comprising 37.9 percent of the total population in Hawai`i, was a matter of considerable concern to people deeply suspicious of Japan and Japanese Americans.[3] The maturation of the ethnic community might have been expected to calm some fears, since each passing year more decisively shifted the balance in favor of the American-born nisei and a growing number of even more assimilated third-generation sansei. In 1925, 55 percent of the Japanese community was nisei. By 1933, the percentage had climbed to 70 percent.[4] Unfortunately, many haole leaders responded by pointing to the "dangers" of this group that not only retained its bloodline and heritage but now also enjoyed the protection and rights of citizenship, especially the ballot, denied its immigrant parents and grandparents.

The world of foreign affairs, including U.S.-Japan relations, that would eventually consume much of their lives lay beyond the interest of the future VVV members, as would the initial organizing efforts of the radical International Longshoremens and Warehousemens Union (ILWU) and the debates about appropriate schooling for the largely Japanese American population of Hawaii's youth.[5] These three larger political issues, however, would determine how and where the VVV could make an impact.

Labor relations between sugar and pineapple plantation workers and the Big Five factors had always been contested, but the 1930s proved an especially difficult decade. The traumatic sugar strike of 1920 had seriously blunted the labor initiatives of Japanese workers. By the late 1930s, Filipinos, the last of the major ethnic groups to be imported, had had several decades to adjust to the new setting and to absorb the sting of class and racial discrimination. They were more than ready to assume leadership roles in the labor movement.

The 1930s also ushered in the age of industrial unionism, as the militancy of the Communist Party U.S.A and the Congress of Industrial Organizations appeared in Hawai`i in the form of ILWU organizers. They pushed for solidarity on an industrywide basis and insisted on absolute interethnic collaboration, even at the expense of bruising the egos of Japanese American leaders who had longer experience and more "seniority." This strategy prevented the Big Five from effectively implementing its divide-and-rule tactic against the different ethnic groups.[6]

This was the decade, too, when a large cohort of Japanese Americans, mostly second-generation nisei, came of age and sought better employment than that traditionally offered by the plantations. But the Depression made prospects for the nisei less than ideal. The economic downturn had virtually ruined the pineapple industry, although sugar was protected with federal subsidies and plantations continued to recruit labor. Unfortunately for the planters, the Tydings-McDuffie Act of 1934, which promised independence for the Philippines a decade in the future, included a key provision terminating this last major source of cheap labor.[7]

Congress had responded to race-based exclusionary pressures, especially in California, and eliminated unrestricted Filipino rights to immigrate to the United States. Hawai`i sugar planters and educators, as a result, tried to persuade the nisei that plantation labor was an honorable career.[8] These efforts were not without effect; the loftiest career goal of most of the best and the brightest at the university in 1941 was public school teaching.

By the 1930s, American fear of the Japanese assumed that blood ran very thick, as later proponents of mass incarceration of all Japanese Americans would insist; race trumped all else, even citizenship.[9] But the Constitution did provide some basic rights for citizens, and there were real problems dealing with a Japanese American population that had become a definite part of U.S. society. The 1924 Immigration Act had re-solved the issue of the first generation by prohibiting almost all Japanese from entering the United States, and the 1922 Ozawa case had con-firmed issei ineligibility for naturalization; thus, the 1930s became the crucial decade to come to grips with the American-born nisei.

Military and civilian leaders seized every opportunity to persuade or intimidate the young Japanese American population into a thorough-going version of Americanism. They were to do so, in the first instance, by severing all connections with Japan. Tragically, this policy extended well beyond any political affection for Japan, or even to its culture or legacy: Where possible, the nisei were expected to disavow links with the Japanese, including their own parents.

The potential for Japanese American political influence through the franchise in Hawai`i was cause for considerable alarm. At the 1932 New Americans Conference for Japanese American youth, Admiral Yates Stir-ling, who had been upset by the original Massie verdict, directly ad-dressed the nisei youth on this issue. He bluntly wondered whether his audience, with its proud heritage as a people, could "truly efface their allegiance to Japan and adopt full loyalty to a nation so different in his-torical background?" At the 1933 New Americans Conference, General Briant H. Wells, army commander of the Hawaiian Department, warned against Japanese designs, including "peaceful penetration" through the voting process. "I can only emphasize the fact that these Hawaiian Is-lands are American Territory; that they will always remain so; and that if foolish individuals or groups, through conspiracy, intrigue, or ambi-tion should aspire to change or modify that status, . . . and the procedure patterned in the 'American Way'; they would inevitably realize nothing but disappointment in the hour of anticipated triumph." This was a truly astonishing remark but one which, in the context of the times, raised very little concern except among Japanese Americans.[10]

The rhetoric reflected a strategy aimed at defusing the possible dis-loyalty of Japanese American youth in the event of war, as well as at con-vincing them to accept an inferior status in Hawai`i. The untenable as-sumption that the issei, or at least their cultural and business leaders, were embarked on a systematic effort to turn their young toward Japan suited the military and Hawaii's oligarchy. As a result, there was a de-liberate move to use "counterpropaganda" techniques to ensure the neu-trality, if not the loyalty, of the American born. But the international context and the eventuality, however certain, of war with Japan was not the only concern. After all, there was the issue of daily life in Hawai'i and the need to absorb this large and problematic group into the body politic.

Former VVV members Hung Wai Ching and Shigeo Yoshida remembered the 1928 Fukunaga and 1931 Massie-Kahahawai cases well. Yoshida felt, keenly, the lack of community power in the Fukunaga case and "definitely the need for a greater voice on the part of Japanese Americans." "And the same thing with the Massie Case . . . but then we weren't organized; we didn't feel capable of speaking out"[11] (12–13).

This dual system of justice was recognized and resented by Hawaii's nonhaole population, but the control exercised by the oligarchy was too powerful, on the whole, to resist. When the VVV and others of the post–World War II generation of Japanese Americans assumed political control, this past was regularly invoked to inspire enthusiasm and encourage dedication to ensure that Hawai'i not "slip back" into that racist past.

Ralph Yempuku, the oldest of the VVV members, was seventeen when the 1931 Massie case occurred. He recalled the basic outlines of the case and the subsequent trials. When I asked how he *felt* about the events, he responded: "The newspapers were all against Fukunaga and they were all against Kahahawai or whatever his name was and, as far as the Massie case is concerned, you get a feeling that they were justified in lynching the Hawaiian guy. And the governor did a great thing commuting their sentence. . . . Yeah. That's how you feel. Because, I think, to read the papers during that period, that's how the stories were given" (10–11).

Ted Tsukiyama remembered the Fukunaga case well because it so directly impacted the Japanese American community. But "I don't recall the Massie case that much because, although it involved one Japanese guy, it wasn't so much directed—the defendants were not Japanese. That was more local or Hawaiian that was being victimized" (7). There were, in fact, two Japanese Americans involved, but Tsukiyama makes an important point: The target in the Massie case was the larger so-called local population. In any case, since Japanese Americans were the vast majority of the local population, they were also clearly on the spot.

The 1930s had begun, then, most inauspiciously. The national climate made it a cultural crime to be of Japanese descent; the local environment clearly sanctioned unequal standards of justice and life, one for haoles and another for "locals." The nisei, in particular, were subject, simultaneously, to assimilationist and segregationist policies: Cut ties to Japan and demonstrate unwavering loyalty to the United States on the one hand, but exercise careful restraint in your ambition to succeed here, on the other, was the message of the 1930s.

The Japanese community made its own efforts to get ahead; there was considerable discussion and dispute regarding appropriate strategies to extend the parameters of ethnic mobility. The debate was an old one: It had begun with the first arguments among contract laborers on the sugar plantations between those who counseled patience and accommodation with their manager-bosses and those who advocated a more militant stance with protests and strikes in the 1880s and 1890s. The debate engulfed laborers and journalists who argued over strategies in the major strikes of 1909 and 1920. It continued into the 1920s, when the struggle over the Japanese-language schools exploded into viciously polarized factions. This was a discourse that reverberated across the United States, and Japanese Americans on the continent participated vigorously.

Unlike the U.S. mainland, however, Hawai`i included significant numbers of well-placed non–Japanese American individuals who were willing to work publicly as well as privately to present the best face of U.S. society and its ideals.[12] Among them were Hung Wai Ching, Charles Hemenway, Miles Cary, John Young, Stephen Mark, and Joseph Lightfoot. Ching, Hemenway, Cary, and Young have become significant parts of this book; Mark, a charismatic Christian minister, was an intellectual and spiritual mentor to many young people in the 1930s, including the VVV's Shiro Amioka and Yutaka Nakahata. Lightfoot was an attorney who, while not particularly fond of the Japanese as a group, devoted considerable legal effort to protecting their constitutional rights. He was especially prominent in representing immigration rights in 1917 and in the language-school case, which he took to victory at the U.S. Supreme Court in 1927.[13]

John Young's experiences as a youthful YMCA secretary assigned to the tough, poor, urban sections filled with Asian immigrant families are helpful in understanding race relations in Hawai`i and the social context in which the VVV members grew up during the 1930s. Racial integration of the YMCA in Hawai`i took a long and tortuous route and by the 1930s still retained a distinctly colonial appearance, with Caucasian funding and domination and a sprinkling of "local" participation.[14] Young's Nuuanu branch became "the only outlet for the Japanese and the Chinese boys. Hoo, how roughneck! . . . my district . . . King Street, Emma, School Street, Liliha; the worst district!" (8).

The work of the YMCA itself, in providing space, programs, and leadership training to minority youth, was enormously important in developing this generation during the 1930s. The Y created room for a young and energetic Hung Wai Ching, for example, to explore career possibilities in a society not widely open to Asians from working-class backgrounds.

Some of the Christian and Buddhist leaders—among them, Reverend Stephen Mark of the Community Church, comprised primarily of ethnic Chinese—were also vital in presenting critical views of society that, they stressed, should not wait passively for the millennium and ultimate resolution but could be addressed in this world, even by children of immigrants. Amioka joined the church and its Hi-Y YMCA youth group, the Tung Lok Hui, which drew Chinese American students from various high schools in Honolulu; Shiro was the only Japanese American member. Reverend Mark created "special book review clubs" and considered himself a disciple of John Dewey, but he also reinforced Amioka's growing sense of religion and Christianity, specifically, as a "moral kind of—the practical day-to-day ethics kind of thing which I found very appealing; . . . it should affect your daily life. . . . I think that had a tremendous impact on me later on" (25).

Charles Hemenway, Big Five businessman and university regent, regularly invited local debate-team members, including Shigeo Yoshida and Hung Wai Ching in the 1920s, to his home. He supported hundreds of local student scholars and athletes through the decades of his devotion to the University of Hawai'i, among them the All-American halfback Thomas Kaulukukui, who later supervised athletic activities for the VVV at Schofield. To Kaulukukui, Hemenway "was like my godfather. He was the one who paid for all my five years of scholarship at U.H. . . . I'd walk in the coach's office today because my registration is tomorrow. I'd say, 'Three hundred dollars.' He'd take [it] out of his pocket" (9–10).

Hung Wai took particular delight in disclosing Hemenway's support to those who believed they were locked in mortal class warfare against Hawaii's ruling oligarchy—the daughter of labor leader Jack Kawano, for example. And the range of support was wide: "When I took over Atherton House [the University of Hawai'i branch of the YMCA], I found this stack of IOUs that thick [indicating about two inches]. This is the money for scholarships and things like that. . . . Two hundred small grants here and there. . . . I just pick up the phone and call Charlie Hemenway, 'I need a kid to go down to Texas . . . Teachers College for one semester, for one year. . . . I got one scholarship already. . . . All I need is some travel money—a hundred bucks.' The kid comes back and in one year's time, talk like a Texan" [He laughed] (48).

Ralph Yempuku worked with the head coach of the university's football team and recalled the way in which support for athletes was managed in the 1930s. "Those days we didn't have a boosters club like the foundation or anything like that and . . . all these football players had to have money to register. . . . So old man Hemenway used to put up the money. . . . I know, because I seen that money. [Otto] Klum, the coach, used to go see him; come back with two or three thousand dollars in cash and lock the door and he and I used to prorate the money amongst the ballplayers" (33).

It was in this setting, then, that the boys lived through the 1930s—for them personally, life was generally uneventful and predictable. For some, as previous chapters have indicated, life was not only smooth but also quite comfortable; there was little sense of insecurity or insufficiency. For others, life was not as easy, as one or another parent died while they were still very young and some households were sustained only by the meager welfare policies of the period. Nonetheless, there was little sense of deprivation, since so many others lived exactly like them. Buttressed by the support of non-Japanese community leaders, Japanese Americans turned in the 1930s to a variety of modes of improving their individual and collective lives. Education, especially public schools, became a major focus of contention.

The education provided by McKinley High School in Honolulu was especially critical. Established in 1896, it was one of only four public high schools on all of the islands until the 1920s, when six new high schools were created.[15] But McKinley remained the only public high school in Honolulu until Farrington High School was created in 1936 (except for Roosevelt, which was on the separate English Standard track). By the 1930s more than half of the public school students in Hawai`i were of Japanese descent. The percentage of nisei at McKinley was much greater—the school was sometimes called "Tokyo High."

Fortunately for the students, it was an unusually good school and inspired thousands of immigrants and their children. Much of the credit is due to Myles Cary, its dedicated and idealistic principal.[16] Many of the

VVV members remembered Cary, who was almost universally respected as an educator and advocate. In opposition to most of the Big Five leaders, who wanted a docile and malleable labor force, Cary envisioned a school whose mission was to infuse young people with goals and visions appropriate to fully participating citizens and to provide the skills for that demanding role.

For some of the students who would eventually join the VVV, Cary was wildly successful. By the time Shiro Amioka had graduated from McKinley in 1940, for example, he was thoroughly imbued with the two principal tenets of progressive education of the times: democratic participation and the scientific method. Amioka felt, as early as his sophomore year, that Cary would support the local youth in their aspirations. "What he really inculcated in us was a real democratic ethos; . . . with all its faults, the U.S. is committed to the democratic ethos and this means that you as an individual are just as important as the other person. . . . There is racial prejudice and everything else but . . . don't take a back seat to anybody; . . . he lived it at school" (31).

This was heady stuff for bright and ambitious young Japanese Americans who were being told, at virtually every other turn, that they should not expect too much from education or their society. Amioka helped his classmates script and perform a play for the Sophomore Day program, May 18, 1938. Entitled "Our Growing Democracy," the piece was idealistic and rhetorical (and sophomoric)—it used various historical epochs, from Egyptian pyramid building to U.S. slavery, to illustrate the need for Hawaii's plantation system to incorporate the scientific method and democratic principles for social progress. As one character Tom (described as "scientifically inclined") says toward the end of the script: "We need the scientific method. We must get our best experts to help us study conditions carefully so that we will make wise changes. . . . Social relationships are so complex, that we will have to study hard and experiment tirelessly if we are to succeed in getting people to cooperate successfully for the good of all."[17]

Amioka was proud of the social conscience reflected in student activities at McKinley. In a September 19, 1938, article for the award-winning student newspaper, the *Daily Pinion*, on the value of strong cooperatives such as those in Sweden, he argued that cooperatives for the fishing industry, for example (his own father had been a fisherman), would dramatically lower the cost to the consumer. This principle would work for poi, housing, and medical care for Hawai'i, he asserted, and ended with an exhortation: "Students of McKinley, cooperatives have made people happy in many places. Why shouldn't Hawaii be included in that list. Here truly is a new frontier for us, the future voters of the territory!!"

Decades later, Amioka recalled the main target of the article: "Why was it so expensive? All the middlemen, which is the capitalist system. Get rid of the middlemen. We form our own cooperatives. . . . Oh, Miles Cary comes charging down and shake my hand and he congratulates me and he says that that's the kind of thinking we need among our young people" (23). Under Cary's progressive and energetic guidance, McKinley implemented a variety of student-run activities, including student deputies and courts, as well as a mutual aid fund for health care at school and for emergency financial assistance (23).

Amioka was "sure there were pressures" on Cary as a result of his "radical" approach to teaching these nisei, but the principal never revealed their existence to his young charges. And Cary did have support from a few other educators. A teacher from Illinois who became a principal in Kona, Hawai`i, Arthur Harris, recalled that he first met Cary in the late 1930s. Cary's influence helped Harris create an environment at Maui High School, his next post, that incorporated core studies and a participatory democratic ethos that "called forth the interest, the cooperation, and the achievements of a student body, a faculty, and a community, unfortunately not often seen in today's school system."[18] Core studies combined English and social studies classes and taught both by examining key topics of the time.

At McKinley's graduation ceremonies in 1940, Amioka read his poem "The Fusion of Cultures in Hawaii" to open a pageant that for decades would epitomize multiethnic inclusivity in Hawai`i: representation of all groups, whether in school performance or beauty pageant. Amioka's poem gave way to remarks by "nine of my classmates, . . . all Americans, but each of a different racial origin . . . [to] express our appreciation, and Aloha, to our parents." In the poem, he suggested that "industry" might absorb or reject the class—940 strong—but that their "heritage and training" would sustain them. Amioka saw his graduating class as a product of differences, "a Golden Mean" forged of extremes of races and cultures that included "ethical principles of Confucianism," "calm contemplation of Buddhism," "Polynesian friendliness, grace and charm," as well as the Western contributions of a "scientific attitude, principles of Democracy, art, literature and ideals of Christianity."[19]

VVV member Yutaka Nakahata, who later became a bank executive, entered junior high school in 1932. He enjoyed the differentiated classes and special periods for sciences and was elected president in his last year, an accomplishment he would repeat as a senior at McKinley High School in 1938 (16–21). His teachers were all haole, "but I don't think they had any prejudice toward us. I don't think any teacher, not that I can detect, had prejudice or superiority over Oriental students." Like Amioka, Nakahata was in regular contact with the McKinley principal. He remembered Cary as someone who "used to call me to his office and encourage me. . . . He was a very kindly person" (16–17).

Core studies also impressed Edward Nakamura, because "you were supposed to learn how to be a citizen."

> I recall Cary as being a visionary. He was always getting up in assemblies and talking about democracy, and this was the first time, of course, we had been exposed to this type of thinking. Lot of heavy stuff and, you know, that again caused confusion. . . . What I recall was that they had periodicals in all of the core studies classrooms. And I spent a lot of time reading all kinds of periodicals—*New Republic, Nation, Christian Century, Asia*—they even had *Amerasia*, which got on the bad list later on, I guess. [He laughed.] You know, just the fact that you read these things helped you, made you think a little bit more about things. You just weren't a sponge, listening to the teacher. (7–9)

Even in high school, Nakamura did not know whether he was headed for college. He guesses that perhaps he enrolled in college prep courses because "it just seemed more natural for me to take those courses" (7–9). But there was no overt encouragement or pressure from his parents to "value" education; for them, at least, high school graduation seemed enough.

McKinley could not have been so successful for everyone, to be sure, and there were VVV members who found the education decent but in no way exceptional. Jackson Morisawa recalled nothing outstanding; still, he was art director for the *Daily Pinion*, the "only daily newspaper— high school newspaper—in the world, in fact, you know. We took it out daily" (12).

Richard Zukemura remembered classmates gleefully disrupting classes at Central Intermediate School. His math teacher told the students, on the first day of class, that she was allergic to gardenias and "please" to refrain from bringing those pungent flowers into the classroom because they invariably caused her severe headaches. Of course, "couple times I remember distinctly some girls brought gardenia and, ah, she just said, 'No, no class today.' Nobody would admit they had gardenia in the room, so we used to get away with it." He laughed. When asked if he felt he had received a good education there, Zukemura replied: "I think so. I had typing. I still can type. That's the only [good] class I had when I was in the eighth grade" (13).

Akira Otani was not a good student either. He was a very quiet kid, sitting in the corner, never bothering anyone: "I struggled . . . I had to work." As far as high school rivalries were concerned, it was "McKinley against the world," although "I think if you talk about rivalry, it must have been with Punahou. Everybody wanted to beat Punahou." He did not know anyone, at the time, who attended Punahou. "I think we were just isolated. . . . We didn't know people from the other areas" (13–14).

Wallace Rider Farrington High School, named for the former governor and then congressional delegate from Hawai'i, became only the second public high school established in Honolulu. Enrollments at McKinley had exploded, almost exclusively driven by nisei demographics. Even with Farrington, Shiro Amioka's McKinley class of 1940 boasted 940 graduates. Claude Takekawa was in the first class to enroll at Farrington. In high school his closest friend was Harry Tanaka, another VVV colleague, who grew up with Claude in Kalihi, a working-class neighborhood.

At Farrington, Takekawa and Tanaka were influenced by a teacher named Mitsuyuki Kido, who became an important leader in the Japanese American community during World War II as executive secretary of the Emergency Service Committee. After the war, Kido became a respected political leader. Takekawa remembered Kido as a core studies teacher with "terrific influence on some of us at the time." He also recalled, in particular, a pretty Chinese woman from the mainland—she may have been about twenty-one or twenty-two, not much older than her high school students—who had a "terrific influence on a whole bunch of us." They were certainly not accustomed to "that kind of wahines at that time; she was very outgoing." As their drama teacher, she introduced them to the exciting world of theater, literature, and books in general. "Sort of gave you the other side of what living was all about. So even after we got into the service and took our furloughs to New York—first thing we did was hit Broadway and go to see all the plays."[20]

Harry Tanaka went from Farrington High to the University of Hawaii knowing he wanted to become a lawyer. He was student-body president at Farrington, and since he was in the first class to form the new school, he would be a "senior" for all three years. Mitsuyuki Kido was one among a number of teachers he thought were "very inspiring." Another was Gertrude Tao, who had transferred from McKinley and who worked closely with Harry as student body adviser. Tanaka also worked on the student paper, *The Governor*.[21]

It is interesting to note the regularity with which the VVV members could recall teachers or administrators who had inspired them. Perhaps it took something extra to deal with talented youth enmeshed in a system designed to blunt ambition. The public school system was assigned the task of providing the nisei with "realistic" goals. But in at least these cases, maverick teachers and administrators inspired youngsters to dream beyond the current realities.[22]

The private schools were different.

By 1925, some 561 nisei were attending such schools, representing 10 percent of all private school students but only 2 percent of all Japanese American youngsters in grades two through twelve. As Tamura points out, they were the most underrepresented of all ethnic groups in Hawai`i in private schools. Yet there was great disparity among the schools, and substantial Japanese American presence in at least a few of them.

Punahou Academy, the elite institution, had very few nisei students, perhaps 2–3 percent in the 1930s. Nearly one-half of the enrollments at Iolani and Hawaiian Mission Academy were Japanese Americans, although in the late 1930s, perhaps because of the worsening international situation, nisei figures dropped precipitously to 10–20 percent until after the war.

Mid-Pacific Institute (Mid-Pac), also small, had a long and steady tradition of Japanese American enrollment; Aiko Reinecke was a student there before heading to Kauai, where future VVV member Herbert Isonaga became her student. In 1925, 119 of 231 Mid-Pac students were Japanese Americans, some 51.5 percent. Unlike some schools, its share of nisei did not decline in the 1930s but in fact reached 60.9 percent in 1937. George Yamamoto graduated in 1934 and joined the ethnic community workforce, putting in long hours at minimal wages at a Japanese-owned store in Honolulu. Masato Doi and Teruo Himoto followed George to Mid-Pac in 1937.

For students like Himoto, fresh off a pineapple plantation, the school was very comfortable: "You know, the students there are mostly Japanese anyway and come from the same type of lifestyle, so we don't feel it [racial prejudice]. The only time we felt it was when the war break out, you know."[23]

Masato Doi, who left the Big Island of Hawai'i in 1936 to start high school at Mid-Pac, had done well at Honokaa School, which offered classes only through the tenth grade. The school had just established the eleventh and twelfth grades, but they were so new that Doi's parents felt he deserved "a more solid high school education. The plantation's Japanese [language school] teacher, he had sent his son to Mid-Pacific and that was the reason my parents got the idea of sending me to Mid-Pacific," which "was a terrific school; I think it still is but in those days, it was almost strictly a boarding school; . . . and for $125 a semester, you could have room, board, and education. . . . I had a working scholarship . . . maintaining the swimming pool and that got me $75. . . . So, although it was a sacrifice, still you know, it was a very reasonable kind of school expense" (5–10).

Doi did well in his classes. He wanted to train as a boxer, "I guess primarily because I was small and, you know, you have to fight by weight in boxing; I was very tiny as I am now, and that's the reason I thought of boxing." Although boxing was not available at Mid-Pac, the school had a baseball team, his other preference, but his acting teacher prohibited Masato from joining it. "See, I was his, sort of, star pupil. You know, he didn't want me to get hurt" (12–13). Nonetheless, Doi managed to break his collarbone playing touch football. But after a running start with drama and oratory back at Honokaa, he found a nurturing environment for the stage at Mid-Pac, and that passion would stay with him.

Doi was student-body president and valedictorian at Mid-Pac; his ambition was to attend the University of Hawai'i. His goal was to become a teacher, like his older sister, and his parents reinforced this bent. Doi felt that, given the realities of the society, "the highest I could advance to in the teaching field would be a principal of a very small school, way out in the country, after maybe thirty or forty years of teaching." He did move on to the university in the fall of 1939 but, he believed, no thanks to Mid-Pac's principal:

As far as the principal of Mid-Pac was concerned, I was, in his opinion, not to be recommended for college work. . . . Maybe, you know, I might—I might get to be a leader who might cause trouble. . . . Well, I was the principal's clerk. And, I would never have thought that he would have that kind of thinking, but as I say, the person that told me about it was just like my blood brother. He was a haole, too. He was my teacher at Mid-Pacific and I had no reason to question what he told me. . . . When I graduated, there's, well, the feeling I have was—Oh yeah, he wants this little Japanese boy just to be a good, nice, quiet boy, doing a good job as a bookkeeper or clerk or something like that. (14–16)

It is, of course, impossible to determine this principal's motivation. It may even be that Doi's "blood brother" was mistaken or, for some personal reason, had misrepresented the principal's remarks about Doi. But, given the place and the time, it is not at all difficult to envision an educator trying to track potential leaders—potential troublemakers—away from threatening the status quo. Doi was fully aware that, because of the racial restrictions, even after World War II "the nisei, even in business, would be, not the top people, but would be, well, maybe supervisors, and the lower level would be about the best they could hope for." So, teaching and, far down the line, a principal's post in a remote locale, were his best hopes for the future. "I had no illusions about where, I would end up. . . . Although I was not bitter, I wouldn't say I liked it. Sure I resented it, but not to the point of bitterness. . . . You hope for the best, but that's about it" (15).

George Yamamoto, a few years older than Himoto and Doi, commuted to McKinley High School from his home in Heeia; in those days, the twice-daily trips across the Koolau mountain range were long and arduous. Reverend Goto, who had helped George's family after his father's death, recommended that he transfer to Mid-Pac, where boarding would make life easier for everyone. Yamamoto transferred in 1932 as a junior, "but MPI was lousy at that time. Only four courses per semester. It was terrible."

I was advised to take bookkeeping. . . . I don't know how come I signed up for Latin. Hey, I was good at it! I liked the damn stuff. But this is a waste of time and effort and it's not going to do you any good, I was told. . . . And those who were going to college somehow squeezed in one math course, and they did have chemistry. Those things I didn't have, because I wasn't going to college. . . . No. Oh, no. I couldn't plan on that. This is the middle of the depression, too. A few went on [to college] from Mid-Pacific, but not many." (14–17)

I asked Yamamoto to comment on the belief that Japanese culture and Japanese people particularly valued education—in Japan, as immigrants, and through their descendants. Members of the VVV had various reactions to this proposition. In Yamamoto's case:

> No, I didn't really get that [feeling]; . . . my wife, after working one year after high school, decided to enroll at UH against the wishes of her father. "Go sewing school, *mo yaku ni tatsu*" [be of practical use]." . . . Only one boy [among her brothers] decided to go to college; . . . certainly they [there were ten children] didn't get pressured to go to college." He laughed. "Well, it might be that compared with Portuguese kids, Hawaiian kids—oh, I wouldn't say that as against Chinese kids— but I was never told, 'Education, you have it with you.' All that kind of thing, I never heard that. I didn't get enough of the right kind of stuff." [More laughter.] (15–16)

The Roosevelt High teachers were all haole—"not very unfriendly or anything. None very special." Yugo Okubo noted that attending Roosevelt—the English Standard high school—separated him from the neighborhood, where the other kids saw him as a bit strange. He was an "average" student in high school. His best subject was algebra, which led to his unfortunate choice of a civil-engineering major in college. He did not participate in extracurricular activities and did not date (8).

Ted Tsukiyama did not appear especially enthusiastic about Roosevelt, although his experience was not as unhappy as Okubo's. He did, of course, notice that there were very few Japanese Americans or other "locals." "In those days, of course, we didn't date, so there was no opportunity, not even the thought of dating interracially. . . . I never had any feelings of superiority or condescension [toward other public school students]. I got along. You might say it was one-way. The others may have felt intimidated or inferior with someone from Roosevelt, but I never felt the reverse" (3–4).

Students at the non–English Standard schools were certainly resentful. Shiro Amioka, president of the McKinley student body, was quick to point out that students felt Roosevelt was "a poor man's Punahou." The use of Standard English rather than the local pidgin was the primary determinant of social class and status among most residents. Shiro himself, after all, would never have been admitted to Roosevelt: "I wouldn't have made it because I didn't talk good English. So I used to say to myself, You folks think you are smart but the only difference is that you talk better. . . . Oh yes. Was us versus Roosevelt and all the other haole types. They think they are hot stuff but wait till we go to the university. We'll show you. I always kept it in my mind. By God, when I got to the university . . . (20–23).[24]

Amioka insisted he had a fully developed determination that he, as a working-class public school student, would never yield to the arrogance of the haole [or other!] students at Punahou, Roosevelt, or even the very few who attended McKinley: "You talk like a haole, but so what? What makes you think you are better than us? . . . I admit you talk like a haole and that's good, but don't translate that to better brains. . . . And I used to tell 'em, I said that the testing ground is going to be going to the university." And, indeed, Amioka recalled having his delicious bit of revenge on the university campus. "I showed them. When it came to the exam, they want to borrow my notes. 'You want to use my notes, go ahead. I don't need them.' Then I tell them, 'Hey, how come? I thought you went to Roosevelt?' Or 'How come, you went to St. Louis, or Punahou?'" (22).

This was an unusually frank outburst. Amioka never mentioned Tsukiyama by name, but they might well have met at interschool activities. Resentment against the English Standard system, at its height in this period just before World War II, was repressed almost entirely during the war and transformed into an active movement to abolish the system soon after the war ended.

I recall feeling the same way—we did not consciously think of it primarily as envy, by the way—toward the Roosevelt students in the mid-fifties when I was at Kaimuki High, a decidedly working-class public school. And this was so even though by then the ethnic/racial characteristics at Roosevelt had been altered beyond recognition. The system's founders would have been most surprised, had they dropped in to observe the school only three decades later, to find most of the student leaders at Roosevelt of Japanese and Chinese descent, just a few years before the demise of the system in 1960. The system died with very little fanfare and even less opposition precisely because it had lost its original function: to provide a linguistic and racial island in an ocean of pidgin and people of color.

Families like the Okubos and Tsukiyamas understood that education was important—both intrinsically and in terms of mobility. But they were exceptions even among the VVV families and certainly in the Japanese American community of the 1920s and 1930s. This is not the impression left by many writers. A value on education, per se, is widely assumed to be among the constellation of cultural attributes brought by the issei from Meiji Japan.[25] Ralph Yempuku certainly believed this to be the case:

> You see, because my parents instilled that thing in me. Because they were both teachers. "Whatever you do, get an education" And this is the big thing with me. I gotta have an education. . . . The Japanese were the ones that would tell their kids you got to get an education. So all of us— I know all my friends, they were Japanese, there weren't that many other nationalities. I think proportionwise, Japanese were the largest percentage. . . . I think throughout, the Japanese appreciated the fact that education was a big thing in the advancement of the person. So they forced their kids to go to the university. (8–9, 17–18)

However, appreciation of education as vital to "advancement of the person" was linked critically to schooling as a means of occupational mobility. Ralph also recalled that he was the top student "graduating" from the eighth grade at Kahuku School and that he was one of a precious few going on to high school. "I would say hardly any except myself. . . . Yeah, because everybody finishes [intermediate school]—they went to work for the plantation" (8–9).

I then offered: "So, even if we talk about Japanese placing a high value on education—even if you wanted your kids to go to school in that period, it was tough, yeah?"

Yempuku agreed. "Yeah. That's right. Fortunately, like I said, my father was a Buddhist minister and the temple, . . . they help their kind, you know, . . . they made room for me there at the dormitory and then afterwards, in fact when I started to go to the university, they made available a room underneath the temple" (8–9).

Yempuku also felt that getting a high school education was "the ultimate" for most of his generation, including Japanese Americans. His case was most unusual—when his parents returned to Japan, they left Ralph with "about $1,000" so he could continue school in the mid-1930s. He worked very hard, of course, to earn his keep—including doing chores around the temple and cleaning classrooms at the Imamura Home, the dormitory for Buddhist youngsters at the Hongwanji. Nonetheless, this was not an insignificant amount of money in that period. Yempuku was also fortunate in having an elaborate support system of Buddhist leaders and temple infrastructure in place for him. This was not the case for youth in other ethnic groups, for nisei girls, or for many other nisei males as well.

And, as George Yamamoto made clear, there was not always a value placed on education itself. Yutaka Nakahata also sensed from his parents no particular emphasis on education. "I don't think that, among my peers, there was this strong urge to go to college. I don't know for what reason, but I said I want to go to college. . . . I never told my mom or brother or anything like that. . . . She didn't push me" (23). This lack of a "push" was true for nearly everyone else interviewed among the VVV members.

It is telling that many future VVV members themselves understood that any emphasis on education on the part of their issei parents was for nisei occupational mobility—that is, as Masato Doi spelled out, a goal that could reasonably be expected, given the limited possibilities of the times. This would be borne out by the fact that only a few of the VVV aspired to other professions upon entering the university: Harry Tanaka and Ted Tsukiyama knew they wanted to be lawyers; Yugo Okubo majored in civil engineering (and hated it); the brightest and most ambitious of the rest competed for cherished slots in Teachers College.

For all of these boys in the 1930s, school was paramount in their minds. While their very youthful years were filled with carefree play, there does not appear to be very much in the way of "social life" in the 1930s. There was the depression, of course, and most of their families had little money. For Okubo and Tsukiyama, Roosevelt High School was a setting that virtually guaranteed little interaction, given the social distance between haole and Japanese.

When asked about dating in high school, Akira Otani simply responded: "Girls? I was afraid of girls!" (Perhaps the emphasis was for the benefit of his wife, who was sitting nearby during the interview.) His attitude changed a bit at the university, but he was sure it was because he was one of the few who had access to a car and so was needed to chauffeur his buddies and their dates (11). Richard Zukemura mentioned the proms but said he did not go out very much "cause cannot afford it those days" and laughed (19).

Yutaka Nakahata never had a "steady" in high school, but he recalled occasional dances in addition to the class proms that, like other major events, were held at the posh Waialae Country Club. Yutaka never had access to a car, so he relied on friends for transportation. "That's why I could not easily ask a girl to go out, because no car." So dating was almost always a group activity, usually a dance, with two or more couples sharing a car. "Some kind of club would sponsor a dance, and most of these were held in the school cafeteria."

> I think we had at least a jacket on and in those days the orchestra was, maybe, a seven-piece [group]. The music was not, you know—bang, bang, bang. It was the soothing kind. The dances, I recall, were program dances. . . . And you signed [dance programs], ask the girl to sign for you. . . . You and your date, you get the first and the last dance but in between— . . . And, of course, after the dance we used to go to these— there are not too many now—drive-ins. . . . You would drive in there and the carhops would come and take your order and you would sit there and eat; . . . you roll up the window and then they'll put the tray on. (17–19)

Shiro Amioka's senior prom was held at a fancy hotel in the city. Amioka's family could never have afforded a car, but Shiro was outgoing and social, active in student government and many extracurricular affairs, so he had no trouble finding dates. Like Nakahata, he recalled that school and club dances were the major dating events. If a date attended the same high school, going to football games would be an option—but it would be a problem if the couple had to root for opposing teams. Especially in the last two years of high school, there might be special movie dates to the new and splendid Waikiki Theater that had opened in the 1930s or, as Richard Zukemura recalled, to a dinner at a restaurant like Kewalo Inn, decent but hardly fancy. For Amioka, the old-time dances, many right on the campuses, had much to recommend them: "Of course, we don't go fancy places like kids today go, but students participated wholeheartedly in decorating the place and making it nice and everything— . . . a challenge. . . . It was much more student-created atmosphere and student-created fun" (17–19).

One of the reasons many nisei had so little time for dates and social life was that their parents found the practice so unfamiliar. This was especially true for the girls.[26] The VVV families tended to be rather more broad-minded or, as in the case of Nakahata, Yamamoto, or Amioka, headed by widowed mothers who had less control over their sons. Except for Tsukiyama and Okubo at Roosevelt, the lack of money and cars was more critical; the level of general dating throughout the society was low enough, moreover, that nonparticipation was not stigmatized.

In the 1930s, then, the mandatory "American" school system clearly overshadowed the Japanese-language institutions. Although most of the

VVV members continued to attend Japanese-language schools through their high school years, *nihongo gakko* assumed much less significance as the years went by. For some, like Ed Nakamura, there was a gradual withering away of parental insistence that he attend and, by the time he was in high school, Japanese-language school was no longer an issue. "From first grade to fifth grade, I was number one," Jackson Morisawa reported. He slipped to number two in the sixth grade, then "started to fool around. You know, other things start interest me." He laughed. By the seventh grade, he had dropped to number ten or thereabouts. "And now, we were in sort of high school and we had more activities going on—football and all that. So, by the time eighth grade—I was about [number] twenty-something." More laughter. "And the last year of [intermediate school], you know, nowhere near. So I quit" (9–10).

In 1928, in a fourth-grade play, George Yamamoto acted the part of Kusunoki Masatsura, the son of Kusunoki Masashige (played by an eighth-grader), who went off to battle knowing he would never return. The famous parting scene in fourteenth-century Japan (following a split in the imperial family and a series of battles to determine which line would ascend the throne) between warrior father and son had become the ultimate symbols of the samurai, completely loyal to the emperor.[27] By the time of Yamamoto's performance, the emperor system was well established in Japan, and the Kusunoki story indoctrinated into every school child in Japan. But this was not necessarily the case in Hawai'i, where textbooks had been revised to incorporate U.S. or Western themes and topics. In addition, it seems that the impact on the students was less the political message of devotion to the emperor than the poignancy of a family tragedy. "Well, anyway, father and son part, the father going off to war [and death] and son knowing he has to remain at home, take care of his mother and become a sturdy loyalist samurai. The moisture on the warrior's sleeve—was it tears or was it the evening dew?" (25).

The cultural lessons of values like *mono no aware*—the sadness in realizing life's transient quality—were easily learned. There was less evidence of inculcation of political chauvinism. Some Japanese schoolteachers did try to instill a sense of Japan's preeminence, especially in justifying its rapacious treatment of Korea, Taiwan, Okinawa, and China, but little of this chauvinism came through for the VVV members.

Yamamoto, for example, did not recall any admonition from his teachers to "remember that he was a Japanese." On Tenchosetsu, the emperor's birthday, his teachers read from the Imperial Rescript on Education, promulgated by the Meiji emperor in 1871, but no one knew what it meant and the sensei never bothered to explain. "Incidentally, I don't recall any gung-ho Nippondaiichi [Japan as number 1] kind of thing . . . or banzai, . . . you know, the flag waving" (14). There is, in contrast, evidence of strong Japanese chauvinism on the West Coast, where some language schools and Japanese-language newspapers were notorious for rabid propaganda efforts. According to Senator Daniel Inouye, however, even one of his teachers in Honolulu exclaimed to his young students in 1939: "When Japan calls, you must know that it is Japanese blood that flows in your veins."[28]

Yutaka Nakahata said, of Japanese school, "Well, I didn't hate it." He attended, along with Zukemura and Morisawa, the Hongwanji "coat" school, so called because it required boys to wear jackets and ties. Nakahata sensed no "nationalist kind of a feeling" among teachers in the younger grades; "perhaps there was some when I went to Hongwanji. Many of these teachers were Buddhist priests, too. So I thought if there was any feeling for Japan, it was more when I was in the Hongwanji" (10–11).

Shiro Amioka did not know until much later that his modest Kakaako neighborhood actually boasted two separate Japanese schools because the issei community had split so decisively over the language schools' court case against the territory, eventually won in 1927. Amioka recalled that in his school: "We had quite a bit of extracurricular activities: . . . *kendo* [Japanese fencing] . . . and every four years they used to have what is known as *gakko geikai*, student performance, . . . it's a big job, you know—put on stage plays; the whole school participated. . . . The principal made it very clear that the Japanese schools in Hawai'i exist to make good American citizens of the students. . . . Right from the beginning. That's his philosophy" (11–12).

The anti-Japanese-school movement, which had lasted from the early 1900s to the 1927 Supreme Court decision, effectively removed most traces of national chauvinism from the curriculum. And while losing the battle to eliminate the language schools, these attacks largely succeeded in their primary purpose, which was to intimidate the Japanese American community into accepting the status quo. Throughout, however, the students themselves, like Shiro Amoka, remained blissfully ignorant of the controversies swirling around them; first, that waged between the Japanese community and the outside world and, second, between opposing forces within the immigrant community itself. The importance, however, of the schools themselves and their significance in the evolution of Hawaii's race relations should not be underestimated.[29]

Most of the future VVV members, who were in high school in the late 1930s when relations between the United States and Japan were deteriorating so rapidly, might have sensed international stresses and been subjected to racial stereotyping. But like many others, Ralph Yempuku "never thought that war would come between Japan and the United States. You know, I thought that everything would be peaceful" (20–21). At the same time, he was confronted with racism at work. When I asked whether there were non-Japanese willing to speak on Japanese Americans' behalf—to address the prejudice or the many discriminatory actions, he replied:

> It was very unpopular at that time to be for the nisei. See, like I say, if your name Odo, you're stereotyped, you're a Jap. There is no, "Oh, you know, he's American. He's born in Hawai'i. He's a citizen."
>
> Back in 1936, '37, '38, I was with the athletic program here. I remember taking trips to the mainland with the football team as the manager. All the niseis on the team, like us, we had to have passports. . . . American citizens, to go to the mainland. The other nationalities don't need [them] . . . [but] the Japanese were different, or nisei were different from the other races. And I don't know how the federal government can do that. (34–35)

Barney Ono remembered that travel requirement well because he had been ready to comply while preparing for a trip scheduled for mid-December 1941. "You know, all the oriental people had to get what we call CC card—Certificate of Citizenship card. . . . Matson [shipping lines] forced the government to require all the Orientals to get the CC card because they didn't want to bear the expense of bringing us back if we couldn't land on the West Coast. . . . Hung Wai Ching, who was head of the YMCA, was gonna send Masato Doi and I to Asilomar, California, for this conference. . . . But my trip got blown up by Pearl Harbor" (1–2).

Ralph Yempuku was correct about the need for documentation, although it was not a passport that was required but certification from the Immigration and Naturalization Service; the federal government was, in this case, responding to local racial politics by assisting the Matson lines, which had a monopoly over passenger service between Hawai'i and the mainland. It may be that Matson, a subsidiary of a Big Five firm,

Alexander and Baldwin, wanted the requirement to protect against business risk, as Barney Ono presumed. Whatever the reasoning, the process was humiliating to the local-born Japanese, who felt it unnecessary and demeaning.[30]

Almost everyone else who eventually joined the VVV sensed tension in the air between the United States and Japan but, like Ryoji Namba, almost no one anticipated a war. When asked when he first realized that "things might be a little tense between the United States and Japan," Namba replied, only partly in jest: "You know, actually, maybe after the war started!" Like so many of the others, Ryoji was a student at McKinley High School in the late 1930s and was exposed to some of the best of progressive education of that era. But all the readings assigned from contemporary magazines and newspapers and all the classroom discussions in their problem-oriented core studies never gave the students a real sense of the impending war (20).

Even at predominantly haole Roosevelt High School, Ted Tsukiyama recalled, the thought of war "never entered my mind. That's why I was so shocked on Pearl Harbor day. Just incredible" (13). Yugo Okubo, at Roosevelt until he graduated in spring 1941, was familiar with hostile attitudes toward Japan and Japanese Americans but "didn't have a sense that anything could lead to a war. I just sort of wished; even at that time I would say, in general, there was still hope in people that there might be a way of having peace." He knew, too, that such a war would have had a severe impact on Japanese Americans, so the hope was especially fervent (16).

Some, like Akira Otani and Richard Zukemura, felt that, at the time, they were simply unprepared to deal with matters like international relations. Zukemura, who graduated from McKinley in 1940, "wasn't too interested in international affairs, to tell you the truth, if these things were not brought up; . . . I didn't have a mind of my own. I didn't care, in other words" (19).

Herbert Isonaga told a somewhat different story. He had gone to the University of Oregon for college in the late 1930s. Realizing he would be drafted, he returned to Hawai`i so he could serve with his friends.

So came '41, I figured, hey, I was twenty-one, ready to be drafted, so I felt that I had better come home. . . . So I returned the summer of '41 and enrolled at the university while waiting to be drafted. . . .

Coming back on the *Lurline*, one of the occupants in my stateroom was a Japanese man. He and his family had lived in Hawaii previously.

And I asked him, "Gee, how come you're going back to Hawaii?" He says, "Oh, I'm going back because a war is going to break out between Japan and America." And he felt that when the war broke out, he'd rather be in Hawai`i. . . . I thought that, gee, this guy, how come he knows so much? And of course, events proved him right. And then I saw him here in Hawai`i during the war and he was driving a cab. . . . And he told me, "Hey, I told you so." [Isonaga laughed]. And I asked him how come he knew. He said, "Oh, well, you listen to all the news and read all that's transpiring, there's no out." So I always said to myself that, gee, this buggah was smart enough, how come we never know? (17)

Masato Doi was an exception. He recalled thinking seriously about the impending war with Japan. When he enrolled at Mid-Pac in 1936, units of the Japanese Army provoked an incident at the Marco Polo Bridge in North China to justify an invasion. It marked the beginning of full-scale war in Asia. Shortly thereafter:

I distinctly remember one day seeing a plane fly over, see. It's one of those commercial planes, but I asked my father, "If there comes a time when there's a war between the United States and Japan, what's my position?" Because, I said, "You know, looks like, there's a possibility that war might come about." And what he told me was . . . well, the way he puts it is, "Omae wa kono kuni de sodaterareta [You were brought up by this country]." (12)

These were very young men; absent unusual encounters like Isonaga's with the cab driver, it was difficult to transcend the official assurances that Hawai`i was impregnable and that the Japanese, while powerful in Asia, were an inferior race incapable of challenging the United States. It was hard enough for them to project their own life trajectories in the face of so much social, political, and economic discrimination. They were intelligent young men who realized that the barriers confronting them were portrayed as cultural traits they had inherited. Even their languages (Hawaiian Creole English or Japanese) were defined as cultural weaknesses or liabilities. Any association with Japan, given this setting, was extremely problematic.

Arguably the most provocative issue confronting the young Japanese Americans was that of dual citizenship. Since Japan, like most other nations, recognized the principle of *jus sanguinis*, the law of blood, American-born Japanese with immigrant fathers inherited Japanese citizenship. Since the United States recognized the principle of *jus soli*, the law of the soil, anyone born on U.S. territory was automatically entitled to

U.S. citizenship. For many Americans, this was an issue as clear as it was critical. As Judge Alvah E. Steadman, who had been a vice-president of the Big Five's Cooke Trust Company, put it: "I cannot see how anyone can be a clean 100 percent American if at the same time he has allegiance to another power existing. . . . It is this dual citizenship that has created more suspicion, more discussions in Congress than anything else."[31] When Congress in 1937 sent a delegation to hold hearings on the issue of statehood for Hawai'i, this question was prominently and pointedly directed at the American-born Japanese.

Within the territory, public and official opinion was virtually unanimous—the nisei, individually and collectively, had to divest themselves of their Japanese citizenship. The elements more hostile toward the Japanese community took the obvious lead, but even its most supportive advocates felt that expatriation was necessary. Miles Cary, McKinley High principal, even invited a representative from the Japanese consulate in 1925 to explain the procedure to his students and to process applications on the campus. Well-known issei leaders joined the chorus. Reverend Takie Okumura, organizer of the New Americans conferences, was outspoken and consistent in urging "every dual citizen to . . . cut off every tie that binds him to the country of his parents."[32] *Nippu Jiji* editor Yasutaro Soga had been urging expatriation at every opportunity. The *Hawaii Hochi* and its fiery editor, Frederick Kinzaburo Makino, had often criticized Okumura and Soga for taking stands that sacrificed the rights of the Japanese community in order to appease the Big Five elite, but not on this issue. A 1939 *Hochi* editorial agreed that nisei were absolutely loyal to the United States but went so far as to endorse a proposal to prohibit employment in territorial, city, and county agencies to anyone with dual citizenship. Another editorial, shortly before Pearl Harbor, warned that "in times like the present there can be no split allegiance, no half-in-half [*sic*] loyalties."[33]

The Japanese government had made major concessions in 1916 and 1924 to placate American protesters, including a number of nisei. The 1916 action allowed nisei, except males aged seventeen to thirty-seven who were subject to Japanese conscription, to expatriate. In 1924, largely in response to nisei who petitioned Japan for reforms, the diet revamped its laws to permit any nisei, at any time, to renounce Japanese citizenship. More important, anyone born to Japanese subjects after 1924 would not automatically become a citizen but had to be registered at the consulate by parents or guardians within fourteen days of birth.

In spite of these actions, the rate of expatriation was unimpressive. By 1933, only 31 percent of the 103,467 nisei in Hawai'i had expatriated. As the movement to encourage expatriation intensified, however, more individuals responded, until in 1940 about four hundred were renouncing their Japanese citizenship every month. As tensions mounted, some nisei leaders began a concerted campaign to gather petitions to urge expatriation; on June 17, 1941, the Campaign Central Committee formally closed operations and its books after gathering more than thirty thousand signatures and spending $424.36.[34] Still, the number of nisei who divested themselves of Japanese citizenship was less than impressive.

The reasons for this relatively low level of expatriation were numerous and varied. Surely a few nisei were proud of their Japanese citizenship and contemplated working and living in Japan, but for most the process was simply too cumbersome, tedious, or expensive. Parents were normally required to accompany nisei applicants to the Japanese consulate; nearly every parent was employed, of course, and for rural residents or, worse, those on neighbor islands, this was an unusual hardship. Sometimes, nisei births were not properly recorded with the territory or the consulate. In that event, it was difficult to undo something that had never officially occurred. Sending for proper documents in Japan was a major problem.

In some cases, there were practical reasons for retaining dual citizenship: Expatriation could mean both financial loss and emotional pain. For families with ties to the ancestral village home, expatriation meant cutting off potential rights to property that had been in the family for centuries. When Ruth Yamaguchi's father went to the Japanese consulate to remove his name from the Japanese record, his mother, Sei Ishibashi (her grandmother—*babachan*), was furious. At first the young Ruth did not understand:

> I thought my father did the right thing. But there was another part to it that we didn't understand; it was my grandmother's part. She said that he being the only child, and he was the male child, . . . the property in Japan was in his name, but when he did that, Japan no longer was obligated to have that land for him. And so she said, in other words, she has no home. . . . For us, we're thinking that, Oh, *Babachan*, no way you— no, no, no, you cannot go to Japan. You have to stay here with us. . . . *Japan dare mo oran kara. Kaeren demo e* (In Japan you have no one there. You don't have to return.). . . . But she is trying to tell us that when my

dad did that, now she cannot go back to Japan. . . . She was an Ishibashi. Her husband died, but as long as that land was in my father's name, he was still an Ishibashi. Japan doesn't think too much about a female who's a widow. And if her son, or there's no family ties now with Japan, they don't think much about you coming back to that family, you see. . . . So it seemed as though she had cut—when my father did that, all ties with the Ishibashi family was cut off to her.[35]

In many cases, then, expatriation was much more than an act of clarifying political loyalties—it marked cultural, familial, and social abandonment or rejection, not only of Japan as an ancestral homeland but of the issei parents themselves. The 1922 Supreme Court decision that rejected Takao Ozawa's application to become a U.S. citizen ended the last hope that the issei could become participants in political life.[36] Thereafter, immigrant Japanese lived with the constant reminder that they might be forced to return to a homeland many did not even remember. In that eventuality, any of their children who had expatriated would be at an enormous disadvantage. Small wonder, then, that expatriation could be a difficult decision. Very few of the nisei understood the anguish of their parents or the material basis of the problem. This issue was but one of many that exacerbated the already considerable generation gap.

For most of the VVV, like most nisei in general, the issue of dual citizenship remained an abstraction and did not become especially important in their lives. With a few exceptions, they did not feel that expatriation warranted the time, expense, and bother required to find documents, travel to the consulate, and pay the fees. Barney Ono and George Yamamoto, however, went to unusual lengths. Yamamoto's case, an extraordinary study in timing, illustrates the bureaucratic problems of documentation that sometimes discouraged expatriation. The case

was very complicated. . . . I never had a birth certificate because at birth I was not reported to the vital statistics bureau in Honolulu; . . . at age sixteen or so I had to be literally born. My mother had to contact the midwife neighbor; she had to give a deposition that "Yeah, I was present at that boy's birth." . . . My father had not reported [my birth] to the Japanese consulate. . . . So, since there was a flurry of concern about dual citizenship and that sort of thing in the '30s, I went to petition the Japanese government for expatriation. . . . This was when I was already twenty-two or -three, just before the war. As a matter of fact, I think it

was the Friday before Pearl Harbor Sunday that I got news from Ko-
matsuya [Hotel] that I was expatriated, and then suddenly it didn't seem
to matter at all. (3–4)

In 1934, just into the seventh grade, Barney Ono similarly decided he
should join the movement to expatriate. His decision was at least partly
in response to an appeal by the Hawai'i Civic Japanese Association, a
group of nisei activists who urged expatriation. "And I told my parents
that I would because I didn't think I could ever go to Japan or have any
feeling about Japan. So, I did; then they said, 'Boy, if you ever go to
Japan, you're on their shit list for doing that.' So I defied them" (3).

The movement to encourage expatriation forced the nisei into a defensive posture; the whole tone of the military and civilian "warnings"
to the Japanese American community in Hawai'i, as Gary Okihiro has
pointed out, was to intimidate it to produce strong and steady signals that
it would cheerfully maintain a subordinate status in Hawai'i. In this context, the nisei who volunteered for ROTC action and Hawaii Territorial Guard (HTG) duty on December 7 and in the weeks thereafter may
be regarded as individuals unwilling to abide by the status quo, engag-
ing in the only form of defiance and resistance that made sense to them.
As each instance of voluntarism for duty was rejected by their country,
it became more difficult to sustain their enthusiasm. Thus, where several hundred Japanese Americans joined the HTG, fewer than 170 could
be convinced to volunteer yet again, for work with the VVV.

But Japan was more than a potential enemy; it was Buddhist. As we
have seen, Christianity played a significant role in the lives of many VVV
members. Of course, there were staunch Buddhists in the group—Ralph
Yempuku's father was a Buddhist priest, as was Yoshiaki Fujitani's. And,
it may be remembered, Buddhism itself had become a major target for
persecution at the beginning of the Meiji era; indeed, there is some evidence that anti-Buddhist sentiment remained and extended to immigrant communities in Hawai'i.[37] But Christianity was a distinctly minority religion within the Japanese American community in the pre–
World War II era. As a result, its adherents had to deal with complexities not required of youth more comfortably entrenched in largely Buddhist communities.

So it made sense that John Young and Hung Wai Ching, two of the
VVV's most important advisers, were strong Christians. Young would
become a reverend and perform weddings for several of the VVV mem-

bers; both men worked out of the YMCA movement. George Yamamoto was clearly affected by the kindness of Reverend Goto, who had become a "good Samaritan" to his family, and the young Yamamoto did considerable work around the church in Kaneohe. Reverend Stephen Mark's intensity inspired Yutaka Nakahata and Shiro Amioka. Ted Tsukiyama's parents had been baptized before arriving in Hawai`i. Ryoji Namba, Yugo Okubo, and Herb Isonaga attended Sunday schools; Shiro Amioka even taught in his Kakaako Sunday school. Masato Doi's parents were Jodo-shu (Pure Land Buddhism) adherents, but his sister married a Christian who taught Sunday school. "So I was taken to that Sunday School when I was a child," Doi said, "and I guess I would be more—I would've been more of a Christian than a Buddhist" (11).

Christianity must have had an impact on these youngsters in the 1930s.[38] Any ambitious nisei would have considered the fact that the United States proclaimed itself a Christian nation. The radical approach of Reverend Takie Okumura and his son Umetaro of the Makiki Christian Church to convince nisei to denounce Buddhism in embracing Christianity was not particularly appealing or successful. On the other hand, implementation of social gospel policies wherein religiosity was manifested in service to society was a powerful message to idealistic youth.

The best of the Christian ministers, like Stephen Mark, and of the YMCA leaders, like John Young and Hung Wai Ching, urged the nisei to "do something" with their lives. This kind of inspiration was what Ted Tsukiyama meant when he referred to his father as a "living or practicing Christian," not having to "show it off," and what Herb Isonaga meant in discussing the "educational" aspects of Sunday school on Kauai. Japanese-language schools and the Buddhist religion both had come under consistent attack as incompatible with U.S./Christian ideals, and both had responded with enormous efforts to reform their institutional and ideological foundations to accommodate their new contexts.[39] If nothing else, these boys who had some experience with life sustained by a "minority" religion understood that some beliefs required unusual tenacity and action in the face of social indifference or hostility.

One last issue in the 1930s regarded the fact that the nisei were sometimes called on to serve as the intermediaries between Japan and the United States. Interestingly, the former VVV men reported no conscious recollection of having been placed in a position to serve as bridges—to use their bicultural heritage to promote better understanding or relations—a burden commonly imposed upon the nisei by their own immigrant parents, as well as by their supporters in the non-Japanese community. Nor was there discussion of the oft-mentioned bamboo metaphor by which the issei are supposed to have trained their children to survive racism, growing strong yet flexible so as not to break before the winds of adversity.

THE 1930S PROVIDED a bewildering set of international, national, and local events and trends through which the men who would form the VVV needed to maneuver. Hawai`i entered the decade as the nation was enduring the Great Depression and facing the mounting challenge of Japan's Asian wars. All the while, these teenage nisei dealt with two kinds of schools, with growing families, and with their own need to make their way in the world. Then, abruptly, Japan's attack on Pearl Harbor on December 7, 1941, put everything on hold.

4

Pearl Harbor

I was real upset, you know. I had never thought that war would start. And to find that your—you know, because somehow you associate yourself with your kind—and to find that your kind is attacking. Hey, you're made real, real sad, and at the same time angry. . . . The goddamn Japanese, you know.

—Ralph Yempuku

alph Yempuku's response to the Japanese attack on December 7, 1941, was classic; he understood immediately that there would be a problem for him and the rest of the Japanese American population because of the "association" with "your kind."[1] But his forthright acknowledgment of the sense of kinship with the attacking Japanese was unacceptable to mainstream Japanese America for many decades after World War II. The prevailing mythology, to this day, emphasizes the thoroughgoing assimilation of the pre-war nisei and the concomitant distancing from the Japanese in Japan.

War between the United States and Japan had long been anticipated on both sides of the Pacific. Military and civilian leaders were swept into what appeared to be an inexorable tidal pull, particularly after World War I, pitting against one another these two dominant imperial powers.[2] The assault on Pearl Harbor was a brilliant tactical victory but a disastrous strategic decision. From a military perspective, the attack was straightforward and masterfully executed. From a broader perspective, as Admiral Yamamoto Isoroku, commander of the attacking fleet, had predicted, this victory guaranteed only that the total industrial capacity and political will of the United States would be focused on Japan's ultimate defeat.

UNTIL DECEMBER 7, while the U.S. military was confident that there would be a war, there was almost no thought that Hawai`i might become the primary target. Secretary of the Navy Frank Knox assured a private gathering three days before the attack: "I want you to know that no matter what happens, the United States Navy is ready! Every man is at his post, every ship is at its station. . . . Whatever happens, the navy is not going to be caught napping."[3] *Collier's* magazine, in its June 1941 issue, featured an article entitled "Impregnable Pearl Harbor," which boasted: "The Pacific Fleet . . . [is] always within a few minutes of clearing for action. . . . We're kept pretty well informed where they [Japanese ships and planes] are and what they're up to. . . . In the continental United States there may be some doubt about our readiness to fight, but none exists in Hawaii. Battleships . . . plow the ocean practicing gunnery, wary as lions on the prowl."[4]

Given this arrogance, the decisiveness of the Japanese military victory made Pearl Harbor even more humiliating. Stereotypes of the Japanese as inferiors who could not challenge European or U.S. superiority had long reigned supreme, although some concern had been expressed, especially after the Japanese defeat of the Russians in 1905, the first modern instance of a nonwhite country defeating a European (albeit Russian) nation. And while an alarm had been sounded about a "yellow peril" that could overwhelm white civilization, Japan's threat was primarily portrayed as that of a technological imitator leading countless hordes of Chinese troops.[5]

At the national level after December 7, 1941, the primary focus became the galvanizing of the population for a total war effort. One result was the scapegoating of the military commanders in charge in Hawai`i at the time—Lieutenant General Walter Short of the army and Admiral Husband E. Kimmel of the navy both were soon dismissed in disgrace. Another was the targeting of the Japanese American population. For a few weeks after the attack, the press and government officials were relatively benign in their assessment of the situation, arguing that the United States needed to distinguish between resident Japanese and the vicious "Japs" who had perpetrated the sneak attack.

But not all media were as reasonable. The *Los Angeles Times* warned on December 8 that California was in particular danger from potential enemy agents since "[w]e have thousands of Japanese here," and "in the light of yesterday's demonstration that treachery and double-dealing are major Japanese weapons."[6] In general the media and public officials were careful not to raise undue alarm about the few Japanese Americans in the larger community. After about a month, however, the political impulse to fix blame became all-consuming, and stories of Japanese American espionage and sabotage became routine explanations for the Pearl Harbor fiasco. This set the stage for the removal and internment of the Japanese, arguably the most deliberate, considered, and prolonged assault on the U.S. Constitution in American history.[7]

In Hawai`i, the steady drumbeat of anti-Japanese scare tactics had succeeded in convincing the military, before December 7, that resident issei and nisei were likely to be more dangerous than any attack or invasion by the Japanese military.[8] One spectacular result of this assumption was the tragic decision to keep fighter aircraft in tight lines on the tarmacs of the airfields, for maximum protection against saboteurs who might infiltrate the airbase from surrounding sugarcane fields. As a result, on December 7, Japanese pilots found row upon row of aircraft, perfectly aligned targets for bombing and strafing runs.

There were other, happily less consequential, examples. Samuel Lindley was walking by the railroad terminal in Honolulu about a week before the attack on Pearl Harbor and noticed the machine guns mounted there. "And instead of facing out to the ocean, as you might expect, they were facing the street, where they figured Japanese in Hawai`i might attack the railroad station. And also, there were machine guns set up in the tower of Kawaiaha`o Church. Where the clock is, there were machine guns facing along King Street, in case there was some kind of local insurrection, I suppose."[9]

The local context and the events that unfolded within it during the war years are better understood when Hawai`i is appreciated as a crucial strategic position in the Pacific, but marginal in every other sense. The military's insistence (and Roosevelt's concurrence) that Hawai`i immediately be placed under martial law, suspending the civilian judiciary and the writ of habeas corpus, was reasonable given the anxiety over the possibility of a second attack or a major invasion.[10] But Hawaii's position relative to the economic and political metropoles in the United States allowed the military to continue martial law in the islands until

October 1944, long after the threat of invasion had passed. It is difficult to conceive of such a long-term "occupation" occurring in, say, Los Angeles, San Francisco, Portland, or Seattle. To be sure, the immediate possibility of a second attack or of an invasion was also taken seriously in Hawai`i, and the landscape reflected this reality with blacked-out windows, slit trenches on school campuses, barbed-wire barricades on the beaches, camouflaged antiaircraft guns, and armed sentries guarding a host of buildings.[11] This was a crisis situation that only gradually diminished in intensity until the decisive Battle of Midway, June 4–6, 1942, which destroyed any serious Japanese capability of launching an invasion against Hawai`i.

But the initial reaction to the blitz, for almost everyone, was shock and disbelief. Among the immigrant issei, the primary emotion was fear of the unknown. For a few days, there was even some jubilation that Japan had delivered a crippling blow to the U.S. military and to U.S. arrogance. Some of the issei characters in Jon Shirota's novel *Lucky Come Hawaii* fairly burst with pride after the Pearl Harbor attack. One, Kato-san, screams out within earshot of a nisei and a rich haole employer: "Japanese airplanes bombing all the ships in Pearl harbor. Banzai! Banzai! Banzai!"[12] On December 8, Ted Tsukiyama's father was embarrassed by an issei acquaintance who yelled out in delight from across the street in downtown Honolulu: "Oy, umai koto yatta zo!" [Hey, what a great job they did!]" (13).

The issei also felt shame and humiliation: Japan's treacherous actions undercut the proud legacy of feudal honor and honesty so methodically instilled in them and which they had so assiduously preached to their children and neighbors. At the same time, the issei felt despair, most notably those who considered themselves loyal Japanese subjects, who felt betrayed by an uncaring native country whose aggression had placed them in such danger.

Early on the fateful morning of December 7, Ralph Yempuku was in Waikiki arranging a sightseeing bus tour for the football team from Willamette, Oregon, which had lost decisively to the University of Hawai`i the day before; the hosts were feeling especially generous. The team from San Jose, scheduled to play the following week, had already arrived and was to be accommodated on the tour. Ralph was assistant graduate manager in the UH Physical Education Department, and it was his duty to take care of the visitors. That morning, however, the attack on Pearl canceled the tour. (Indeed, many members of both visiting teams found themselves on a long, unplanned Hawaiian "vacation"; some of the athletes volunteered for military service or took jobs in Hawai'i for the duration of the war.)

Driving home, Yempuku was flagged down by several navy fliers, hung over after a night of carousing, who were desperately trying to find their way to Pearl Harbor. He drove them through Honolulu on the way to the naval base but stopped on Middle Street, where traffic was clogged with trucks bearing the wounded and dead, bound for the city hospitals and emergency medical centers. "I got so scared, I dropped them off and went back. It was my baptism by fire" (24–25).

After the attack, every available person was recruited for assistance. Since nearly 40 percent of the population was Japanese American, it was impossible to avoid their involvement at many critical levels, in contrast to the situation on the West Coast, where their marginal status made internment a relatively simple matter. The future VVV men who attended the University of Hawai'i had been required in their first two years, along with all other able-bodied males, to participate in its Reserve Officers Training Corps, the ROTC. A few, like Yutaka Nakahata, had been excused for physical reasons. But most of the Japanese Americans had accepted the requirement with little thought; some, like Ted Tsukiyama, had elected to stay on as upperclass officers. The duties were not especially onerous, and the drills and lessons, after all, took place amidst the beauty of the campus in Manoa valley.

On December 7, a frantic radio summons called the ROTC students to the campus, where they gathered at the armory. It was rumored that Japanese paratroopers had just landed on St. Louis Heights, the line of hills defining the campus's eastern rim. The students were handed old Springfield rifles—this time with firing pins, which they had never used—and one clip containing five rounds of ammunition. Then, although most bore Japanese faces, names, and heritages, they were marched into anticipated combat against, as Ralph Yempuku indelicately put it, their "own kind." The University of Hawai'i ROTC thus would become the only such unit in U.S. history to be awarded a battle streamer.

Fortunately for all, the rumor of paratroopers was as false as most of the others that circulated at the time. By the afternoon of that day, the ROTC students were recalled and asked to join the newly organized Hawai'i Territorial Guard (HTG). Most of them enlisted. The HTG became necessary because the territory had lost its National Guard units to the U.S. government when Hawaii's 298th and 299th regiments were federalized on October 15, 1940. At that time, the regiments' 126 officers, lone warrant officer, and 1,616 men were primarily of Hawaiian, part-Hawaiian, Portuguese, or Chinese descent, because Japanese Americans were discouraged from enlisting.[13]

But after the draft was imposed in October 1940, many Japanese Americans were inducted into the National Guard. Others enlisted in 1940 and 1941 because they expected that they would eventually be called. Ben Tamashiro, for example, volunteered in late 1940 and was scheduled to go on reserve status just about the time the Japanese attacked Pearl Harbor.[14] Like most of the other nisei, he stayed on to fight.

In spite of this recent infusion of Japanese Americans, there was a critical shortage of trained troops capable of defending Hawai'i against attack. After December 7, every available fighting man was needed. In addition to troops on the front line, there was limited manpower for protection of waterfronts, military installations, airfields, hospitals, power plants, reservoirs, food-storage centers, communication links, and many other vital areas.

Hung Wai Ching was not surprised by the phone call from his brother, Hung Wo, telling him that the war had finally begun. Director of the Atherton YMCA, next to the Manoa campus of the University of Hawai'i, Hung Wai had been involved for over a year with top FBI and military intelligence officers preparing for the outbreak of hostilities with Japan. He recalled a meeting held on December 16, 1940, almost exactly one year before the attack. The group met at the exclusive Pacific Club and included Robert Shivers, head of the FBI in Hawai'i; Charles Hemenway, a member of the university's Board of Regents; civilian officials like Ernie Kai and Ted Trent; and the chiefs of Army and Navy Intelligence.

> We planned our activities throughout the year and the program was for us to organize to go after the Filipinos in the plantation, to go after the defense workers in Red Hill [above Pearl Harbor]. Do you remember prior to 1940 we imported a tremendous number of mainland workers to take Red Hill [and build fuel] storage tanks? . . . In case of emergency, our message said, don't do anything until we tell you what to do. So we passed the word down the plantation to the Filipinos: "Sure, sharpen up

your cane knives. But don't you use them [on the local Japanese Americans; he laughed] until we tell you what to do." (4)

This comment would not have been at all amusing immediately after Pearl Harbor, when local Filipinos learned of Japanese military atrocities in the Philippines; more than a few must have been tempted to go after the Japanese in Hawai'i out of frustrated rage. Local Koreans and Chinese had at least as much reason to hate the Japanese, who had colonized Korea in 1910 and had taken Manchuria in 1931 before invading North China in 1936. Keeping the lid on these potentially explosive ethnic and racial tensions was critical. Making the point that the Japanese in Hawai'i were not responsible was going to be necessary but extremely sensitive and exceedingly difficult.

Hung Wai's wife, Elsie, was seven months pregnant and very apprehensive on that December 7. Hung Wai left her in their Wilhelmina Rise home overlooking Honolulu to drive down to the McCully area. There, "friendly fire" in the form of defective U.S. antiaircraft shells had destroyed a few buildings, although at the time it was assumed that Japanese bombs had been dropped on civilian targets. Some of the shells had been fired without timing devices, exploding upon impact rather than in the air. Crowds had gathered, and the FBI wanted Hung Wai to be sure that there was no suspicious quality about them. He reported that everything was in order. The buildings were on the campus of Lunalilo Elementary School, which suffered $40,000 in damages to several classrooms and its library.[15] Hung Wai went there as soon as he heard of the explosions and fires. "I went right in to see the principal and the principal was a gal I knew at the University of Hawai'i, . . . and she was bitching: 'Of all things, why can't they burn down my schoolroom? They burned down my library!' [He laughed.] Funny how people react, huh? [More laughter.] Stick in my mind, 'You burned my library!'" (8).

Later, at about 9 P.M., Elsie called to tell him, "I think the baby's coming." Then she went into labor, and Hung Wai was finally forced to take her more seriously. Since there was a blackout and curfew, no civilian cars were permitted on the roads. Ching checked with another brother, a sergeant on the police force, who said: "Hey, I'm on duty. There's going to be another attack." In desperation, Hung Wai finally called the commanding general, Walter Short, to obtain permission for Elsie to get to a hospital (6). Decades later, Elsie continued to tell anyone who would listen about her neglectful husband; several of the VVV members, including Ted Tsukiyama and Ralph Yempuku, recall that she reminded the "boys" of Hung Wai's dereliction at every one of their reunions.

Native Hawaiian Thomas Kaulukukui was "at home in Kaimuki and . . . heard that Pearl Harbor had been bombed. . . . It was up somewhere about Twenty-first Avenue where I was living. . . . And pretty soon I heard the planes coming and . . . saw the big red sun underneath. . . . In fact, they were right over my head" (5–6). Kaulukukui later wrote a short story, "I Am a Volunteer," about a fictional VVV member, Minoru Oyasato. Largely based on his involvement with the VVV in 1942, this is an interesting account from the perspective of an empathetic non-Japanese participant. Minoru, from a poor but proud sugar-plantation background, was stunned by Pearl Harbor but soon recovered to join his ROTC comrades on the Manoa campus, thence to join the Hawai`i Territorial Guard: "To say I was frightened is putting it mildly. With knees rattling like castanets and cold sweat running down my forehead I received my fighting equipment and orders to guard a public utility building. My two months of R.O.T.C. training did not prepare me for the duty I was to perform and as a result my fears mounted. They did not last, for to my surprise I found my nerves steady and no longer felt afraid." Kaulukukui's short story helps confirm and add another dimension to the oral histories of the VVV participants and casts their statements in a different light; for example, Minoru shares the fear that others relate but adds, as no VVV members did, a concern for life and death: "Perhaps I would be shot. All the dreams of a career vanished like bubbles in the air."[16]

Just before eight o'clock on the morning of December 7, Yoshiaki Fujitani, son of the bishop of the Jodo Shinshu sect, was dressed in the standard uniform for a pickup game of baseball among local youths: corduroy trousers, a sweatshirt, and bare feet. Fujitani had been told that practice antiaircraft rounds produced white smoke; when he saw the black smoke and heard the explosions, he realized that this was no ordinary exercise.

> We were quite frightened, of course, you know, and then we began to hear reports that Lunalilo School in McCully area was hit. . . . The drugstore there was destroyed. A bomb fell in Leilehua Lane, and my classmate and friend was killed. There was an Edward Kondo living there and he was killed. . . . We got a call on the radio saying all ROTC students, university ROTC students, report to the school. I wasn't sure, so, just dressed like that, barefooted, I came up to the university. . . .

Then we were shipped down to the armory. You know, the armory used to be where the capitol is now. . . . I walked there from twelve midnight to seven in the morning. . . . But we walked the beat with a rifle and five rounds of bullets. That's all they'd give us—five rounds. And we were told if anyone comes, if we hear someone coming, to just say, "Halt, who goes there?" In the morning, that was when we were really frightened, because there were some workmen who had come to the library and they looked toward me as though *I* were an enemy. Well, anyway, that day ended all right; . . . I think that evening I placed a phone call from the armory to let [my parents] know. (18–20)

Jackson Morisawa, who was studying for an exam scheduled for Monday, December 8, lived in the area to which Fujitani and his friends had driven to watch the "maneuvers." It was close enough for him to walk over to see the damage. "I remember seeing an airplane flying and—with the red, red, you know, ball. I didn't think anything of it. I didn't connect anything. Then there were, you know, those ack-ack bursts in the air. . . . I remember running out around there to see better what was going on. And there were some shell bursts in the McCully area. . . . So, curious, you know—we were curious guys, so we went to look what was happening" (17).

Ted Tsukiyama remembers trying to sleep in on that Sunday morning. Even from his home in Kaimuki, just below Hung Wai's residence and some distance from Pearl Harbor, the attack was impossible to ignore:

There had been a junior dance, I think, the night before, and so we were kind of sleeping it off and we heard this rumbling, like thunder—thunder that didn't stop. It finally got so that you couldn't sleep anymore, so I went out in the yard and looked and see this black smoke coming from that side. . . .

The radio announcer is frantically saying: "Take cover. We are being attacked by Japanese warplanes. This is the real McCoy. Take cover." And that's when I felt numb. Just numb. . . . They called us out into our units, and our unit was captained by Nolle Smith, the black guy, and I was first sergeant, and I don't know if it was then that we got the tin hats but anyway we got rifles with ammunition and the first order or assignment we got was that Japanese paratroopers landed on top of St. Louis Heights and that we were to deploy and await the advance of the enemy. . . .

Scared? Yeah, we were scared. But with the feeling of fear was one of anger, I guess. Anger. How could they do this? First of all, we didn't think they were that stupid to go and attack us. And then to do it the way they did, it was sort of shameful. But, you know, not one that I would feel shame, because I didn't identify myself as a Japan Japanese that I did something to be ashamed of; rather, you know, there was no question in my mind and I could see by the response in the other people's minds that we were Americans and that America is under attack, an attack in a very sinister and shameful way. And we were going to defend. There was no question about what we were supposed to do or what our duty was, where our loyalty lay.

They knew that 80 percent of that ROTC was Japanese. They didn't ask questions. They didn't give us a loyalty oath, you know. They didn't interview us, screen us. They just said turn out, and we turned out. And then HTG—same thing. They just automatically swore us in. We may have had a chance to say, "I ain't going to join" and go home, because I don't know what they could have done to us, but it was just, you know, somebody was making the decision that they could use us. We were needed to defend and there was just no thought given to it. (15–18)

Tsukiyama's testimony underscores the difficult position in which many nisei believed themselves to be trapped; his comments about the attack being "shameful" were followed immediately by disclaiming any implication that he was personally embarrassed. Most of the future VVV members understood that others would associate them with Japan— there was, after all, a long history of such guilt by association. Ralph Yempuku's reaction was different in that he acknowledged a sense that the Japanese were "our kind."

I recall that, as a third-generation sansei growing up in the 1940s and 1950s, we had similar conflicted reactions when watching Hollywood World War II films about the treacherous "Japs." Similar emotions were evoked among fourth- and fifth-generation Japanese Americans when U.S. media criticized Japan's killing and consumption of whales and, later, its trade practices. These incidents were more commonplace among Japanese Americans on the mainland, although fifth-generation students have told me that they had similar reactions in Hawai`i.

George Yamamoto, who was in an urban shantytown bungalow in Palama, very close to Pearl Harbor, did not remember hearing the attack. Like Morisawa, he was studying for an exam scheduled for the next day. Although he was not particularly alarmed by news of the attack, his mother certainly was: "Oya oya, kore, komatta no [Oh, oh! This means trouble!)": "My! I remember I had a huge American lit. book that we had to read hundreds of pages out of, an impossible kind of thing. It was a nice, good relief when Pearl Harbor occurred. Later, I heard of people having to bury samurai swords or *hata* [Japanese flags] and this and that and all kinds of presumably subversive stuff. We didn't face this, because our home was threadbare. No possibly subversive literature to be burnt" (33–35).

The Yamamoto family did, however, surrender its shortwave radio— "Sears, table model"—to a nisei policeman. Many Japanese families had radios with shortwave bands that could receive programming from Japan. The military immediately ordered all of these sets to be turned in, along with fireworks, firearms, cameras, and binoculars, to the nearest police station. In February 1942, another order prohibited the possession of shortwave radios in any home to which enemy aliens might have access. Some saw this order as unnecessarily draconian. Interestingly, the most effective protests came from haole employers of Japanese domestic servants. Richard Zukemura's father took his shortwave radio set to the medical office where he worked and asked one of the doctors to hide it for him. Eventually, the order was modified; the Army Signal Corps removed shortwave bands from about thirteen thousand sets so their owners could retain the radios.[17]

This order was a problem for the issei. There was very little in the way of communication in Japanese, since all Japanese radio programming was prohibited and newspapers were strictly censored. But wartime conditions made news, music, and regional information from Japan even more critical to the immigrants. Henceforth, there was no way they could learn of conditions affecting hometowns and families in Japan.

In some cases, Japanese American families were extremely frightened and destroyed their property or left it, anonymously, on police station doorsteps. My own father, who was *kibei* nisei (born in America, reared in Japan, returned to America), was able to keep our family's shortwave radio. A few neighborhood issei men would surreptitiously climb the stairs after nightfall to our residential quarters over the Odo grocery store to hear Japanese broadcasts during the war.

Future VVV member Anki Hoshijo's parents had come from Okinawa. On that Sunday morning, Anki was a very lucky young man. Already a highly promising amateur boxer, he was working at Pearl Harbor after the 1941 summer pineapple-harvesting season. As his son Leonard explained: "On December 7 our father had a morning weigh-in for a fight that night that took him out of the Kukui Street Gym, where training boxers were hit by falling antiaircraft shells. That was one of a few combinations of events and luck that my mother, brother, and sister, and I are glad for."[18]

Akira Otani's father owned the fish-wholesaling section of Aala Market in Honolulu. A reception for friends was held on December 6, 1941, to celebrate the rebuilding of the fish market after a fire earlier in the year, and a grand reopening was scheduled for the morning of December 7. Pearl Harbor intervened—family and guests immediately dispersed and the gala reopening was never celebrated (16). This disruption was only the beginning of the Otanis' wartime problems. Akira's father, Matsujiro Otani, was not in good health and had gone home as soon as he could after the attack. Akira, worried about his father, left soon thereafter and joined him in their Waialae residence. Within a few hours of the attack, the FBI and army agents arrived to arrest Matsujiro. Years before Pearl Harbor, the FBI had identified those to be rounded up as soon as war broke out; Matsujiro Otani was evidently at or near the top of that list.

> I think I remember fairly clearly that there must have been about three or four people. . . . And my dad, as I say, he was sick in bed. So he came out in his kimono and a Japanese-style jacket and wanted to know what it was all about. They just shoved a pistol or revolver right in his gut and said, "This is no joke," you know. . . . And he didn't know what was what, you know. Then we—I have a brother-in-law who lived right in the back and I said to somebody, "Go call him," because he was a police detective. . . .
>
> So we called and he came rushing over. He said, "What's this all about?" And they shoved the gun right in his gut too and said, "You keep out of this." He said, "Well, I'm a police detective." "That's nothing. Get out of here." For some reason or other they kept on shoving that darned revolver in the gut and then you realized that there wasn't much you could do, so they were pulling my dad away to the car. And so my mother said, "If you're going to take him, take me along too." And they said, "You keep out of this," you know. And they kept on shoving the darn gun. . . . "You've got to take me." "Oh, no, no, you stay away." So she ran back to the bedroom and I think she grabbed a raincoat or an overcoat or something plus a pair of shoes and tried to give it to him. She finally threw it into the car, you know. . . . Well, you know, to us it was real harsh. It seemed real unnecessary, you know. But they said, "Don't you know Japan has declared war on us?" and this and that and so forth. What can you do? (17–18)

Matsujiro Otani wrote of his ordeal in his autobiography, beginning with his detention in the immigration center in Kakaako and his travels through several War Relocation Authority and Justice Department camps on the mainland.[19] His arrest and detention were among the relatively few carried out in Hawaii's Japanese American community. Indeed, unlike the mass incarceration on the West Coast, only about 1000 individuals, along with another 1000 family members, were eventually interned from among Hawaii's 160,000 Japanese Americans (among them Yoshiaki Fujitani's father in 1942).

Since Akira had just witnessed his father's arrest, a question often put to VVV members was doubly poignant in his case: What drove you to volunteer for service in the face of repeated rejection?

> Well, I tell you, as far as I'm concerned, I turned right around and volunteered for the Territorial Guard, . . . right after that. . . . I can't explain to you why. I wasn't with the university boys at all. . . . I had two years of ROTC in high school and two years at the university. And I was in my senior year at the U already, so as far as ROTC was concerned, it was all a thing of the past. . . .
>
> I think I must have felt, gee, my country needs me, you know. They were calling for people; I had some ROTC training, therefore I go. I don't know; I never did analyze the why or how come or whatever. And today, when you think about it, I think my kids must think I'm a stupid person or whatever. Here, to see your dad get taken away and turn right around and volunteer for a country that took your dad away. . . .
>
> Yes, there were quite a few other walk-ins. And there were all other nationalities. With the university boys, you saw a lot of Orientals. But in the walk-in place, you know—Puerto Ricans, Hawaiians, Portuguese, and what not. . . . You just sign up and they're giving you—shoving a rifle, shoving a helmet, shoving this, and shoving that, and you put on clothes way too big for you. (18–20)

Shiro Amioka was shocked by the December 7 attack: "It was a traumatic experience." A Sunday school teacher, Shiro was already at the Kakaako Mission near his home close to the waterfront in the community of Japanese fishermen. He did not learn of the attack until he dismissed his class and got home at about 9 A.M. By then, radio announcements were ordering ROTC students to the campus. He put on his uniform and found his way to Manoa, although, like many others, he could not remember how he got there. Amioka never thought about the possible implications for people of Japanese descent. All he could think of was: "Oh, we got a war on our hands now and we got to go and re-port now" (45).

Amioka could not remember the men with whom he served on that December 7. He did not recall "fear or anything like that. Just that we had to be on our toes. All blackout, you know. It's an eerie feeling." He may have talked to his mother just before reporting to the ROTC unit but remembers that it was some time before he was able to talk to her again. Had she expressed any resistance or concern? "No. No. No." School was, of course, out, and "at that time we didn't even think about those things" (47).

Herb Isonaga was one of the students who did "think about those things." One of Hung Wai Ching's young charges at the YMCA com-plex, Atherton House, he remembered that he and some friends had just returned from breakfast in Hemenway Hall's cafeteria. Someone yelled, "Eh, the war broke out!" and the group clambered onto the roof to watch the fireworks. Herb took it "very calmly":

> I wasn't upset. So we're at war, you know. And, of course, took stock of—What now? Is school going to start? you know, you start worrying, thinking about those kinds of things rather than concern over the gen-eral upheaval or how do the political issues. . . . Yeah, yeah, What am I going to do now? How do I do it?
>
> And later on that evening, the word got out that "Hey, they sighted some paratroopers on St. Louis Heights!" I—I debated whether to join the Territorial Guard or not. . . . Well, I'll just wait. . . . No, no particu-lar reason. Well, I guess in the decision-making process, I decided not to walk down and volunteer primarily because I think I didn't have anyone alongside me to go with. If I had somebody, . . . I would have gone. (20–21)

Unlike some of the others, Isonaga recalled thinking deliberately through the practical problems imposed by the war. Perhaps he had had some practice; after all, he had decided to transfer from the University of Oregon shortly before Pearl Harbor specifically in order to be drafted into the army with friends in Hawai`i. But Herb also seemed to be more reflective in general. A recurring theme in his interviews was that of luck or fortune or chance. The notion that chance dictates some important options in life is difficult to reconcile within an American culture that prides itself on achievement and meritocracy and responsibility. But Isonaga is comfortable with, as he recalls it, happenstance determining whether he would join the HTG. At the time, he had a job at the *Honolulu Star-Bulletin*. "So, next day, Monday morning, went down to my job. . . . The advertising department had a big meeting and the gist of the meeting was: "Hey, you guys, you know, just because there's a war on, you know people have to advertise. You have to go out and solicit." He laughed. "Yeah. I thought that was funny" (21).

By the Pearl Harbor attack, Yugo Okubo had been a freshman for several months and was going nowhere fast. His original goal—a degree in civil engineering—required courses like chemistry and spherical trigonometry. Yugo discovered that he hated math and the sciences and so was "miserable." For him, December 7, 1941, was an even greater relief than for George Yamamoto, who was dreading his next English exam. Yugo, a reclusive type all of his life, had a keen sense of irony; only partly tongue in cheek, he thought the Pearl Harbor attack "saved my day" (17).

For Yugo Okubo, the chance to participate in a meaningful way in the war represented "big excitement." This was an opportunity "to serve in the U.S. armed forces, . . . a positive thing because up to then, you never get a chance to be, you know. . . . But there was no questioning. Just we got to go. We got to go. We didn't even think about any anti-Japanese feeling or anything." He took the bus to the campus and, uniformed and armed, was deployed at a water-pumping station in Kapahulu, a suburb between the university campus and Waikiki beach (17–19).

ON DECEMBER 7, 1941, these young men began to play their own particular roles in what would become the greatest watershed period in the twentieth century. In the days and months to follow, some 169 Japanese Americans would come together as part of an effort to show the world that Japanese Americans could and should be counted upon to play responsible roles in this great struggle. For some, the war obliterated any thoughts of school or career. Both Ted Tsukiyama and Shiro Amioka felt that the general response was concern for the welfare of the country—as "good Americans." Like Akira Otani, several men commented that their children or the younger generations might have thought them "stupid" for volunteering in spite of the racism they and their families faced immediately after Pearl Harbor. They had no explanation except to say that their reactions seemed necessary at the time.

5

Hawai`i Territorial Guard

or the first few years of the war, the European theater was the primary concern of the United States. When it became clear that the Nazi onslaught had been blunted and an Allied victory was inevitable, the Pacific finally took center stage in the overall U.S. strategy. In the meantime, Hawai`i played a critical role as the staging area for the Pacific war, and the impact on these tiny islands was dramatic.

The Japanese American community was critical. First, it was the largest single ethnic group in the territory. Second, it had demonstrated powerful forms of cultural maintenance in the face of assimilationist pressures. Third, it was, at least culturally, related to a homeland that was non-European, nonwhite, militarily powerful, and a wartime enemy. And fourth, it would largely shape the future of Hawai`i: The 160,000 people of Japanese descent, mostly American born, included a majority of the workforce and of the territory's youth, who were destined to have a major influence at the ballot box in the future.

Under wartime conditions, the "Japanese question" assumed monumental proportions. One important aspect of this history, the wartime experiences of Japanese Americans in uniform, has been explored in great depth.[1] This chapter explores the six weeks after Pearl Harbor, an intense and unsettled period during which Hawaii's capacity for racial tolerance would be sorely tested.

117

Until Pearl Harbor, the Big Five/Republican/haole oligarchy used a wide variety of strategies and tactics to maintain hegemony, as we have seen. Even the one institution formally representing the interests of the immigrant issei, the Japanese consulate, was almost invariably aligned with the oligarchy against Japan's own subjects. This was the case from the earliest labor disturbances in the 1890s through the major strikes of the twentieth century and the battles over culture maintenance such as the language-school controversies. And when persuasion was not enough there were other means. As recently as 1938, dozens of longshoremen and their family members, including many Japanese Americans, were wounded while peacefully demonstrating in an incident still referred to as the "Hilo massacre."[2]

IN HAWAI`I, where the Japanese community was both feared and needed, Pearl Harbor could have unleashed racial dynamics that dramatically impeded the war effort. Hung Wai Ching was particularly sensitive to the possibility of some aberrant behavior by another Myles Fukunaga: "What if we have one guy that—that after December the seventh, just suppose some Japanese American do something crazy?" (61). There had been, to be sure, considerable thinking about this general issue well before Pearl Harbor. The military as well as local and federal governments had several decades to develop concrete and detailed plans in anticipation of war with Japan. But these plans focused on the small number of Japanese community leaders who might pose a threat—no one had seriously considered the vast majority of ordinary Japanese Americans or their potential assailants, including immigrants from the Philippines, China, or Korea, as well as whites. So there was good reason to fear racial disorder.

One of the strategies crafted during the December 1940 Pacific Club meeting referred to earlier, Hung Wai recalled, was the judicious use of respected Big Five leaders to support specific government and military measures. These policies had to reassure the resident haole population that the threat of espionage, sabotage, and, worst of all, an uprising from the local Japanese community was being contained. Those at the meeting spent much less time thinking of ways to convince the majority of the Japanese that there was room and reason for cooperation and demonstration of dedication, loyalty, and sacrifice.

When the attack finally came, maintaining racial tolerance was a precarious enterprise. In part this was a function of the means the enemy employed (the surprise/sneak attack) and the devastating effectiveness of the Yamamoto-led blitz, in part the logical outcome of nearly a century of white supremacist ideology and practice. Since the military had repeatedly assured everyone that Japan, largely an "imitator" power, was incapable of penetrating the defense shield around Hawai`i, it was altogether too tempting to suggest that only "unfair" tactics or disloyal residents could account for the disaster. As a key army report put it: "Hawai`i is more than a melting pot. It had, and still has, potentialities for a first class racial clash which can seriously hamper the prosecution of the war in this theater." This reaction may have been partly self-serving, since the military insisted that potential disorder justified martial law. However, oral testimonies and contemporary documents attest to the fact that both military and civilian leaders were convinced that racial unrest was a distinct possibility.[3]

Perhaps the most critical decision of the new military government was the creation on December 18, 1941, in the Territorial Office of Civilian Defense, of a Public Morale Division, the result of planning by the informal Pacific Club group, which had been meeting for about a year prior to the Pearl Harbor attack. The group included Robert Shivers, head of the local office of the FBI, Captain I. H. Mayfield of Naval Intelligence, Colonel William Marston of Army Intelligence, and various business and community leaders, as well as Loomis, Ching, and Yoshida.

A committee headed by business leader and university regent Charles Hemenway nominated three individuals for the new Morale Division: haole YMCA leader Charles Loomis; Chinese American YMCA secretary Hung Wai Ching; and Japanese American school principal Shigeo Yoshida.[4] The mission of this trio was deceptively simple: "(1) to serve as a liaison between the Army and the civilian community on matters relating to public morale; and (2) to work toward the maintenance of a unified and cooperative community." These were particularly crucial issues in the war effort because of the "heterogeneous character of the local community" and the absolute necessity of maintaining racial peace and a united front to prosecute the war to the maximum. It was also, very early on, considered important to work toward the solution of "possible problems of post-war Hawai`i" through the deliberate use of strategies that employed cooperative and unified planning.[5]

Designated the Morale Section, the trio soon moved into the office of the military governor and reported directly to Colonel Kendall

Fielder, assistant chief of staff for intelligence (G2). Its members shared a number of characteristics: They were from the major ethnic or racial groups—haole, Japanese, and Chinese—whose cooperation would be critical in the war effort; they were highly educated and articulate; they were trained leaders of respected public entities; and they were identified with, but not principally beholden to, their own ethnic groups. There is no evidence that this last feature was a deliberately considered qualification, but it made very good sense to secure men with ultimate loyalties to the overall Morale Section effort rather than to the sectarian needs of any single group.

Charles Loomis was a respected haole outsider who had come from the mainland, someone who would not have been included in the exclusive circles of the *kama`aina* (native-born) elite. Hung Wai Ching was the son of Chinese immigrants, a YMCA administrator with strong ties to individuals like Hemenway. Shigeo Yoshida, born to Japanese immigrant parents, had excelled as a debater at the university under the tutelage of Hemenway and others and had risen to become one of the few nisei administrators in the territory's Department of Public Instruction. Unlike men who were executives of Big Five firms or ethnic organizations, these were leaders by virtue of their associations beyond their own ethnic boundaries. Loomis was the official director of the Morale Section, but Ching was clearly the dynamic leader.

It was appropriate, given the character of these three men and their jobs, for them to remain behind the scenes and, as Captain Mayfield's final report put it,

> without representing themselves officially as representatives of an Army office, to shun publicity and to work through the existing agencies and leaders within the community, thus giving credit, in many cases, to these groups and individuals when, as a matter of fact, the original ideas and plans and the driving force behind the activities were theirs. . . . The general public does not know that the initiative and part of the "brains" behind many of the things which have happened in this community since the outbreak of the war have been supplied by members of the Morale Section. . . . Varsity Victory Volunteers, Emergency Service Committee, neighborhood units of the O.C.D. [Office of Civil Defense], Hawai`i Defense Volunteers and certain war research activities at the University of Hawai`i are some examples.[6]

Mayfield's report made clear the degree to which the army and the community at large had relied on Hung Wai. For example, Yoshida and Ching asked Kendall Fielder, head of army intelligence, to arrange a meeting in Honolulu in 1942 with Eleanor Roosevelt for the two of them, as well as for two representatives of the Japanese American Emergency Service Committee, Yoshida said.

> So we chatted with Mrs. Roosevelt, told her what we were doing, told her that story of the Triple V and also about how the racial situation was being handled by the army and by the FBI and that there was no single case of sabotage up to that point. . . . So, after we got through talking with Mrs. Roosevelt for about half an hour or so, she said, "I think this whole story should be told directly to the president." We thought, gee, that was a good turn of events. . . . So she assured us that she would get an appointment for one of us to go there. Because of travel restrictions [for Japanese Americans], Hung Wai was the only one who could go. (6–7)

Ching was sent to Washington, D.C., in early 1943 and again in 1944. While not an official representative of the Morale Section, he was clearly on missions directly related to its basic purposes. Ching indeed conferred with President Roosevelt, as well as with Assistant Secretary of War John McCloy, Secretary of the Interior Harold Ickes, General S.L.A. "Slam" Marshall (then a lieutenant colonel), and several senators and representatives in the U.S. Congress. He also worked to convince numerous publishers and editors of newspapers and magazines that "the Army policy in Hawai`i was unique and for the best interest of the people of Hawai`i, that Hawai`i should be allowed to work out its own problems without outside interference, and that the soldiers of Japanese ancestry . . . were absolutely loyal and needed the cooperation of the various communities and officials of the mainland."[7]

In the weeks after Pearl Harbor, the situation in Hawai`i was chaotic and volatile. Less than three hours after the attack, Hawaii's governor officially formed the Hawaii Territorial Guard. The adjutant general, Perry M. Smoot, became its colonel. He was instructed to "take command of the R.O.T.C. units in the Territory of Hawai`i and along with other volunteers, to organize, train, equip and command the Hawaii Territorial Guard. At midnight, 7 December 1941, the force was placed in the field, uniformed, armed and equipped."[8]

There were 363 men available on that day. The largest number ever in the field was 1,375, on January 20, 1942. On December 9, Smoot reported to Governor Poindexter that "the Hawai`i Territorial Guard is now in service with approximately thirty-three (33) officers and five hundred sixty-six (566) enlisted men. Of the above number of enlisted men, approximately four hundred (400) are sufficiently trained to perform active military guard duty." Smoot acknowledged several problems: "What the Hawai`i Territorial guard sadly lacks is communication personnel and equipment. It is hoped that the Commanding General will authorize at least a portable radio (key and voice set)." Smoot's memo to the governor disclosed a variety of potential problems. The officers, for example, were drawn from an unusual pool but nearly all came from the ROTC: "The present officer personnel of this Guard is composed of one officer, regular Army; several of the Army of the United States; several of the regular Army Reserve; some of the inactive Territorial Militia; all officers of the senior unit of the University of Hawaii R.O.T.C., and a few officers appointed in the Hawaii Territorial guard, exclusively."[9] Smoot's casual reference to four hundred men "sufficiently trained" is generally contested by those VVV members who had been part of the HTG. They tell instead of a sorry state of disorganization.

Perhaps the disarray felt in the ranks reflected the shifting position of the HTG in the newly emerging configuration of territorial and military governments. It was placed under the command of the department provost marshal on December 11, 1941. The military governor also authorized, on December 15, the territory's governor to "continue to call out the territorial militia and place so much of it in the active service of the territory as may be determined and selected by the Adjutant General of the Territory of Hawai`i." Finally, General Order No. 44, issued on December 26, 1941, placed the HTG directly under the commanding general, Hawaiian Department, "for instruction at once." The HTG was not an inexpensive operation. On December 17, Smoot estimated that the first eight days of operation had cost $33,512.41, most going to salary and rations.[10]

The HTG took its work seriously. It guarded vital installations, according to a Smoot memo written on Christmas Eve of 1941, including Washington Place (the governor's residence), the territorial archives, bridges, wells, reservoirs, pumping stations, water tanks, and high schools. Some of the high schools, like Punahou and Farrington, were being used as emergency hospitals. Guardsmen were also deployed at telephone exchanges, electric substations, the FBI office, the courthouses, and even the headquarters of the Hawaiian Pineapple Company. One individual was assigned to guard the Fort Armstrong Post Exchange, while the largest number, twenty, went to the Kaneohe Hospital to secure its water tank.[11]

One of the HTG's responsibilities was to oversee the eviction of Japanese Americans from approximately thirty areas considered militarily sensitive. One location was Lualualei Homesteads, adjacent to a munitions storage facility not far from Pearl Harbor. It is unlikely that any nisei participated in the following HTG order of December 8, 1941:

a. Removal of all Japanese families from Lualualei Homesteads by December 14, 1942.
b. Admission to the Homesteads during daylight hours of such members of these families as may be useful field laborers, for the purpose of working their fields.
c. Effective measures to prevent unauthorized entry to the area by routes other than the regular road; either day or night.
d. Patrol of the area during working hours to insure that subject Japanese proceed to and remain at their respective properties and do not congregate.
e. Maintain sufficient surveillance over the operations of the farms to insure that the farms are seriously worked and not used as subterfuge by subversive persons.[12]

One of the enduring ironies of the first months of the war was the decision to arm so many Japanese Americans and place them in areas of strategic importance. Military bases themselves were usually but not always off limits to those of Japanese descent. When Akira Otani's father sent two trucks to help with the wounded at Pearl Harbor, his Japanese American drivers were not admitted onto the base. At the same time, however, nisei skilled laborers such as carpenters and electricians were retained for defense work on bases, albeit forced to wear distinctive and much-resented black-bordered identification badges.

The ROTC and HTG represent striking contrasts to the mainland experience, where entire Japanese American communities remained in limbo and would be summarily removed to assembly and concentration camps en masse. At the time of the attack, Japanese Americans were being treated very differently in Hawai`i. Chaos and the perceived crisis may help explain this apparent anomaly. The December 7 attack had been a complete surprise; the carefully laid plans for war with Japan had not anticipated a direct assault on Hawai`i, and adequate troops were not available.

Asked to join the HTG as a lieutenant, Richard Lum—older than the future VVV members, the son of Chinese immigrants, and with several years of ROTC and National Guard experience—did not recall much apprehension over the fact that nisei were armed. "Well, I don't think there was any fear except that you had to keep a close vigilance, that's all. I don't think there was any fear, otherwise they wouldn't take the people. My observation was that there was only some suspicion" (11). That suspicion, given time and space, would grow.

Tommy Kaulukukui, the Native Hawaiian All-American running back, remembers going to the armory to volunteer for the HTG a few days after Pearl Harbor. With no military training, Kaulukukui nevertheless became a second lieutenant after a brief stint guarding a watershed area in Wilhelmina Heights, above Honolulu. He recalled that everyone was welcomed into the HTG, including the Japanese Americans. "There was no discrimination. . . . I think they had to take everybody. . . . They had no choice at that time. Until, two or three months later they stopped to analyze the situation and they probably said, 'Hey, maybe we made a mistake.' I'm not sure" (7–8).

Like Richard Lum, Ralph Yempuku was more acutely aware of the disorganized state of the HTG than were many of the college students who came directly from ROTC duty on December 7. He had been making about $150 per month in December 1941 at the University of Hawai'i and had no other ambitions. The money was good for the times and the future looked solid enough, so he had sufficient reason to stay on the sidelines and he had already been declared 4F—ineligible for the draft due to physical condition. Yet he joined the HTG. "You know, it sounds trite, but I felt I wanted to do something for my country. . . . Yeah. It wasn't because I felt that the Japanese were invading that I went to the HTG. No. I went to the HTG because I knew they needed people and I wanted to serve my country. If you tell people that today, they say, 'Oh, you're full of shit'" (26–27). Ralph's parents were in Japan, so he had no one to consult before joining up. "I think it was more of everybody doing an independent action; . . . going to the HTG was . . . [a] spontaneous thing" (28).

Unlike many of the others, however, Yempuku was clear that being of Japanese descent was an important factor for him. "I wanted to be counted. Being Japanese, that's why. . . . Oh, yeah. Being Japanese, I wanted to be counted" (26). Other VVV members did not recall this sense of guilt by racial association, but it is likely that some such feeling existed.

Both Yempuku and Lum were older and became officers. As a lieutenant, Ralph toured posts where the young guardsmen were stationed. It was a frightening experience. "Oh, shit. It was a nightmare," he laughed. "They issued everybody weapons and 90 percent of the guys never used a rifle before. They have a roll call at night, especially, and you hear guns going off all over the building there. . . . Hey, it was scary. . . . See, we had rumors that the Japanese were coming in—like paratroopers. . . . So this was the only group that was going to protect the city. . . . At night you would go out in a jeep with hardly any lights and make sure the guys aren't sleeping and it scared the shit out of you. They say, 'Halt!' you know, and then you hear the gun go click, huh? . . . These were untrained, undisciplined—and they didn't know what they were doing" (27).

Not everyone felt he was in a dangerous situation. Yugo Okubo and two of his brothers volunteered for the HTG. Yugo was assigned to the Kapahulu water-pumping station, very close to Waikiki Beach. He and eight others created a defense perimeter of sand bags around the station and sat around, smoking and talking. There was nothing especially "memorable" but he felt it was an empowering experience. "I wasn't even thinking about being scared. . . . There were [rumors], but I can't recall anything like that putting fear in me. The big deal is you got a gun, you got a uniform." He welcomed the opportunity to participate in the military, even though "we didn't know what war was, the shooting, the killing." (19-21)

Edward Nakamura, who also joined the HTG on December 7 and had been a member of the university's ROTC, marvels at the thought of being "given the rifle and five rounds of ammunition. That's what everybody had; . . . we felt scared. Yeah, you wondered what you were gonna do if it should happen" (16). His HTG duty was to guard a building that belonged to American Factors, a prominent Big Five corporation "in Kakaako, which was being guarded because it was a food warehouse. I recall all things burning, out Pearl Harbor way. . . . After the first week or so, . . . I was at the power substation up here on Emma Street and there was a perimeter of tents there where we slept, the whole squad of people" (17).

Nakamura knew that many youngsters of Japanese descent were serving with him in the HTG, but they, like the others, never discussed or even thought about themselves, armed, as a potential issue. "There were a couple of Hawaiian kids. They weren't all from the university. Some high school students apparently volunteered. I recall a Filipino. I don't recall that they displayed any suspicion. Everybody all got along very well" (23).

Shiro Amioka, the Sunday school teacher from Kakaako, went from the ROTC directly into the HTG, and things after that were something of a blur. "I don't know how long it took before we finally got a chance to get in touch with our parents" (47). Someone in his unit took his orders seriously and shot out a light in a residence after curfew. One of Amioka's college professors also worked in the HTG and brought Amioka into headquarters to work on personnel files. When I asked whether he had a sense of contributing, he said: "Oh, this was war! Oh yeah! That's why we got so mad when we were discharged" (49).

Tamotsu "Barney" Ono led a unit in the HTG, probably because he had been an officer in the ROTC. His contingent spent most of its duty guarding water tanks on Alewa Heights, overlooking Pearl Harbor, "and it was pretty good duty." The men were invited to share meals with the residents, and since the neighborhood was largely professional—doctors and businessmen—and generally Asian American, they ate very well. Like most of the others, Ono had no sense of the growing unease over so many Japanese Americans bearing arms, even though they were woefully untrained. "I don't think I felt any, anything, except that, doggone, this the only country—land—I knew. If anybody was gonna come, you know, . . . I mean, nothing patriotic, unfortunately. I mean if somebody's gonna invade my home, the only place I know, I'm gonna fight to protect it" (7).

For about six weeks after December 7, then, several hundred Japanese Americans constituted a plurality of Hawaii's multiethnic volunteer force, most of whose members were barely out of high school. But while the HTG was doing its wartime part, calls for disarming the Japanese Americans steadily increased, and on January 21, 1942, Military Governor Delos Emmons, commander of the War Department in Hawai`i, suddenly ordered the HTG disbanded. The next day, Emmons reformed the unit, pointedly leaving out the nisei. This decision reflected the general distrust of Japanese Americans and prepared the way for a new stage during which they would be required to reposition themselves in Hawai`i and the United States.

Some three decades after I played on Nolle Smith's junior varsity football team as an uninspired sophomore quarterback at Kaimuki High School, I called Coach Smith on October 26, 1991, to talk about his recollection of the Japanese Americans being kicked out of the HTG on that early January morning. He was in the original ROTC group ordered to defend St. Louis Heights and one of the first to volunteer for the HTG. When the order came down to dismiss the nisei, Smith was personally assigned to roust them out of their pup tents in the predawn darkness in the Koko Crater firing range where they were bivouacked for target practice. Smith recalled the anguish he felt on informing his comrades that they were no longer acceptable in the HTG.

Ralph Yempuku had been vaguely aware of the rising tension caused by the armed nisei patrolling Hawai`i immediately after Pearl Harbor:

> Then, in one month or two, the haole troops started coming in from the mainland. And they came to Honolulu and they had HTG guys guarding the waterfront, . . . and [they] see these Japanese, yeah. They thought, "jeezus, we're too late." They still had that feeling, you know, that Japanese cannot be trusted. . . . So somebody came up with a great idea. They said, "Okay, tomorrow we'll disband HTG." So they—without anybody knowing anything—they disbanded the HTG. . . . Yeah. And the day afterwards they said, "Okay, we're going to form the HTG again." Now they don't let us Japanese in. . . . Of course, we could say that it's not constitutional and all that bullshit, but those days, martial law and all that, there is nothing to do. And this is how the VVV was formed, you see. Or why. (28–30)

Sociologist Andrew Lind, in a work published immediately after the war, noted a report that at least one Texan, startled to find so many Japanese Americans in Hawai`i, exclaimed: "My God, we got here too late. The Japs have already got the place."

Yempuku's initial reaction in our discussion was to gloss over the Japanese Americans' dismissal from the HTG, but it did not take long to discover that the humiliation of the action had weighed heavily on his mind for many years. He had reflected on the circumstances of the war at that juncture and the very real danger Hawai`i faced if the Japanese military had followed up on their initial success.

> Well, hey, you old enough to realize at that point that they are giving you a raw deal. You say, jeezus, I joined this thing because I like my country. All of a sudden they kick you in the ass. And this is when you say the hell with them. You get the feeling you don't want to do nothing. . . . Very bitter at my country; . . . I was just bitter against the people and the system that wouldn't trust me because, when we first went out, like I say, on the seventh, maybe the eighth or the ninth, there was a feeling that the Japanese was going to land. . . . And if they had landed with five thousand troops, they would have taken Hawai`i, . . . no problem. But, fortunately, they didn't. . . . We thought we were going to encounter Japanese paratroopers; . . . nothing in my mind that said, "they are Japanese; I'd better not kill them." They were the enemy. And then to

have them throw us out when you had that feeling, hey, that made you very, very bitter. (29–30)

Ted Tsukiyama remembered that Smith had delivered the bad news (19); he spoke of being mustered out of the HTG as the single worst day of his life. "If a bomb had exploded in our midst, it couldn't have been more devastating," he would say later.[13] He believed deeply that the valiant participation of Japanese Americans in the ROTC and HTG efforts immediately after Pearl Harbor would trump anti-Japanese feelings. As a result, the failed idealism rooted in a romanticized notion of U.S. democracy plunged the university junior into despair. "We got the word that all niseis were going to be released. . . . They put us on trucks and brought us back to the university and that's where we were going to be discharged. . . . As I described it once, the bottom dropped out of my life; . . . I think we cried. Sure. Just, you know, frustration, anguish, disappointment, the feeling of rejection . . . that you are being distrusted by your own country, and all the fine things you learned about democracy—and I used to enter essay contests and all that. We were waving the flag, . . . and because the enemy had the same kind of face like you, suddenly you are distrusted" (19–22).

Nolle Smith told them that the army wanted the Japanese boys out. They had been "like a family," Nolle said in our 1991 phone conversation, and an outstanding military outfit—"probably the highest IQs of any company like that." His devotion to his Japanese American comrades was much appreciated, and, although himself African American, would try to join the men of the 100th Battalion when it left for further training on June 5, 1942.

Only five days after being removed from the HTG, Tsukiyama wrote of his experiences to a close friend on the mainland. In the letter he commented on the tough duty within the HTG when there was so much anxiety and work and so little sleep. But most of the HTG was made up of boys from the University of Hawai'i, and "intelligent enough to know right from wrong so there was no need at all to domineer or bully them." The unit had tremendous spirit and morale was extremely high. The men even volunteered for KP or fatigue duty, and they could "march and drill with snap and precision." Even the town toughs—the stevedores, boxers, and gamblers—were part of "one happy family." In all, "the army brings out the true man in anybody and even among my friends I have seen them made or broken. Mine has been a most pleasant and profitable experience."

Ted and the others knew full well the reason for their rejection, but his letter could not be entirely forthcoming because he knew that all correspondence was being scrutinized by censors.[14] "Boy," he wrote to his friend, "it sure was hard to break up after we had learned to live and sweat together; . . . some of us actually cried when it came time to part but the spirit of Company B will carry on!"

Invariably, the men kept their sorrow and bitterness to themselves. They had not discussed the decision to join the HTG with anyone else, and they did not discuss the impact of their dismissal. Ed Nakamura related his sense of the discharge; his group, too, was told of the decision by one of the non-Japanese in the HTG.

> I remember Charles Frazier was an officer in the Territorial Guard. One of the high-ranking officers. I think he was from a very well known family. He came out and spoke to the men and boys of Japanese ancestry and expressed regret that they had to be mustered out: "It's too bad that this had to happen." . . . Everybody felt disappointed. I think, at that time, to be told that, look, you weren't going to part of this group because of your ancestry, it was a big blow. And I think more than anything else, your pride was hurt. So, I guess, [I] just went home and went back to school. . . . I don't recall that I was bitter, particularly bitter, or anything like that. Just disappointed. (23–24)

Shiro Amioka was at HTG headquarters and "mad as hell, . . . that's a crock of bull, you know. . . . To see Japanese Americans with rifles, with live ammunition, was inconceivable to some people up there." Like many of the other students, Shiro went back to the university, although studying was not a priority. "Well, basically, it was a grave injustice and although an order is an order, . . . it was a bitter experience for me, you know. I was always brought up that I was just as good as anybody else. And now you're being treated differently, see. Strictly on race. That's something that came particularly in high school from Miles Cary. The whole curriculum is based on the democratic ideals" (49–52).

When I asked Shiro if this "didn't disillusion you about the society you were living in," he replied emphatically: "No. No. Not that so much as a kind of a bitter experience. No, I didn't lose faith in the whole system. . . . We still believe in the basic . . . , you know. This was a bad mistake. Like, you know, the evacuation [the mass internment of Japanese Americans on the West Coast] was a bad mistake. An aberration in a sense, but we still had faith in the system" (49–52).

This attitude—that the experience was an "aberration," a terrible distortion of the ideals toward which the United States should be and was, in fact, striving—kept these nisei on task. Barney Ono, like Ralph Yempuku, had heard rumors that soldiers arriving from the mainland were making racist remarks. "'What the heck, this place is already taken by the Japs.' . . . Those were rumors. But we didn't pay too much attention until the orders came down saying that the Japanese boys were to be released" (24).

When Barney heard the order to disband, it was "told to us in no uncertain terms that the order was that all the Japanese boys would turn in their guns" (24). That rejection was difficult for him, "not only complete surprise; it was a shock. Like I say, I've never had that kind of feeling—that, geezus, the whole bottom dropped out. . . . Where you gonna go? If your own country, place where you're born, not gonna accept you? . . . I don't know if I was mad or not; I mean it was just out of frustration. What the heck am I supposed to do? That kinda thing. You know, get mad at whom? It wasn't a matter of getting mad; just, doggone, I don't know what the hell I'm gonna do. Am I gonna stay here or what?" (23).

Of all of the men, Barney summed up this feeling best. Beyond angry, beyond disappointment, beyond sad, beyond all of these, was a great sense of frustration. After all, they had done their part. Their ordered world, at least the world that had been ordered for them in school and at home, had disintegrated. The worst of it was the lack of other viable options to serve the country in crisis. The ROTC and then the HTG, for many of the Japanese Americans, had at least been conditional acceptance, since they were all aware that no unit of the U.S. military would accept them.

Yugo Okubo was one of the HTG members who was not particularly upset when discharged. When Yugo was summoned to the armory, the chaplain, Father David Bray, was there to sympathize with the boys. "He was the one standing at the doorway of the armory expressing his . . . regrets that the army kicked us out, and he shook hands with each one of us" (21). For Okubo, the dismissal was not a major problem—except that he had to go back to the dreaded science and engineering classes from which the Pearl Harbor attack had rescued him. The only consolation was that the university provided credit for all courses in which students were enrolled before December 7, even though the rest of the semester had been canceled. When I asked him about his reaction, Yugo remarked: "You see, at that time, you are really not disappointed because you got kicked out" (22).

Herb Isonaga had not joined the HTG—probably because there was no one at the time to accompany him to the armory. He remembered the boys coming back after having been discharged, because "a lot of guys who were in HTG were in A House [the YMCA Atherton House] residence. So, you know, when they were booted out they came back over there." He does not recall any discussions about the event and, in fact, "if you ask me they were glad to get out. . . . They were, because they were pulling some lousy detail, you know." He felt, however, that he would have been "greatly disturbed" had he been in their position and suggested that whatever their feeling, "they didn't express it, wasn't expressed, wasn't expressed" (22–23).

Racial policies in Hawai'i, in which the nisei were to play a central role, were being deliberated at levels far removed from the direct experiences of the men of the HTG. General Delos Emmons, commander of the army and military governor of Hawai'i, served nearly uncontested in the early months of the war. Under martial law, relatively free from the historical constraints of Big Five rule, there was a new and more flexible terrain on which to design and implement racial policies. Hung Wai Ching marveled that three Southerners played such crucial roles in mitigating the racism directed against the Japanese in Hawai'i: Robert Shivers, head of the FBI in Hawai'i; Joseph Farrington, former governor and territorial delegate to Congress; and Emmons. Hung Wai recalled, however, that the relative tolerance toward the local racial environment did not appear to affect their traditional prejudice toward African Americans.[15]

In spite of the careful groundwork laid by the army and by civilian leaders like Ching and Shivers, the weeks immediately following Pearl Harbor were marked by anxiety, especially with regard to potential racial unrest. The replacement of General Short by Emmons was not reassuring. Emmons, after all, had ordered the expulsion of Japanese Americans from the HTG on January 21, 1942. He would later authorize the formation of the VVV on February 25, 1942 and support the creation of the 442d Regimental Combat Team. But in the first few weeks of his tenure, Emmons was buffeted by a wide range of advice and it was not clear how he would treat the local Japanese American population. Even well into 1942, Emmons was capable of fiercely anti-nisei sentiments. In May, for example, he wrote that nisei in the uniform of the U.S. military in Hawai`i "would be shot immediately by the American troops" in the event of a Japanese invasion.[16] Fortunately for the Japanese Americans, the FBI's Shivers and the head of Army Intelligence, Kendall Fielder, were convinced that they were trustworthy.

According to a 1979 interview with Fielder, Shivers had commanded great respect and exerted much influence on the military. Fielder thought that the order for Emmons to discharge the nisei from the HTG must have come from the War Department; later, Emmons "came around." The decision to form the VVV only one month later must have been one of the turning points. Fielder believed himself to be instrumental in convincing the army chief of staff, General George Marshall, to "give the boys a chance" in forming the nisei 100th Battalion in June 1942. Later, Fielder encouraged formation of the volunteer 442d Regimental Combat Team. He recalled taking considerable criticism for standing by the Japanese American soldiers—and being much relieved when they fought so well in Italy.[17]

In the meantime, the Morale Section was hard at work. Hung Wai Ching, Charles Loomis, and Shigeo Yoshida spent long hours deliberating strategies that would, by maintaining racial equilibrium, further the war effort. A memo dated December 16, 1941, the day before Emmons replaced Short, revealed the fragility of racial harmony at the time. The Morale Section's first suggestion was to create an informational network through which key leaders of ethnic and national groups could be reached, separately or collectively, quickly and easily. It was vitally important to be able to "get certain matters of importance verbally to any section or group of the population," because this process would "greatly facilitate the directing of public thought." After all, "already the Filipinos and especially the Koreans are taking advantage of the emergency."[18]

The memo noted that Filipinos, "because of a lack of calming advice from their leaders," had become a serious potential problem on Oahu and the Big Island of Hawai`i. The major fear was the threat of random or organized violence directed against local Japanese. Hung Wai took great pride in his personal approach—telling the Filipinos to sharpen their machetes but to wait for official word before using them on the local Japanese Americans. The Koreans "present a wholly different problem. They are taking advantage of the present emergency to harp on their desire for independence [for Korea]." The problem with this approach, according to the Morale Section, was particularly acute with

Korean Americans, who were acting more like Koreans than Americans. They were urged to work in concert with other Americans who sympathized with all peoples and nations under enemy domination, and not primarily with any particular homeland.

Chinese Americans would also need assistance, the memo suggested, since they would "be tempted to think in terms of their ancestral homeland" now that China, some of which was occupied by Japan, was essentially a military ally of the United States. They too would need to be reminded of the "desirability of associating themselves with America and *as Americans* to direct their focus on China's struggle" (emphasis added).

Thus, the strategy was established of using formally constructed ethnic, racial, or nationality groups with flexible venues of communication, especially informal and verbal. The Morale Section did not publish material directed at any particular group or groups, because "often matters are too delicate or direct and specific to treat all groups alike."

On December 18, only two days after this memo was circulated, another directive from the Morale Section underscored the delicacy of the racial situation. There were, it seemed, instances of unintended negative consequences that stemmed from misguided goodwill. A few haoles had "leaned over backwards" to demonstrate impartiality and friendliness to "their Japanese domestics and hired assistants." While these gestures were initially met with favor, there soon emerged attitudes of "indifference, suspicion and in many cases cockiness and hostility" on the part of the servants. Most of this "ingratitude" was manifested by nisei who, it was alleged, had been significantly influenced by their issei elders. It was feared that too many of these cases would constitute a nucleus of discontented nisei "whose loyalty may be described as one of more bewilderment than actually of alienation." With proper guidance, the document suggests, the younger generation would regain its senses, especially when "a constructive morale program is developed and the actions and advice of their elders is stopped."[19] Until such a state was achieved, however, the military believed that much depended on the neutralizing of issei influence.

The existence of influential issei compounded the "Japanese problem" in the early war years. Every significant organization in the Japanese American community was dominated by these immigrants, from associations of entrepreneurs and business leaders (hotel owners, merchants, and physicians) to language schools, the media, cultural organizations, and religious bodies. While the war quickly curbed the influence of traditional ethnic community leadership, issei attitudes and behaviors would surely prove extremely important in the Japanese American community.

The Morale Section addressed this issue in an important document, "Propaganda Among the Japanese Aliens," dated January 15, 1942, exactly one week before General Emmons abruptly discharged the nisei from the HTG. It acknowledged the existence of a minority of aliens who were "strongly nationalistic, strongly loyal to Japan, and dangerous." Nonetheless, the "large majority" was characterized as fearful, insecure, frustrated, humiliated, abandoned, appreciative of fair treatment, law abiding, and resigned to the situation.[20]

The alien Japanese, according to this report, were living in intense fear—especially of the unknown—given the potential of more Japanese attacks and reaction against them and their children from the authorities or other racial groups. Many had been fired from their jobs and had difficulty finding employment; some, like the fishermen who dominated Hawaii's fresh-fish and tuna-canning industries, had boats and equipment confiscated; others were evicted from homes and fired from jobs because of racial animus. A number, like Ryoji Namba's parents, who depended on trade with Japan, were made destitute by the war. "Many are deeply humiliated by the treacherous way in which Japan has started this war." A few muttered darkly about Japan's lack of concern for Hawaii's Japanese—demonstrated by the attack on Pearl Harbor.

Many issei appreciated the relative tolerance shown them by the U.S. government and felt that the regulations imposed, under the circumstances, were reasonable, the report noted. They were philosophical and resigned, certainly not prone to "cockiness" over "Japan's temporary success in the Far East. Some undoubtedly are elated and proud of the achievements thus far of the Japanese war machine, but these have not shown it or have cleverly concealed it." In the end, according to the Morale Section, "most of them are still loyal at heart to the emperor." This loyalty would not erupt in overt behavior but "lies deep in their hearts in the form of a certain mystic reverence for the emperor."

To neutralize this group, the report urged a propaganda program that would stress issei obligation to America; remind issei of their children's welfare as Americans; manipulate their appreciation for fair treatment under difficult wartime circumstances; compare U.S. democratic values with the current militaristic totalitarianism in Japan; urge them to live up to the "best in Japanese traits (obedience, respect for constituted authority, sense of appreciation, etc.)"; follow their nisei children's lead; point out the ruinous course being pursued in Japan, especially given the enormous disparity in resources between the United States and Japan; stress the consequences of noncompliance or subversion; and emphasize the value of ultimate victory to their families and community. This was an extremely detailed plan. In fact, the military managed to go beyond its recommendations and actually include many issei in war-related roles—paid employment, as well as volunteer activities such as rolling bandages for the Red Cross or clearing trees on the beaches.

In the process of drafting this ambitious plan, the Morale Section was fortunate in having an unusual informant, Alberta Tarr, an American who had "adopted" Japan as her own country years before Pearl Harbor. The Morale Section found her particularly useful because of her sympathies with the immigrant Japanese and her haole background. While no direct evidence links interviews conducted with Alberta Tarr to the strategy to neutralize the issei, both timing and content appear beyond coincidence. Tarr was interviewed in the first two weeks of January and produced a written report on the same date as the Morale Section document.

The interviewers were the Morale Section's Charles Loomis and Shigeo Yoshida, who visited Tarr and discussed ways in which these "enemy aliens," the issei, could be induced to cooperate most fully with U.S. war efforts. They asked that she put her thoughts on paper and, about a week later, on January 15, she did so in a formal report, although "chasing hither and yon, trying to get in touch with the right people to help suggest activities for 'enemy aliens' at this time has taken more time than I had thought it would."[21]

Tarr noted, first, that she had approached Red Cross executive Mrs. Richard Cooke to see if the issei could work on projects such as rolling bandages. Cooke's initial response "was that she was not at all sure that they would want aliens working on [these] materials." Tarr insisted they should be utilized and was sent to see Mrs. Molyneux, head of production, who was "gracious, cooperative and commendable." Throughout the war, issei women devoted many hours at the Red Cross.[22]

Alberta Tarr had spent considerable time and energy on the mainland trying to articulate, if not defend, Japan's position when it first invaded China. Then, however, "when I returned to Japan, I was most interested to note that those of us who had been away from Japan and on the defensive for Japan had an entirely different attitude from those who had been there all the time and had been subject to the propaganda and pressure that the press was bringing to create loyalty and support. Again, the most reactionary and nationalistic of our Christian leaders were the men who had been on the Mainland and had had to explain Japanese actions and try to find some defense for them. Those who had been at home [in Japan] all the time and under pressure to be regimented were much more outspoken in their denunciation of the war on China."

But it was equally important to understand that pushing the issei too far on the defensive would be counterproductive, Tarr suggested; for example, newspapers could refrain from urging that the Japanese support "defeating Japan" to demonstrate their position, since the important ideal was that democracy prevail over imperialism or totalitarianism. "I think the ordinary Japanese here does not realize that the government of Japan has been, for years, taken out of legitimate civic channels and completely controlled, or increasingly controlled, by a right wing of the army." The community in Hawai`i thus had scant knowledge of the fact that most of Japan, even some within the army and navy, "have long been weary of the activities in China and are eager for peace. To expect a first-generation Japanese, however long he has lived here, to show enthusiasm for 'defeating Japan' is expecting the emotionally impossible, I think. A different terminology could achieve it, however, without making him feel disloyal to the homeland." In the meantime, the Morale Section was anxious to get an accurate reading of the issei community. In this, Tarr was especially helpful.

The "predominant emotion is that of fear," Tarr explained in the interview. The issei were afraid of all authorities—police, army, any government officials. Their status as aliens "ineligible for naturalization" had always been insecure; as "enemy aliens" it was immeasurably worse. Rumors, especially the propaganda emanating from Japan, were rampant, and those with shortwave sets gathered clusters of friends to listen in clandestine groups. There was fear of violence, especially from Filipinos, Chinese, and Koreans who might be tempted to "take the law into their own hands" and "square accounts" on a national basis. Many Japanese women were especially fearful of leaving their homes.

The Japanese were afraid of "social discrimination," Tarr said. They had always been, she felt, "a singularly sensitive people, quick to feel slights that are not intended sometimes." The nature of Japan's attack on Pearl Harbor heightened the antagonism toward them, and even those who did not understand English "understand the contempt and hatred in the tone of voice often addressed to Japanese."[23] Finally, there was fear for the future for themselves and their children. The issei understood that there was considerable economic discrimination, even against their American-citizen children, and it was not clear how conditions would be resolved.

On the other hand, Tarr observed a sense of "deep appreciation" for government procedures and the tolerance and fair play displayed by authorities in the month since Pearl Harbor. She noted, also, "childlike gratitude and appreciation for friendship shown by those of other racial groups, especially Anglo-Saxons." Some had even expressed shame and humiliation: "Now you see why we are ashamed of our Japanese heritage!"

One section of the Tarr report deserves particular attention. It conveys the issei's sense of abandonment by their own government and reflects the feeling issei had expressed for decades, both in Hawai`i and on the mainland.[24] By U.S. law, they could not become naturalized Americans; at the same time, as the Japanese government grew increasingly assertive in its singular quest for major power status, its overseas subjects became ever more insignificant. Tarr felt their

> feeling of disappointment or hurt, about which they do not often speak: it is the natural sense of being deserted by the homeland they have idealized through the years. They had felt so secure here in the Islands, and had been confident that, no matter where Japan might strike, she would never strike the Islands, because THEY were here. "Oh, why didn't Japan leave us alone here in Hawai`i, where we are happy!" is the cry of older second-generation mothers, who report that this is the attitude of their alien parents and friends. As aliens, they have always felt somewhat "out" of things, and perhaps comforted themselves with the thought that the mother country, at least, loved them. Now the attack on the Islands proved that their welfare, safety, and happiness do not matter, even to the mother country. As a result, they are feeling cast off and cast out.

One of the few institutions to render support to the Japanese American community, especially to the issei, was the American Friends Service Committee (AFSC)—the broad outreach effort of the Quakers. William Morris Maier, a conscientious objector from Philadelphia, was sent to oversee AFSC activities in Hawai`i. Gilbert Bowles, who had been a Quaker missionary in Japan for forty years, was already in Hawai`i, and the two spent considerable energy working with the issei. Hung Wai Ching recalls a visit from Maier, who explained that his mission was to serve the Japanese American community because the Quakers knew they would be under siege (2–3). A descendant of William Penn and a trustee of Haverford College, Maier even talked to Ted Tsukiyama about attending his school, a Quaker-affiliated institution.[25]

Amid the strident calls for drastic action against the Japanese Americans in Hawai`i, the Japanese community needed every friend it could find. Perhaps the most notorious public figure who called for removal and internment of the entire Japanese American population was John Balch, president of the Mutual Telephone Company, who in July 1943 published a vitriolic pamphlet entitled "Shall the Japanese Be Allowed to Dominate Hawai`i?" Ray Coll of the *Honolulu Advertiser* was sometimes the object of protest and asked to tone down the rhetoric of his anti-Japanese columns.[26]

Hung Wai Ching recalls that he confronted General Emmons at one point, threatening to resign, because someone had wiretapped his telephone conversations (as well as Shigeo Yoshida's) and had been following him around. It turned out to be a "local haole" army officer who had been tapping these lines on his own and who was, as far as Hung Wai knows, reprimanded and ordered to stay away. There was more— prominent local haole families were able, under cover of military exigency, to seek arbitrary detention of Japanese who had displeased them. Ching found anti–Japanese American sentiment in the military: "Now that the war is over I can say this now. Not all of the local haoles were friendly to our local Japanese Americans. . . . You know, some of them were intelligence—Naval Intelligence, Army Intelligence. Those were the guys that I felt would give me a hand, you know. No way" (22–26).

There were many ways in which anti-Japanese sentiment could be expressed. Individuals were free to submit to the FBI or military governor names of individual Japanese they had reason to suspect or simply resented for some past insult, real or imagined. On the basis of race alone, many Japanese were terminated from their positions or never hired or promoted.

At the government level, this movement could be seen in a variety of forms. The first and most obvious was the call to remove the entire population of residents of Japanese descent either to American concentration camps or to the island of Molokai, where they could grow their own food and where the turbulent ocean waters would eliminate the possibility of escape. Less drastic measures included removing significant numbers, perhaps fifteen or twenty thousand, to the continent.[27] It took some doing, in fact, for General Emmons to delay implementation of such draconian measures and convince President Roosevelt that the situation was under control.

Perhaps the first open indication that the non-Japanese population was growing uneasy with so many armed nisei came exactly one month after Pearl Harbor. On January 8, 1942, E. D. Bourland of the Hawaiian Electric Company wrote to express concern over security issues; he suggested establishment of a separate "provisional guard" of white men in the event of a Japanese uprising.[28]

Two days later, on January 10, Colonel Smoot, head of the HTG, responded to Bourland, noting that Emmons had already authorized formation of a special reserve. Soon thereafter, Bourland was placed in command of the Businessmen's Military Training Corps (BMTC) which was provided khaki uniforms, armed, and trained by the army. The BMTC was comprised exclusively of haole and part-Hawaiian men and conducted its own military exercises.

Smoot agreed that Bourland's idea of having businessmen in each residential area acting as a form of block guard would be of value in reassuring residents of Honolulu in normal times and might be of considerable value "in the event of an emergency." Indeed, Smoot noted that "at the present time the Hawaii Territorial Guard is used to guard installations and no protection from this source is afforded residential districts. Despite the effort being made to train the Hawaii Territorial Guard, it has two difficulties, namely, inexperience *and that a portion of it's* [sic] *personnel are orientels* [sic]" Within two weeks of its formation in January 1942, the BMTC had 1,500 men, many of them very prominent, including the seventy-six-year-old former chief justice of the territory. "One of the BMTC's primary missions was the immobilization of enemy aliens in case of invasion. It compiled elaborate data on the alien population and the city in general and maintained a 10-foot map showing areas with vital installations and large concentrations of Japanese."[29]

Even Tarzan's creator, Edgar Rice Burroughs—a resident of Lanikai Beach in Kailua, Oahu, since April 1940—got into the act. On December 7, 1941, Burroughs and his son, who was visiting, responded to calls for volunteers and shouldered Springfield rifles at Kewalo Basin (the ROTC was thus not the only unit to face possible combat with these old weapons). Later, the military asked Burroughs to write a newspaper column to help boost local morale; called "Laugh It Off," it ran intermittently in both dailies. Some of the pieces were offensive to the Japanese

American community, especially when Burroughs complained in print about the use of nisei in the HTG.

Burroughs wrote directly to the military governor's office sometime before January 24, 1942, to question the wisdom of arming Japanese Americans. On that day, Colonel Thomas Green wrote Bourland, founder of the BMTC, that Burroughs had suggested "formation of an organization such as you are now organizing in the form of the Honolulu Business Men's Military Corps, and I suggest that you send him an application blank to join your organization."[30]

By mid-January 1942, the nation was deeply engaged in a frenzy of anti-Japanese activity, including lurid and invented cases of espionage and sabotage. In spite of constant statements in Hawai`i newspapers and nationally, by the FBI as well as General Delos Emmons, insisting that no espionage or sabotage had occurred, the media, politicians, and special interest groups continued the assault. These groups included economic competitors of mainland Japanese American fishing or agriculture ventures, as well as opportunistic politicians and racist/nativist groups. Together, they developed an intensive campaign to target Japanese Americans for removal to inland concentration camps.[31]

The January 5, 1942, issue of *Time* magazine had featured stories of sabotage by Hawaii's Japanese community: "Fed on tolerance, watered by complacency, the Jap fifth column had done its job fiendishly well and had not been stamped out." Two weeks later, *Time* sympathized with the 105,000 haoles for whom invasion "loomed as a very real threat. What would the Islands' Japanese do then? Islanders who remembered that Jap high-school boys from Hawaii had helped pilot the planes that attacked Pearl Harbor looked uneasily at Hawaii's thousands going freely, imperturbably about their business. What about the houseboy, the cop on the corner, the farmer down the road? What about the Japs [in the HTG] set to guard the Islands?"[32]

In the end, with no significant opposition, the momentum to remove the Japanese Americans from the HTG was unstoppable. On January 21, 1942, Colonel Thomas Green, aide to General Emmons, issued orders to "inactivate" the HTG "due to the fact that the police force has been augmented and improvements in the protection of vital installations have been increased." Colonel Green also demonstrated some concern for the welfare of the men being discharged and the need for scarce wartime labor. On the day of inactivation, he called and then wrote to the head of the Army Engineers headquartered on the Punahou School campus to urge hiring of the Japanese Americans: "There would be as many as 500 men who would be desireable [*sic*] of having jobs, it is requested that such men be employed by you, if practicable, on projects which are being constructed for the Military Government. I have particular reference to those in the evacuation areas and the trenches which are being constructed."[33]

Headquarters unit was kept intact and, officially, at least one Japanese American, First Lieutenant Katsumi Kometani, was temporarily retained. Shiro Amioka and Masato Doi recalled that they also stayed on to continue typing out discharge papers for their nisei colleagues. A report to Governor Poindexter dated March 26, 1942, a month later, indicated that Kometani was still on the payroll at $260.27 as force dental officer.[34]

THE HTG PROVIDED a stopgap military solution to Hawaii's defense problem in the first anxious weeks after the attack on Pearl Harbor. The public was mercifully unaware of the group's lack of training and discipline and, for December, at least, too frightened to comment on the large numbers of armed nisei. There was little money or glory in standing guard over hospitals and reservoirs, but there was a deep sense of satisfaction among the HTG's Japanese Americans in having been accepted, however marginally, during the national crisis. Their subsequent dismissal was, ironically, a sneak attack at the hands of their own government, and there did not appear to be much that they could do about it.

6

The Varsity Victory Volunteers

The year 1942 was pivotal for World War II in the Pacific. In January and February, the war was going badly for the United States, and a vast reservoir of existing prejudice was deployed to generate maximum hatred against the Japanese as a distinct and vile race. It was not surprising, therefore, that the order to dissolve the HTG was issued, on January 21, in the midst of a national surge of anti-Japanese outrage that would engulf the tiny minority of Japanese Americans on the mainland and threaten their counterpart community of 160,000 in Hawai`i.

Local zealots as well as racists on the mainland were demanding that all Japanese Americans be detained. The commanding general of the army and military governor, Delos Emmons, eventually determined that it was necessary to conduct a holding action, arguing against any substantial internment while offering up modest numbers of Japanese Americans—a strategy that succeeded in protecting the majority of Japanese Americans from internment.

Still, this protection came at a fearful price. As Roland Kotani suggests, the rights of 1,875 Hawai`i residents of Japanese ancestry—those who were sent into concentration camps—were "actually sacrificed by Emmons to placate the bureaucrats in the nation's capital."[1] Like their counterparts on the North American continent, they were neither charged with nor convicted of any wrongdoing. But where the 120,000 Japanese Americans interned on the mainland could reassure themselves that they were collective victims of injustice, the Hawai`i internees became an embarrassing blot on the otherwise stellar wartime performance of the ethnic community. They were an unexplained problem in the transformation of the nisei from prewar threats to postwar heroes. The postwar myth of racial tolerance required that their experience be minimized and marginalized, expunged, if possible, from the historical record.

PRESIDENT FRANKLIN ROOSEVELT'S Executive Order 9066, which cleared the military path for mass internment of Japanese Americans on the West Coast, was issued on February 19, 1942, almost exactly one month after Japanese Americans were removed from the HTG.[2] The president had a long history of anti-Japanese sentiment, and his personal bias was quickly reinforced by private and public calls for the removal and detention of the Japanese by nearly every politician, newspaper, labor union, patriotic association, and business organization on the mainland. The few exceptions, like Harry P. Cain, the mayor of Tacoma, Washington, were removed from office in the next election.[3] The American Friends Service Committee of the Quakers, along with the Black Muslims, were the only religiously affiliated organizations to protest the internment. Even the American Civil Liberties Union, except for a few individual members, crumbled in the face of massive hostility toward the Japanese. All of this public pressure to remove the Japanese en masse occurred in spite of adamant testimony from J. Edgar Hoover, head of the FBI, as well as Curtis Munson, author of a crucial 1941 report on the potential loyalty of Japanese Americans in the event of war, that wholesale internment was unnecessary.

Public opinion in the first month after Pearl Harbor, as measured by column inches in newspaper articles and editorials as well as letters from the public, reflected substantial concern for fair play for the Japanese. But suspicion that the resident Japanese could not be trusted jumped dramatically in January and throughout February 1942, first on the West Coast and then throughout the country. This shift was largely caused, it appears, by deliberate lies about Japanese American espionage and sabotage spread by influential journalists and radio commentators, as well as by public officials like Frank Knox, secretary of the navy, and Earl Warren, then attorney general of California.[4]

In Hawai`i, the newspapers were more guarded, and there was little public outcry with regard to the ultimate disposition of the large and strategically placed Japanese American population. Still, the overall sentiment was hostile; John Reinecke remembered that "it looked as if there would be no opportunity to prove that loyalty—when the *Advertiser* was applauding the West Coast evacuation to concentration camps, when the government said nothing to contradict the lying rumors about sabotage on Pearl Harbor day and the OMG [Office of Military Governor] treated Japanese-Americans as barely tolerated second-class citizens."[5]

Advertiser writers Ray Coll and Earl Albert Selle were remembered as having been especially vicious. Barney Ono recalled that Selle was directly responsible for causing his mother great pain, literally. Selle occasionally wrote to criticize issei who continued to wear slippers and other Japanese garb after Pearl Harbor. "You know, he fuss about our parents. . . . I know my mother used to cry for having to put shoes on her farmer's feet. . . . Tried to put shoes on and her feet hurt so bad." At one point, Ono organized a group to confront Selle but the reporter refused to meet with them (19).[6]

In early spring 1943, Keiji Kawakami wrote to the *Advertiser* to protest one of Earl Selle's columns. Selle had admonished Japanese Americans for not "being more boisterous in their denunciation of the Japs." Kawakami objected to this peculiar index of good Americanism; it was "like saying I am a good Christian because I damn the other sects." Moreover, Kawakami wrote, he had volunteered for combat and was "willing to give my life, if necessary." Unlike Selle, he was not given to "lip patriotism or noisy chauvinism" and was not sitting "behind a typewriter" to "pound out my patriotism."[7]

The *Star-Bulletin*, under the leadership of editor Riley Allen, was widely appreciated as much more fair-minded. Allen prohibited the use of the epithet "Jap" in his newspaper through the war years. Even the December 7 issue, on the Honolulu streets within hours after the attack, spelled out "Japanese." Two reporters on his staff were Japanese Americans, Lawrence Nakatsuka and Ken Misumi, and they continued to work at the paper after Pearl Harbor. Even under Allen's enlightened leadership, however, there was pressure from within to demonstrate an appropriate level of race baiting.

In one telling instance, twelve staff members asked in a petition to Allen "that we once more be allowed to refer in our stories and headlines to the enemy Japanese as Japs." They listed five reasons: (1) all other newspapers in the territory were using the term and "our failure to use the word sets us apart and defeats the very purpose of the plan, which was to help allay race feelings"; (2) both the army and navy used the term in their press releases; (3) the competing *Advertiser* elected to make this an issue by publishing an editorial pointing to the different philosophies; (4) Admiral Chester Nimitz referred to "Japs" without fear of "race riots—and he should know"; (5) finally, any "race feeling" that "might have been stirred up by us was *due more to the overplay of our AJA stories, than to our infrequent use of the word Jap when referring to the enemy*" (emphasis added). The two Japanese American reporters, Nakatsuka and Misumi, were among the twelve who signed the document; in the context of such widespread resistance, it would have been difficult for them not to. Much to his credit, Allen refused to back down and the policy stood.[8]

On January 26, five days after removing the nisei from the HTG, the military governor's office granted "permission" for the "University of Hawai`i to open on February 2nd."[9] General Emmons had decided that the absence of crisis also meant that education could be resumed. In the days after their discharge from the HTG, some of the students left the Atherton YMCA and crossed University Avenue to sit under a banyan tree to "talk story," as Hawai`i locals put it. At one point, Hung Wai Ching left his office in the YMCA and walked over to join them. They told him they were going over, in their minds, the injustice of the government's actions and wondering what they should do. Hung Wai refused to commiserate. "'Well then,' I said, 'if you guys feel so hurt about it, nothing you can do about it. Then you want to go the second mile. Like good Christians.' I think that kind of startled them a little bit. . . . The guys say, 'What are we going to do?' I say, 'Go the second mile; show them, the powers that be.' 'So, okay, so what do we do?' 'Come down, let's write a petition; I'll get it to the general'" (36–37).[10]

In fact, Hung Wai had already been talking with John Young of the Nuuanu YMCA, Shigeo Yoshida, and members of the Emergency Service Committee, the Japanese American group organized to provide information and support in the war effort. The HTG discharges were a serious setback to a unified, multiracial war effort. Now, these leaders felt, they needed a positive, morale-boosting, dramatic initiative to reverse the negative momentum. A small group of students met with Ching and Yoshida at the Central Branch of the YMCA.

They accepted the idea of a petition offering voluntary service, and Ted Tsukiyama worked on a draft that presented a heartfelt plea:

> We are Americans of Japanese ancestry recently discharged from the service of the Hawaii Territorial Guard. We understand the reasons and motives that lay behind our subsequent discharge but we understand this as a means to

the achievement of the ultimate goal—the impregnable defense of our Territory.

Our services have been sacrificed for the fulfillment of this goal but our loyalty remains untouched. We stand more resolved to defend with our lives, if necessary, this land of our birth, our homes, our education, our loved ones and our happiness, with much more vigor and determination than any imported defending force. We desire to contribute our share toward the defense of Hawaii. If our services are not required in the Territorial Guard, we wish to offer them to be used in any other phase of defense of our country.[11]

Tsukiyama's rhetoric reflected his youthful idealism. Shigeo Yoshida produced a simpler and more elegant version that drew heavily on Tsukiyama's intent and phrasing and has come to symbolize the frustration, dedication, and ultimate triumph of steadfast devotion. Only after repeated and direct questioning toward the end of his life would Yoshida admit that he had personally crafted the final petition. "Well," Yoshida said in our interview, "now that you ask me, I'll have to say yes. You can't expect a bunch of university kids to come up with something like that in a short order. . . . I already knew what they wanted me to write because we had discussed it so I quickly drafted it. . . . So, it's not just me writing it. It's just me putting into words what the boys had already expressed" (4). It read:

Honolulu, T.H.
January 30, 1942

Lt. Gen. Delos C. Emmons
Commanding General,
Hawaiian Department, U.S.A.
Fort Shafter, T.H.

Sir:

We, the undersigned, were members of the Hawaii Territorial Guard until its recent inactivation. We joined the Guard voluntarily with the hope that this was one way to serve our country in her time of need. Needless to say, we were deeply disappointed when we were told that our services in the Guard were no longer needed.

Hawaii is our home; the United States, our country. We know but one loyalty and that is to the Stars and Stripes. We wish to do our part as loyal Americans in every way possible and we hereby offer ourselves for whatever service you may see fit to use us.

> Respectfully yours,
> (signed)
> University students

In the next week or so, 130 university students signed the petition; soon by word of mouth came the news that a volunteer unit might be formed. On February 11, another petition was submitted. This time, individuals who "were not members of the Hawaii Territorial Guard also wish to express our loyalty to the country of our birth and of our choice, the United States of America, [and] do also sincerely wish that you will use us in any way you see fit" (TTC). At the same time, a more formal recruitment effort was initiated and a meeting of university students was called for the next day, February 12. In addition, Ralph Yempuku circulated a letter, also dated February 12, to friends of the core group, the first public affirmation that linked loyalty and the Japanese American community:

> In view of the serious situation now confronting the security of these islands, it is urgent that we Americans of Japanese Ancestry demonstrate our loyalty in concrete ways.
>
> We need the active cooperation of every American of Japanese ancestry and we urgently request that you be present at a meeting called to consider this matter at the Nuuanu Y.M.C.A. auditorium, Sunday morning, February 15, 1942, at 10:00 o'clock.[12]

The Emergency Service Committee noted, in early March 1942, two separate meetings relevant to the establishment of the VVV. The first was the February 12 meeting at the University of Hawai`i attended by approximately two hundred "university Boys"—an impressive turnout. At the second, on February 15, about seventy-five "Former H.T.G. Boys" gathered at the Nuuanu YMCA.[13] These meetings were watched closely by the Morale Section—by Ching and Yoshida, especially—and carefully reported to Emmons, probably via Kendall Fielder, head of Army Intelligence. The army moved rapidly; negotiations were concluded with Colonel Albert Lyman to secure a home for this anomalous outfit within the Corps of Engineers. There is nothing to indicate whether Emmons needed or secured authorization from Washington to establish this segregated Japanese American labor battalion; Hung Wai Ching suspected that he did not (44–45).

Ralph Yempuku and the rest of the men were unaware of the negotiations being conducted between members of the Morale Section and General Emmons. Indeed, they did not know that it was Emmons himself who had given the order for the Japanese Americans to be purged from the HTG. And they could not have known of the dramatic pressure being applied on Emmons for the mass removal of the entire Japanese American population to mainland concentration camps, or, at least, of large numbers to a separate location like the island of Molokai. On February 1, 1942, for example, the War Department proposed that all soldiers of Japanese descent be separated from active duty. Emmons responded that he had already discharged the nisei from the HTG but would leave in place the 1,400 who were in the 298th and 299th Infantry Regiments of the Hawai'i National Guard, as well as several hundred others in engineer and service units.[14]

On February 9, the War Department ordered Emmons to suspend all civilians of Japanese descent who were employed by the army; Emmons demurred, explaining that "the Japanese were an irreplaceable labor force in Hawai'i." Complying with that order would have cost the military about eighty percent of their construction workers. The War Department later rescinded the order.[15]

This was, in fact, a very serious issue. In July 1942, Drew Paulette wrote a draft history of "Martial Law in Hawai'i: The First Eight Months"; though never published, it is a revealing document. Paulette alluded to the Japanese American presence in terms of the "employment of aliens and citizens of Japanese ancestry in restricted areas," "particularly . . . as it affected work forces on the waterfront."[16]

Restricting Japanese American stevedores, for example, severely impacted the movement of food, construction materials, and war supplies. But sugar was the primary industry in Hawai'i, and the Big Five was anxious to retain its labor pool. Martial law froze "critical" workers to their jobs, and the Hawaiian Sugar Planters' Association (HSPA) managed to have agricultural plantation workers placed in that category; they were even exempted from the draft. Nonetheless, by the end of January 1942, plantation owners were complaining of "heavy losses" of labor and equipment diverted to defense projects. The HSPA agreed that war efforts deserved priority but reminded General Emmons that sugar was the only food to be rationed and that approximately 60 percent of the plantations' 7,321 unskilled laborers had been lost or were loaned for defense work.[17] Conversely, workers tied to their jobs found their frozen wages steadily losing ground to inflated wartime prices. In the end, General Emmons was forced to ask Admiral Chester Nimitz to "obtain some relaxation of the restrictions applicable to the employment of Japanese."[18]

In this hostile environment, the nisei critically needed influential haole support to make any headway. Leslie Hicks, president of the Honolulu Chamber of Commerce, became a key ally. Ted Tsukiyama was so moved by a speech Hicks delivered to the local Rotary Club, published in the *Star-Bulletin*, that he wrote to thank him, on February 11, just one day before the large meeting of students at the university. His letter, a copy of which he kept, captures the men's sense of rejection and the desperate need for hope and support.

> It was a most encouraging message coming as a ray of light in times darkened by war hate and hysteria. Your speech, spoken like a true American, only served to emphasize the aims and ideals which we fight for—the preservation of principles of justice and humanity, the essence of our American way of life.
>
> I sincerely admire your courage to stand up and speak out your own, honest convictions in the face of an overwhelming majority, swept by emotionalism and un-thinking prejudice. I admire your sense of justice—your sticking up in defense for a loyal group of Americans, unfortunately and unjustly damned. . . . Finally, I admire the depth of understanding with which you analyze and interpret this crucial race problem confronting our territory and our nation, and your recognition of the unmixed and wholehearted loyalty to the United States that lies in the hearts of those born in Hawaii. You expressed the need of stimulating this allegiance by positive means—by faith and trust; likewise, you know that "suspicion does not breed loyalty" whereas not many others do. The greater majority of them need not stand under shadows of suspicion—they will continue to live and will die as true Americans!
>
> As an American of Japanese parentage, I feel deeply gratified and indebted to you for such an understanding and inspiring message coming in trying times as these, as do many others of this group with unspoken sincerity, for it has given us all the more "fight", hope and determination to share an active part in America's war efforts. We will fight, then, to the very end, not only to preserve our American way of life, but furthermore, to prove our loyalty to all unbelievers with undisputable certainty, and not least of all, to fully justify the faith, trust, and confidence with which real Americans as yourself have upheld in we, Americans by conviction and by heritage.
>
> Very sincerely yours,
> (signed)
> Ted Tsukiyama
> Student, University

As with their decision to join the HTG, most of the boys never discussed with their parents the effort to create the Varsity Victory Volunteers. John Young, their Nuuanu YMCA leader, recalled that at least some of the parents were unhappy. These issei had already watched their sons serve with distinction in the ROTC and the HTG, then be removed under circumstances that appeared to disgrace and dishonor their families and race. When the boys joined the VVV, "lots of their parents didn't approve of it, I know that. . . . The parents, frankly, thought that they were stupid when the American government . . . didn't want them. Why should they pay to be taken by the government. Well, I had a lot of trouble with the parents on that regard" (20).

Young's dedication to these youth made him accessible to them, as well as to their parents, and endeared him to the Japanese American community. Among those who adored him were the mother and father of Daniel Inouye, not a VVV member, who would later become senior senator from Hawai`i. Mrs. Inouye wrote to Young, informing him of the battlefield commission that promoted Inouye to second lieutenant: "I thought this was an occasion to write to you since you've been very good to him in his forming age. I am sure his able leadership came from your training and your influence. I didn't express this to you before, but I was always thankful to you for his being a good boy in that not too laudable surroundings of his."[19]

Young wrote to me that he remembered Japanese mothers telling him: "'You know, *sensei*, children and dogs like you!' . . . when I left for Japan in 1947, Ted Tsukiyama's mother and Dan Inouye's mother and some of the old women that I had loved for years, they were down at the airport. They had a huge banner: 'Sayonara. Honoruru no kodomo no taisho.' All the old people called me 'general of Honolulu's children.'"[20] He was, in short, one of the few non-Japanese privy to issei concerns about their wartime treatment and to the decision of their sons to volunteer for labor duty in the VVV.

In February, the tide finally turned. Civilian and military leaders agreed that restoring avenues for the inclusion of the Japanese American community had become a priority in Hawai`i. Creating the VVV was the first significant step. Officially designated the Corps of Engineers Auxiliary, the VVV was attached to the Thirty-fourth Combat Engineers Regiment in the U.S. Army Corps of Engineers. No one now remembers how it got nicknamed the Varsity Victory Volunteers, although the name must have been adopted soon after the men's arrival at the Schofield army base in Wahiawa. The three barracks to which the VVV was assigned quickly became Varsity, Victory, and Volunteers. For the next eleven months, as the war intensified, the VVV men were classified 4C—aliens ineligible to serve in the armed forces of the United States—a designation formally imposed on the American-born Japanese in March 1942.

The community leaders who convinced Emmons to establish the VVV were united in their assessment that the nisei could be trusted and that the long-term racial health of the islands depended upon just treatment of the Japanese American community during the war. Men like John Young, Bob Shivers, Kendall Fielder, Charles Hemenway, Charles Loomis, Miles Cary, Stephen Mark, Leslie Hicks, and Riley Allen were sure that the fragile climate of racial stability in Hawai`i hung in a delicate balance in the weeks and months after December 7, 1941, and they sought desperately to prevent its wholesale destruction.

Morale Section member Shigeo Yoshida remembered John Young as the first to bring the plight of the young university men to his attention:

> As I recall it, it was one day late in February 1942 that we got a call from John Young who was then executive secretary of the Nuuanu YMCA and when I say we, I mean the Morale Committee. And John Young said, "I got a bunch of university students here. They got kicked out of the Territorial Guard. They don't know what to do about it now. Will you folks be willing to talk to them and help them if you can?" So we said, "Yes, Young, send them down. Maybe we can work something out."
>
> So five or six boys came down . . . and talked to us. We explored the various options they have under the circumstances. One is to just take it lying down. Another option would be to at least write a letter to the commanding general bringing out how you feel about such an obviously discriminatory action. Another would be to do that plus offer themselves for whatever service the army still desired for them. So after talking around the table, the boys came to the conclusion that option three would be about the best thing to do. . . . They wanted to offer something constructive or more of a challenge to the army now. Put the monkey on their back, so to speak, you know. Here we are. What are you going to do about it?
>
> And so the boys left and went back to the university to get signatures to the petition. Meanwhile, we kept Kendall Fielder informed and he fully approved. Hung Wai and I thought about it and said, Well, if they're going to be accepted by the army in whatever kind of work the boys can do, it will be very important that the boys be attached to a unit that would be sympathetic with what they were doing. . . .
>
> And, just at that time, the U.S. Corps of Engineers, which is the big army unit that did most of the construction work, was commanded by General [Albert Kualii Brickwood] Lyman. Lyman of the famous family in Puna on the Big Island. So Hung Wai . . . visited with General Lyman, gave him the background. . . . And he asked General Lyman if he

could help . . . with a group that is at least sympathetic and, further-more, if possible, get Hawaiian officers for them—not just any officer from the mainland—to be the liaison . . . that's how you happened to get Captain . . . Richard Lum and the two part-Hawaiian staff sergeants. . . . Well, we figured we would need another officer. So we decided, well, Tommy Kaulukukui should be a good one. He knows the boys. The boys know him. Let's see if we can get a commission for him and have him placed with the boys also. And we asked Kendall Fielder if that could be done. He felt that he was pretty sure he could get him a com-mission and assigned to the unit. And that's how Tommy came to be a part of the organization. This illustrates the sort of work we were doing as members of the Morale Committee. Most of the work was behind the scenes. (2–3)[21]

(According to Hung Wai Ching, Yoshida was known as a skilled writer. When General Emmons asked Ching to draft speeches related to racial harmony and the war effort, Hung Wai relied on Yoshida. It is one of the delicious ironies of the war, then, that some of the military gover-nor's most eloquent and important speeches relating to treatment of Japanese Americans were written by a nisei.)

Hung Wai Ching is usually credited with motivating the university students to "do something about it."

So they gave me the damn petition; I gave it to Wooch [Colonel Kendall] Fielder and I said, "Hey, Wooch," I said, "Look, you could use these kids. You'd be surprised how many kids we can get."

And so he called General Lyman and General Lyman's first crack: "Give me all the kids you can find. I'll take care of them." . . . This was a very strange, unique situation. It's most unusual. Somebody could write it up in the annals of the United States military. They are under the jurisdiction, under the discipline of the army. Imagine! They got a cap-tain; a first lieutenant, and a second lieutenant to run 150 kids, 160 kids. And, wait! Two master sergeants or three? Look, we're overstaffed! And, on top of that, I had to go and hustle Ralph Yempuku to be a straw boss. . . . We needed labor. And the boys even paid for their own *kaukau*, their own food. What the hell? How they get cheap labor, coolie labor? They were like prisoners—all they were lacking was a POW designation; oh, no joke, it's true, of course that they got back at three o'clock P.M. and could play golf, but still . . . (38–39, 45)

Another significant VVV ally, Charles Hemenway, was a crucial link among several critical elements in Hawai'i during the war. He brokered the tense peace between the Big Five business community and the local working-class communities; he was essential to the smooth operations of the FBI and the Honolulu Police Department; he understood the importance of maintaining the fragile peace as the war exacerbated difficult relations between Japanese Americans and everyone else. Hemenway was particularly important in convincing his Big Five peers that the nonhaole groups were needed as participating actors in the war.

Richard Lum became the senior army officer in direct command of the VVV. Individuals like him and Ching were crucial to the VVV effort because they were but one generation removed from China, then being savaged by the Japanese military. Their active participation was a moral and political statement to the population at large to encourage cooperation rather than the repression under way on the mainland. It need only be recalled that some Chinese and Koreans were sporting badges that proclaimed their non-Japanese ethnicity to understand the importance of this policy and their individual commitment. With General Lyman's cooperation, Tommy Kaulukukui as lieutenant, and George Aikau and Bill Jarrett as sergeants, there was substantial Native Hawaiian participation. And haole support was evident at the very top. Frank Judd, a scion of an influential Big Five family, became first lieutenant and executive officer, reporting to Captain Lum. At the time, it was less critical to involve the other ethnic groups because of their lack of numbers or status in society.

In the end, however, it remained the decision of the former ROTC/discharged HTG boys to form the Varsity Victory Volunteers.

Ralph Yempuku became the single most important figure in the VVV. As "civilian supervisor," he was more accessible among the nisei volunteers, and he transmitted orders, including daily work assignments, from the army to the boys. He understood the nature of his assignment and the factors that made his service indispensable: Ralph was about six years older than the students and could assume the leadership position without arousing peer jealousies and factionalism; he was well known as administrator of the intramural athletics program on the campus, at the time a flourishing operation, as well as assistant manager of the football team. At less than five and a half feet tall, he managed a commanding presence. Volunteering was not an easy decision for him. Men like Ching and Yoshida knew he would be essential, but the HTG experience was still a raw wound for Yempuku.

> Yeah. Yeah. Yeah. They had to talk me into it because I . . . I was pissed off. . . . Geezus. They kicked you out and then—you know that they had

the 100th Battalion, the National Guard there, they had federalized, and they wouldn't give them guns. So this is why I say, when Hemenway talked to me and told me that sometimes you got to do the obvious things like go out and wave the flag before people will accept you. And I guess to say, "This is my heritage, my born right that I be treated equally like the haoles or whatever," is not going to get you anything.

It was very unpopular at that time to be for the nisei. See, like I say, if your name Odo, you're stereotyped, you're a Jap. There is no, "Oh, you know, he's American. He's born in Hawai`i. He's a citizen." . . . And to come out at that time took a lot of courage because not only the federal government but in Hawai`i, you know, I presume 90 percent of the Hawaiians and everybody were anti-Japanese.

When we went in, we knew that we weren't going to be given guns. I knew that they had to do backbreaking labor. . . . They had to have people do all this road building and fence fixing. . . . But I don't recollect them telling us how much we gonna get paid. . . . No. No. None of that. And it wasn't a case of looking for a job; . . . at least I went there with my eyes wide open that whatever they say you gonna do, you gonna do. Whatever they pay you, you gonna take and you not going to strike or have any complaints. . . . But how much work, what work, I didn't know. (33–37)

Yempuku had been on his own since his family returned to Hiroshima in 1934. He was accustomed to a life of discipline and self-discipline and understood that the road ahead would not be easy.

For the non-Japanese like Richard Lum and Thomas Kaulukukui, joining the VVV was a declaration of their usefulness to the war effort; like the two sergeants, George Aikau and Bill Jarrett, along with Lieutenant Frank Judd, they shared distinctive ethnic and racial characteristics which would suggest that all of Hawai`i stood united in this effort to rehabilitate the nisei. Of course, these men had their own sense of duty and responsibility as well. Kaulukukui, for example, felt that he needed to respond in some fashion—he had been in the HTG and was willing to serve in spite of the fact that he had only recently been married. Surprisingly, Tommy was considered physically unfit for military service. "I volunteered because it was an emergency. I wasn't going to volunteer for the army. I couldn't even get into the ROTC. . . . My right leg was shorter than my left. I couldn't pass the physical for the ROTC" (11).

Perhaps his uneven legs helped disorient would-be tacklers in Kaulukukui's distinguished gridiron career. In any case, Tommy was provided instant officer status as a second lieutenant. The rest of the VVV members had a variety of reasons for joining the group. On the long ride to Schofield Barracks on February 25, Kaulukukui

> observed the boys, it was kind of like when you are finally given an opportunity to do something that you thought might never happen. I think the fact that they were taken out of the Territorial Guard, that particular moment, maybe there was a kind of either sadness or bitterness or some state of shock. And then a second time, they said, "Okay, now we'll accept you." . . . [On the way to Schofield] the only conversation I could remember was, "I wonder where we are going? . . . And how is it going to feel with all those other soldiers from other places?" (16–17)

For the most part, the motives of the Japanese American VVV members fell into three categories: "personal" reasons, just "following along," and a sense of historical mission.

Masato Doi was not involved in the earliest negotiations but "when they approached me on that I immediately signed up" (27). Barney Ono missed the first meeting on campus but in downtown Honolulu ran into Hung Wai Ching, who encouraged him to join the small group of five or six who would meet with Shigeo Yoshida to consider their options. Hung Wai offered the Central Branch of the YMCA as a site, since martial law prohibited more than a few persons of Japanese descent from congregating in public. When his zoology professor, Chris Hamre, advised Barney to continue with his pre-med course of study instead of volunteering for the VVV because "we're gonna need doctors," Ono could not agree. "Look, you guys can talk like that, but you know, being Japanese under these circumstances, we just got to go all out" (30).

Ed Nakamura joined the VVV because it just "seemed like it was the right thing to do, . . . but I don't think I had a sense of a mission. I don't think I was that mature. . . . Remember we had all registered for the draft and all that" (19). Claude Takekawa had been in the HTG and surmised that the VVV came about because "some influential people wanted to get something going. . . . I don't think too many of us had any strong feelings about—go fight for the country and things like that."[22]

Unlike most of the others, Himoto regularly conferred with his parents on his decisions, and they were upset about his joining the VVV. "Well, my dad wasn't too happy because after we got thrown out of the Territorial Guard he said, 'What the hell you doing volunteering again.

They don't want you in the army,' you know. 'Why you have to go and volunteer your service a second time?'"[23]

Akira Otani, whose father had been detained by the FBI on December 7, knew that the HTG discharge deliberately targeted the nisei. He was "mad as hell" and went back to campus for his last semester of college but never thought that volunteering for some indeterminate period of service with the VVV was any sacrifice. "Apparently I didn't analyze all this. You just did things, you know. They were looking for people. Fine, let's go. You know the country needs you or whatever—you felt, by golly, let's go." He announced his decision to his mother, who was "very sad," but Akira "didn't give her a chance to tell me whether she liked it or not. It was just a case of telling her I was going." He would eventually be able to tell his father of his decision—but only as a G.I. when "I got in the 442d and I saw him in a concentration camp [in Santa Fe, New Mexico]" (22–23).

After being rejected by the HTG, Yoshiaki Fujitani "didn't do anything. We just stayed at home. Nothing. We kind of felt lost, you know. We were out." The opportunity to join with friends in a meaningful way was "a kind of a salvation, you might say, for—especially for those who were in the HTG. . . . So when they organized the Triple V, then this was something that buoyed our spirits" (22). This sense of personal comradeship was an important element for many others as well.

George Yamamoto enrolled at the university after having worked for five years beyond high school graduation. He was a soft-spoken man of slight build; "I didn't weigh more than a hundred pounds, you know." He had not joined the HTG and did not volunteer for the VVV with the original contingent. George read about the group in the newspapers and knew some of the members—Masato Doi was a good friend, for example—and was able to talk to them when they returned to Honolulu on their breaks. After a month or so, sometime in March 1942, Yamamoto "thought I can't stand just working down there. I have to do my part, I gotta go!" George went to Shigeo Yoshida to inquire about joining the VVV. Yoshida noticed on the application that Yamamoto was from Palama. He looked up and frowned slightly, then read on and was reassured when he saw that Yamamoto was also a university student (37–38). Yoshida at that meeting inadvertently revealed tensions between the university boys and the "street" kids recruited to "balance" the membership.

Yoshida's comments to Yamamoto indicated he was not altogether convinced that incorporating the "Bethel Street gang," as the university

VVV members called them, was such a good idea. (Bethel Street in downtown Honolulu was notorious for its bars and pool halls.) But Ching had more on his mind. Evidently, Hung Wai Ching had decided that a few nonstudents should be included to indicate to the general public that the VVV was broadly reflective of the entire Japanese American community and not merely the "cream of the crop," a term he regularly used for the university boys. Hung Wai was also, although he rarely mentioned this, concerned that the number of volunteers might have been too small to make a positive impact and that this would reflect badly on the loyalty of the Japanese American community: "To be honest with you, I was very disappointed at only 176 kids [actually, 169] . . . I said, 'You bums.' I told them to go back and work some more and get me 500 kids. I didn't put pressure. I thought 500. . . . When you think about it, 176 is not much. I though I'd have to go get some of the gambling, some of the bad kids too, you know. . . . Yeah, save face, too. Come on, not *my* face!"[24]

Hung Wai recruited less than a dozen of these tough and streetwise boys, most from what we would now call an urban ghetto area in Palama, who developed a reputation for being tougher, louder, cruder, and more boisterous than their university counterparts. Several were outstanding amateur boxers, including Anki Hoshijo and Richard Chinen. Hoshijo had a brief professional career in the ring after the war; Chinen, territorial amateur bantamweight champion and a national contender, trained several others to championships in the all-Schofield boxing tournaments.

Yugo Okubo felt that signing up with the VVV had been naïve: "I remember I talked to a guy I always admired. This guy, his name was Sato. He was a very intelligent guy and a friendly guy. He said, 'You volunteered once, why are you going to go for?' We trying to get out there, I said. 'Ah, they don't want you. Why go?' But it didn't register on me at all. I wasn't thinking at all. Let's go. . . . It's a matter of youth. . . . I remember I'd sing the song—the air force had a song, and the last line would go, 'Peace and happiness for all.' And one guy said, 'Eh, this is shit'" (22–24).

Okubo had been reared in a family with strong social justice concerns and was relatively insulated from any sense of cynicism. "You might say . . . I had my Christian hymns speaking to me." He laughed. He recalled the emphasis on being young leaders and on their responsibility as they were being recruited for the VVV.

I remember that they said we were the cream of the crop. That we owed something [he laughed], being the cream of the crop. There was a heavy emphasis on the phrase "social consciousness." . . . They said they were going to have a meeting of all the nisei students. . . . Word of mouth. Oh, guys like Ted [Tsukiyama]. . . . And I think Hung Wai and Yoshida came and spoke to us. . . . At that time, you appreciated anybody coming to help in a cause like that. I remember the few people who did speak up for the Japanese community. I remember Charles Hemenway. I remember the guy who used to speak out against you too [John Balch of Hawaiian Telephone], . . . the American Legion and all those assholes. (22–27)

Yugo was among the 155 original members at the short recognition ceremony on the steps of the university's Hawai`i Hall. Immediately afterward, they boarded a truck for the long ride to Schofield Barracks. He sat next to Masato Doi and recalled bits of that conversation. "I was really praising war. . . . Oh, it was a wonderful thing. It got rid of my miserable life. Boring, unexciting life. Oh, Masato went, but he had a girlfriend and everything else, . . . [so for him] war is bad." Yugo laughed. "[Me], I'm really gung ho. What was I? Eighteen?" (25–27).

Ted Tsukiyama emerged as the principal spokesperson of the university boys and of the VVV as a unit. His English Standard Roosevelt High School education was useful, and his Christian upbringing imbued him with a particular sense of mission. Tsukiyama was uniquely aware of the potentially momentous nature of the VVV. His private experience became the public model of VVV emotion, motivation, dedication, and success. In part, this was due to the peculiar usefulness of his individual case to the social construction of a nisei myth; in part, it was his personal quest for meaning in a world turned hostile and vengeful.

One result is that Ted is often called upon to write and speak of the VVV experience. I sense that this is sometimes resented by a few of his comrades, but no one else seemed willing to invest the time and energy in writing the articles or giving the speeches. In any case, Tsukiyama became the chronicler of the VVV from its inception. He took photographs, kept notes and copies of speeches delivered in 1942, filed copies of letters he wrote to newspapers and public figures, preserved his pay stubs and tax returns from the period.

Ted most dramatically exemplified the disillusioned student whose life was shattered by the HTG's action on January 21: "Overnight you are rejected and you are cast out in that ash heap of society, because of your race and your name and your color" (24). He and a few others were on campus "feeling very down and sorry for ourselves" when Hung Wai Ching persuaded them to move positively. Ted insisted that Hung Wai's contribution be properly acknowledged

> He was one of Charlie Hemenway's boys. He was a Christian worker, a YMCA secretary, and I guess he has his ideals. But the thing about this—he didn't have to do these things. Most of the Chinese can sit back and just try to avoid being mistaken for Japanese and just reap up because the Chinese really made out during the war. Land and business, restaurants, and so forth. They had a great opportunity to make money, and he could have done the same but he was in YMCA work and, of course, he was appointed to the [military] governor's Morale Section and I think that's what he did most of his day. And to this day, his wife resents the fact that he spent so much time serving others. She's quite resentful. Every time we sit down and talk to her she talks about how she was with the first one [child] right after Pearl Harbor and Hung Wai, instead of staying home, would be out at Schofield with us. (25)

When the opportunity to join the VVV appeared, it was a godsend for Ted. "For me, there was no choice. Education was secondary. Now you had something to prove. You going to do it by just keep on going to school or you going to do it by joining this group who, as Hung Wai says, like the Christian, you turn the other cheek" (27). Not everyone felt the same way; many students elected to stay away from the VVV. Tsukiyama was quick to suggest that everyone had the right to make his own decision. "I did what I thought was right for me. They did what they thought was right for them. Who am I to second-guess them? They had to live their lives" (29).

> Every now and then I get somebody coming up to me and saying, you know, we were in the HTG—lamenting and half-apologizing why they couldn't join us.
> Yeah. The fact that 150 of them spontaneously responded in the same manner to me indicates the correctness of and appropriateness of the decision. . . . If the Triple V never happened, I possibly would have joined the Red Cross or gone to join the Corps of Engineers or something. Go out and work. It would make me feel better. I mean, that was not the time to think about education or to think about self-betterment or self-promotion and aggrandizement. . . .
> But some of them stayed back and I always got the feeling, when we used to meet the guys who stayed back and when they saw us, especially

at dances and things like that, they would avoid us because they . . . kind of realized that they were looking after themselves. (28–29)

Ted had staked out a clear position, and at the time his peers respected that. As the university contingent was honored on campus on February 25 just before boarding the trucks to Schofield Barracks, he was asked to speak on behalf of the VVV. Tsukiyama tried to incorporate the feelings of the other students and, in so doing, to articulate their thoughts in the form of a public manifesto.

> We regretfully leave you today to respond to a greater and more immediate task to fulfill. We are foregoing our education and our personal aims and ambitions temporarily that we may answer to the vital needs of the victory efforts of our nation. Meanwhile we ask that you remaining here pursue your studies with greater initiative and dedication, with full appreciation of the fact that it is a great privilege to be able to continue your education in crucial times as these. We will appreciate and welcome any word of remembrance and encouragement from you—never forget that you can do lots to keep up our fighting trim.
>
> As you know, most of us are veterans of the HTG since the outbreak, very much disappointed in the fact that our services were no longer needed there, yet always looking for the possibility of proving ourselves useful in some other phase of our war efforts.
>
> We have been accepted as a labor corps under the Army Engineers. We leave today to assume our new role and share in our nation's all-out victory efforts. We leave then with roughly three aims or purposes in mind.
>
> First, of course, to take an active part in the scheme of national defense and to do our part toward achieving our ultimate victory. Second, through such action, we will demonstrate the extent of our Americanism in its concrete, constructive and active form.
>
> Finally, but not the least important, to set a good and living example of what good Americans can do to help in his country's war efforts and to set the initial pace, to show the way, to break the ice for other groups to demonstrate their Americanism. . . . No matter how tough the going gets, we will always keep in mind those words that were born out of the founding of our great nation, then reiterated and re-emphasized by our own president a few days ago at a time when great American principles of democracy face its acid test, that "the harder the sacrifice, the greater the triumph." (TTC)

This speech was delivered only five weeks after President Roosevelt issued Executive Order 9066, which paved the way for the mass internment of everyone of Japanese descent on the West Coast. There is no indication that Ted received any guidance in drafting this speech. But the month of intense meetings and discussions with men like Yoshida and Ching provided or reinforced several key concepts which appear for the first time in this speech and became cornerstones of the postwar nisei myth. First, the selfless dedication to duty: Ted reminds students who have not volunteered that it is a "great privilege" to continue their schooling in a time when it is "almost imperative" for Americans to respond in some "concrete" fashion.

Second, they are volunteering in the face of unjustified rejection from the HTG. The Japanese American community is the clear focus here. Third, the response is heroic; it will set an example, set the pace, "break the ice," and "show the way." Finally, they are extending the principles of Americanism. There is a determination to appropriate the basic tenets of the nation to validate their cause. The document provided considerable support for those attempting to maintain the fragile racial peace in Hawai`i.

For some of the VVV, like Jackson Morisawa, this interpretation later seemed to reflect the self-serving glorification of unheroic actions by ordinary young men. When Morisawa learned of the original oral history project, he wrote to Yempuku to vigorously denounce the effort. I eventually persuaded him to submit to a videotaped interview, but only after a lengthy discussion of the goals of the project: to explore the real world of Hawaii's nisei males between the 1920s and the 1950s through the device of the VVV experience. With continuing reluctance, Morisawa discussed his version of the meaning of the VVV:

Well, the nucleus of guys forming [the VVV] was mostly university guys and, lot of 'em, I ran around with, so through them I learned that they were going to form; most of us didn't have anything to do, we all joined. [He laughed.] Not thinking any loyalty or anything; I mean honestly, I don't think any of 'em had that in mind.

If people had presented the whole Varsity Victory Volunteer adventure as a serious "We gotta save the Japanese American population" thing. . . . Well, we had something of that sort, but we were really not seriously into that kind of thing; we didn't really think of being patriotic or any that kind of stuff.

Yeah, and after you join, because everybody's doing it you wanna go in there and be part of it, okay. Then maybe afterwards, you going start thinking of what you did and then you find out, maybe, you did the right thing. . . . But at that moment, I don't think anybody felt like that. (20–22)

Ryoji Namba shared Morisawa's sentiments.

All this thing about we should go petition. We should show them that we are loyal and all that stuff. Frankly, it didn't make any difference to me [but] I stayed with them. I wasn't one of them guys who rebelled against anything like that. "It's a good idea. Let's go!" . . .

Me, I think we were too young; not like these days. Nowadays kids are, they are so concerned about environment and like that. They all gung ho. Those days we weren't so, to me anyway, sincere about those things or so engaged. To me, Hung Wai and them and Shigeo Yoshida—those guys were more concerned or gung ho about these things. (28–29)

Shiro Amioka, to his death, maintained a complex understanding of the formation of the VVV, although he did not recall much of the period between the HTG discharge and that formation. Well into late January, Amioka remained in the HTG processing exit papers for his nisei compatriots. As a result, he was not among the handful that began discussions with Hung Wai Ching, Shigeo Yoshida, and John Young. His mother was not unhappy to see him out of the HTG, because she thought it would lead to resumption of his university career. But Shiro quickly teamed up with his old friends. His mother was "not happy about the idea of giving up school" (53).

Amioka was interested in discussing the significance of voluntarism, of its meaning at the time and the complexities that were not necessarily evident to everyone.

Sure it's comfortable going to the university and all that. . . . Why, essentially why do it, you know. You are not wanted. That's the other side of the story. Why do it when you were rejected on unfair grounds? . . . Kind of a justifiable cynicism. Here we tried and they kick us in our teeth. Why go back, why give them the other cheek. [He laughed.]. . . .

Well, you know. We really meant it. . . . Now in the Vietnam years, people would read something like that and people would think, What kind of nonsense is that? but we really meant it, you know. . . . As I said, we weren't skeptical of the system—we, just this aberration we had to counteract, have to come up with something other than just pouting. You got to show them, is the attitude we had and this is one way of doing it.

We didn't know what we were getting into. Whether it would be successful or not. As it turned out, it turned out beautifully all the way around but nobody knew it was going to happen. We didn't know what kind of treatment we were going to get at Schofield, how we would operate. (53)

John Young recalled that everything since Pearl Harbor "was such a shock to them. Half of them didn't know why they . . . were in the VVV. They were so glad to be accepted somewhere; . . . of course, they had no idea that they would be in the army, you know" (10–11). Herbert Isonaga suggested that the VVV record be placed in a context that includes women who rolled bandages for the Red Cross and issei men who were clearing *kiawe* (algaroba; mesquite) trees from the shorelines to deny potential invading forces any cover. "So you know if they were doing that, something like that as aliens, and we as citizens join with the Triple V or even volunteering for service, there really wasn't any conflict" (27). But Isonaga added that Hung Wai was also concerned about the imminent danger to the Japanese community in Hawai`i and "gave a spiel about, you know, how important it was to respond to the negative action taken in the case of the HTG. And, I guess, to counteract future similar actions. And of course Hung Wai, trying to develop this concept of volunteers, he impressed greatly with the real threat of relocating all the Japanese in the territory" (24).

Fewer than one-half of the Japanese Americans who were in the HTG volunteered for the VVV, and it seems reasonable to assume that many simply were too disgusted or hurt to volunteer yet again. There is but one contemporary account of one of these men, who said he had been severely disillusioned by the fact that "we served for a month during the time of greatest danger from invasion; then, when our usefulness was over, we were thrown out. It was probably the shock of being discharged that made us so unreasonable in our attitude; and I really admire those boys from the university who joined the VVV in spite of their conviction that they had been unjustly discriminated against; . . . the eight months have mellowed my attitude considerably. No longer do I feel the weight of crumbled idealism on my shoulders as I used to."[25]

After a day's notice, some 155 university students assembled for the short and simple farewell ceremony on the steps of the university's Hawai`i Hall on February 25, 1942. Their membership varied slightly through that year, but 169 young Japanese American men eventually served in the VVV. The acting president of the university, Arthur Keller, on behalf of President Gregg Sinclair, offered the best wishes of the campus community. As we have seen, Ted Tsukiyama responded on behalf of the VVV.

The Morale Section immediately seized upon the VVV's significance. On March 5, in the Morale Section's "Third Progress Report," the first item referred to the new group:

> One of the most significant activities of the Morale Section has been the formation of the auxiliary labor corps stationed with the 34th Engineers under

Colonel Lyman at Schofield Barracks. The preliminary stages in the organization of this corps which the boys have termed the triple "V" Corps required over two weeks of consultation and conferences. It was not an easy matter for the boys to make the decision they did because of uncertainty as to the reaction of the public, their parents and the possibility of their plan not being acceptable to the Military authorities. For many also this meant sacrificing their schooling just after they had reentered for another semester.

Whatever qualms may have existed in the beginning, the experiment seems to have more than justified itself for there appears to be practically unanimous praise from all quarters. The boys have been genuinely accepted by the engineers with whom they have become associated and they keenly enjoy their work. Public comment has also been on the whole favorable. There are a few skeptics who maintain a wait and see attitude but thus far no unfavorable comments have come to the attention of the Section. (SYC)

The military governor concurred that the two weeks of "consultation and conferences" seemed to be paying handsome dividends. In our interviews, the VVV members themselves studiously avoided discussing the kinds of conclusions noted in the report.

The Emergency Service Committee, in its March 6, 1942, report, also listed the formation of the VVV as one of its major accomplishments. Some of the ESC members evidently worked with Hung Wai in the organizing efforts, having "conferred with Colonel Lyman and other military authorities on matters pertaining to their [the VVV] status."[26]

FOR THE VVV, the remaining ten months of 1942 would constitute the real test: a combination of disciplined labor along with astute public relations actions designed to reintegrate Japanese Americans into the body politic.

World War II begins for Hawai`i. Front page of first extra by the *Honolulu Star-Bulletin* on December 7, 1941. Unlike its rival, the *Honolulu Advertiser*, this paper deliberately refrained from using the term "Japs." Hawaii War Records Depository, #2174-10A, Hamilton Library, University of Hawaii at Manoa. (Courtesy of the *Honolulu Star-Bulletin* and courtesy of the University of Hawaii.)

Hickam Field, December 7, 1941. The U.S. Army Air Force lined up its fighter planes in the middle of the tarmac to deter possible Japanese American "saboteurs." US Army Signal Corps. Hawaii War Records Depository, #1623, Hamilton Library, University of Hawaii at Manoa. (Courtesy of the University of Hawaii.)

University of Hawaii students on steps of Hawaii Hall before leaving for Schofield Barracks as the Varsity Victory Volunteers. *Honolulu Advertiser* photograph, February 25, 1942. Hawaii War Records Depository, #61, Hamilton Library, University of Hawaii at Manoa. (Courtesy of the *Honolulu Advertiser* and courtesy of the University of Hawaii.)

The young men of the VVV worked at a wide variety of manual-labor tasks, including constructing entire buildings on the army base itself. This carpenter gang was led by Unkei Uchima. Courtesy of Ted Tsukiyama (Ted Tsukiyama Collection [TTC]). All following photos courtesy of Ted Tsukiyama and from his collection unless otherwise noted.

For backbreaking work, the VVV sometimes insisted on their "local"gear, stripped down to shorts, period.

Ponds and lakes close to the job site provided welcome breaks for the VVV gangs working on roads and culverts.

Athletics became the major recreational outlet at Schofield Barracks. This outstanding boxing team competed successfully against regular army units on base. *First row, kneeling, l to r:* Takashi Kajihara, Joe Matsunaga, Richard Chinen, coach; *second row, standing, l to r:* Yugo Okubo, Jimmy Miyake, Fumio Serikawa, Wally Nagao, Hiroshi Kato, Dick Uyemura.

The "unlimited" team, one of two VVV teams that competed and did well in Hono-
lulu leagues. It included some players under 135 pounds. *First row, l to r:* Thomas
Shintani, Masaichi Sagawa, Edward Watase, Katsumasa Tomita, Ted Amioka,
Richard Chinen, Yoshio Nakagawa, Claude Takekawa, Eddie Higashino; *second row,
l to r:* Ted Tsukiyama, Stanley Watanabe, Jenhatsu Chinen, Lincoln Masato "Camel"
Yoshimasu, Kenneth "Cannonball" Kawate, Toshiro Kawabe, Raymond Nogawa,
Shiro Amioka, unidentified, Yoshimi Hayashi; *third row, l to r:* Saichi Zakimi, Ronald
Sakamoto, Hiroichi Tomita, Tamotsu Akimoto, Seichi "Champ" Ono, Jackson Mori-
sawa, Warren "Blubba" Higa, Akira Otani, Sumu Furukawa, Hiroshi Minami, Wal-
ter "Joe" Okumoto, Chiyoki Ikeda.

The 135-pound barefoot team playing against Waialae. Note the standard Hawaii-
style uniforms.

The Triple V basketball team, shorter by far than their army counterparts. *First row, l to r:* Hiroichi Tomita, Ed Higashino, Stanley Watanabe, Tsugio Yoshimoto, Jackson Morisawa, Seichi "Champ" Ono; *back row, l to r:* Richard "Sus" Yamamoto, Walter "Joe" Okumoto, Edward Watase, Toshi Nakasone (a "ringer" borrowed from the 232nd Engineers!), Claude Takekawa, Yasuhiro Fujita.

Sukeyoshi Kushi, at one time the territory's nisei golf champion. VVV played after work and continued until, in the 1990s, several were still trying to "shoot their age."

After working without uniforms for a few months, the VVV designed their own. Ted Tsukiyama is in the work denim version at his family's Kaimuki home.

They were mostly college boys, after all: Dick Uyemura in macho stance.

The quarry "gang," under the leadership of Junichi Buto, had the roughest assignment, breaking rocks. *L to r:* Shiro Amioka, Ken Kawate, Ryoji "Bull" Namba, Wally Doi.

"Sus" Yamamoto's gang on the steps of Victory Hall. *First row, l to r:* Hiroichi Tomita, Melvyn Nagasako, John Takara; *second row, l to r:* Tokio Yamaguchi, Ronald "Pippip" Sakamoto, Jackson Morisawa, Ranceford Matsumoto; *top row, l to r:* Yeiyu Miyashiro, Richard Yamamoto, Stanley Watanabe.

Junichi Buto's gang on the steps of Varsity Hall. *First row, l to r:* Shiro Amioka, Teruo Himoto; *second row, l to r:* Hiroshi Minami, Dick Uyemura, Junichi Buto, Atsushi Fujitani; *third row, l to r:* Calvin Tottori, Edward Okazaki, Edward Watase, Wallace Nagao, James Oka; *fourth row:* Ryoji Namba; *top row, l to r:* Hiroshi Kato, James Miyake, Kenneth Kawate.

Masaichi Sagawa's gang on the steps of Volunteers Hall. *First row, l to r:* Jenhatsu Chinen, Saiji Zakimi, Edward Uyemura; *second row, l to r:* Ma Sagawa, Taketo Kawabata; *third row, l to r:* Harry Sato, Ted Amioka, Takashi Kajihara; *fourth row, l to r:* Hideo Kuniyoshi, Kaname Takemoto, Tom Morita; *top row, l to r:* Akio Nishikawa, David Fujita.

Claude Takekawa's gang on the steps of Volunteers Hall. *First row, l to r:* Henry Nagahisa, Henry Morisako, Edwin Higashino, Seichi "Shadow" Hirai; *second row, l to r:* Walter Okumoto, Takashi Shikuma, Yoshimi Hayashi, Claude Takekawa; *third row, l to r:* Raymond Nogawa, Wilfred Mita, Fumio Serikawa; *fourth row, l to r:* Thomas Shintani, Shoso Kagawa, Shigeru Ishii, Akira Otani; *top row:* Isamu Kitagawa.

Robert Kadowaki's gang on the steps of Volunteers Hall. *First row, l to r:* Kikuji Himeda, Tamotsu Akimoto; *second row, l to r:* Shigemitsu Nakashima, David Miura, Yoshio Nakagawa; *third row, l to r:* Tsugio Yoshimoto, Stanley Ichihara, Terry Suzuki, Daniel Betsui; *top row, l to r:* Tom Maeda, Robert Kadowaki, Yasuhiro Fujita.

The VVV boys are ready for a weekend on the town, about four o'clock on a Friday afternoon.

Yuriko (Shimokawa) Tsunehiro, a VVV friend who helped with the luau for Wisconsin GIs at Schofield. The VVV spearheaded an effort to host them in appreciation for the decent treatment accorded to the 100th Battalion nisei who trained at Fort McCoy, Wisconsin, in 1942.

Picnic in Moanalua Gardens in Honolulu, not far from Pearl Harbor. The VVV eventually won over the men of the 34th Engineers, to which the VVV were officially attached. Several, including Harold Molberg (kneeling in middle) and Al Cataldi (standing), became regular participants at VVV social functions.

Many of the VVV pledged to purchase one war bond a month. *L to r:* George Tokuyama, Henry Oyasato, and Yoshiharu Mikami, June, 1942.

Beer bust with some 34th Engineers. Captain Richard Lum, in army uniform, seated on bottom step.

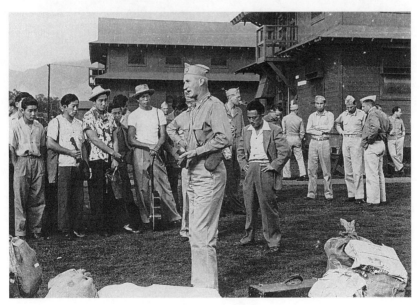

Colonel Silkman, 34th Combat Engineer Regiment, thanking the VVV at deactivation in January 1942. Recognizable, from left: Akio Nishikawa, Hiroshi Minami, Richard Uyemura, Kats Tomita, Hiroshi Kato. Ralph Yempuku is to Silkman's right.

Deactivation ceremonies at Iolani Palace, January 1943. *L to r:* Gregg
Sinclair, president of University of Hawaii; Captain Richard Lum;
Ernest Kai, acting governor, Territory of Hawaii; Lieutenant Thomas
Kaulukukui, Ralph Yempuku. Hawaii War Records Depository, #770,
Hamilton Library, University of Hawaii. (Courtesy of the *Honolulu Star
Bulletin* and courtesy of the University of Hawaii.)

1

Schofield Barracks

or about a year, at Schofield Barracks in Wahiawa, Oahu, the
men of the Varsity Victory Volunteers worked on a wide variety of tasks, from painting buildings and constructing field
iceboxes to quarrying rocks in the nearby mountains. In this
same year, approximately 120,000 residents of Japanese descent on the West Coast were being forcibly removed to concentration camps in the North American interior. Two-thirds
were U.S. citizens. No one was charged with any crime and
none was provided any hearing. Thousands more were being herded into even worse conditions in Canada, while hundreds of Japanese Latin Americans, mostly Peruvians, were
kidnapped from their countries and brought to the United
States.

For at least a year, no one could be sure what would become of the 160,000 Japanese Americans in Hawai`i. Indeed,
the formation and behavior of the VVV became part of a resolution avoiding the mass internment planned by many, including some of President Franklin Roosevelt's key advisers.

Japanese Americans were a problematic group in Hawai`i.
They comprised the largest single ethnic group and had the
potential to become either a highly charged force in the
American war effort or a military nightmare. The year 1942
would be critical to the war effort in the Pacific and the future of race relations in the islands. It was primarily in this
year, therefore, that the "Japanese question" was resolved in
some very intricate ways; this chapter seeks to unravel the
most important of them.

181

ON THE DAY the VVV left for Schofield, February 25, 1942, the *Honolulu Star-Bulletin* provided front-page coverage with a photograph. The accompanying article reported that, with "simple ceremonies marking their entry into a new patriotic endeavor and symbolizing a display of unselfish contribution to the territory's defense, 155 Americans of Japanese ancestry, many among them former Hawaii Territorial guards, were tendered an aloha program by a University of Hawaii convocation." In an unusual move, the paper printed all the names of volunteers who had been part of the HTG. The same issue included an editorial that addressed the significance of the event:

> This is more than an incident for passing notice.
> It is an illustration of one of manifold ways in which Americans of Japanese ancestry can serve their country in time of emergency. . . . The remedy for their difficult situation is basically with these young Americans of Japanese ancestry themselves.

First, the *Star-Bulletin* editorial insisted, Japanese Americans had to realize that it was Japan that had "forced this situation on them and on all Americans." Second, they had to accept as inevitable a degree of suspicion among Americans, especially those with little exposure to this "second generation." Third, Japanese Americans must behave absolutely beyond reproach and bear "cheerfully the inconveniences to which they may be put." Finally, "they must do as this group of 155 young citizens has done—seek out and find a way to serve their country." This editorial encapsulated the ideological underpinnings of the entire strategy of absorbing Japanese Americans into the Hawaiʻi body politic.

Simply put, the analysis and resolution of the problem ran as follows. The *Star-Bulletin*, along with the Big Five and the military, had inherited a terrible situation precipitated by the attack from Japan. The identity of the enemy created a difficult situation for Japanese Americans, but they, in spite of their victim status, must be responsible for improving their lot through "loyal conduct" and "absolute regard for the spirit and the letter of our laws and regulations." Thus, the VVV became a metaphor for exemplary behavior for any victimized minority and the starting point of a generalized ethnic myth to be used in transcending racism.

This new strategy established a particular racialized order that continues to dominate Hawaii's race relations. It has become a system that requires a general tolerance of racial differences but insists that victims of social injustice bear the burden of overcoming its barriers—as the VVV and the entire nisei generation had presumably demonstrated. This ideology essentially validates the status quo, requiring little from power holders. In 1942, however, the VVV and the nisei did not reconstruct the racial climate on their own; they had a variety of supporters among the military and Big Five.

Officially designated the Corps of Engineers Auxiliary, the VVV was attached to the Thirty-fourth Combat Engineers Regiment commanded by Lieutenant Colonel William Sexton. A largely New York outfit whose varied history dated to World War I, the Thirty-fourth was part of the Hawaiian Department of Army Engineers commanded by Colonel Albert Lyman, the first Native Hawaiian to graduate from West Point. It was Lyman who had approved the request to have the Japanese Americans attached to the engineers as a volunteer labor battalion.[1]

The VVV were federal civil service employees and received monthly wages of about $100, against which various charges were levied. Ted Tsukiyama kept his pay envelopes. His statement for the month of June 1942, a typical one, included an itemized breakdown of deductions, including food, laundry, war bonds, quarters, retirement, and $1 for an "organization fund." This left him with $45.75 take-home pay. As unit leaders, Tsukiyama and Yempuku earned somewhat more than the other VVV men, who were paid $90 per month. The men even paid for their own clothing; in mid-1942, they designed a uniform of sorts but bought their outfits. Even at these wages, the men of the VVV earned enough to pay federal and territory income taxes for the year; Ted kept receipts for $25.50 paid to the U.S. Treasury Department and $2 to the territory tax collector (TTC).

Serious economic discrimination plagued large segments of the Japanese American community. But for other ethnic groups, even the teenagers among them, war-related jobs paid well. Agnes Chun, for example, was a sixteen-year-old Chinese American who dropped out of McKinley High School to work at Pearl Harbor as a messenger for $90 a month. Mary Samson Hendrickson, fifteen years old, was released from school to work in the Women's Air Raid Defense unit on Kauai and collected $120 each month.[2]

Captain Richard Lum, army liaison in direct command of the VVV, appeared at Schofield on February 28, three days after the VVV itself arrived on base. He knew that he was the second choice for the job. "It was rumored from Hung Wai and the other boys that Colonel Gilbert, professor of military science and tactics up at McKinley High School, was first chosen. They found out he was kind of prejudiced—didn't like Japanese boys, see. They scrounged around and picked me for this duty" (9).

Captain Lum reported to Colonel Sexton and relayed daily assignments to the VVV via Ralph Yempuku; he also acknowledged, much later, a covert responsibility: censoring VVV mail, observing the men, and providing intelligence for the entire Schofield base. In his intelligence capacity, he reported directly to Colonel K. S. Vandergriff, head of G-2 at Schofield. "That's the officer who spoke to me about vigilance and my taking over troops," Lum remembered. "They had a group of all Japanese boys who volunteered as laborers in the post. And if there was anything unusual, I thought was wrong, I had to report it. . . . I was assigned as assistant S2 with the regiment. I was also the censor officer of the VVV. . . . I read all the mail in the regiment, including the VVVs that left Schofield. No one could use the phone. So all had to write letters back, right?" (8–10).

Lum was directly ordered to be alert for communist activity; he had operatives throughout Schofield spying on the rest of the troops for possible "subversive" doings. "We had a lot of instructions, a lot of directives on the communism [threat], as I told you. Now I realize the part I participated in have some bearing. . . . Much more so than watching the boys. And we got a lot of reports from certain troops; . . . yes, communism was moving in and our intelligence was concerned" (10). By the beginning of World War II, then, the U.S. government was actively engaged in anticommunist surveillance among the troops, presaging the post–World War II terror unleashed against left-wing movements throughout the nation, including a concerted effort in Hawai`i.[3]

Hung Wai Ching said he was not aware that Lum was performing an intelligence function while commanding the VVV, and the nisei themselves were certainly not apprised; whether they would have resented this is unclear. With half a century of hindsight, they accept that such surveillance was a reasonable precaution, given the temper of the times and the high stakes of the VVV experiment. Ching recalled: "I go and eat with you guys several times. . . . One of my jobs anyway. Let's put it that way—to talk with the boys." Would this qualify as informal surveillance? "Yeah. That's what it was. No more than that" (18).

Selection of the officers serving with Lum became another key element. Lieutenant Frank Judd served for a time. From the prominent, missionary/Big Five–descended Judd family, he provided impeccable haole credentials. His father had been a chaplain for the National Guard and his uncle was a former governor, Lawrence M. Judd.[4] Frank Judd also played in the 1930s on the offensive line for the University of Hawaii.

Lieutenant Thomas Kaulukukui had served with many of the boys in the HTG. Hung Wai felt that his athletic and ethnic attributes were powerful public relations assets and negotiated with the army for an instant commission. Ching also made another point: "I had something to do with [selecting] Tommy. I said, 'Wooch [General Fielder], make him a second lieutenant.' . . . Make him feel good, you know. Shit. He doesn't have to go out [to Schofield]. Why should he go out? He had a full-time job here. . . . I think he liked the kids. He's impressed. He want to do his job. That's Tommy" (40).

Tom Kaulukukui was married in 1941, and so left his new bride to volunteer both for the HTG and the VVV. At Schofield, he had VVV member Kenneth Saruwatari, who later became a judge, drive him home nearly every afternoon and back to base in the morning. Kaulukukui never regretted the decision to volunteer. "It was not by an order. . . . When they said, 'Well, we are going. Won't you come along with us?' 'Yes,' I said, 'I'll go.' . . . To me, as I observed the boys, it was kind of like when you are finally given an opportunity to do something that you thought might never happen; . . . they were taken out of the Territorial Guard, that particular moment, maybe there was a kind of either sadness or bitterness or some state of shock. 'I live here all my life and now they tell me I cannot [serve].' And then a second time they said, 'Okay, now we'll accept you'" (14–17).

Minoru Oyasato, the fictional protagonist in Kaulukukui's short story mentioned earlier, reflected on the ride to Schofield, which was "uneventful and everyone present was silent. . . . Somehow my mind was filled with thoughts of the future, the futility perhaps of this sacrifice when all was over. Will my sacrifices be in vain? Will there be a place for me and my friends in this community when our side has won? Will the fact that but a small minority of 135 boys help in this proof for loyalty?"[5]

Kaulukukui's piece is solidly based in historical experience in nearly every verifiable aspect, from descriptions of the barracks to real names of characters and descriptions of work and sports events. (Most of the VVV men saw Kaulukukui as a friendly but relatively inconsequential officer attached to provide recreational direction; I think they underestimated his interest in them and his keen insights.) As the volunteers were assembled at Schofield and introduced to their barracks, Kaulukukui's story describes an abrupt transition to a world of bunk-lined buildings, although his protagonist is relieved to find "hot and cold water facilities and all the conveniences of home. Setting up cots, foot-lockers and nails for hanging clothes took up most of the day; . . . the least of my expectations was being served beans at my first meal."[6]

Ralph Yempuku recalled his own first impression:

> It wasn't too bad because I had been living like that all of my life. But I felt for the other guys. . . . Some of them came from pretty well-to-do families, like Akira Otani like that; you know—Otani market. He's got a beautiful home and all of a sudden he's got to live with twenty, thirty people in the same room
>
> After we started living up there in Schofield, we used to have quite a few—not altercations, not fistfights, but confrontations with haoles. (38)

Kaulukukui recalled that these confrontations were anticipated and that restrictions were designed to minimize unsupervised contact between the nisei and the rest of the troops at Schofield.

> I think the tension mounted when they got there. . . . They told us that the guys in the next area were from Arkansas and other places. They don't know how a Japanese look like; they haven't even seen a Japanese. "So don't venture out." . . . For me and the others in uniform, it wasn't so bad . . . because we were in uniform, . . . the same uniform as everybody else. But all the boys, they were not in uniform.
>
> Captain Lum was the one who issued the bulletin and he's the one that told Ralph that the orders were from the top brass not to go "over there" [beyond their barracks]. When it was dark, the boys had their area. The three barracks were line up like this. There's one, two, three [in a row] and there was another barrack for the cafeteria with a kitchen and the office. . . . About ten or fifteen yards on either side of the barracks was an imaginary line with a warning for the boys not to go beyond it. . . . It was a safety measure. I don't think they made any verbal objection. Maybe deep down inside they might have resented it at the beginning. . . . There was a PX but they couldn't go in there either. (17–22)

Kaulukukui sympathized with the Japanese American volunteers but understood that there was ample potential for mischief. The restrictions were relaxed as their reputation for hard work spread and they became part of the routine at Schofield. Tommy also recalled that every truck transporting a VVV work gang included armed guards.

> My first reaction really, at that time, was that it was too bad that every time the truck went somewhere, two regular army men went along. One sat in front with a carbine and one sat in the back on the truck with the boys. . . . As the year went by, it was kind of relaxed; . . . the guy never hung on to his rifle like before. . . . The attitude changed. To me, it was not the other guys who caused the change, but the friendliness of [the VVV]. (22)

Of course, the navy had been hardest hit at Pearl Harbor; as a result, the animosity was intense. Buses between Honolulu and Schofield stopped at Pearl. The buses were filled with troops returning from weekend leaves with a few last drinks under their belts. Yugo Okubo was part of the kitchen gang, which did not require any guards. But he did remember the bus rides back to Schofield after his weekly days off in Honolulu: "I used to hate the rides back to camp. You had to ride the bus full of GIs and sailors. . . . Well, they made all kinds of [racial] cracks. . . . And you are in civilian clothes too. . . . Most of the guys are quiet; once in a while you find assholes" (38). It is, in retrospect, surprising that the presence of one—or a few—Japanese Americans on the buses did not trigger serious incidents.

These were no more than weekly episodes for the VVV, but for the bus drivers, some of whom were Japanese Americans, it was a difficult daily grind. Fred Kaneshiro was among the bus drivers grateful to be hired by the Honolulu Rapid Transit Company, a company widely known to have discriminated against Japanese Americans before the war. But the wartime labor shortage forced employers to change their practices as so many non-Japanese moved on to more lucrative jobs in the defense industry, especially at Pearl Harbor's naval shipyard. Kaneshiro recalled the problems he encountered while driving busloads of drunken servicemen back to their base:

> And when these service guys—marines, soldiers—when they get little high, oh, they see you're an Oriental. They throw all kind of wisecrack. And you can't do nothing, you alone, . . . but those days we were protected by roving protectionists. Had big Samoan guys, Hawaiians. Tough guys. They just follow some small drivers, see that they are okay. 'Cause I have seen these guys that go out and protect us. I've seen how they've beat up some soldiers and marines because they were giving the young, small oriental drivers bad time.[7]

Teru Himoto related encounters with GIs that illustrated racial stereotyping but indicated something of the humorous context in which it could at times be located. "There wasn't a lot of actual prejudice. . . . And they didn't know one Japanese, you know. They think me—I was Portuguese! 'Cause mainland haoles, they don't know what one Japanese look like anyway. . . . 'Oh shit, you're not a . . . ?' One said, 'I know when I see a Jap.' He said, 'They all get slant-eye.' I said, 'You dumb haole. You go in the battlefront, you never going find one slant-eye Japanese. By the time you recognize, you'll be shot,' I told him."[8]

Ralph Yempuku was the key figure for the VVV at Schofield; Ted Tsukiyama was his executive assistant, and Hank Oyasato helped with paperwork. Yempuku was a serious taskmaster; Hung Wai called him "Nap," for Napoleon, and many of the VVV men fondly referred to him as "Caesar" and "Dictator." The twelve work gangs were identified by their gang leaders: Junichi Buto, Richard Chinen, Masato Doi, Chiyoki Ikeda, Robert Kadowaki, Sukeyoshi Kushi, Henry Oyasato, Masaichi Sagawa, Claude Takekawa, Harry Tanaka, Unkei Uchima, and Richard Yamamoto.

Most of the gangs developed some form of expertise, including carpentry and cooking. Perhaps the most notable was Buto's quarry gang, made up of the brawniest members, that spent the year breaking boulders, shoveling rocks, and building stone walls. When Assistant Secretary of War John McCloy visited Hawai'i in late March 1942, Hung Wai Ching personally escorted him up into the mountains to ensure official recognition of the serious dedication to task and country being demonstrated by these young Japanese Americans. Watching the VVV at work may have reduced McCloy's own misgivings about including the nisei in combat units. Within a few months of that visit, McCloy played a key role in the decision to form the segregated nisei 442d Regimental Combat Team.[9]

Among the quarry-gang members were Teru Himoto, Bull Namba, and Shiro Amioka. Himoto recalled seeing McCloy visit while they fed rocks into the crusher up at Kolekole Pass—the gap in the Waianae Range through which Japanese planes flew en route to Pearl Harbor. As one of the larger and stronger volunteers—more than five and one-half feet tall and about 150 pounds—Teru Himoto broke and shoveled rocks for most of the eleven months. Himoto was known as one of the hardest workers in the group. But not everyone was as diligent.

Ryoji Namba knew there were "goof-off" types, the perennial army "goldbricks." For some reason, Namba thought, Ralph Yempuku actually liked these guys who drifted off when work was to be done or who feigned illness with the best. But they were certainly not in the quarry gang, which had a fierce and tenacious work ethic: "I tell you, we worked! . . . I mean, we put in good eight-hour jobs" (37–38).

Shiro Amioka decided that "busting rocks" was the gang for him. At just over five feet and barely 130 pounds, Shiro stood out as a cub among bears. In fact, "Cub" was his nickname, according to the booklet published by the VVV as it disbanded in February 1943. In the publication, some twenty-eight men were targeted with personal, often cutting, highlights—much after the then-current fashion of providing such tidbits for graduating seniors in high school yearbooks. The booklet informed readers that Cub "was the toughest, the sweetest and the workingest little guy in the quarry gang."[10] Yutaka Nakahata, the editor, was in the Kadowaki gang, which did some heavy work, including building roads, "but not as heavy as the quarry gang; . . . see, those were the big guys and I was surprised that Shiro Amioka was in that gang, you know. Shiro is not a big guy. But that group had a lot of husky guys and I heard that they had a tough job" (47).

Amioka had served in headquarters duty with the HTG—filing and typing. He had good administrative and clerical skills, but when Yempuku tapped him for office work with the VVV, Amioka objected.

> You see, I'm small and Ralph Yempuku was a civilian director and he figured I'm small and of course I have this personnel background. . . . So I told him, "Ralph, hey, no way . . . I didn't come out here to work in an office. This is a volunteer labor battalion. I want the toughest outfit you can find. I want to be with the quarry gang." . . . He looked at me. "Well, you're too small." I said, "Well, we'll see. We'll see." He says, "Okay. If you want to go, you go." Hard work—I tell you. Oh, the first day I came back, soon as I came back, I took a shower bath; I was dead. [He laughed.] They kind of laughed because it was rough. Fortunate because it was early—get in the bunk and sack out. . . . Oh, I died a thousand deaths. But me and my big mouth. I asked for it. . . . Oh, you develop strength. So it was a good experience. (61–65)

Young men of the quarry gang took great pride in the "manly" nature of their task, and Hung Wai was quick to exploit its pick-and-shovel image to the fullest with influential visitors like McCloy.

The soldiers assigned to guard the VVV quickly became their comrades. Masato Doi recalled that "we got along very well with the people that were directly in contact with us" (30). Sergeant Al Cataldi, one of the guards, became a good friend and appears in photos of the VVV members on social outings, along with nisei coeds at picnics and parties. For the twenty-fifth VVV reunion in 1967, Raymond Ginnetti, another guard, was invited back to Hawaiʻi to join the men he had guarded in 1942. He recalled that "at first it was strange for both sides—with the GIs wondering what their purpose was and the Japanese boys wondering what would happen to them next. But the relationship between the two sides was remarkable; there was never any conflict."[11]

Perhaps the most visible and best known gang was the kitchen crew led by Richard Chinen, the tough boxer, described in the VVV booklet as "the bull of the kitchen. His menacing presence in the mess hall made even the worst GI beans taste decent." He was also "a swell guy in any man's army."[12] Several of his kitchen crew were extremely forthcoming with stories about this remarkable man and his gang. They all had vivid memories of Chinen, who by the time of our interviews had suffered a stroke and could not participate. Ed Nakamura thought he was extraordinary, a

> highly intelligent guy who had not had the opportunity to go to college. He—if you talked about people with a sense of mission, maybe you could talk about people like him. Here's this guy who's a boxer. He's coming into this group of all college kids and he's leading this kitchen crew and everybody would be depending on him to feed the group. He could be a tyrant but at the same time he was a very compassionate person. People in the kitchen were very loyal to him; . . . every now and then he would get tough with the kitchen people that he thought weren't doing their jobs. And I think the group was better for having people like that. All of the university kids finding out a little bit more about the other kids. They were all part of the same thing. (20–21)

Herb Isonaga volunteered for the kitchen crew, having cooked for his family on Kauai and developed an interest in cooking. Herb recalled that Richard Chinen was "a wonderful person, but he was not an easy person to get along with." "I think there was this conflict in terms of university versus nonuniversity feeling. Richard was an independent person. So I think it was a constant between Richard and Ralph [Yempuku], where Ralph would have to tell Richard, 'Eh, Richard, you know we can't do it that way.' For example, Richard was in charge of the Triple V boxing team and he had an excellent boxing team. . . . Ralph would do whatever he could for the team but there were limitations; . . . maybe

Richard would like to schedule a match, taking the boys on a working day into town to have training or whatever" (35–36).

Yugo Okubo weighed a mere 120 pounds when he joined the Triple V: "I looked at all the food and I volunteered for permanent KP; . . . I couldn't think of a better place. . . . Being with the kitchen—it was kind of a small group, you know. You were always kind of free" (28). Richard was "an organizer and he likes to be in the limelight. Likes to be around people. He likes to have twenty people in the kitchen working, even though they're not working. Being intellectuals, we cut the crew down into half. We worked every other day" (35). While everyone praised the quality of the food and Chinen's legendary ability to barter and secure treasured staples, especially rice, there were some concerns about the diet, Okubo said. "It's just that Richard cooked only starch. We never had any training or anything. We just cooked the way we cooked at home . . . macaroni, hamburger, sandwich, coldcuts, . . . beef stew, beef tomato. One time, Richard Chinen was the mess chief; he made rice, spaghetti, and potato salad and there was a big uproar. 'You can't use a starch diet.'" He laughed. "Oh, it was the college-trained sense of nutrition" (29–32).

Rice, spaghetti, and potato or macaroni salad would today still make an acceptable "plate lunch" for many Hawai`i residents, although this lo-cal version of fast-food take-out platters now includes more protein and, at times, salads or vegetables. There is, however, a venerable working-class tradition of tasty starches, which were both filling and inexpensive, and it took some courage to complain to or about Chinen. Yutaka Naka-hata recalls leaving the table a bit hungry at times and being disappointed with the occasional lunch, especially when it featured white rice topped with sardines right out of the cans.[13]

John Young, from the Nuuanu YMCA, made regular trips to visit the VVV. He recalls arriving at about seven in the evening and leaving at ten—just to talk: "I mean, I just tried to be a good friend. You couldn't do much more." Young drove into Schofield with news and gifts from VVV families. Just before leaving the army base, he often backed his car close to the kitchen and Richard Chinen "arranged" to have his trunk stuffed with cans of tomatoes, coffee, and other foods that were difficult to secure in wartime Honolulu. "But these boys never liked tomatoes," Young said. "They didn't drink much coffee and . . . , of course, you know the army. You're given a certain amount and if you don't use it, they throw it away. Well, Richard Chinen was smart. But I just realized at the last of the war, if those guys [the guards] had opened [the trunk of the car]. . . . Either Richard would have been shot or I would. . . . It was a crazy thing to do. It was fun" (11–12).

Richard recruited several other young men, including Anki Hoshijo and Roy Nakamine, also excellent boxers. Hoshijo's son, Leonard, recalled that his father was available partly because "no Japanese were allowed in Pearl Harbor, no job."[14] Chinen once quit and left for Honolulu, an incident some of the kitchen-gang members do not remember, but it was of major import to Ralph Yempuku, who immediately left to retrieve his chief cook. Yempuku recalled that Chinen was upset by the seemingly endless meetings to discuss the war or current events or morale within the VVV; Chinen "didn't care for that. You know, he figure, I'm here doing my job and that's enough. I was much closer to Richard than anybody else. I knew him very, very well. I figured, 'Hey, without him we'd be in trouble.' Anybody else can go out AWOL and goodbye, but not Richard. So I went out there and finally got hold of him and talked to him, talked to him. And, finally, I brought him back." He laughed. "Yeah, I tell you, Richard was real upset for awhile but then he cooled off and then he organized a boxing team."[15]

Yugo Okubo, who was among those who did not remember this incident, suggested that one precipitating factor may have been the few university types who voiced objections to the recruitment of the Palama–Bethel Street urban toughs, Chinen's good friends. Okubo "was very close to him. He might have left temporarily and it might have been big at that time, but as I look back, it was a very small matter. But he took it very personally when some people objected to his buddies coming into the outfit." Richard Chinen evidently liked Yugo, however, and made him "mess sergeant and all that. I had an easy life." Yuko laughed. "And he used to take me to the fights, too" (34).[16]

The kitchen gang quickly reduced its tasks to a routine. Its two crews, working on alternate days, could go every other day into Honolulu, lounge around the barracks, or play golf. On those off-duty days, Yugo Okubo would sleep late and fix himself a great breakfast, "which the other people never ate." Then he would "play golf, come back, eat your lunch. . . . Some of the guys working used to give me dirty looks" (35). Even during working hours, there was opportunity for at least a few to take evasive action. Yugo remembered that they called Ralph Toyota "Houdini." Why? "Every time there was work, he disappeared" (31). Kitchen-crew member Warren Higa, who was sometimes physically taunted by Chinen, provided fun for the VVV booklet: "More fat than brawn, slower than an ox cart, he was aptly named 'Blubber.' He had a thundering voice, full of sound and phooey. He loved to mold himself into a chair, especially at work."[17]

Still, the kitchen gang had to be up at three or four in the morning, well before the other men, to fire up the oil-burning kitchen stoves to prepare breakfast, as well as lunches for those who would be out in the field. Herb Isonaga helped scramble the eggs, usually powdered. The bread was brought in, but Kats Tomita baked their pastries. The VVV booklet praised Tomita as a "paragon of goodness. Kats had his lighter moments but he was usually serious. He took his baking seriously. He took his reading seriously. And he took his girls seriously."[18]

Isonaga remembered the worst of the jobs: "Yeah, and the bacon came in cans thick with fat, hardly any meat portion, which we had to slice by hand—terrible stuff," he laughed. "Or Spam" (30–31).[19] Dinner was served early—about 5:30 P.M.—so cleaning up could be left to some while others joined sports, poker, movies, lectures, or other activities.

Ralph Yempuku felt the kitchen gang worked as hard as the others. "After all, what did they know about cooking?" He laughed. "The same thing with these other men. They didn't know how to pound nails or saw wood or anything. But they had to learn in a hurry, because they started the very next day."[20]

A few of the VVV men left during the course of the year. Taketo Kawabata, for example, returned to Kona on the Big Island of Hawai`i for four months to help his family with its annual coffee harvest, an extremely labor-intensive process. He sent several ten-pound bags of pure Kona coffee for the VVV and returned in mid-January 1943, shortly before the group disbanded.

Yoshiaki Fujitani eventually requested a discharge. He worked in the Kadowaki gang and remembered being "very, well, happy at the end of the day, all pooped out" (23–25). The roller-coaster ride of highs and lows in early 1942 had affected the young Fujitani deeply. Participation in the ROTC on December 7 and service in the HTG were positive memories; being discharged was disquieting; joining the VVV gave him a sense of being useful, working with his comrades. On the first day at Schofield Barracks, he went to the PX to buy a box of cigars for his father, then the bishop of Jodo Shinshu Buddhism in Hawai`i. This bit of extravagance did not strike him as odd, even though his father "never smoked cigars. Crazy." When his father was arrested by the FBI and removed to the mainland as a "potentially dangerous enemy alien" in April,

Yoshiaki was stunned and simply gave up on the VVV. "Suddenly, I thought, heck with it. . . . And so immediately I asked for a discharge" (23–25). No one questioned his decision or tried to dissuade him.

There were a few unusual assignments for the VVV members. For six weeks in the summer of 1942, Masato Doi and Barney Ono worked on a YMCA project, the Junior Victory Brigade, which employed boys aged twelve to fifteen. The project was proposed as early as May 6, 1942, to deal with boys not yet old enough to be employed but certainly capable of mischief. The Morale Section anticipated problems with this group because so many parents were at work and home life was unsupervised; the schools, police, health, and other social agencies were also concerned. These junior high school boys, provided room and board at Central Intermediate School in Honolulu, worked in the mornings and enjoyed supervised recreation in the afternoons and evenings.[21] Ono and Doi were evidently on loan from the VVV to help supervise—the boys maintained vegetable gardens and public facilities, including the bomb shelters that had been dug everywhere; they also earned pocket money by doing yard work for families willing to pay. This project fulfilled two objectives: First, it helped to maintain wartime morale by providing supervised employment and recreation while school was out; second, and more important, it publicized the value of nisei contributions, actual and potential.[22]

On at least one occasion, some of the VVV were farmed out to build furniture for a community child-care facility supervised by Jane Albritton (then Jane Christman). On December 7, 1941, Albritton was busily creating a small library for a preschool program in Teacher's College but the war put a halt to that venture. She then went to work at the Quartermasters Corps at Fort Shafter, an army base in Honolulu, where she quickly convinced her superiors that establishing day-care centers would free up many mothers for the labor force. They used former Japanese-language-school facilities, and Albritton was assigned to one of them, along with Pearl Kaneshige (now Yamashita), Irene Elam, and Ruth Kuwata. Two of these women were of Japanese descent; the men were not alone in rendering wartime service. "We needed cots—oh we needed lots of things," Albritton wrote to me, "*AND* it was the *VVV Boys* who made everything for us. They were wonderful . . . (who in the world would doubt that kids of any ancestry growing up in Hawaii were loyal)."[23]

On at least one occasion, there was official recognition for the VVV contribution. Four of the men received a special commendation from Lieutenant Colonel William Sexton, regimental commander of the Thirty-fourth, "for the skill and speed with which they constructed the Adjutant's Office." George Oka, Edwin Honda, Shuichi Hashizume, and Edward Okazaki "planned and constructed the office in a period of four days; . . . [they] voluntarily worked from three to four hours overtime every day."[24]

The VVV's first major assignment was the construction of prefabricated houses. The Volunteers graduated to six large warehouses and a large repair shop. In the space of a year, they strung miles of barbed wire to defend against potential invasion; quarried tons of rock; crafted numerous articles such as field iceboxes, desks, chairs, tables, lamps, blackboards, bulletin boards, mess-hall furniture, and trophy cases. Yutaka Nakahata recalled that for several days, he and Johnny Takara moved coils of barbed wire around the base (49). The VVV completed one road project and began two others. The men built a washing ramp and renovated their regimental headquarters, as well as the regimental supply office and officers' quarters. They "blacked out" the Post Bowl.[25] (Buildings that were potential targets of nighttime bombing raids often had their windows painted black to keep the light from giving away their location.)

Life at Schofield was highly structured. The VVV six-day, forty-eight-hour workweeks were systematically supplemented with social activities, educational opportunities, recreation, and highly organized athletic contests. Much of the men's activity was chronicled in yet another of their "extracurricular" efforts, a newsletter, *The Volunteer,* first published on May 16, 1942, about ten weeks after their arrival at Schofield. Edited by Yutaka Nakahata, it ran faithfully through number 37, dated January 23, 1943, when the group disbanded. Other contributors included Soji (Jackson) Morisawa, Kenichi Uyeda, Shoso Kagawa, Shigemitsu Nakashima, Wilfred Mita, Melvyn Nagasako, Hiroshi Tokuyama, and Henry Oyasato. The first issue ran an editorial, "Lest We Forget . . . ," which included the text of the original petition to Emmons. Nakahata implored the VVV to remember that the public was "likely to judge our loyalty in terms of the effort and energy we put into our work." He also reminded them: "If this were any country other than America, we would never have been given the opportunity to demonstrate our loyalty. That opportunity to demonstrate our loyalty, that opportunity which has been granted us is a trust. It is, as well, a challenge."[26] The first editorial column announced a competition for names for the paper; by the June 6 edition, one had been selected: *The Varsity Victory Volunteer (The VVV)*.

Since the VVV had no official uniform, they held a contest to design an emblem—Junichi Buto's entry (a soaring eagle encircled by stars) was judged the best. Nakahata was the logical choice to edit the newsletter, he told me, since he had worked on the University of Hawaii's student paper, *Ka Leo O Hawaii* ("The Voice of Hawaii"), as well as the school yearbook, *Ka Palapala* (32). The army censored the newsletter, of course. Nakahata once playfully tested the censors by including an article on nicknames of the VVV members, one of whom was known as Chinpo (Japanese slang for penis—"dick"); perhaps it was reassuring to learn that the offending passage was detected and deleted (52).

Other contests through the year included a call for slogans—one each for work, the barracks, and overall use. Kenichi Uyeda won the grand prize with "Work up a sweat, and the sun will set." Stanley Kimura's "Cleanliness leads to Healthiness," won for use in the barracks, and Walter Iwasa's "Let not our efforts be in vain" took honors for general use (*The VVV*, May 30). (Sloganeering does not appear to have been one of the VVV's special gifts.)

The social calendar for the VVV—primarily young college men— sometimes resembled that of a typical fraternity. Although dates, dances, and parties were reserved for weekends, nearly every issue of *The VVV* included a report of a previous party, plans for the next dance, or notice of an upcoming event. Some of the dances were hosted by women on the university campus, especially Japanese American coeds from two of the dorms, Hale Laulima and Hale Aloha. These dances were generally held on Sunday afternoons at the campus center named for Charles Hemenway, the university regent so supportive of Japanese American and other students.

The VVV of September 19 included a reminder that there was to be a "social" the next day, where they would "dance to the music of Corporal Gordon 'Red' Smith's Sunspotters, a 17-piece orchestra noted for its fine, 'in-the-groove' brass team, and novel string section made up of violins." It would be held from one to five P.M. Kats Tomita led the delegation that would escort the women from Hale Aloha and Hale Laulima to the dance in Hemenway Hall. The cochairs were Daniel

Betsui and Minoru Ikehara. There were a few evening affairs but a cur-few was in effect—gradually relaxed until it was finally revoked in July 1945, just one month before the end of the war.[27] At least once there was a dance hosted by an individual in the community—an afternoon social held at the home of Dr. K. Hosoi on June 7 (*The VVV,* June 6).

By July, some five months into their stay at Schofield, the young men had established many of their own social organizations. They formed a glee club, and their orchestra, led by Henry "Hank" Nakama, featured the "boogie-woogie" at a monthly dance in July, as the July 18 *VVV* noted. Soon, according to the September 3 issue, Hank was consider-ing innovations for his orchestra, among them sixty new pieces of mu-sic that included percussion, clarinet, and saxophone, as well as Roy Kobayashi on the violin, Eddie Yamada on steel guitar, and Walter Miyake on acoustic guitar.

In addition to periodic expeditions to the university campus for dances, the VVV maintained constant contact with the students. On June 11, Ted Tsukiyama wrote to thank his classmates in the "Class of '43" for a shipment of books, which "promptly added to our small but growing library out here. . . . Right offhand, the Collier's volume seems to have the broadest and most popular appeal, but Spaeth's guide to sym-phonies is not without devoted followers." Tsukiyama signed off, "Still one of you" (TTC).

Contact with fellow students on campus was salutary. It provided good support, especially from the young women, but it was also a con-duit for healthy doses of the political and racial reality in Hawai`i. Yuriko (Yuri) Tsunehiro was a sophomore at the university and a friend of several VVV members when Pearl Harbor was attacked. Both of her parents had been Japanese–language school teachers on a Big Island plantation, and her father frequently helped less educated issei with im-migration matters through the Japanese consulate. An early target of the FBI, he was arrested the day after the attack and interned on the mainland. Yuri's reaction to Pearl Harbor was similar to that of many of the VVV: "All the schools were immediately closed, and I left Honolulu [for Hilo] not knowing what my future would hold. I remember my first reaction was to yell under my breath in anguish to the unseen enemy, 'How dare you do this to me!' I felt terribly betrayed."[28]

Her non-Japanese classmates were "rushing to take on good paying jobs with the defense installations which mushroomed all over the island. What chance did I have with a Japanese face and a Japanese name, and a father held in detention?" Among her worst memories were the regular reminders that they were "Japs." Like many others, Yuri recalled the humiliation of being removed from flights on Hawaiian Airlines whenever some non-Japanese arrived too late for a reservation. And since there was only one airline, with but one flight per day among the islands, being bumped was more than a minor irritant.

During the war, passengers with reservations gathered early at the airlines office and waited for official approval from the provost marshal of the military governor's staff. After securing clearance, "the airlines agent called off the passengers for that flight. It became clearly evident that the names were called by race, . . . first the Haoles, then Portuguese, Chinese, Hawaiians, Filipinos, and lastly, the Japanese, in that order. If a Haole came in at the last minute, he was accommodated, and the Japanese at the bottom got bumped with no explanation or apologies. This practice was a daily occurrence." For Yuri, this experience reinforced the "humiliation and helplessness of being Japanese. For a local company to carry on such a policy is so shortsighted, there had to be a bigot at the top."[29]

Some VVV social events served also as important public policy statements. The Triple V celebrated its "half-year anniversary" with a major luau in August 1942. Colonel John Silkman sent a congratulatory message; so did Captain Lum and Supervisor Yempuku. *The VVV* published a short history of the organization for guests at the party, who represented a veritable who's who of the military governor's office, beginning with Lieutenant General Delos Emmons, Hawaii's military governor, and Brigadier General Thomas Green, as well as Colonel Kendall Fielder and the top brass at Schofield, including colonels Silkman and George Bicknell. The Morale Section topped the civilian invitation list: Hung Wai Ching, Charles Loomis, and Shigeo Yoshida were joined by the FBI's Robert Shivers and the University of Hawaii's Charles Hemenway and its president, Gregg Sinclair. Businessman Leslie Hicks and YMCA and Christian leaders like John Young and Stephen Mark were invited. The two-day celebration included athletic events and a dance, as well as the luau (*The VVV*, August 22). It was an opportunity to remind the VVV and its leaders that the experiment was proceeding smoothly and that the public should continue to be aware of the VVV's dedication to country. Reporting on the event, *The VVV* for August 29 provided its usual collegiate humor:

Kenny Saruwatari fasted for at least a week before the luau. In fact he is now known as the Mahatma Ghandi of the VVV. . . . Jackson Morisawa and Edward Emura were barbers and Stanley Watanabe, James Kashiwada and others took a chance. Many were turned down—only a size 6 7/8 bowl was available. Warren "Blubber" Higa and Shigemitsu Nakashima were heard arguing over who was to take a certain wahine to the luau. They decided to toss for her and Shigemitsu won so Warren had to escort the girl.[30]

Not all social occasions focused on coeds. Captain Richard Lum and Lieutenant Tommy Kaulukukui already had brides before joining the VVV; Lum handed out cigars when his first child was born—"the stork, on Sunday, August 2, had fetched a descendant to the Lum family and an heir to the fortunes of the Lums," the August 8 *VVV* reported. One VVV member was married before joining—Kongo Kimura, who left in September to take a position with the Department of Public Instruction. Ralph Yempuku married Gladys Ito in September and invited the entire VVV to a reception in Honolulu. Every member contributed to a gift for the newlyweds, who received a total of $255 (*The VVV*, September 17, 26).

Individual dating took place, although group outings were more common, since not all the men had access to cars. Several of the men established solid reputations as smooth operators. Shiro Amioka's profile in the VVV booklet noted that "Cub" was always "a big hit with the girls, he was the pride and joy of Hale Laulima"; Herbert Isonaga "got rough, he got drunk, but he was always a gentleman. The boys liked him, the girls, more"; Robert "Wacky" Kadowaki "was the undisputed leader of the wolf pack that haunted Hale Aloha on Sundays. Too bad he wasn't as good as a lover"; as noted earlier, Kats Tomita of the kitchen gang "took his girls seriously"; and Ted Tsukiyama allegedly resolved, on New Year's, to "concentrate on one girl, but never quite succeeded. His wolfing expeditions were the talk of the camp."[31]

While never directly discussed, it seems that at least a few of the men lost their virginity while in the VVV—with prostitutes in Honolulu—sometimes after trips into Honolulu to donate blood.

It certainly would not have been difficult for the VVV or for the thousands of servicemen and defense workers to find prostitutes, for they were clustered in officially sanctioned (and regularly inspected) establishments. Gwenfread Allen reports that there were "twenty houses, with 250 'girls' [who] were registered with the police, fifteen of them in the small area bounded by River, Nuuanu, Kukui, and Hotel Streets. Unregistered houses were scattered throughout the city. It was estimated that their gross income was $10,000,000 to $15,000,000 a year; that the girls averaged $25,000 annually and the madames about $150,000." Lines of civilians and servicemen in uniform waited on the streets for their turn.[32]

Hotel Street in Honolulu became the notorious center of prostitution, bars, and tattoo parlors, a lonely place for the women, who were prohibited from any semblance of life other than sexually servicing upwards of a hundred men every working day, between 9 A.M. and 2 P.M. Their customers paid three dollars and were expected to complete their business within three minutes.[33]

The VVV often had substantial support from the outside community for their social events. Shigeo Yoshida visited them "every other week." Other friends arrived periodically, and new recruits were interviewed from time to time. The Emergency Service Committee reported that "various gifts such as radios, magazines, and cookies have been received on behalf of the boys and sent to them."[34] George Higa, the owner of the Honolulu Cafe, a popular family-style restaurant, provided the food for the VVV Christmas celebration on December 23, as *The VVV* announced on December 12. Dinner was the main attraction, but a grab bag (limit 25 cents) was another highlight. Another donor provided a piano, a gift for which Barney Ono was especially grateful—he was an enthusiastic beginner and became somewhat proprietary about the instrument. "I've always liked the Brahms *A-Flat Waltz.* I said, 'If nothing else, I'm gonna learn to play that song.'" He laughed. "So many guys—so we had to fight to get the practice time. . . . Doggone, I thought. . . . I was getting kinda mad."[35]

Although gambling was forbidden in the barracks, the "street" influence (including gambling and drinking) exerted by the nonuniversity group recruited by Hung Wai and later by Richard Chinen was a concern—although Yugo Okubo thought the atmosphere was pretty clean-cut: perhaps some gambling but not much drinking (29). Ted Tsukiyama recalled that there was "a gambling den somewhere where most of the Hawai`i guys used to congregate out at Schofield." When I asked how much gambling went on in the VVV barracks, Ralph Yempuku reacted in mock horror: "Not in the barracks!" He laughed, then elaborated. "Gambling was not permitted in the barracks. No, I don't say there was no gambling, but it was not permitted."[36]

Shiro Amioka never developed a taste for cards or dice but remembered that the town boys "taught us how to gamble." He laughed. "There was a guy called 'Pro' [Shigeo] Fujioka. He was a real pro gambler, . . . good at the dice; . . . they used to do it pretty regularly" (66). George Yamamoto knew that there was at least one recreation room operated by the "regular" army engineers where some VVV members went to shoot craps. "One guy, well, he said so himself—he was several thousand dollars in debt. But some guys may have made money" (44–45). Masato Doi was part of the group that played poker regularly. "Bull" Namba, who played poker with his quarry gang in the barrack recreation room, said: "It didn't bother the rest of the guys. Our quarry gang, you know, we were too tired [to play very late]" (39–40).

Tommy Kaulukukui's fictional Minoru Oyasato celebrated the end of restricted movement for the VVV on the base by going to "Boomtown," the social facility for enlisted men in the regiment. Upon entering the room, Kaulukukui's protagonist immediately encountered a blast of "stifling warm air and smell of tobacco." There were ping-pong games and soldiers in fatigues or sweats laughing and talking. Oyasato moved toward a small bar only to be disappointed that "cokes were the only drinks for sale." Then he discovered one of Boomtown's attractions: "The blaring of a radio with the hums and whistle of men sitting around it all but drowned the faint clink of ivory cubes as they rolled leisurely across the smooth velvet covered table. Peeking between the bulky forms of two soldiers, I was amazed to see the rolls of bills stacked on the table."[37]

Kaulukukui, known for his strict personal code against gambling and drinking, could not resist moralizing in the story. His protagonist bets his "last dollar bill" and agonizes over the roll of the dice, only to come away a dejected loser. "Leaving the building, I turned to gaze at the large sign over the entrance which read 'Boomtown,' and from my lips came a vow that hereafter Boomtown will have to boom without my help."[38] Not many of the VVV, however, shared Tommy's convictions.

The men who drank tended to stay with more conventional fare like beer from the PX, but there was one interesting exception. Ryoji Namba recalled the homemade brew made by the head of the kitchen gang who, conveniently, had access to all of the necessary ingredients: "Richard Chinen—he lived downstairs, see, in our barracks. He used to make pineapple swipe and all that stuff under his bed. And we used to go down and drink the damn thing when it was raw, you know. Put some raisins inside and when that thing fermented, we just put a towel over the bottle opening to filter out the raisins. . . . Oh, it wasn't too bad. . . . In a gallon jug and all. And then, of course, we used to give blood, because every time we donate blood, we can have a few drinks" (39–40).

On the more serious side, the VVV organized many opportunities for continuing their education while away from the campus. In August, the members were surveyed to determine what courses would be most welcome. Perhaps they felt a bit nostalgic after having missed the spring semester, facing the prospect of skipping fall classes as well; no one knew, after all, how much longer they might be in the VVV. The most favored discipline was English literature, followed by philosophy, mathematics, history, and psychology, *The VVV* reported August 15. Several courses were offered for credit during the year. The first, for one credit, was "Post-war Worlds," offered by Professors Paul Bachman and Charles Hunter of the University of Hawaii and held on six successive Sunday mornings, beginning on June 21, at the Nuuanu YMCA. The Board of Regents, perhaps spurred by chairman Hemenway, approved a 50 percent reduction in tuition for the VVV, thus charging each student only $2.50 for the course (*The VVV*, June 20).

Reverend Stephen Mark, who knew several of the VVV men from his Community Church congregation, was a lecturer in the university English Department and brought another one-credit course, "Religion and Literature," to Schofield Barracks. It met on six Tuesday nights, and enrolled twenty-four students (*The VVV*, August 29). They were required to read five of the following: Crane's *Red Badge of Courage*, Dreiser's *Sister Carrie*, Wharton's *Ethan Frome*, Cather's *Death Comes for the Archbishop*, Wilder's *The Bridge of San Luis Rey*, and Cabell's *Jurgen*. Tommy Kaulukukui also offered college credit for physical education. The final course was Mathematics 149—algebra—taught at Schofield on Monday nights by Shigeo Okubo (*The VVV*, September 12).

The ride between Honolulu and Wahiawa was long and arduous, the roads bad and unlit, and only tiny blue slits in the headlights were allowed during blackout hours. The VVV were especially appreciative of instructors willing to make that journey (*The VVV*, January 9, 1943).

Kenso Uyeda, among those enrolled in Reverend Mark's course, earned enough credits to graduate with degrees in business and economics and even marched with his classmates at graduation ceremonies on June 4, 1942, as *The VVV* of June 6 noted. By the end of 1942, twelve VVV members had earned bachelors' degrees.[39]

Some of the most important learning took place informally. With so many men sharing such close quarters in intense work and play, there was bound to be a considerable amount of intellectual cross-fertilization. It was not unusual for the men to recall just how impressed they were with their "smarter" colleagues. In the VVV booklet, for example, George Yamamoto was described as "the human encyclopedia. He was so unobtrusive that no one realized how much he knew until he came out with some incredible knowledge." Barney Ono turned into one of Masato Doi's admirers: "You know, we'd wait for the bus and here's the Declaration of Independence [on the building wall]; he read the thing and he can quote you, comma for comma, every damn thing." He laughed. "Lunch time, one hour lunch—one day, he'd pick up a book of poems, Gray's 'Elegy'—next day, he'd repeat the damn thing!"[40]

It was appropriate, then, for Yamamoto and Doi to be asked to lead a "bull session" titled "Preparing Ourselves to Face the Post-war Problems." This Monday-night discussion was open to all VVV members, as *The VVV* announced on June 13, to serve as prelude to the one-credit course "Post-war Worlds."

Meanwhile, Harry Tanaka won the university's Annual Berndt Extemporaneous Speaking contest on May 21 with "Preservation of Free Speech." Two months later, in an oratory contest within the VVV, he won the open competition with a speech entitled "The Road Ahead," in which he warned that the "road ahead" would test their faith in democracy, a faith which "must be stronger than the Nazi's dream of a larger and more powerful Reich and the Japanese' ardent faith in their emperor God, for democracy will triumph only when people are willing to work and die for it." Grover Nagaji was runner-up with "Above All Nations Is Humanity" (*The VVV*, July 18). The idealism was clear, pronounced, and unabashed.

There was even a novice division for the oratorical contest. The quarry gang, perhaps intent on proving they had more than brawn, captured all three places, with Hiroshi Minami, Ryoji Namba, and Dick Uyemura placing in that order. Minami won with a speech entitled, appropriately enough, "Physical Fitness for Victory." Namba startled the group with a frank discourse, the "Deterioration of Morals During Wartime." First-prize winners in both divisions received twenty-five-dollar war bonds.

Masato Doi and Ted Tsukiyama submitted essays for the 1942 University of Hawaii Banks Memorial Prize, which had as its theme personal experiences and ideas "arising from the war," *The VVV* reported on June 6. The contest was established to encourage and reward creative-writing efforts among undergraduates. Doi did not have a copy of his second-place essay, "Frankie," but fortunately the library kept a microfilmed copy. "Gee," Doi said, "only thing I can remember about that essay was that it really hurt going into a bus and see other Orientals carrying signs—Korean, 'I am a Korean' sign. And another saying 'I am a Chinese.' . . . Nobody wanted to be a Japanese," he laughed (29).

The essay, framed as a letter to a "haole" friend, began with a sense that the war would be won but that Japanese Americans would face more trouble: "Our Ship will ride out the Storm, yes. But for me I can see no placid seas. I am an American—but of Japanese ancestry." Masato was, therefore, grateful to his friend "when you, an 'haole,' so frankly declared that the war had brought no change in our fraternal bond of former times." And could not this friend recall "how frequently my inferiority complex would rise to the surface and I would close up like a clam whenever any 'haole' was around?"

> The other day I was on a bus. A drunken Caucasian American got on. He immediately accused the driver of being a "Jap." The driver remained silent. Whereupon the other began on a tirade of vile abuse and curses and, without any provocation on the part of the driver, threatened to "knock him clear off his seat." "Well, you're a Jap, aren't you?" he shouted. "Nope." "What are you then?" "Korean." "Korean? You sure?" "Yep." "You sure?" "Yep." "Well, why'en't you say so in the first place?" "Makes no difference." "Would it make a difference if I'da knocked your block off?" Silence. I did not find out whether the driver was really a Korean or whether he was lying to avoid a brawl. It was only small consolation that the Caucasian-American was drunk. Perhaps liquor had only rubbed off restraint and had brought to the surface the true feeling of the American masses. And my answer to such abuse can only be a tightening of the muscles around the jaws.

Doi continued by noting his HTG and VVV service and his dedication to the "principles of Democracy and the American Way of Life" but wondered about a future with "the mud of racial prejudice" so readily at hand to keep the waters murky. For Doi, the future looked bleak and the only saving grace seemed to lie in thinking on the joys of the past and the personal "hand of friendship as a beacon to guide me through to whatever the future holds." This was a sensitive and idealistic young man. The language is flowery and romantic, no doubt a reflection of those "halcyon" days of English composition:

> Dear friend, do you not wish for those halcyon days gone by? . . . Then was a time when we were able to build Dams to determine how our River of Life shall run. . . . Does it mean nothing that I volunteered in the Hawaii Territorial Guard, that I joined emergency units, that I am in with the Varsity Victory Volunteers? Does it mean nothing that I was born and raised in an American community, that I was educated in American schools, that it is to the principles of Democracy and to the American Way of Life that I hold? Are there forever to be cursed minorities branded throughout life by and from birth because of the gross stupidity of other men? . . . Happy have been the Days That Were, dark is the color of Now.[41]

Doi was wrestling with the racial demons of the times and, while the prose may have shaded into purple, his words reflected the real anguish of contemplating a society so thoroughly imbued with racism.

Ted Tsukiyama kept a copy of his submission, "We Must Win the Peace," three single-spaced pages that spelled out his notions of the war being waged and the peace to be won. It was an exercise that called for the upholding of principles: "We are thus, carrying a crusade against totalitarian evils in which we, armed with the weapons of justice, reason, and human rights, seek to crush the false philosophy of power, lust, and hatred of totalitarian despots." He begins by referring to several incidents he had heard about or perhaps created to highlight the feel of the times.

The first was a "group of workingmen mercilessly beating up two men of Japanese ancestry. The faces of the assailants were savage with a burning hate, much more terrifying to look at than those of the bruised and bloody victims; . . . that was my first taste of war." Whether the incident was fictional or not, Tsukiyama could honestly relate that he had been plagued by that feeling many times, "as expressed in the minds and actions of people."

The second incident came from Tsukiyama's HTG experience. Another Japanese American volunteer described how he had come by the scars on his back: "Bayoneted out of the Pearl Harbor gate when I reported for work on the eighth." The last involved a soldier in town who pushed his way through a group of little Japanese American children: "Out of my way, you damn little Tojos." Tsukiyama ends with quotes from a congressman demanding that all Japanese in America, regardless of citizenship, be deported after the war, and with an appeal for the

United States to avoid the tragedy of post–World War I politics: to "lay down the terms of a just and honorable and lasting Peace."

Masato Doi also mentioned the congress member's demands for Japanese deportation, reported in the newspapers and the target of an editorial in *The VVV* on September 26, in which the congressman is identified only as "from the Pacific northwest": "It is not the American Way to destroy the privileges of those who are born and live on American soil. It is not the American Way to reduce people to a state that they live in oppression and at the mercy of discriminating edicts. That is too much the way of Nazism. And America hates Nazism!"

These essays indicate the pain and anger that lingered well after the first months of the war. Idealistic youth like Doi and Tsukiyama were especially stunned by the ferocity of the racism unleashed by Pearl Harbor. They were two of the more self-consciously and assertively mobile and acculturated nisei, products of educational backgrounds that encouraged a heightened sense of relationship to a world beyond the working-class environments of, say, McKinley or Farrington High Schools. For them, the shock of rejection and hostility was proportionately greater.

Tommy Kaulukukui summed up this group as one that "didn't want to just sit and do nothing. Always making plans for somebody to keep them . . . going mentally and spiritually. This is why—that's how, to me, they were outstanding. They were not just another army group going there and, after work, sit in the barracks and do nothing. These guys are always thinking that we gotta have a course. Somebody gotta come here to lecture" (36).

Academic courses, bull sessions, visiting speakers, essay contests, and intellectual discourse were normal fare for the university types, but it was clear to all that other forms of recreation, especially athletics, would be essential. Indeed, that was Kaulukukui's primary responsibility, although he also supervised the building of dozens of model aircraft that were used by military observers and civilian "spotters" to distinguish U.S. or British aircraft from German and Japanese.

The VVV reported on October 31 that fourteen VVV men received certificates from the U.S. Navy Bureau of Aeronautics for crafting these intricate models. They included Seichi Ono, Harry Sato, Robert Kadowaki, George Oka, Soji "Jackson" Morisawa, Thomas Shintani, Shoso Kagawa, Robert Kikawa, and Allen Yamada. Yoshio Nakagawa and John Takara became "honorary ensigns" for building at least two models each.

Nakagawa personally had built five of them by early June (*The VVV*, June 20). According to Kaulukukui, the models were exhibited in the mess hall and later displayed at the Honolulu Academy of Arts.

But athletics became the social glue that held the unit together. The VVV booklet declared that sports was "foremost in popularity and participation, . . . divided into the following classes to encourage as much participation as possible by the group: Inter-barracks competition; intra-regimental competition; Regimental teams, and the VVV teams."[42] The boys had been part of a university system that encouraged a wide variety of intramural competition—Ralph Yempuku had been in charge of that program, and Yutaka Nakahata had reported the scores for the campus newspaper—so it was relatively simple to replicate the system. Each of the six floors (two floors to each of three barracks) competed for points, awarded to individuals and groups.

Competition was genuine and fierce in everything from badminton and ping-pong to barefoot football and boxing. The bookish lads, who weighed in at about a hundred pounds, were expected to participate; individuals like Richard Chinen, who had won boxing titles at the national level, joined the football team. A number had competed under Tommy Kaulukukui on varsity football and baseball teams at the university level. (Jyun Hirota, a gifted athlete in both sports, went on to play professional baseball in Japan.)

The outstanding athletes competed in circles well beyond the VVV or even the base. Hirota and Wallace Doi, while part of the VVV, played for the University of Hawaii football team against Na Alii (the chiefs) in the annual classic, the Shrine game, on November 22. Hirota at left half-back, operating out of the then fashionable T-formation, peeled off a forty-two-yard run in the second quarter that led to the first touchdown. In the third period he returned a punt sixty yards for a touchdown (*The VVV*, November 28).

For many in the VVV, golf became a lifelong passion; their regular postwar reunions invariably featured tournaments. Sukeyoshi Kushi, one of the best golfers in the territory—he captured the Maui island title in 1942—provided lessons to the rest of the VVV. According to the VVV booklet, he "lived with his golf clubs. Goosie golfed every afternoon but he could never keep his waist line down. . . . He never had a girl but always talked about them."[43]

The VVV boxing squad walked away from the Schofield championships with a runner-up trophy for Teruo Himoto and three titles—

for flyweight Wallace Nagao, featherweight Anki Hoshijo, and middleweight Richard Kato—a major triumph for this tiny unit. Richard Chinen coached three fighters for AAU championships in the territory: Anki Hoshijo and Roy Nakamine were bantamweights; Joseph Matsunaga was a flyweight (*The VVV,* June 6).

Team sports drew the most interest. At the regimental level, the VVV was well represented by Hirota, Doi, and Edwin Higashino, who all started for the baseball team—no small feat during the war, when numbers of professional athletes enlisted or were drafted and played for military teams. The Schofield team played against, for example, Staff Sergeant Joe DiMaggio of the New York Yankees, at the time center fielder for the Seventh Air Force.[44] Tommy Kaulukukui, who coached the regimental baseball team, recalled a racial incident that almost got out of hand. "There was a boy we had catching. His name is Doi—and Wally, he was catching one day; . . . somebody, see, this is the kind of things our boys get to hear: "Oh, I think the guy is a spy." . . . He was ready to throw down his gear and go after the guy. . . . He played football. And he was going to go after the guy. . . . He was pretty big, a tough boy. Those are some of the things the VVV boys had to contend with" (23–25).

The VVV fielded a basketball team which was 5–3 in a truncated season. (It might have had a chance at postseason play but for the VVV's disbandment in January 1943.) This, too, was extraordinary, given the relatively short stature of the nisei. Starting forwards were Walter Okumoto and Hiroichi Tomita; Claude Takekawa was the center; and Sus Yamamoto and Toshi Nakasone were the guards (*The VVV,* January 23, 1943).

It was football, however, that captured the imagination of most of the VVV, which fielded two teams that competed at Schofield and beyond: the 130-pound barefoot team and the "unlimited" squad that competed against all comers.

Barefoot football boasted a long tradition in Hawai'i, with roots probably extending back to sugar-plantation leagues established by management to provide an outlet for the boys and entertainment for themselves. I recall playing in many barefoot games well into high school—we had nothing but old clothes, a football, and a field. Competition was heated and fistfights were not uncommon. Organized barefoot leagues incorporated all the usual football equipment and uniforms except socks and shoes.

Shiro Amioka, who played on the VVV team, recalled that Kaulu-kukui was an excellent coach who "believed in condition." So after a full day of shoveling rocks at the quarry, Shiro joined the team to work on conditioning and plays. They competed against others in a twelve-team Honolulu league and some military groups as well (69). The team won three and lost two games before disbanding. The "unlimited" team was undefeated in several scrimmages and games against two high school teams: Farrington and Roosevelt. The grand finale was a game between the VVV 130-pound team and the Chow Hounds (so called because of their legendary prodigious appetites) of the 1399th Engineer Construction Battalion, made up of nisei draftees.[45]

An important contest because it provided bragging rights to the "locals'" championship at Schofield Barracks, the game was played on New Year's Day 1943 in Honolulu Stadium, the city's major sports venue. As the *VVV* crowed on January 9: "The Chow Hounds tasted crushed pine in the Bowl on New Year's Day . . . and when the animal was fat and well-fed, the Varsity Victory Volunteers feasted on hot dog. . . . Lt. Tommy Kaulukukui's VVV administered the crushing defeat, 27–0, and won the mythical Schofield barefoot football championship." Ken "Cannonball" Kawate, Chiyoki Ikeda, Joe Okumoto, Kats Tomita, Stanley Kimura, and Eddie Watase all put points on the board. One play featured the left end, future supreme-court justice Yoshimi Hayashi, who took the ball on a trick end-around play. The January 9 *VVV* article ended with a tribute: "Masao 'Moonkachi' Ono smashed his nose, but cut the enemy to pieces before he was rendered hors de combat. His performance that day was the standard for all-American tackles."

While boxing and team sports yielded the most exciting press, the membership was involved in sports activities on a daily basis. One of the most avidly attended events was the Varsity Golden Gloves, with sixty contestants, nearly one-half of the total VVV membership. AAU boxers like Hoshijo and Nagamine were, of course, barred from participation. The elimination rounds were viciously contested and the championship bouts drew a crowd of two hundred, including Hung Wai Ching. Theodore "Pump" Searle, who was in charge of the athletic program at the university, attended, as did Al Karasick, a professional-boxing promoter in Honolulu.[46]

Ralph Yempuku teamed with Junichi Buto to capture the doubles tennis crown, defeating Ted Tsukiyama and Kaname Takemoto. August was a busy month for Ralph; Yempuku also won, with Jyun Hirota, the doubles volleyball tournament (*The VVV*, August 15). Softball, golf, ping-pong, and badminton were also on the agenda, with points carefully tallied for group and individual awards.

Sports provided a morale boost to the VVV and also gave the men a chance to compete in citywide leagues, within the Thirty-fourth Regiment, or, for a few, as part of the regimental team competing with other outfits at Schofield Barracks. As Kaulukukui's earlier anecdote about Wallace Doi suggests, VVV members had their patience tested by racist remarks, and they were exposed to other racial tensions as well.

One particularly tense confrontation occurred during a football game between the VVV and a predominantly African American contingent—"colored" or "Negro" in the parlance of the times. Several individuals had vivid memories of the game, although their descriptions varied. The principal figure in this fracas, "Trigger" Thompson, was a southern white GI from a unit quartered close to the VVV. He evidently loved sports and practiced with the VVV whenever permitted. Teru Himoto played in the game, Ralph Yempuku was a spectator, and Tommy Kaulukukui was the VVV coach as well as OD (officer of the day), armed and in uniform.

Teru Himoto recalled Thompson as someone who "wanted to play football in the worst way, so we let him join us to play that game. And he get no use for colored. He told us this. And the other team had about 50 percent, I think, was colored players, yeah." Trigger was a halfback; on one play he was tackled on the sideline near the opposing bench. "So when they tackled him, this guy on the sideline—the colored boys, they don't like southern haoles—so they told him, 'Kick his teeth in.' And what he [Thompson] said when he got up was, 'Not today, black boy.' Whoa! Then the whole group—sheez, I saw some guys with knife cut all over their heads. So, I telling you, I never felt that they got that rattled up; at that time, you know, calling a colored person 'black boy' was a no-no. 'Black boy' and 'nigger' was two terminology they cannot use."[47] That realization did not stop the VVV from using the latter term as a nickname for a particularly dark-complected comrade who later became one of several judges from the VVV ranks. (This was not an uncommon practice in Hawai`i—we were certainly still guilty of this racism in my childhood—and unfortunately, it has not yet ended.)

Ralph Yempuku's account of the incident was at least as vivid as Teru's:

He got tackled—and the black said something, and he said, "Not today, black boy," or something like that. And they were losing. We had them;

they were so behind, you know. So now they had an excuse to go after the white guys, so we got involved. So I don't know who it was that shot the gun up in the air to stop the rioting. . . . They were going to kill us. . . . Well, I suppose so, because the white guys were on our team. . . . I wasn't playing but I was there. It scared the hell out of me. All these black guys, you know. One officer or someone shot the gun off in the air. . . . [He laughed.] Black against the Japanese. (42–43)

Tommy Kaulukukui, the officer in charge, gave a more measured account of the incident, although he by no means downplayed its importance. Tommy remembered Trigger Thompson as a southerner who liked the VVV and was well liked in return. Kaulukukui's account paralleled the others' to the point when Trigger was tackled and responded to someone on the sideline, "Not today, black boy":

Immediately fans rushed onto the field. It looked like a riot. . . . I was the OD, you know. I was trying to separate these guys because I was in uniform. Anyway, our boys didn't get involved. No, it wasn't a fight. They were just going after Trigger. . . . They weren't going after all the others—not our boys. . . . Oh, the bench cleared; everybody runs in the field. Anyway, we pushed him out of the way; . . . finally, I had to put him in the jeep and drive him away. (23)

This incident reveals something of the dilemma the nisei faced as they were increasingly and inexorably drawn into the largely black/white world of U.S. race relations during World War II. Few of the nisei had ever met an African American other than Nolle Smith, the star football player and fellow volunteer in the ROTC and HTG. Their prejudices were generated from their Japanese heritage, which stressed, as Yempuku's interview has indicated, the superiority of cultures from nations that were powerful, as well as from their acculturation into America with its pervasive racist images of blacks. Himoto's images of "knife cut" and Yempuku's of riot conditions with "all these black guys" are logical, given this background. It may not be possible to reconstruct an objective picture of the incident, but Kaulukukui's representation needs to be respected, especially his sense that the rage was focused on Trigger Thompson and not on the nisei.

In general, sports helped introduce the VVV to the wider world of U.S. military life and the GIs they would later live with in the 442d or in the Military Intelligence Service. At the same time, the Schofield GIs had a chance to interact with Americans of Japanese descent in a controlled environment and over an extended period of time. Athletics became a major part of this cultural exchange. Richard Chinen's importance in this venture is difficult to overstate; his rough-and-ready background fit the profile of other Schofield army men better than the university types within the VVV, and his reputation as a boxer worked wonders. His genius in scrounging food and supplies from other units was legendary, and his patented fried rice attracted many friends from the Thirty-fourth.

But the VVV was more than a worthwhile project to boost the morale of young and discouraged Japanese Americans. It was important in a larger strategy to rehabilitate an ethnic group linked indissolubly, it seemed, to a fierce and implacable enemy. Because some individuals in Hawai`i supported the national agenda of systematically scapegoating the Japanese community—as in the wholesale internment of the entire group living on the West Coast—it was crucial to provide an alternative perspective. The success of the VVV venture depended first and foremost on the ability of the young men of the VVV to function as a unit with a reasonable degree of effectiveness and enthusiasm. Toward that end, sports, education, and social events were provided, but the VVV members themselves understood that living and working together for an indeterminate period would require discipline and planning. They even formed a morale committee of their own, the M.C., which became the sounding board for the organization because their monthly Monday-night general meetings tended to be too large and unwieldy. Unkei Uchima chaired the committee until other responsibilities became too burdensome; at its June 9 meeting, the M.C. recognized Shiro Amioka as the new chair (*The VVV*, June 13).

Most of the day-to-day complaints were resolved by the work gangs themselves or Ralph Yempuku. The others went to the Morale Committee (TTC). Some were specific: Place blue globes in their barracks for some light during frequent blackouts; run more water through the urinal, "and deodorants would help a great deal in reducing the helluva stink when too many guys piss at one time." Someone was disgusted by the practice of the kitchen crew of setting out the tableware after each meal in preparation for the next, because the utensils were knocked on the floor when the mess hall was used for films or speakers and simply replaced on the table or had cockroaches crawling over them at night.

Other complaints were more substantial. One ongoing concern was the need for more activities, with a bit more variety: "Do you folks realize all the recreation we have are muscular? After a day's work, I for one don't feel like going out to lift the bar bell, punch the bag or play base-ball. How about some light recreation such as a 'pool table'? I guaran-tee you if we have a pool table it will be the most popular practice in the VVV." The same individual suggested that work be apportioned on a contract basis so that gangs that finished early by working hard could take the day off. Perhaps this fellow had been watching the kitchen crew and noticed that they had split into two crews, thus enjoying alternate days off.

Another suggested that leaders "study the individuals more closely. If this be done, our problems concerning gold-bricking, low morale, dissatisfaction, etcetera, could be more adeptly handled. It shouldn't be hard because the foremen shouldn't find it difficult to study their men—*especially* with their university background."

There was some griping about poker games and bull sessions that continued after lights out at 9:30 and kept some individuals awake. One angry note requested ("maybe should be *demand*") that a certain indi-vidual, loud and obnoxious, be removed from the top floor of Barracks #3 because the area was bad enough, but "with his arrival—you can guess the rest. Feels just like hell, especially when one is feeling rotten." This outsider was particularly resented because he "belonged" to Barracks #2, downstairs. Perhaps in rebuttal, another member just as angrily protested the arbitrary ending of poker games at 9:30 and invoked the wholesale assault on Japanese Americans as part of his argument against any generalized crackdown:

> We're supposed to be university men. Let's act so. Poker games can be played quietly. Let them continue. To heck with guys who have some-thing on their minds and can't sleep. If this is to be done fairly, a vote is the best way out. This is simply a case of a few guys who can't sleep forcing an early curfew on the whole bunch. It's the same thing with us. A few ignorant Whites who have "loud-mouths" are bringing pressure to bear on us. Why bring speakers to tell us about equality and stuff if we can't have it here. There's no sense in learning anything about it.

On May 21, the Morale Committee discussed the "Case of [Richard] Chinen–Hung Wai Ching." This was evidently the dispute regarding re-cruitment of more nonuniversity "street guys." While not explicit, the minutes of that meeting suggest that Richard was angry because Hung Wai felt they should cease recruiting anyone who would lower the "in-tellectual level" of the group. Evidently Chinen was still actively invit-ing his friends. The committee "observed that Mr. Ching has some say in organization and tho sincere and earnest, perhaps a bit arbitrary." The committee decided to resolve the issue by establishing "an entry board of review," being mindful that the qualification to join should be "the desire to work in patriotic service" rather than college education. Otherwise, there would be problems of "cleavage, factions, dissatisfaction and broken morale." This issue apparently was a factor in Chinen's decision to leave Schofield Barracks for several days, until Yempuku was able to convince him to return.

At least a few of the problems never made it into open discussion at the meetings and certainly not into the group's minutes. One VVV member, James Oka, regularly listened to Radio Tokyo on his shortwave set—"an eccentric guy," according to Bull Namba. Of course, shortwave radios had been confiscated from the issei community, and Oka's habit "used to burn some guys, you know; . . . the guys thought that was disloyal or something like that." Namba laughed. "You know, you get caught up in that patriotic fever." A few made a point of expressing their displeasure, but Oka simply turned the volume down and continued to listen. Namba thought that Oka had "lived in Japan for quite some time. He just like to listen to Japanese" (44–46).[48]

The success or failure of the experiment involving the VVV, of obvious import to the Japanese community during the war, also had enormous implications for postwar society in Hawai`i, as well as for race relations policy in the United States as a whole.

To accomplish the difficult task of reintegrating the large Japanese American population into postwar Hawai`i, a wide variety of groups and key individuals representing them needed to be assembled, many of whom have already been mentioned: the military governor and his command; Bob Shivers of the FBI; Leslie Hicks, president of the Honolulu Chamber of Commerce; Charles Hemenway, Big Five executive and arguably the most important member of the university's Board of Regents; Riley Allen, editor of the *Honolulu Star-Bulletin;* Gregg Sinclair, president of the University of Hawaii; Miles Cary, principal of McKinley; John Young of the YMCA. Another important participant was Jack Burns, a captain in the Honolulu police department and liaison with the "contact group" of Japanese American leaders during the war. (Burns, with the critical help of the nisei, later built a Democratic Party that captured political control of Hawai`i in the 1950s.)[49]

The various non-haole ethnic groups would also be crucial: Native Hawaiians, Chinese, Filipinos, and Koreans. The Portuguese, Puerto

Ricans, and African Americans, while relatively small in number and influence, were included in the deliberations. Finally, the various sectors of the Japanese community itself had to be persuaded to contribute their enthusiastic support.

The Chinese, Koreans, and Filipinos retained extremely strong ties to their homelands, all under the control of or under siege by Japan. Hung Wai Ching helped with the younger Chinese American leaders, especially the Christians. All three immigrant communities were actively pursuing national liberation struggles through fundraising, political lobbying, or military training.

But while Japan was the common enemy, U.S. objectives did not automatically coincide with the goals of our Asian allies—as the turbulent postwar period would demonstrate. One of the first orders of business, therefore, was reinforcing the "Americanness" of these Asian immigrant communities in order to reduce the risk of racial incidents and to focus their energies on an American perspective in the war against Japan. To this end, the Morale Section established separate nationality/ethnic group committees to serve as coordinating and liaison bodies: Puerto Rican, Portuguese, Filipino, Korean, Chinese, and Japanese. As Hung Wai Ching recalled: "My assignment was to work with, not only with the aliens and Japanese Americans—citizens of Japanese ancestry—but with other races too: the Koreans, the Filipinos, and the Chinese and not so much with the haoles" (1).

The other ethnic groups were smaller and relatively powerless except in their potential capacity to damage the racial harmony needed for the war effort. Even relatively minor and spontaneous racial incidents would have required serious diversion of resources. And while still a sizable and significant group, Native Hawaiians had long been marginalized and were largely dependent upon haole leadership. Most were unlikely to resist the tide in any open fashion. Further, as Davianna McGregor has argued persuasively, many Hawaiians who were least subordinated to the haoles had withdrawn to rural enclaves—an important form of resistance. Thus, there was no perceived need to create a specific liaison committee for Native Hawaiians.[50]

The VVV's public image in this campaign became more important than its members' day-to-day hard labor at Schofield Barracks. The media made much of the VVV regularly donating blood and purchasing war bonds. The men went in groups into Honolulu to donate 350 to 500 cc of blood. "Some went to escape from work for the day and the meal that came after the operation, but the great majority because they wanted to do their bit for a worthy cause."[51] Whether donated for a meal, a day off, the cause, or a couple of drinks, the blood was appreciated.

Hundreds of victims of the Pearl Harbor attack still needed blood, along with increasing numbers of wounded returning from the Pacific. In addition, there were the inevitable accidents that attend military maneuvers and construction taking place at a frenzied pace. In the immediate aftermath of the attack, the enormous surge of donors forced the blood bank to operate around the clock, seven days a week. Later, public enthusiasm waned and there were occasional pleas for donors; under martial law, military provost courts commonly ordered blood drawn from those convicted of minor offenses.[52]

To scotch a persistent rumor that the Japanese community was reluctant to participate in the blood-donor program, Shigeo Yoshida occasionally gave speeches in the larger community to promote unity. On December 2, he talked to students at the elite Punahou Academy, overwhelmingly haole, informing them of Japanese American contributions—the VVV, the volunteer service units, the purchase of war bonds, and the donations of blood—23 percent of the blood donated, "according to figures released two or three months ago. (This is less than the record of the Caucasian group but more than the percentage of several other large racial groups.)"[53]

Investing in war bonds became a major pastime in the territory. In the year before Pearl Harbor, islanders bought about $3 million worth of bonds. Every subsequent bond drive was oversubscribed—in fact, the U.S. Treasury declared Hawai'i the best region, per capita, in the country over the course of the entire war.[54] In the ten months from April 1942 into January 1943, the VVV bought $27,850 worth of war bonds. Each bond cost $18.75 and would be redeemable for $25 in ten years. Participation was excellent; nearly everyone bought a bond each month. Ted Tsukiyama, for example, who kept all of his pay stubs, bought a bond in all but two months.

Not everyone was happy at the pressure to buy bonds. Barney Ono recalled resisting the efforts by Ted Tsukiyama and Ralph Yempuku to "push it." He told them, "The heck with you guys," because, first, it may have been okay to encourage blood donations, but the money issue was a private matter: "Lot of us were really in bad shape. I mean, . . . my father couldn't get a job; . . . at that time my family consisted of twelve to thirteen kids, plus both parents. The salary you bring in, whatever could be brought in, you know, helped."[55]

Barney's private complaints created not a ripple. The VVV's image as a self-sacrificing unit of Japanese Americans was furthered by war-bond purchases, and their leaders continued to urge participation. The pressure extended deep into the Japanese American community. I recall, as a first grader in 1945, being swept up in that patriotic tide; the periodic drives for us to purchase war stamps which could be accumulated into bonds were occasions for impassioned pleas to my parents for an extra dime or two to take to school.

VVV members gave speeches to community groups—especially Japanese Americans—to "boost morale" by providing a model of exemplary behavior under trying conditions. Shiro Amioka, for example, was invited back to his alma mater, McKinley High School, in May 1942 by the principal, Miles Cary, to address the students about the VVV experience. Harry Tanaka was doing more than his share by winning the University of Hawaii speech contest on May 21. Both Tanaka and Ted Tsukiyama were asked to speak to plantation communities (*The VVV*, May 30). Ted noted that Jack Burns, the Honolulu police captain who would become governor of Hawai`i, was involved in arranging some of the meetings: "Some of us were picked to go out and talk to plantation camps at night. And that guy who took us around was Jack Burns. . . . He would come in his car with black-out lights and he and either Baron Goto or Hung Wai and one of us [would go]" (41).

These speeches were prepared by the VVV men and submitted for approval to Captain Richard Lum. In a detailed outline for one such presentation, obviously for a Japanese American audience, Tsukiyama traced the history and purpose of the VVV and described their work and community service functions. He explained that they formed the VVV because (1) some saw the Japanese in Hawai`i as a security threat; (2) there was pressure to intern them; (3) community leaders like Leslie Hicks defended their loyalty; and (4) "positive and loyal action [was] now necessary to establish and prove their position and place in the Hawaiian community." Tsukiyama ended with an appeal to his community to validate their efforts: "We are not just the V.V.V. We are yours, the community's, the nation's representatives in a unique war effort. We need your support, your confidence, your good will, your approval that what we do is right."[56]

The summer boys' program in which Masato Doi and Barney Ono participated was another example of VVV service in the wider community.

In one event—carried out on a grand scale—the territory hosted a luau on January 24, 1943, for all military personnel from Wisconsin to demonstrate Hawaii's appreciation for the welcome extended to the 100th Battalion while it trained at Camp McCoy. The VVV were prominently involved. Herb Isonaga and Clarence Hamaishi prepared 150 pounds of poi; Richard Chinen supervised the meal, which included kalua pig, fish, and chicken. Later in the afternoon the Wisconsin GIs were treated to a dance, with Ted Tsukiyama in charge of the "hostess committee" (*The VVV*, January 23, 1943). Some of the official USO dances in Hawai`i for white GIs featured white-only hostesses; at the luau, the Caucasian Wisconsin GIs danced with Japanese American coeds.

It was especially important that the larger Japanese American community be perceived as supportive of the VVV project. The young men were carrying the banner of loyalty for the entire ethnic group. The Japanese Emergency Service Committee, in its first progress report, March 6, 1942, noted that efforts were ongoing to "collect materials which will meet the recreational needs of the [VVV] boys and to get more prospective enrollees and other individuals and organizations interested in the Corps" (SYC). The VVV was acutely aware of events, especially those affecting Japanese Americans, unfolding beyond Schofield Barracks. The members were not in a position to do much more than watch and learn, but they did try to incorporate those lessons into their lives.

Finally, in January 1943, it was announced that the United States would establish a volunteer segregated unit of Japanese Americans for combat duty. An initial call went forth for 3,000 volunteers from mainland concentration camps and another 1,500 from Hawai`i. From the camps, just over 1,000 volunteered; in Hawai`i, the number approached 10,000.[57] If positive participation in America's war effort was the goal, these numbers vindicated the Hawai`i path. In a brief meeting, the VVV decided that this was the opportunity toward which they had been working and elected to disband. One year after forming the VVV, they organized an anniversary dinner to bring most of the members together one final time before most volunteered into the new 442d Regimental Combat Team. On January 28, 1943, an invitation was extended:

> You are cordially invited to join the Varsity Victory Volunteers in observing their first anniversary which will be a semi-formal dinner and dance beginning at 5 o'clock P.M. on February 1, 1943 at the South Seas on Kalakaua Avenue, Waikiki.
>
> We are extremely sorry that this invitation is so sudden but since the majority of our members are considering volunteering into the Armed Service

in the very near future we have found it necessary to observe our anniversary, which actually falls on February 25, at such an early date.[58]

SINCE SHORTLY after the attack on Pearl Harbor, Hung Wai Ching and Shigeo Yoshida had worked tirelessly on a shared vision that became a major part of the making of modern Hawai`i—the disciplined, self-willed transcendence of racial barriers by a victimized Japanese minority. For Yoshida, this was a pragmatic reversal of his belief in a positive "melting pot" in which ethnic groups completely lost their salience. The war forced the change, because "we Japanese were singled out and we had to accept that as a fact that we were the children of enemy aliens. You couldn't get around that fact and so in addressing any problem concerned with the Japanese Americans at that time, we had to speak for ourselves as the Japanese group or the Japanese American group. There was no getting around that" (20).

The goal to transform Japanese Americans from victims to models was a brilliant vision, but one which could not have been accomplished solely by the Japanese. The various forces within Hawai`i were generally in concert, from the military government and the FBI to a few key local haole leaders and the other Asian ethnic groups. The final and determining element was the U.S. government itself—the president and the War Department.

In his report on the Morale Section compiled in 1944, Captain I. H. Mayfield described the extraordinary lengths to which Hung Wai had gone to convince government and national media leaders that the Hawai`i approach to the Japanese problem was correct. Along with their lobbying of Assistant Secretary of War John McCloy, Ching and Yoshida managed to carry their message of a special brand of racial tolerance to the White House itself. McCloy's visit to Hawai`i in late December 1942, when Hung Wai Ching escorted him to Kolekole Pass to observe the VVV "quarry gang" at work breaking rocks, may have been decisive. Lyn Crost, distinguished World War II reporter, suggests that McCloy returned to Washington with this image fresh in mind, and that the experience ultimately helped Army Chief of Staff General George C. Marshall approve the creation of the 442d Regimental Combat Team on January 1, 1943.[59] Ultimately, President Roosevelt put aside his considerable prejudices and approved the project.

8

The Front Lines
Battlefront and Home Front

When the United States formally entered World War II after Japan's attack on Pearl Harbor, Winston Churchill was confident that "Hitler's fate was sealed. Mussolini's fate was sealed. As for the Japanese, they would be ground to powder." But, as Paul Kennedy has argued, victory in the Pacific was not assured until the 1942 naval battles of the Coral Sea in May and Midway in June destroyed the possibility of Japanese domination.[1] By the end of 1942, the Allies were destroying the Axis forces in North Africa, and the push up the Italian boot would soon commence. As it became apparent that the war ahead would consume enormous numbers of resources and fighting men, some thought was given to the untapped pool of Japanese Americans.

More important, deploying nisei as combat troops had considerable significance in realigning official U.S. government practice with constitutional values of racial equality. The mass internment of Japanese Americans on the West Coast and their exclusion from the armed forces were embarrassing. Japanese militarists were achieving altogether too much success deflecting criticism of their aggression in Asia and the Pacific by defining their role as racial liberators. They successfully courted collaborators even in conquered nations like Korea, China, and the Philippines by pointing to America's bleak—and continuing—record of anti-Asian racism. It was no coincidence, then, that 1943 also witnessed the first break in the long litany of anti-Asian immigration laws—with a token annual quota of 105 Chinese.[2]

THE DECISION TO CREATE a segregated, all-nisei, regimental combat team proved a major turning point in the rehabilitation of Japanese Americans in U.S. race relations. The army and the VVV proudly acknowledged their roles in that process. When General Delos Emmons made the official announcement of the creation of the new regiment, he congratulated Hawaii's Japanese Americans for their loyal participation in the war effort, specifically including the VVV along with the 100th Battalion as important contributors. In spite of their being subject to "distrust because of their racial origin, and discriminated against in certain fields of the defense effort, they nevertheless have borne their burdens without complaint and have added materially to the strength of the Hawaiian area. . . . Their representatives in the 100th Infantry Battalion, the Varsity Victory Volunteers and other men of Japanese extraction in our armed forces have also established a fine record."[3]

On February 26, 1943, a year and a day after the VVV was activated, Ralph Yempuku sent mimeographed letters to all members to notify them that the "Army intends to give preference to the boys of the V.V.V. in the Volunteer Combat Regiment." Yempuku urged them to send appropriate information to the army contact office immediately and to pass the word to buddies, since a number had moved and might not receive the news.[4]

Some VVV members were asked to encourage volunteering for the 442d. Ted Tsukiyama gave me a copy of the handwritten speech he delivered in Hilo, on the island of Hawai`i, in which he outlined the history of the VVV, pointing to its three basic purposes: to contribute toward winning the war, to prove their loyalty, and to provide for their place in the future. But focus of the speech was to stress that any credit the VVV had secured should be reflected back to "you all—if any good or benefit has come from its existence, it is also for the good for Japanese people in Hawai`i." Ted carefully acknowledged the "hometown" men, especially Thomas Kaulukukui, whose superb coaching helped them win the Schofield 130-pound barefoot football championship and place third in the basketball league. In addition, only "last Friday night, coached by another Hilo boy, Richard Chinen, [we] won 3 championships and 3 runner-ups in the army boxing tournament." Tsukiyama was proud of the fact that all had received honorable-discharge certificates signed by "a General, a Col., and a Captain." The army band had played "Aloha Oe" and "3 companies of soldiers presented arms as our convoy moved out" (TTC).

Harry Tanaka recalled that in the two months between the dissolution of the VVV and induction into the 442d, most of his time was spent shooting pool on Bethel Street in Honolulu. Ralph Yempuku interrupted this long vacation with a message that Shigeo Yoshida wanted to "get in touch with you about this volunteer business." "So I called up Shigeo Yoshida; he told me, 'You know, we went to all the trouble to see if the U.S. government would allow people of Japanese ancestry to serve in the U.S. Army and we have an opportunity now and we wanta be sure that it won't be a flop. We want to be sure that there be sufficient number of boys volunteering and all that, and I'm asking for your help.' I said, 'Doing what?' He says, 'Well, the stevedores having a meeting next week and they wanted somebody to speak about that, so would you be willing to go?' I said, 'Well, yeah, yeah, yeah, yeah, okay, I'll go.'"[5]

It made sense for the VVV to spearhead recruiting drives directed at Japanese Americans, but this time it was for combat duty and not a labor battalion. Hung Wai Ching vehemently denies that he was part of any attempt to solicit volunteers for the 442d: "I swear to God, I never recruited one single guy. You see, I have to say to myself, Hung Wai, you have no business telling the guy to join the army or go to combat" (52). Hung Wai may not have recruited anyone personally but it was clear that a strong turnout would be welcomed. He had been disappointed, after all, in the relatively small number of VVV volunteers.

As Dorothy Matsuo points out, the men who volunteered for the 442d did so for a wide variety of reasons, from a deeply felt need to demonstrate their Americanism and a commitment to fight fascism to a host of more mundane personal motives. Ralph Yempuku, the supervisor and dedicated leader of the VVV, who was one of the first to sign up, failed the physical examination because of a knee injury he sustained in college. But Ralph had spent more than a year in the HTG and the VVV to convince the government to accept the nisei for combat duty. For him, sitting the war out would have meant bitter defeat. Yempuku turned to Hung Wai Ching.

Then Hung Wai went to see some general or some colonel and they say, "Okay, we'll give him a chance. If he can go through Ranger training for one month and come out with his knee in one piece, we'll let him join, give him his commission." So I remember going to Schofield. Every morning, as a civilian, no pay but go through the training. There was a guy called Sam Wallace there and I knew him and he knew me. . . . Yeah. A Hawaiian boy. So he took it easy on me. . . . I saw the colonel— the doctor—and he said to get on the table. I jumped down. And he said, "Oh, you are okay." I could have done that before I went to Ranger training. [He laughed.] So I got my commission. (52)

Ted Tsukiyama hailed the opportunity to enlist almost as an act of redemption. "We were sort of held up as shining examples of loyalty. . . . And that led to the 442d and a chance to fight and even die for the country, which eight or nine hundred of the niseis did and, to me, that's the bottom-line answer to people of 'Who you gonna fight, or where does your loyalty lie?'" (30).

Shiro Amioka agreed that this was a momentous and historic occasion and felt it vindicated the Japanese Americans' trust in the ultimate reasonableness of U.S. democracy. He knew that some VVV members felt the need to consult with family but found it difficult to sympathize: "At the VVV we had big meetings, you know. There were some guys who were saying that before they join the army they got to go home and talk to their parents. Why? They have their own minds!" (73). For Amioka, the entire VVV enterprise, following on the heels of the HTG dismissals, was simply the prelude to military service. "Deep down in our hearts this was our ultimate goal—that the aberration of racial discrimination in respect to military service that hit us would be gotten rid of. In fact that was our basic motivation—to show them that we were worthy of them." When Amioka told his mother that he would be volunteering into the army, "she was mad." But she accepted his decision when she realized how determined he was. For him, there was no question but that the VVV had "had a lot to do with" the decision to accept Japanese Americans into the army (75).

Masato Doi recalled being "told that the reason why we were being deactivated was to give us an opportunity to volunteer into the 442d. . . . I felt good that—I felt good about it, yeah" (34). Yugo Okubo felt the same way: "It was kind of good to get a chance to go in the army" (36).

George Yamamoto remembered that Hung Wai Ching had convened a gathering in January 1943 for a straw vote, asking how many VVV members would volunteer should a combat infantry unit be formed. "Well, the majority of us, we didn't know what we were committing ourselves to if we did say yes. . . . Well, interestingly, not too long afterwards, the announcement came out," he laughed (39). George's mother had been a single parent for many years and was unhappy at his decision to volunteer. There was, however, no "long pro-and-con discussion." He simply told her: "I got to go. Besides, look at all my friends. We had more going in than staying out" (39).

Claude Takekawa decided to join but was apprehensive about telling his father, who was "real pro-Japanese," and so delayed the confrontation until the last moment. "I woke him up—I think was the day before I was gonna go, . . . sat down by their bed. I told them, 'Gonna join, 442.' I was taken aback when my father said, 'Well, it's your country, you know, that's the right thing to do.' And I was really surprised. Although when I came back from the service and came back from Japan [after serving during the occupation], he tell me, 'Who, who won the war?'" Takekawa laughed.[6]

Not everyone felt that joining the 442d was an expression of patriotism or service of any kind. Like several others, Ryoji Namba recalled that ideas of loyalty or heroism were not especially important; he thought: "Well, everybody was joining up, so I joined up" (49). Indeed, Jackson Morisawa was reluctant to be interviewed precisely because he felt that too much was already being made of Japanese American World War II heroics. After the VVV was disbanded, joining the 442d was "sort of a continuation. . . . I don't think those of us had any patriotic thoughts . . . in fact, you felt that if you didn't go with the guys, you felt like you not part of something, you know. I don't think anybody went into it with the sense of 'Hey, I gung ho,' you know, patriotic move and all. I don't think most of them felt like that" (26).

Ralph Toyota tried to enlist but was rejected. He later made it into the Military Intelligence Service as one of about three thousand nisei who translated Japanese documents and interrogated Japanese prisoners. Yoshiaki Fujitani, who had left the VVV in anger and resentment in April 1942 after his father was arrested and interned in a mainland concentration camp, was not about to join the 442d. Fujitani had learned to make eyeglasses for the American Optical Company. In January 1943, he was still very bitter; he knew that many of his buddies in the VVV would be joining the 442d, "but I was adamant. I said I have nothing to do with that anymore. . . . I think people understood that it was kind of an incongruous situation where I'm there and dad is an enemy alien, . . . but Hung Wai Ching talked to me. I don't know exactly what he said . . . he tried to persuade me, though" (25).

Hung Wai has consistently denied any recruiting for the combat unit, but even into his nineties, he was such a commanding presence that he could appear to be twisting both arms even though he might simply be making a statement. Much later, Fujitani did enlist.

> So at the end of '43, thereabouts, I noticed that all of my friends had gone. They volunteered. And more and more I got to feel kinda lonely, you know. So when the call for the Military Intelligence Service was made, I volunteered. . . . Yeah, and we were inducted on January 3 of 1944. And the thought that I had at that time was not one of patriotism—"My country right or wrong" or that kind of stuff. It was "Gee, I'm lonely!" . . . I guess, during that time, I began to accept the reality. You know, after all, dad is dad, and I am myself. I have to do what I feel I ought to do. So, while I left Triple V with a particular reason, a year later I decided, well, that didn't matter; . . . at that time it was the proper thing to say—that you were patriotic, my country at any price, et cetera. But the reality for me was simply that without my friends, life wasn't very comfortable, and so that was the main motivation in my going. And I think that's part of my Hawaiian heritage too. (25–26, 30)[7]

This is a remarkable and remarkably human testimony. Akira Otani's father had also been interned, but the timing was different. Because Matsujiro Otani was arrested on December 7, 1941, Akira immediately confronted the dilemma of serving the country that had unjustly incarcerated his father. Fujitani, on the other hand, saw his father interned even as he himself was engaged in months of volunteer manual labor. After he left the VVV, he had months to reflect. That so many of his friends were volunteering into the military suggested two things: first, the United States was changing its original hard-line policy against the nisei; second, the bonds of friendship were extremely powerful. That unity of identity is what he meant by "Hawaiian heritage."

When Harry Tanaka had agreed to speak to the group of stevedores to recruit other nisei for the new combat unit, he wondered whether they might not ask if the speaker himself had already enlisted. If not, Tanaka's personal stance and the integrity of the recruitment effort might be compromised. So, "on that very day," he stopped by the local draft board and became the first nisei in his district to sign up. The draft board officials had to call headquarters for information regarding proper procedures for accepting Japanese Americans.

Yempuku was enthusiastic in encouraging fellow nisei to volunteer. Charles Oda, who was not a member of the VVV, remembered that

Ralph was "instrumental" first in securing him a scholarship at the university and later "in getting us to volunteer": "He glorified war and returning as heroes. We got taken in by that. . . . Actually I didn't feel I had to volunteer but did so because Yempuku told us we should."[8]

Not every VVV member enlisted. While in the VVV, Richard Zukemura had often invited Seichi Ono, who was from the island of Maui, to spend weekends at his home. Richard came down with the mumps just as the VVV was disbanded and was forced into quarantine on the base. Seichi, of course, informed Richard's parents and urged them to keep their son, an only child, from volunteering. Armed with this information and advice, Richard's parents insisted that he remain home. The height of enthusiasm for volunteering had subsided by the time Zukemura was released from quarantine, so he complied. "If I was at the barracks," he commented, "I may have volunteered" (33).

Teru Himoto faced formidable opposition from his parents. Unlike Amioka, he insisted that parents deserved the "courtesy" of serious deliberation before such a critical decision was made. One of the hardest working and most enthusiastic of the VVV while at Schofield, he found the decision to remain out of the 442d difficult:

> I almost signed up but when I went home—discussed this with my parents—I'm the only child now. I'm adopted. So, you know, my dad and I had a real long discussion. He wasn't too happy. . . . But it was my mother that stopped me from joining. She almost snapped. She started running around the house, and I said I can't have a crazy mother while I'm on the battlefront. So I told my friends that I'm not going to sign up. I said, you know, my family and I are as important as joining the army. . . . I feel so downhearted so I worked in a pineapple plantation. . . . I thought right through that I would get taken but agricultural employees were given 5-C, some kind of classification where they were considered important labor force. . . . So I never got drafted. (6–7)

Himoto's account suggests the variety and complexity of nisei responses to the 442d and raises the question of the transmission of traditional cultural values. Did Japanese immigrant women simply defer to males? Did cultural norms such as honor and duty inevitably hold sway over private and individual interests? Teru's issei mother surely knew the much-heralded tale of the Japanese mother who saw her son off to the front lines during the 1904–1905 Russo-Japanese War. While still visible to her son, who was waving goodbye from the troopship, she jumped into the ocean and drowned herself so that he would never worry about her and lose focus as a soldier of the emperor. This became a public morality tale of immense benefit to the militarizing government of Japan, but clearly it was not universally embraced.

On March 28, 1943, almost three thousand nisei, with a handful of haole officers, assembled at Honolulu's Iolani Palace for a ceremony to mark their induction. Former VVV members were honored by being placed in the front row for the ceremony and the official photograph. Perhaps fifteen thousand relatives, friends, and spectators thronged the palace grounds for the occasion. Within a week, the men trudged off to Honolulu harbor, where they boarded the *Lurline*, a luxury liner converted to a troopship, for the voyage to San Francisco. On that occasion, the men were in virtual disarray, not yet in good physical shape but forced to shoulder large and heavy duffel bags from the railroad station to the pier. Many felt disgraced before their families, who had lined the streets for a last look. Daniel Inouye, the future U.S. senator from Hawaii, described the scene as humiliating and pitiful.[9]

Hung Wai Ching took great pride in seeing off the former VVV members at Honolulu harbor. He then arranged to be flown immediately to San Francisco to meet the men as they disembarked. "I got permission to fly up on the plane with some admirals ahead of the arrival, and I come off the plane, without an overcoat, cold as hell" (29–31). Ching reported to General John DeWitt, the notoriously bigoted head of the Western Defense Command, who was responsible for issuing the orders that removed Japanese American communities from the West Coast.

DeWitt "scared the hell" out of Hung Wai by declaring his visit unauthorized; Hung Wai finally arranged his own release by requesting that DeWitt assign someone to accompany him. Finally, he learned the timetable for the rail trip to Camp Shelby in Mississippi, looking for a way to divert the basic-training site out of the Deep South and into Colorado or Minnesota, where he felt the racism would not be as pronounced or provocative. Hung Wai was afraid that, in the South, the Hawai`i Japanese Americans would be treated as badly as the blacks and that there would be "a hell of a morale problem . . . riots and fighting. . . . Some guy lose their temper and then let's go take it out on them fucking haoles or something like that; . . . when you get our local boys mad, we can be terrible. . . . We suppress ourselves but local ethnic behavior—I'm telling you, there is something about us, you know" (29–31).

This was not an unwarranted fear. These were working-class kids from fields, farms, and tough urban neighborhoods. Physical confrontations were common and often took the form of group participation—and, importantly, they came from a society in which whites had never been the majority.

Ching arranged an appeal to change the training site through the offices of Hawaii's territorial delegate to Congress, Joseph Farrington. The request went to Assistant Secretary of War John McCloy, who then traveled to Mississippi for a personal investigation; Lieutenant Colonel S.L.A. "Slam" Marshall was also sent. McCloy decided to stay with the original plan. As Hung Wai recalled, McCloy regretted that the concern had been raised too late. More important, as Hung Wai related, McCloy insisted: "'Your boys are American, right? And Mississippi is a part of America, right? . . . Don't you think they ought to know about the South too?'" (34). Unconvinced, Hung Wai made one last attempt; this time he spoke directly with Eleanor Roosevelt, whom he had met in Honolulu the previous year.

On May 24, 1943, Mrs. Roosevelt wrote to Colonel Marshall conveying Hung Wai's reservations about Camp Shelby. By now surely more than mildly annoyed at this persistent intervention, McCloy responded to Mrs. Roosevelt on behalf of Marshall on May 31, explaining that the War Department, "prior to and soon after Mr. Ching's visit, . . . sent qualified Army officers to inspect conditions at Camp Shelby and report on the morale of the Japanese American soldiers; . . . there have been no untoward incidents between the citizens of Hattiesburg and the Japanese American soldiers." McCloy did, however, acknowledge problems.[10]

McCloy explained that the major issue was between the nisei and some of the "white soldiers" stationed there. "These are the occasional tendency [sic] on the part of some of the white soldiers to refer to the Japanese American soldiers as 'Japs' or some opprobrious term identified with enemy Japanese. Since they are very sensitive about their loyalty, this is resented by them." Nonetheless, since the problems "appear to stem more from the fact that the reported incidents grow out of a Japanese *enemy* consideration rather than a Japanese *racial* consideration" (emphasis added), there was no need to change the site. This line of reasoning made it possible for McCloy to insist, to the end of his life, that the World War II internment of Japanese Americans was neither racist nor unreasonable.[11] Finally, McCloy suggested that the "Hawaiian Japanese" were experiencing a new and strange situation causing them to "have an exaggerated sensitivity." So things would settle down, he reassured Mrs. Roosevelt. The 442d continued training at Shelby through the end of the war.

Hung Wai Ching had good instincts about race relations in general, but he was wrong about Camp Shelby and the nisei. McCloy's decision was ultimately vindicated by the successful training record established by the 100th and 442d. Hung Wai's fears of widespread racial unrest or riots came to nothing, although there were many incidents between the nisei and the white GIs or the white community of Hattiesburg. Eleanor Roosevelt continued in her role as a steadfast supporter of Hung Wai and the Japanese Americans. In later press conferences, she used the positive nature of race relations in Hawai'i to urge dismantling of the War Relocation Authority camps and resettle Japanese Americans in colleges, farms, towns, and cities across the United States, even as the war was still being fought.[12]

Widely scattered among the various units at Camp Shelby, former VVV members nevertheless kept in touch with one another. The men of the 442d quickly earned the respect of their officers, as well as of the troops against whom they were pitted in war games. The VVV were nearly indistinguishable from other 442d volunteers except for the preponderance of university men and for their semi-military labor during the past year. That experience was not inconsequential, however, because they had become accustomed to hard physical work, as well as to army life and regimentation. It was logical, therefore, for many to assume leadership roles at the squad and platoon levels. In their group meetings, courses, and general college orientation, VVV members had acquired a wider perspective on the global war, a sense of the discipline required of military life, and a certain status that encouraged leadership both by example and persuasion.

Like so many of the youngsters from Hawai'i, the VVV were struck by the open racism of the segregated South. Nearly every returning veteran had stories of being shocked by the indignities heaped upon his black army comrades and the black residents of Mississippi. Some veterans still revel in stories of Hawai'i nisei who took matters into their own hands—throwing some white driver out of his own bus, for example, when he refused to board a black soldier or pushed a black woman off the vehicle.[13]

Shiro Amioka provided an unusual twist on this theme. As in much of the South, African Americans in Hattiesburg were restricted to the last few rows on the bus; when these seats were filled, drivers often refused to board other African Americans, even when the rest of the vehicle was empty. In Hawai`i, young males usually regarded the rear of the bus as their turf—a tradition I vividly recall as a teenager in the 1950s. In Mississippi, the army made it clear that the nisei were to use "white" sections of movie theaters and buses, as well as "white" water fountains and bathrooms. Whatever their views on race relations or segregation, the nisei from Hawai`i were not about to let others dictate their place on the bus. Amioka noted that it took a while before they realized that their insistence on following their old patterns was inadvertently causing black residents great inconvenience. "In Hawai`i, automatic to us that we go in the back. But what we didn't realize in the beginning was that when we did that we denied the Negroes to get on the bus. . . . We didn't like the system, but if we take them up [the rear seats], they can't get on the bus. . . . So after a while we just took the regular seats and let them get in the back, you know" (80–84).

When John Terry of the *Honolulu Star-Bulletin* was sent to observe the 442d in training in August 1943, he reported that the men were doing well both in training and with the local citizens. He met, among others, Norman Tsukazaki, Masaichi Sagawa (who was in an antitank squad), and Sukeyoshi Kushi, whom he remembered as the outstanding golfer from Maui. Richard Chinen made a distinct impression; he became the 442d Regiment's boxing coach and told Terry that "we are doing all right. We'll make Hawai`i proud of her sons."[14] Chinen and Kenji Nobori coached fifty Japanese American boxers, who dominated the lighter weight categories in Shelby tournaments. Prestigious *Ring* magazine featured the group in its September 1943 issue.[15]

Chinen and his buddies had already met Earl Finch, who acquired a reputation as a generous benefactor to the Hawai`i nisei and was royally treated by them in Hawai`i after the war. Finch became a legendary figure for his relationship with the 442d troops. Claude Takekawa knew him well.

> He'd go up and down the company streets all through the 442d passing out watermelon. And there would be an open invitation for anybody, anybody in the 442d, . . . to come to his house. . . . One time, he said, "Why don't you guys form a band, Hawaiian band?" Because a lot of the 100th and 442d boys were already coming back wounded and going hospitals. . . . I played the ukulele. . . . He said, "I'm gonna have you guys go up to New York and Washington to the hospitals; . . . he put us up at the best hotel, the Waldorf. Can you imagine? . . . Then we went to Washington, D.C. And again he put us up at the nice hotel, the May-

flower. Then we went to Walter Reed Hospital to play. . . . We used to call ourselves the Triple V Serenaders. [He laughed.][16]

On one occasion, Chinen was treated to a day on the Finch farm near Hattiesburg, where he was introduced to some strange traditions. "We went off into the woods on horses. . . . We had a hunting dog. He did a lot of barking, but we never got the 'possum. Mr. Finch said the red fox scared him off. I never had so much fun in my life. That day was the first time I ever heard hog calling, and what I mean, the hogs came running. They came from everywhere."[17]

Richard Chinen mentioned the tensions between the Hawai'i GIs and the Japanese Americans from the mainland but was optimistic that the friction was subsiding. "We are getting to understand each other. We are getting to be pals now. One thing—the mainland boys speak much better English than the Hawai'i boys. We couldn't express ourselves like they could. But everything is going to work out."[18] In the beginning, at least, there were serious problems between the Hawai'i-born "budda-heads" and these *kotonks*, as the Hawai'i GIs called mainland Japanese Americans. It seemed to the VVV, for example, that the noncommissioned officer positions—corporal and sergeant—were reserved for the *kotonks*. Shiro Amioka was outraged. "*Kotonks*, . . . my feeling was why were all the noncommissioned officers mainland people? Why didn't they pick some of the Hawai'i guys? That was my feeling. I was mad as heck; . . . when I saw Hung Wai, . . . I would run down the hall, the street, and say, 'Hey, Hung Wai, I want to talk to you.' I'd let him have it. . . . He'd try to calm me down. . . . Well, it changed later in the sense that after we got through basic training, then some of us got promoted" (78–79).

There was a real difference in behavior, as many 442d veterans point out, after the Hawai'i boys were invited to the concentration camp at Rohwer, Arkansas, one of ten maintained by the U.S. War Relocation Authority. Directly experiencing the conditions from which the *kotonks* had volunteered for combat duty allowed the Hawai'i boys to understand why the mainland Japanese American contingent was both smaller than Hawaii's and less likely to exhibit a "go for broke" spirit. (In all, approximately thirty thousand Japanese Americans, volunteers and draftees, served during World War II.) "Go for broke," a crapshooters' term, became the regimental slogan.

Charles Hemenway, longtime friend, maintained a steady correspondence with the young men he had supported while they served in the VVV, and, he continued to write to various individuals at Camp Shelby, including Unkei Uchima, former tackle for the UH Rainbows: "I know how occupied you will be from now on and do not expect to have many letters from you, but, whenever you feel inclined, remember that I would be very glad to know how things are going."[19] Ralph Yempuku, who had joined the 442d in May 1942, wrote a lengthy letter to Hemenway on June 13, confirming the rigors of the training "from 6:30 in the morning . . . till late at night." Yempuku noted that the younger boys would gripe about the heat and the training until he reminded them that there were "quite a few" men in the regiment who were thirty-five and thirty-six years old. Chastened, they quit complaining.[20]

The camaraderie built during the previous year carried over to Camp Shelby for the VVV. Claude Takekawa's VVV Serenaders was only one of many manifestations. After the initial period of neglect noted by Amioka, the men became logical choices to serve as noncommissioned officers. As Yempuku wrote to Hemenway: "We are planning for a weekly get-together of the VVV boys on Wednesday evenings. The gang sure miss the old life in Schofield and will probably have a bull session every week. A great many of the V boys are squad (sgt.) and assistant squad (cpl.) leaders. My ambition is to see this 442d Combat Team become the best infantry regiment in the United States and if I can get this into the heads of the men I know that this ambition can be achieved."[21]

The Triple V public service tradition continued. When Hemenway responded to Yempuku, he noted that he had received from Captain Katsumi Kometani a clipping from the *New York Times* that showed the boys buying war bonds at Shelby. Kometani, with the 100th Battalion, wrote to Hemenway: "The VVV boys are holding a little gathering and they were kind enough to ask me to attend and say a few words."[22] When the Honolulu chapter of the National Foundation for Infantile Paralysis solicited funds for its polio campaign, the former VVV men took the lead. Colonel Charles Pence, the 442d commanding officer, noted: "I take great pleasure in sending herewith a check for $7,098; . . . 2nd Lt. Ralph T. Yempuku of Honolulu called together former members of the Varsity Victory Volunteers now in the combat team and mapped out a similar opportunity for our soldiers to make donations to this worthy cause."[23]

The record of the nisei who fought in World War II forms, along with the history of the internment of Japanese Americans, the most intensively researched and published area for this ethnic group. (Indeed, there are occasional allegations of publicity overkill.) Some of the VVV members went on to serve on European battlefronts with distinction. When the governor of Hawai'i asked for statistics in fall 1944, the study revealed that Japanese Americans, about one-third of the population, comprised 60–65 percent of armed-services personnel from the territory. They were also dying in wildly disproportionate numbers as well; about 400 nisei had been killed in action in the single year between September 1943 and August 1944, while a total of 72 Hawai'i non-Japanese were killed in the three years between December 7, 1941, and August 1944.[24] For all of World War II, the total number of military nisei deaths was 506—63 percent of the total deaths from Hawai'i. Japanese Americans were being killed, in short, at better than twice the rate of other ethnic groups.[25]

Seven of the VVV died in Europe, among them Grover K. Nakaji, a student in the university's Teachers College and a "darn good" carpenter while at Schofield Barracks. On June 26, 1944, Nakaji and the 442d, led by the 100th Battalion veterans, encountered German troops in Suvereto, Italy. Nakaji helped to destroy an enemy tank and was killed in the ensuing explosion.[26]

On the Fourth of July 1944, there was a vicious battle for Hill 140 overlooking a main coastal highway in Italy. Sergeant Howard M. Urabe, according to the citation for his Silver Star, awarded posthumously, "crawled 25 yards through sparse undergrowth to reach a position in front of an enemy machine gun. . . . Urabe suddenly stood up and fired a rifle grenade into the nest, killing the machine gunner and destroying the gun." Urabe then killed two others fleeing from the nest before destroying yet another machine-gun nest with a rifle grenade before he was killed by sniper fire.

On the next day, the battle continued, as 442d troops struggled to reach the seaport of Leghorn through coastal roads covered by German fire from the Apennine mountain range. Dislodging the enemy from heavily fortified strongholds was a costly campaign; one of the casualties was Sergeant Jenhatsu Chinen, one of Daniel Inouye's closest friends. Senator Inouye later wrote that Company E of the 442d "had to go from one ridge and attack the enemy on another ridge. That's not easy. They were shooting down at us. On that day, a couple of my best friends died. One of them was Jenhatsu Chinen. He played the guitar and I played the ukulele. He was in the process of teaching me how to play the guitar during our breaks. We were very close."[27]

In the battle for Hill 140, Private First Class Akio Nishikawa, a medic, was awarded the Bronze Star for gallantry for helping wounded comrades under artillery fire. Soon thereafter, the nisei pressed forward, meeting stiff enemy resistance through the Italian countryside. The citation for his second medal, the Silver Star, reads: "Nishikawa ran for a distance of 100 yards through concentrated 88mm artillery and mortar shelling to render first aid." Yelling "Gotta go!" despite pleas from his platoon to wait for the barrage to cease, Nishikawa was mortally wounded.

Hiroichi Tomita was a fine math student at the university before he joined the VVV, then the 442d. Near the spot where Nishikawa was killed, Tomita was seeking shelter in a farmhouse from German artillery shells. Private First Class Tomita was killed instantly by an 88mm round that pierced the building and exploded in a brilliant flash.

In August 1944, the 442d was pulled back from the front lines and the veterans were training replacements for their next assignment in France. Daniel Betsui, a musician and composer, was explaining German mines. After the demonstration, the mines were loaded on a truck. A detonating device may have been inadvertently loaded together with 1,800 pounds of various forms of German explosives. Betsui and ten others were instantly killed when the entire truckload blew up.[28]

Robert S. Murata was a freshman at the university when he joined the VVV. In the 442d, he became a small part of the grand drama surrounding the rescue of the Texas "Lost Battalion" in the Vosge Mountains in northeast France, as the retreating German troops fought desperately to keep the Allies from their home borders. His company—Company L, Third Battalion—was nearly wiped out by the rescue mission, so details of his death are not available.

Anki Hoshijo, who had fought in campaigns in Italy and France, was severely wounded just before the 442d was committed to the "Lost Battalion" campaign. Like most veterans, Hoshijo rarely told war stories to anyone but his combat buddies—not even to his curious children. At Anki's memorial, his son Leonard delivered a eulogy laced with affection and wry humor. "The anti-personnel mine he stepped on didn't explode properly, shooting upward through the legs and ripping his raincoat off his back, but luckily for us [his future] children, not hitting other particular points. . . . He went through a series of hospitals. . . . As with most of this story, we didn't hear much of it until recent years. For that reason, we didn't know that one effect of the mine explosion was a permanent hearing impairment. He didn't wear a hearing aid. Imagine teenagers getting frustrated thinking their father was turning a deaf ear to us, and finding out later he really was!"[29]

Ed Nakamura and Ed Honda found themselves in the 522d Artillery Unit, which, in the process of chasing the remnants of the German army back toward Munich, stumbled upon some of the Dachau camps and discovered at least one of the reasons they were fighting the Nazis.[30] Both later became lawyers and judges; they were also valuable because their *kotonk* officers could understand their English—the pidgin spoken by many others was unintelligible to those limited to Standard English.[31] Ryoji Namba was assigned to the 206th Army Ground Force Band, in which he played the string bass. The band played at church services, parades, concerts, and memorial services. Their ranks included ukulele virtuosos and GIs performing as cellophane-skirted "hula dancers."

Many of the VVV members were assigned to the Military Intelligence Service, selected and trained to use their Japanese-language background to interrogate prisoners and translate captured documents.[32] For decades after the war, the MIS was rarely recognized because so much of its work had been classified. But, according to Lieutenant General Charles Wiloughby, the World War II head of Army Intelligence (G-2), these men were extremely valuable to allied efforts against the Japanese in the Pacific and Asia. Several thousand nisei were deployed in Washington, D.C., Europe, throughout Asia and the Pacific (including assignments with Merrill's Marauders in Burma), and on loan to units in allied armies or governments.[33]

Most of the VVV members who joined the MIS were recruited as they were completing basic infantry training in Mississippi. By late 1943, the translation and interrogation teams had more than proved their value to General Douglas MacArthur and the Pacific theater, and there was great pressure to recruit more nisei. The war in the Pacific ranged over half the globe, since Japanese troops had been deployed as far north as the Bering Straits, southward through Siberia, Manchuria, Korea, and China, across dozens of archipelagos in the Pacific, through the Philippines, and into Southeast Asia. It was critical, then, to have a basic idea of the location of Japanese troops and their movements at any given time. As the combined allied forces increased the pace of their counteroffensives, the sheer volume of captured documents and prisoners jumped dramatically—making sense of this enormously valuable resource required facility in spoken or written Japanese.

A school for training Japanese-language specialists had opened shortly before the Pearl Harbor attack at the Presidio in San Francisco under the strict supervision of nisei John Aiso. It was subsequently moved to Camp Savage, Minnesota, and later to Minnesota's Fort Snelling. Harry Tanaka was in a group ordered to Savage in August 1943. The move from Mississippi was dramatic, he reported. Among Tanaka's most vivid memories was the difference in race relations: The absence of a black "problem" in Minnesota created a space for more flexible and positive white attitudes toward the nisei. Tanaka was amazed when, in a crowded streetcar, a middle-aged white woman stood up and offered her seat: "'Why don't you sit down, because you in the military, you must be tired.'" He refused, of course, but the image remained indelibly etched in his mind. Tanaka completed his six months of intensive training—his spoken Japanese was not great, but twelve years of Japanese-language schooling had provided a good background in reading the characters—and was sent to Australia. Later, he was offered a promotion to officer status when the military realized the nature and extent of nisei contributions, but a physical examination revealed a serious case of tuberculosis. Tanaka underwent a lengthy period of hospitalization, returned to complete his undergraduate work at the University of Hawaii, and went on to acquire a law degree from Yale University.[34]

Yoshimi Hayashi had never been a particularly good student at Japanese-language school but was ordered to Japanese-language specialist training in Minnesota with Harry Tanaka. The nisei were joined by non-Japanese who were considered good language students, many straight from college campuses. Most of this group had neither combat training nor Japanese-language background of any kind and were generally considered inferior on both counts by the Japanese Americans. The disparity in ability was understandable, but there was resentment toward these white linguists, because "when they graduated, they graduated as second lieutenants; we graduated as corporals. When we go to the front, they become team leaders; we be the workers."[35] (Perhaps ironically, several of these white officers went on to become the first generation of U.S. scholars of Japanese language, history, and culture who were thoroughly trained in the language.)

Hayashi, remembered as one of the "least likely to succeed" among the VVV, recalled with glee the day that they first were served a meal in the Camp Savage mess hall, "You know, we go through the line, and the people would serve you. 'Put more food on [we demanded].' They won't, so we get mad; then, what we do is get the tray, we turn it upside down and demand more food. And we threaten them so they give us more food." Colonel Kai Rasmussen, the camp commander, finally brought Hayashi and the other ringleaders before him and set them straight.

Yoshiaki Fujitani, who enlisted after considerable soul-searching over his father's internment, went directly to language training in Minnesota. But he hurt his knee playing football and could not be sent to the Pacific battlefront. Instead he went to Maryland, where he translated captured Japanese documents. One of his assignments was to describe an architectural rendering for buildings used in the fortification of islands in the Western Pacific. After the war, he met a cousin in Japan who had used that precise plan to build structures for the Japanese military (27).

While in Maryland, Fujitani witnessed the spectacle of nisei GIs running through the woods outfitted in Japanese military uniforms. "Their job was to run around like that and be viewed by American soldiers. . . . To give them an idea of what Japanese were supposed to look like out in the field. I thought, My goodness, I wouldn't enjoy that kind of work as an American soldier!" (28). This was a milder version of a 1943 project designed to train attack dogs to identify enemy Japanese soldiers. The assumption was that the Japanese possessed a distinctive ethnic aroma and that citizenship would not alter the smell; nisei from the 100th Battalion then training in Wisconsin were sent to remote Cat Island in Mississippi to simulate the enemy and their body odors—the project was a dismal failure, but the subjects enjoyed the sun, the fishing, and the beer, away from the Wisconsin winter.[36]

Ted Tsukiyama was ordered to join the MIS because of his Japanese–language school experience. He complied reluctantly, since he would "miss out" on the opportunity to fight for the nation and "to convincingly demonstrate loyalty. "So I resented very much that I got pulled out and sent to this so-called cushy job of being an interpreter; . . . we got sent to India and here we are behind the lines and I'm in the air force, which is like the country club of the army, . . . very safe. I always had a bad—felt a bad conscience about that" (30–31).[37]

Ted wrote regularly to his parents and to supporters of the nisei soldiers. The Emergency Service Committee received his letters from Burma and made copies for all members.[38] Some of his letters, translated into Japanese and printed in the Japanese-language daily, the *Hawaii*

Times, informed the issei that their sons were contributing to the war effort and that the Japanese military was being defeated.

Claude Takekawa took a most circuitous route to the MIS. His unit, the First Battalion of the 442d, was depleted after basic training by orders to replace men wounded and killed in the 100th Battalion in Italy. There were too few left to constitute a regular battalion, so the First was cannibalized to supply more replacement troops and to train new enlistees and draftees. In Europe, the 100th became the First Battalion of the 442d, although, in recognition of its outstanding battle record, it retained its original designation. As a result, the 442d Regimental Combat Team was comprised of the 100th, 2d, and 3d Infantry Battalions.[39]

Takekawa was first kept at Shelby to train new recruits and later asked to join forty or fifty others, including Akira Otani and Unkei Uchima, to attend Officer Candidate School at Fort Benning, Georgia. He was then sent to Fort McClellan, Alabama, where "I think I trained three cycles of young haole boys from New York and Ohio. And the funniest part about the whole thing was when I told them that I was Japanese, they—they wouldn't believe that."[40] It was only toward the end of the war that the need for translators in the Pacific forced Takekawa into the MIS.

The most dramatic World War II stories came from Ralph Yempuku, who joined the 442d in Mississippi and was recruited for Officer Candidate School at Fort Benning. While there, he was asked to join the Office of Strategic Services (OSS), the precursor to the Central Intelligence Agency. The OSS wanted nisei who could join covert and guerilla actions behind Japanese lines in the Pacific and, if needed, in Japan itself. The OSS was sending language specialists all over German-occupied Europe: "Yugoslavia, Germany, every place. So they figured they could do the same thing in Japan. So when they recruited us, that was the idea." Yempuku then underwent a six-week crash course in Japanese-language at Camp Savage in Minnesota. "Oh, I never studied that hard in my life. From early morning to late night, I learned Japanese all over again. Then after that they sent us to radio communications school to learn dot, dash, dot—you know, all communication stuff. And after that they sent us to Catalina Island, off California. And they had a secret school there for training—a physical training school. Demolitions and guns and hand-to-hand combat and all that" (53).

Yempuku was then sent to Miami and assigned to Burma (Myanmar), where the Japanese were in retreat. For decades after the war, Ralph was ordered to keep the stories quiet. "But OSS—they weren't part of the army. They could do anything they wanted. Most of the time I was in Burma, we were behind enemy lines. A price on my head." What followed?

> We were training native troops—guerrillas. We had two or three battalions of guerrilla, native troops. I suppose they recruited us for the simple reason that they wanted, when they captured the Japanese prisoners of war, they wanted somebody to talk to them. Also they were talking about paratrooping us into Japan. . . .
>
> Well, the Japanese were almost defeated. We were ambushing them, killing them, . . . harass, interdict, and ambush. . . . If the Japanese appeared in any sizeable numbers, then we disappeared into the jungle. If they had one and we had fifty, now, we were strong. I had thirty or forty guerrillas under my command. . . . There was a guy there. "Namba" is a Japanese name, but this guy was a Burmese—Namba. . . . They had to go to school and learn Japanese. When I got in there nobody could speak English. This kid said he could speak Japanese, so he and I conversed in Japanese.
>
> We had about half a dozen other haoles with me and they thought it was the greatest thing. Here you are fighting the Japanese and I'm talking Japanese with this guy. . . .
>
> So anyway, after we got the Japanese practically all out of Burma, I went to China. The night the war ended—the following day—we went down to Hainan Island [off the southeast China coast] by plane. I was parachuted into the prisoner-of-war camp there because we heard that the Japanese were going to slaughter the American prisoners of war. We had about three or four mercy missions. . . . I was with the six of us that went down to Hainan Island. I was the only Japanese, . . . and there weren't any Americans there in the first place. They were all Australians and Dutch. But we rescued them. And then I came out—a British destroyer took us out to Hong Kong. While I was in Hong Kong, the Japanese were going to surrender to the British and present the sword to the British at the Peninsula Hotel, the most famous hotel in the Orient. Four or five of us Americans were up in the balcony watching this ceremony. Unbeknownst to me, my brother is in the Japanese army. He's the interpreter for the Japanese general or admiral who was giving the sword to the British. He sees me up there. . . . He recognizes me but he doesn't want to say anything because he knows the British will never understand. . . . So anyway, he's in a prisoner-of-war camp, and I fly back to Kunming [in Yunnan Province, southwest China; headquarters of Chiang Kai-shek's Nationalist Army]. . . .

No. I didn't see him. So I get back to Kunming, China, and a couple nights later one of my friends, Uyehara, comes over and says, "Hey, Captain, you got a brother?" I says, "Yeah. I have four brothers." He said, "You know a strange thing happened. . . . I'm acting as an interpreter for the British and I'm in the prisoner-of-war camp in Hong Kong interrogating these people. . . . I see a guy exactly like you." He says, "At first I thought you were masquerading because I know you were in the OSS and you folks do all that kind of stuff and you are in there trying to get some information about war crimes." . . . So he says, "I didn't want to go up to this person. But I couldn't stand it so I called him and asked if his name was Yempuku. He said yeah. I asked him if he got a brother called Ralph in Hawai`i. He said yeah. I asked if he knew that he was alive. He said, 'Yeah, I saw him the other day.' And so I said, 'Jeesus.'" So when he told me the story, I said, "What a small world." (52–58)

The fact that the Yempuku brothers fought on both sides of the Pacific war has received notice both in journalism and fiction.[41] In Japan, one widely read novel, *Futatsu no sokoku* [Dual homelands], depicted the brothers meeting on the battlefield instead of in Hong Kong. A television version was later serialized for NHK Television. In spite of all of this publicity, Yempuku noted that his children, in their thirties at the time of the interviews in 1985, knew next to nothing of his war stories. One of the things he wanted them to know of war behind enemy lines was "how scared you were, you know. How frightened you were most of the time" (57).

The VVV in the MIS and OSS fought from behind their desks in Maryland and Europe, on the battlefields of the Pacific, behind the lines in Southeast Asia, and in Japan during the U.S. occupation. Their weapons were dictionaries and years of experience with immigrant parents and Japanese-language schools in Hawai`i and in North America. They also fought as part of the 442d band and in the artillery or engineers. Some were killed in combat in Europe. And while many of them insist that they were ordinary folks with no intention of seeking honor or glory for their ordinary deeds, they were aware that they had elected a means of pushing a society to meet its own professed ideals and that they were in good company.

In the meantime, the battle to end racism continued on the home front even as the war raged overseas.

World War II marked the end of a Hawai`i tightly controlled by a small close-knit haole oligarchy. Perceptive individuals understood, even by the 1930s, that change was inevitable, but no one could foresee the precise contours of the new society in the making. One thing was certain, however; the way in which issues involving the Japanese American population were resolved would be critical. Most accounts of Hawai`i during World War II emphasize the anxiety of Japanese Americans and the heroic measures they adopted to demonstrate their political loyalty—leading to what many called "200 percent Americanism."[42] A neglected part of this history is the way in which Japanese Americans deployed an array of antiracist weapons, one of which was exemplified by the initiative and drive of the VVV. And even within groups like the VVV or the ESC, it is possible to detect strategies beyond those of assimilation and cooperation, including a stubborn refusal to remain passive or accommodating. As a result, even during the wartime period, there were numerous opportunities for struggle and confrontation.

In Hawai`i, the nisei and the general public knew that the military would continue to be a key factor well into the post-war era. First, martial law lasted almost as long as the war itself, and the military fought a bitter, protracted, battle to maintain its position. Second, the military's economic power was immense. Many of the sugar plantations still depended heavily on Japanese labor; martial law was used systematically to freeze wages and mobility so that the Japanese were secured in positions that once more resembled indentured servitude.[43]

Further, what the military bought and whom the military hired became critical alternatives to the closed system controlled by the Big Five. One unintended consequence of the military's presence, for example, was substantial growth for local entrepreneurs, especially more established groups like the Chinese. The overall result for Japanese Americans was decidedly mixed, but for some enterprises—farms, restaurants, wholesalers, contractors, retail stores—catering to the vastly enlarged population of military personnel and workers with ready cash and the urge to spend created an economic boomlet. Herb Isonaga remarked wryly that his parents found that revenues at their general store "increased after the start of World War II in direct proportion to the degree of racial prejudice shown toward Americans of Japanese ancestry." Isonaga thought it ironic that until that time "it was a struggle to keep the store functioning. They started to make money when the war began because of the business from the thousands of troops who were stationed on the island."[44]

The sheer number of military and civilian personnel arriving from the mainland drastically altered the traditional demographic ecology in which, for example, there had been relatively few Caucasians. By 1940, about 25 percent of Hawaii's resident population was white, up from five to ten percent in the early 1900s.[45] Where Japanese Americans had been by far the largest single ethnic group on the islands before the war, the Honolulu Board of Health estimated that by mid-1945, Caucasians actually outnumbered them, 35 percent to 32 percent.[46]

One of the inevitable and interesting results of this extraordinary population shift in favor of whites was a dramatic drop in the prestige and status formerly enjoyed by Hawai`i haoles. Until the 1930s, it seemed that almost every white person encountered in Hawai`i belonged to the powerful Big Five by virtue of family or business or both. But defense workers doing manual labor and GIs from poor white families commanded little respect or awe: The powerful mystique of haole supremacy was irrevocably shattered.

During the war, Hawaii's nisei on the mainland and in Europe bought sex from white prostitutes, fed white beggars, fraternized and brawled with white GIs, married white women, and killed white enemies. Race relations could never be the same thereafter. On the home front, too, the influx of so many whites plus a modest but noticeable number of African Americans introduced possibilities for new dynamics. Segregation, U.S.-style, became one of the many potential problems that had existed only in relatively mild form in pre-war Hawai`i.

Charles Loomis of the Morale Section "brought up the growing problem of Jim Crowism in Hawai`i and how mainland problems and practices are coming in faster than Hawai`i can absorb them."[47] Jim Crow—racial segregation by law or policy—had not been necessary in a Hawai`i where the small haole elite enjoyed de facto separation in housing, education, business, recreation, and most other aspects of life. One reason the new racial dynamics could so threaten the established order was that the preceding decades had witnessed an exquisite refinement of racial and class stratification. The traditional elite was haole and Native Hawaiian of the chiefly class. There was no substantial haole working class and therefore no need for legally segregated facilities or residential areas—the one exception was the establishment of English Standard schools in the 1920s, and even they were not strictly segregated.

One ironic result of this racial shift was qualified Japanese American support for martial law, even though the military used its antidemocratic provisions to its own advantage in dealing with "questionable" nisei. In June 1942, Colonel Thomas Green, executive officer to the military governor, wrote to Assistant Secretary of War John McCloy: "The criminal courts here should remain completely closed. For example, we now have detained here on Sand Island over a hundred persons who are citizens of the United States [more than four hundred issei had been shipped to the mainland]. Hence, if the criminal courts were open for any purpose the judges could rightfully grant writs of habeas corpus and we would be powerless to retain custody of these people whose loyalty we have seriously questioned."[48]

Yet while authoritarian and antidemocratic in nature, military rule had opened new windows of opportunity for groups previously excluded on the basis of tradition and heritage. One neighbor island response was typical: "Maui does not favor civil government in practice at this particular time. The provost marshal has won [over] the civilian population. Twice a week a resident may get a pass to stay out until twelve midnight."[49]

More seriously, the military also portrayed itself as the champion of Japanese American rights in hostile territory. Thus, Colonel Green in his letter to McCloy was skeptical whether anyone of Japanese ancestry could receive a fair trial, given Hawaii's racial climate compounded by wartime animosities. In May 1942 a Japanese man (Green did not note whether citizen or alien) was convicted in military court of raping a child on the Big Island and sentenced to life imprisonment. And unlike the furor caused by a celebrated case of a Native Hawaiian man accused of murder and convicted in a military court, "we have not heard a murmur concerning this case; . . . in the case of a Japanese it would be utterly impossible to now obtain an impartial jury trial, and if Japanese were excluded from the jury panel the trial would be illegal. Taking into consideration the fact that people of Japanese ancestry compose the largest single segment of Island population, and further considering the amount of anti-Japanese sentiment out here, I believe the safest course to pursue is to keep criminal justice in the hands of the military for as long as Hawai`i is a theater of operations."[50]

Dual citizenship maintained by the nisei continued to be an issue through the end of the war. Since there was no Japanese consulate, no official petitions for expatriation could be submitted, although Swedish vice-consul Gustaf Olson permitted individual nisei to file an intent to "expatriate himself or herself from Japanese Nationality." Consulate records were kept from May 1942 to June 1944 to determine the numbers of applicants; 461 filled out the form, 243 males and 218 females. The only notable blip was a major increase in the month of February 1943, when recruitment for the 442d was at its height.[51]

But these gestures were clearly not enough to quell anti-Japanese hostility. Dual citizenship was continually used to justify discrimination against the nisei in both private and public sectors. Some businesses required "every American citizen of Japanese ancestry to show proof of expatriation or of steps taken toward expatriation before he or she is employed." Some personnel offices simply made this criterion a de facto part of the hiring process. The only government agency officially to do so was the public school system, the Department of Public Instruction (DPI), which had long prided itself on being the quintessential "Americanizing" institution, successfully transforming children of all immigrants, including the Japanese, into good U.S. citizens. Moreover, Shigeo Yoshida was employed by the DPI as principal of the Ala Moana School and had essentially received its blessing to remain on the payroll while he spent much of his working day with the military's Morale Section.

The DPI's discrimination was a serious contradiction of its policy, and Yoshida himself tried to resolve the issue. Minutes of the January 26, 1945, meeting of the ESC report conversations with the superintendent of the DPI in which Yoshida urged that the discriminatory policy be rescinded.

> Mr. Yoshida and Mr. O. W. Robinson discussed as members of the DPI the regulation now requiring AJAs to show proof of expatriation before being put on the payroll. This regulation is unique with the DPI and not required by any other branch of service in the federal or territorial governments. Mr. Robinson was impressed that the situation be corrected. . . . The ESC felt that either the regulation should be abolished or that all other races be submitted to the same procedure. If no action is taken by the DPI on the regulation, the ESC will take the matter up at the next session of the legislature. (SYC)

On February 10, 1945, Yoshida wrote officially as a member of the DPI to seek a change of policy. He reminded Robinson that the policy had been implemented about twenty years earlier (at the height of actions against Japanese-language schools) and that some Americans born to Chinese, Swedish, German, and Italian immigrants were dual citizens as well. Further, the United States did not recognize dual citizenship: "Either a person is an American or he is not." After an extended discussion of dual citizenship and expatriation, Yoshida continued:

> There is nothing theoretical, however, about what has happened since December 7, 1941 to prove the loyalty of the Americans of Japanese ancestry; . . . if this war has proved anything, insofar as the Americans of Japanese ancestry are concerned, it has proved beyond any reasonable doubt that they are as loyal as any group of Americans. . . .
>
> There is nothing theoretical also about the fact that the Department of Public Instruction has been the staunchest and most consistent champion of the products of its public schools, including those of Japanese ancestry. . . . It seems rather inconsistent, then, for the Department of Public Instruction, to proclaim in one breath the loyalty of this group of citizens and, in the next breath, say to them that they are not good enough citizens until they have expatriated from the claims of a foreign country. (SYC)

Yoshida noted in his letter that Japan was the only country to have simplified its laws to accommodate Americans who wished to expatriate. But his major argument was that dual citizenship signified nothing with regard to political allegiance; one was an American citizen or not, and neither rights nor obligations were affected in any way. He concluded by reminding the superintendent that the U.S. Army, "when it inducts our young men of Japanese ancestry into its ranks," does not distinguish "between those who are dual citizens and those who are not."

For the Emergency Service Committee, the expatriation issue, according to the minutes of the January 26 meeting, was simply one of the numerous and "various discriminatory measures" that in the aggregate constructed the most pressing morale problem (SYC). Perhaps the most offensive and best-known example of discrimination was the use of black-bordered badges to identify Japanese American workers in "sensitive" areas.[52]

The anti-Japanese sentiment was especially galling to the occasional active-duty nisei in Hawai`i, just back from or en route to combat assignment. Richard Oguro, an MIS veteran who had interrogated Japanese prisoners in California, recalled being delighted with "a chance to visit my family in Pearl City and enjoy local food. I even got carried away and got married." The racism, however, was difficult to stomach. "What distressed me at this time was the Anti-AJA sentiments expressed by some in the local dailies. In spite of the great number of us in uniform putting our lives on the line!" Oguro, attached to the marines, soon left for a tour of duty that saw some of the most bitter fighting of the war, including Iwo Jima.[53]

But the media was not monolithic in its treatment of Japanese Americans. The two Hawai'i dailies fought an ongoing duel over the issue. The *Honolulu Star-Bulletin* was often praised, in our interviews, for its relatively even-handed treatment of Japanese Americans during the war. But VVV members never forgot that the *Honolulu Advertiser* regularly resorted to scapegoating Japanese Americans. Reporter Earl Albert Selle, mentioned earlier, evidently led the successful charge to tear down the famous Phoenix fountain in Waikiki's Kapiolani Park simply because it had been donated by the Japanese government after World War I.

None of the news media made an issue of the most serious problems of racism and discrimination faced by the Japanese American population during the war—that directed against the vulnerable issei. Wartime conditions created severe workforce shortages, but there was general unemployment among Japanese Americans due to "precautionary and discriminatory restrictions." This was especially true for the issei who were "enemy aliens."

Not only did every issei fisherman have his boat confiscated, as we have seen, but also issei in related businesses, such as fish peddlers, were instantly deprived of their livelihoods; few had transferable skills.[54] Farmers evicted from areas next to military or strategic bases, including Pearl Harbor, found themselves without homes or work. The issei were also excluded from defense jobs and projects where they might make other workers feel "uneasy." All businesses dealing with Japanese goods and services, including that of Ryoji Namba's father, went under. Unfortunately, this anti-issei rationalization could lead seamlessly to the barring of nisei as well, since the key element was the "feeling" of "other employees."

By mid-June 1945, there were regular accounts of 100th/442d battleground heroics and nearly daily lists of the wounded and killed in action. Although the Selective Service System was inducting increasing numbers of young men of all backgrounds, considerable publicity was accorded nisei inductees. It had become customary for family and friends to host a boisterous farewell party for the new GI, who after all might not return. The local Japanese community soon developed a new "tradition": parties that involved equally generous portions of alcohol, machismo, and loud camaraderie. There were complaints, an especially vehement one from Bill Norwood, the ESC minutes for June 22, 1945, reported, who telephoned the ESC's executive secretary, Mitsuyuki Kido, about "the many parties that are given by the Japanese people. He also said that he was told that these parties were much too elaborate. Mr. Kido suggested that an editorial be written in the Japanese language papers advising moderation of these parties" (SYC).

Kido was not nearly as accommodating on other fronts. The ESC began, as the group's May 9, 1945, minutes reflect, to study ethnic representation among the territory's political appointees. World War II was still being fought on the battlegrounds, but the nisei were already looking toward postwar racial representation. Kido "summarized the Governor's appointments to boards and commissions. There were 256 appointments of which 200 were Caucasians (78 percent), 41 Hawaiians and part Hawaiians (16 percent), 8 Chinese (3.1 percent) and 7 Japanese (2.7 percent)" (SYC). By this late date there was no danger of Japanese attacks, and the distinguished nisei combat record was well known—although it might also be argued that any official Japanese American representation in wartime was something of a triumph.

The last major wartime policy barrier for the nisei was exclusion from the Selective Service System—the draft. On December 18, 1943, the ESC noted in its minutes a formal request for the inclusion of Japanese Americans, noting that the last draft to call up nisei was in February 1942: "We are willing to grant that conditions at that time may have been such as to make it advisable, *in the opinion of the military and selective service officials,* to leave out the Americans of Japanese ancestry from the draft" (emphasis added). The ESC insisted Hawaii's Japanese Americans could have been trusted, criticized the current policy, then highlighted the exemplary records of the 100th and the MIS as well as principles of fair play and racial justice. It quoted FDR, who, in announcing the formation of the 442d, the ESC suggested, set in motion "a natural and logical step toward reinstitution of selective service procedures which were temporarily disrupted by evacuation of the west coast."

Finally, the ESC made a point of the unintended negative consequences of highlighting Japanese American enlistments. Specific publicity and praise for the nisei to the exclusion of others "has tended to place the former in an embarrassing limelight and has also resulted in a great deal of unfair criticism by the latter." Other groups always had the right to volunteer but sometimes accused Japanese Americans of special privileges. Thus, as far as the ESC was concerned: "From the standpoint of post-war Hawai`i, it is best that our veterans should have been called to the colors on a common basis and should have fought together without any distinction as to color or racial extraction." The letter was signed "Masa Katagiri, Secretary" (SYC).

As the Pacific war continued, the ESC became much more assertive, even though Japan's surrender was not necessarily in sight. Its July 13, 1945, minutes report a discussion of the navy policy that "barred AJAs from becoming captains of fishing boats. It felt such a discriminatory policy ought to be corrected." Director Kido was asked to gather more information. At the same time, however, the ESC noted new incidents of anti-Japanese racism.

Lanai, a small island, was almost entirely owned and controlled by Dole Pineapple. There, two Japanese American families were victimized. "Dr. [Ernest] Murai reported that the Okamoto Store on Lanai was asked by the Pineapple Company manager to give up the store in thirty days about three months ago [early February 1945]. Mr. Okamoto got legal help to extend the eviction for ninety days."At about the same time, "the Hasegawa family on Lanai was asked to leave the Island simply because Mr. Hasegawa was interned. The members of the Committee felt that these actions were very arbitrary" (SYC). Minutes of subsequent meetings do not disclose how or whether these cases were resolved.

It is within this context of shifting and ambiguous messages about the proper "place" of Japanese Americans in Hawai`i during World War II that the Morale Section worked so consistently to forge an operating principle of racial tolerance. The military governor's office was easiest to convince because it was directly accountable for civilian morale and the general war effort. More responsible elements within the Big Five were also supportive of this strategy, although, as the debate between the two newspapers demonstrated, there was plenty of room for disagreement over strategies and tactics.

Throughout the war, the Morale Section's Ching, Loomis, and Yoshida met with official boards and agencies as well as private parties who could help reduce discrimination against the Japanese. By early 1942, meetings had already taken place with the Social Security Board, the U.S. Employment Service, the U.S. Engineering Department, the Hawaiian Constructors, and other agencies. Miles Cary, the sympathetic principal of McKinley High School, offered his cafeteria as a meeting place. In many cases, it was suggested at these meetings that a "more sympathetic and honest attitude on the part of the dismissing employer or potential employer" could prevent much of the alienation and anger (SYC). The method could be as important as the message.

Simultaneously, Yoshida, Ching, and Loomis were making many individual appeals to the haole business community urging fair treatment of the Japanese. They supported the positive efforts of the Businessmen's Committee, the Rotary Club, and the Chamber of Commerce, although they did lament that, even in early 1942, "these expressions on the part of business have come too late to be of maximum service."[55]

In his conclusion to one mid-1943 document, "Looking Ahead," Yoshida was already anticipating the end of conflict and prospects for interracial harmony. For the Japanese in Hawai'i, he predicted, the situation would "become progressively worse rather than improve in the days to come. As the war gets closer to Japan after her European partners are defeated and the full fury of our war machine is concentrated on her, the feeling against anything Japanese is going to grow more and more intense. No one can predict what may happen even here in the islands. Race riots are not outside the realm of possibility."[56]

In spite of persistent and gnawing problems both within the Japanese American community and between it and the larger society, the Morale Section could point with pride to the many signs that the racial climate was capable of absorbing or deflecting the worst of them. One could even find plantation managers who incorporated the nisei in positive fashion. On the Honomu plantation on the Big Island, for example, the plantation newspaper, *Leo O Honomu* (Voice of Honomu), was shut down after the Pearl Harbor attack but resumed publication in March 1942. A lively and informative paper, its editor, co-editor, and sports editor were all nisei.[57]

Instances of blatant anti-Japanese sentiment sometimes backfired. McKinley High School principal Miles Cary became an administrator at the concentration camp in Poston, Arizona. He returned in fall 1943 to resume duties at McKinley at a time when some nisei were permitted leaves from the camps to attend colleges in the Midwest and on the East Coast. To support that cause, he presented a slide-illustrated public lecture sponsored by the Society of Friends (now the American Friends Service Committee) at the Church of the Crossroads, and the Central Union Church. At the lecture, donations were solicited to help fund scholarships.[58] Outraged, the *Honolulu Advertiser*, as well as members of the American Legion and the Legion Auxiliary, called the contributions a public disgrace; their attack inspired an additional round of contributions.[59]

THE MORALE SECTION was committed to a strategy to harness the energies of all ethnic groups to further the war effort and to establish a baseline modus vivendi that would minimize the potential for racial/ethnic division both during and after the war. Military exploits were widely publicized and paired with skillful homefront politics. The formation and experiences of the VVV and the World War II Japanese American military units became the metaphor for the effort. For the time, it was a wildly successful strategy. But while the strengths of ethnic social organization were adroitly harnessed, social fractures and racial fault lines were papered over. This strategy, then, also laid the foundation for a society that continues to find it difficult to discuss problems of division. During the war, however, there seemed to be no alternative but to establish a working harmony, especially with regard to a problematic Japanese American population.

9

After the War

fter World War II, it became almost immediately evident that the VVV and their nisei compatriots would participate in transforming race relations in Hawai`i and the nation. So many of them were admitted into elite U.S. law and graduate schools that they constituted a major pool of social, educational, business, and political firepower. Where only a few outstanding nisei had graduated from prestigious universities in the decades before Pearl Harbor, the VVV ranks alone produced attorneys, Ph.D.s, and MBAs from Yale, Northwestern, Columbia, Minnesota, Illinois, and Chicago. Ryoji Namba, Shiro Amioka, and George Yamamoto returned to teach at the University of Hawai`i. Edward Nakamura and Yoshimi Hayashi led a large contingent of returning lawyers by becoming two of the five justices on the Hawai`i State Supreme Court.

AS THE WAR DREW to a close, Shiro Amioka was training replacement troops for the European front, still anxious to get into combat. After Germany's surrender, the MIS in the Pacific seemed to be his only remaining option, so he left for Minnesota's Fort Snelling. His class graduated on August 18, 1945—three days after Japan's surrender. Amioka felt cheated; only half joking, he said: "I was sad. I was one of the few guys who was sad." He laughed (88). He did get to Japan during the occupation and was stationed on the northern Japanese island of Hokkaido, where his main responsibility was collecting intelligence on Japanese communists in the population—"the Russians were sending agents . . . get a hold of some who, maybe, left a relative behind or something" (90). Like Richard Lum, who did surveillance work on suspected leftists in the U.S. Army in 1942 in Schofield Barracks, Amioka was an early recruit in the cold war. Later, he went on to complete his undergraduate education at the Universities of Minnesota and Hawai`i and earned a Ph.D. at Illinois.

Claude Takekawa also trained replacement troops; like Amioka, he was transferred to Minnesota for MIS training when the war in Europe ended. From there he was sent to Japan, where his major responsibility was to keep relations smooth between the occupation forces and the Japanese neighborhoods—which included doing surveys and giving preventative talks on venereal disease: "It was good fun."[1] Takekawa returned to the University of Hawai`i in 1947 to complete his bachelor's degree in education and went on for a master's at Springfield College in Massachusetts.

Some of the VVV pursued careers well outside Hawai`i. Jyun Hirota, an outstanding athlete, went on to play professional baseball in Japan. Chiyoki Ikeda went into the "new" Central Intelligence Agency and was killed on duty. Richard "Sus" Yamamoto and Kanami Takemoto earned doctorates and lived in Maryland, where they worked as research scientists for the National Institutes of Health. Several in the Military Intelligence Service served in the occupation of Japan.

On their return from the service, the men rarely spoke of their war experiences except with one another. The only war story Anki Hoshijo told "with relish," according to his sons, "was of five to six Hawai`i guys taking on everyone else in a bar in Marysville, near Sacramento, while waiting for discharge. A Hawaiian soldier they'd met was pushed in the back of the head, starting them wrecking the bar, chasing sailors down the street, trying to get at them at the station after being arrested. He made sure not to tell the story while we were young."[2]

Many of the VVV returned to the Manoa campus, where it did not take long for them to find one another and to form a club. The early penchant for reunions and dances had become a tradition. The first "anniversary dance" for the VVV was held in Hemenway Hall on April 27, 1946. Ted Tsukiyama was the new president of the club, while Shigemitsu Nakashima chaired the program committee, Melvin Nagasako handled ticket distribution, and Edward Nakamura was in charge of refreshments. It was an important event, marking the return of the former students and reestablishing their presence on campus. Ryoji Namba, who had been a member of the 442d band, arranged for music by his colleagues, the Torchers, who took their professional name from the 442d shoulder patch that featured the torch of the Statue of Liberty. The guest list confirmed the importance to the VVV of men like Charles Hemenway, Andrew Lind, and Gregg Sinclair, all associated with the university; top brass of the military like William Marston, Kendall Fielder, George Bicknell, and Kenneth Vandergrift; civilian leaders like Leslie Hicks, future governor Jack Burns, and Bob Shivers of the FBI; Morale Section members Hung Wai Ching, Shigeo Yoshida, and Charles Loomis; non-Japanese who had served in the VVV, including Richard Lum, Thomas Kaulukukui, Frank Judd, George Aikau, and William Jarrett; and, finally, the Japanese American community leaders who had been crucial to their success, including Masaji Marumoto, Masa Katagiri, Ernest Murai, and Mitsuyuki Kido.[3]

This was a surreal period for some of the VVV men. They were back in the classroom with youngsters utterly naive in the ways of combat, international travel, multiracial (or other) sexual encounters, or the rigors of military discipline. No wonder so many of the VVV men, far more sophisticated and motivated, excelled. Some took the time to carouse as hard as they studied. At least a few became notorious in their seemingly unrelenting quest for coeds.

One core group included Ted Tsukiyama. "Toyota, Tomita, Takekawa, Isonaga, and we were real, you know, in terms of worldly wise, we went back to school and you know we were goodtimers. Didn't study much. This was the half a year that I was home; . . . mostly Triple V guys, we called ourselves . . . and we still call ourselves, . . . CCM" (42). The initials, they explained to outsiders, stood for Concerned Christian Men. Privately, however, CCM stood for the Japanese epithet *chin-chin mushi*, impossible to translate but evoking the image of male organs in active pursuit of their female counterparts. Jackson Morisawa was studying at the Chicago Art Institute but remembered hearing about his buddies congregating back home under a tree—they were sometimes referred to as the "under-the-tree gang"—and harassing the coeds: "The girls used to be scared passing in front of them!" (33).

It was not, however, all fun and games. One of the unpleasant tasks was contacting families of VVV buddies who had been killed overseas. From Maui, Mitsuko Nishikawa wrote on June 3, 1946, to thank the men for the photo of her brother, Akio. Ted Tsukiyama kept her letter:

"Akio and the family are very fortunate to have such nice boys behind him. Holding service occasionally and doing and giving things heartly, which will be preserved, and to be shown for generations to come. Specially for father and mother it really brought back courage anew, to receive undying memory put in frame, and to put noble facts about Akio in mind. It seems as though they are living in such emptiness. Only getting pleasure in praying morning and night and to look at Akio's and sister's picture" (TTC).

For Tsukiyama, the generally frivolous environment soon became too seductive. "I found out that this, what's the word, not epicurean but hedonistic life was not doing me any good, so I split and went to the mainland for school" (42). Tsukiyama eventually graduated from Yale Law School and returned to become Hawaii's top labor arbitrator. Fellow lawyer-to-be Harry Tanaka, who had contracted tuberculosis in the Pacific at the end of the war, was sent to Denver for a year of recuperation before returning to the University of Hawai'i to complete his undergraduate degree. Like Tsukiyama, he attended Yale Law School, returning to a private law practice until being appointed by Governor George Ariyoshi to the Intermediate Court of Appeals in 1981.[4]

Masato Doi completed Columbia Law School via a curiously circuitous route. After his return from Europe, Doi responded to a frantic call for help from the wife of one of his high school teachers: His mainland haole mentor had suffered a nervous breakdown. His wife insisted that Masato was the only one who could help, so he stayed with the family on Kauai for the next three weeks. Doi's former teacher was a Columbia University graduate who secured an application form for Masato, who by now was thinking of going to law school. "I pick New York City because I'd never seen New York City, not even while I was on the mainland on my furlough." Transportation was still a problem because of troops and casualties returning home, but "my teacher friend with the mental illness, he had connections, so he got passage for himself and for me as his medical attendant and so we flew out on one of those [Pan American] China Clippers" (40–47).

During Christmas break of 1945, Masato Doi entered the dean's office at Columbia and was met by an astonished administrator: "Well, didn't you get our letter rejecting you?" Doi explained that he had not applied elsewhere and had no other options; sympathetic, the dean suggested he wait. A few weeks later, Doi was admitted. He used up "every last dollar" of his GI Bill benefits at Columbia and then at Columbia Law

School, graduating in 1950 as the Harlan Fiske Stone scholar for outstanding academic achievement.

When Doi returned to Hawai`i, Hung Wai Ching introduced him to
attorneys at one of the most prestigious firms in town. Smith, Wild,
Beebe, and Cades gave him a polite fifteen-minute interview and told
him, "Don't call us, we'll call you." They never called. Some things even
Hung Wai Ching could not change. Doi then went into politics as one
of the first Democratic Party candidates in the 1954 elections, later
known as the "bloodless revolution" for having unseated the haole Republican Party after half a century of unbroken rule. Included in his slate
of six running in the Honolulu District were Dan Inouye and Sparky
Matsunaga, both later elected to the U.S. Senate. Doi recalls no personal
sense, however, of any historic turning point with that election. He did,
however, remember the uproar caused by the Democratic speaker of the
house, Charles Kauhane, a Native Hawaiian, who looked out upon his
nisei colleagues and voiced concerns about "another Pearl Harbor" and
how they might have been members of the Japanese "diet" (45–46). Doi
soon moved on to the County Board of Supervisors, now the Honolulu
City Council, until his unsuccessful run for mayor in 1964.

Yoshiaki Fujitani, who translated enemy documents in Maryland before being shipped to Japan, found the U.S. occupation painful because
of Japan's children—"kids who were starving, practically"—who were
begging for food; after all, they "look so much like we do, you know."
Later, he decided to take advantage of the GI Bill by going to "an expensive school. So I chose the University of Chicago." He took and
flunked most of the entrance exams but was allowed to enroll because
of good math scores. He studied religion, enrolling in courses that provided scholarly confirmation that his father's Buddhism had validity.
Thus emboldened, he went to Kyoto to become an ordained minister
(28–29).

Shiro Amioka became a professor in the University of Hawaii's College of Education, interested in the philosophy of education and especially in John Dewey. Amioka had married a Japanese woman during
the occupation and was proud of his knowledge of the language and society. He served on several national committees, representing the United
States in education meetings with Japanese officials, and was also tapped
to become superintendent of the entire Hawai`i school system.

George Yamamoto became a professor in the UH Sociology Department but never forgot that his own professors had discouraged him

from pursuing his true intellectual love, literature and literary criticism. Ryoji Namba's encounter with the racism of the time was more direct. Namba returned to Hawai`i with a University of Minnesota Ph.D. in entomology in 1953. In Hawai`i, where agriculture was still the dominant industry, he should not have had trouble finding employment, but his initial attempts were rebuffed. "They were still prejudiced against an Oriental. . . . I knew that . . . because right after I went around, they hired someone else" (55). Fortunately, Hung Wai Ching was once more strategically positioned. Namba talked to him about the situation and, as usual, Hung Wai sprang into action. Ching, by then on the university's Board of Regents, went directly to President Gregg Sinclair, insisting that "a local boy just come back with a Ph.D." and should be hired. Namba got his appointment:

> Entomology. Just so happened that there was an opening and so I got hired right then. No such thing as search committee or anything like that. The word come out from the top, 'Hire this guy,' that's it. So there was some resentment, you know. . . . There is always some resentment when you get something shoved down your throat. . . . That pissed me off. That ticked me off. And I know those guys who could have given me a chance, and they didn't give me a chance. (56)

Anki Hoshijo fought professionally for a while; he quit the ring when he lost one bout—to Dado Marino, who went on to become world flyweight champion. Hoshijo joined the ILWU as a longshoreman and took part in the famous 1947 San Francisco dock strike. The union made good use of his background by assigning him to the "flying squad," which did not walk the picket lines. The handpicked crew would "sit around and play cards, drink coffee. If there was trouble at a picket line, then they would jump in a truck and go down. They could be [at once] lazy and militant." He later used the GI Bill to complete a BA and MBA at Northwestern, not always easy an easy path for him because other veterans were constantly intent on having Hoshijo join them for a few drinks or a game of pool. "Being on the way to school was not a good excuse," his son wrote to me. "His solution was to carry his books in a bowling ball bag. 'Going bowling' was a more acceptable excuse." Later, Hoshijo took a job with the Internal Revenue Service—a matter of financial security for the family, "not necessarily his dream job." Like the more self-consciously radical Yugo Okubo, Anki and his wife "consciously embraced the reborn hopes of the day: No racial discrimination. Democracy. Education. No glorification of war. Some things that haunted us later upon realizing the world was not that way quite yet. Treating daughter and sons as equals. . . . He talked about right and wrong, about guts."[5]

A number of the VVV went on to successful careers in business, including Teru Himoto, Herb Isonaga, Yutaka Nakahata, Claude Takekawa, Akira Otani, Jackson Morisawa, and Ralph Toyota. Ralph Yempuku became a well-known promoter in Honolulu. He brought a wide variety of entertainment to Hawai'i, including sumo and the Takarazuka troupe (for which Shiro Amioka's wife once performed in Japan), and toured U.S. groups like the circus in Japan.

Yugo Okubo became a supporter of and worker for the *Honolulu Record*, a left-wing labor newspaper. His life took a dramatically different turn from those of the "mainstream" VVV members. Openly critical of their accommodation to postwar Hawai'i and what he considered their complicity in revising the social order only enough to permit nisei participation, he dedicated his life to advocating for working-class and social justice issues. His views are rendered in some detail because they provide the only substantiated critical views from inside the nisei/VVV experience.

Unlike the agony of his experience with civil engineering before Pearl Harbor, Yugo thoroughly enjoyed his political science and history courses, although he had little respect for most of his professors, who taught courses that were "simple and simple-minded." Learning and memorizing the courses' main points led to stress-free academic achievement. The only faculty member who gave him trouble was the liberal Alan Saunders, a leader of the local American Civil Liberties Union. Okubo recalled that an essay topic on one exam was the "similarity between communism and fascism. That kind of bullshit used to go on more in those days. . . . I put in all the typical bullshit and got a good grade." In his first semester back, the ILWU was engaged in the bitter 1946 strike on the sugar plantations. Many of the strikers were former army buddies, and Okubo tried to generate support for them on the campus. "But the university didn't give a damn" (49).

Even before graduating in 1949, Okubo had fairly well developed views about the failings of American society and the disappointingly moderate direction his VVV and 442d comrades were taking. In a paper written for sociologist Andrew Lind, he predicted that the Japanese American veterans' clubs (by then almost always referred to as AJAs) would go the way of old American Legion groups with no backbone and conservative stands on important issues. This was an unorthodox view at the time and Lind took exception: "He said that I got it wrong; that they do have a different goal in society. They were going to be different because of this." Professor Lind then concluded that Okubo was both a "bad sociologist and poor prophet" (50).[6]

While Okubo was at the university, the McCarthy-era anticommunist witch hunts began in earnest. Okubo read about the 1948 firings by Hawaii's public school system of Aiko and John Reinecke, progressive teachers, and was appalled at the lack of support from the local population. Unannounced, he went to their home simply to say that he honored their position. By the time of his graduation, the bitterly fought longshoremen's strike of 1949 was under way. Yugo decided he wanted to be a part of the evolving multiethnic working-class movement and signed on to work at the *Honolulu Record* (53–55).

At the *Record*, Okubo joined editor and Communist Party member Koji Ariyoshi. Yugo did a bit of everything: printing, typesetting, delivery. When I mentioned that Ted Tsukiyama, fellow VVV, now believed that Koji Ariyoshi was a courageous man and regretted not getting to know him better, Okubo was not impressed. "It wasn't a matter of being courageous. . . . It's because Ted tied in with the establishment. . . . Patsy Mink [formerly one of Hawaii's two representatives in the U.S. Congress] wasn't afraid of coming down because she's outside of the establishment. In '56 she ran her first campaign. She came down to the *Record*. . . . She wasn't afraid of coming down. But the thing is, she's a woman. She's an outcast in a way. But she didn't give a damn. But as far as the men, they are all full of shit" (56).

In 1959, the ILWU took over the *Record* and Okubo quit—for personal and political reasons, he said. He had some unkind words about some of the union leadership, including Jack Hall, who was "a jackass; uneducated, and unable to keep up with all the twists and turns of the political things." The ILWU leadership is credited, in conventional accounts of postwar history, with crafting a multiethnic strategy by mandating equal Filipino/Japanese leadership in all units. Okubo thought that the real agenda was diluting the nisei leadership: "Filipinos, Portuguese, not because they wanted representation in leadership. They wanted someone they could control." . . . It wasn't a matter of racial equality. . . . I definitely believe that" (59).[7]

Yugo Okubo was an exception among the VVV and his entire nisei generation. Most of his former colleagues found far more conventional careers. In addition to Tsukiyama, Tanaka, Doi, and Nakamura, there were other attorneys. No VVV member was surprised that Edwin Honda, for example, became a successful lawyer or judge, but they were amazed that Kenneth Saruwatari and Yoshimi Hayashi ever made it through law school. Hayashi, in fact, reveled in stories of his wayward youth and was clearly delighted to have joined Ed Nakamura on the bench of the Hawai`i Supreme Court. Richard Zukemura and Barney Ono went on to careers in civil service.

On the personal level, no one doubted that the year spent in the VVV was an experience of intense feeling and great value. Even Yugo Okubo admitted that the VVV helped him grow up: "For my own thing, it was good" (60). Akira Otani called that period as "maybe a high point in my life, too, because I met some people that are still some of my very best friends" (39).

Yoshiaki Fujitani, who left Schofield Barracks in anger and disappointment after his Buddhist priest father was arrested and interned, was deeply touched by his stint in the VVV, "a very important part of my life" (29–31). Fujitani was proud the "handful" of men was willing to move into action. "And we did set the tone, you might say, for the kind of Americanism that maybe only in Hawai`i we were able to have." Surely, he noted, this could not have happened on the continent, and moreover it should not be interpreted as simple-minded patriotism but as an insistence to have others "accept us as we are." Fujitani had made the point earlier that enlisting in the 442d was motivated largely by wanting to join his friends and attributed this to an upbringing that stressed "the Japanese spirit." Not only courage and loyalty, he suggested, but a sense of "esprit de corps" and of "not wanting to let your buddy down," all part of the culture of the time, of the "Hawaiianness" of the place, and, regrettably, perhaps missing in the later generations.

Ralph Yempuku thought the significance of the group lay in the timing. "If we had waited for another six months or another year, I don't think the effect would have been as great as to come in when we did right after we got kicked out of HTG; . . . the fact that we were all Japanese and the fact that many of these were university kids; they could have gone to the university and continued and nobody would have said anything because they got kicked out. . . . I think that caught [everyone's] fancy" (50).

In his retirement speech in 1985, Shiro Amioka mentioned the VVV experience and told the large gathering that it "made me aware that meeting the problems and challenges of a crisis has tremendous educative potential."[8] Like the others, Amioka felt the VVV year was "fantastic. In fact, many of our lasting human relationships were really solidified there" (91). This camaraderie held especially true for Amioka, because his military experience was fragmented and he never developed ties with any particular outfit. But he made great claims for the VVV as a whole, men who, in the depths of despair, still had "enough faith, enough courage, spirit, and foresight to see that the battle was not lost but just begun." They helped to build a new attitude toward the AJA, which culminated in the acceptance of AJAs as volunteers in a combat unit. And many had gone on to substantial achievement. "What does this mean? It means that democracy is still alive, in spite of the difficulties we face. More specifically in Hawai`i, it means that the effort of the VVV has contributed to a bloodless social revolution in Hawai`i, where the individual potential is given full sway. It means that the public school system has done its job well in serving as the bulwark of democracy. . . . Needless to say the task is not over. For the creation of a better world is a never ending task."[9]

But at least a few VVV members had some cautionary remarks. For Herb Isonaga, the VVV was "very significant because I made many lasting friends during that period; . . . as people in the Triple V became active in politics, that we held together very well, singular in purpose, ideals and goals, . . . when the chips are down, you can count on them because you have similar philosophy, similar goals, similar wishes for the betterment of the community." But at the same time, Isonaga was troubled by those who tried to take too much individual or group credit for what he called the "fortunes of circumstances." After all, he suggested, the VVV was primarily "a vehicle for the Emergency Service Committee, who represented the general community in terms of its relationship with the military powers that be to protect the Japanese community. . . . And, as such, I think, unfortunately, maybe our efforts were, say, overpublicized, overmagnified. . . . Well, to bring it down to bare bones—it was just a publicity stunt, you know" (43–51).

Ed Nakamura, reflecting on the ways in which some of the nisei veterans regularly congregated to "talk story," knew he would never forget the scenes of cadaverlike survivors of Dachau his artillery unit encountered in Germany. But he told his wife that he stopped going regularly to veterans' groups because recollections and retellings of the story "get bigger. People begin to forget the bad things . . . and to remember only what they want to remember. . . . The stories kept getting bigger and better and I know it really wasn't like that" (26). Nakamura's sentiments are akin to the feeling that Jackson Morisawa expressed when he first protested the VVV oral history project. The VVV, he insisted, was positive and important for him personally, but he objected to the overtones of self-promotion. "It's not for us to say, Hey! and shove it on to them and say, Hey, this is what we did; why don't you guys let the whole world know about it" (37). Eventually, like Yugo Okubo, Morisawa was willing to participate in the project, ironically, in order that his testimony might keep this perspective in view.

MOST OF THE 169 VVV men served in the military during World War II, either in Europe with the 442d Regimental Combat Team or all over the globe with the Military Intelligence Service. Seven of them died. The rest came back to a postwar United States that immediately embarked upon an undeclared war with global and domestic communism and socialism. One of the VVV, Yugo Okubo, became a victim of that conflict. Most of the others did extremely well in their work and lives. And while they did not actively seek to create a "model minority," their achievements, as well as the roles assigned to them in the postwar era, became integral to that new racial construction, first in Hawai`i and later in the nation.

Conclusion

I n the 1950s, just one decade after the end of World War II, the nisei nearly became America's model minority and the first group of color to enter its family of "white" ethnic groups. Their collective success in educational, family, and occupational terms provided a convenient counterpoint to charges that the United States was fundamentally incapable of racial equality. Led especially by African American leaders, civil rights movements begun during World War II began to confront determined resistance to change, not only from diehard racists but also from erstwhile liberal allies increasingly concerned about the depth and reach of reforms. Much of this occurred in a context in which leaders like President Franklin Roosevelt had used the model of U.S. freedom to rally patriotic fervor against Axis fascism.[1] As resistance to class- and race-based reforms mounted, critics pointed to aspects of U.S. society that seemed impervious to change—made up, it appeared, of fixed hierarchies defined by race, class, and gender.

The liberal response was to emphasize an America moving toward democracy and equality. A formerly oppressed minority group that had "made it" provided crucial evidence that race did not inevitably restrict mobility. Just released from U.S. concentration camps and still largely identified with a demonized and defeated enemy, Japanese Americans became the ideal group to send this message of hope. That Japan had been redefined from archenemy to stalwart junior

265

partner in the U.S. system that reached across the Pacific played a major part in this new calculus.

By the end of the 1960s, the civil rights movement was joined by black power advocates as well as feminist, Native American, Asian American, and Latino activists. Above all, there were fierce demands to end U.S. wars in Southeast Asia. For defenders of the status quo, especially the ideologically and politically liberal supporters of minority advancement, the challenge seemed overwhelming and the need to reaffirm the basic value of American society became irresistible. At this critical juncture in U.S. history, then, the nisei nearly became the symbol of continuing and potentially limitless opportunity for people of color in the United States.

IN POLITICS, education, and the media, the myth of the model minority gained widespread currency and extended beyond the Japanese to Asian Americans as a whole. But it has been difficult to promote the model-minority myth for other Asian ethnic groups because they all include substantial numbers of recent immigrants and the economically disadvantaged. This was not true for Japanese Americans and, as one result, there appears to be little inclination to contest the narrative of their "successful" acculturation but to emphasize instead the reasonable nature of their transition from victims to victors.[2] The implication that inherited cultural traits and a passive strategy explained Japanese American success infuriated many third-generation sansei activists. More recently, works like Tamura's *Americanization* argue that the nisei managed to deflect the worst elements of wholesale "Americanization" efforts by the haole elite while maintaining their ethnic identity and thereby contributing to a healthy acculturation process. This revision has been very helpful. I suggest that a critical analysis of the genesis of this myth is important to any understanding of why and how U.S. society at large saw fit to elevate the nisei. And that story is largely built around the history of World War II Hawai`i.

Japanese Americans did not, of course, become "white." In the first place, many did not want this "privilege." Between those who had been victimized by mass internment and a small but articulate group of younger activists who identified with "third-world" communities of color across the nation and the world, there was serious resistance to this assimilationist direction. Second, the physical and cultural relationships with other Asian American groups, at the time largely Chinese and Korean, made separation difficult if not impossible. Finally, while U.S. liberal intellectuals may have found the project useful, the larger society was not ready for such a drastic redefinition of "race." Nonetheless, I believe it important to emphasize this project as among the ways in which race can be seen as fluid and manipulable. This analysis may also help us understand the apparently fantastic commitment to U.S. ideals and promise on the part of some, like then-leaders of the Japanese American Citizens League, in the face of ongoing prejudice and discrimination.

The early chapters of this book devote substantial attention to the cultural baggage brought from Japan by the issei immigrants and presumably absorbed by their nisei children. Postwar successes prompted an ahistorical attribution of upward mobility to cultural values embracing education, children, or both; deferring gratification; stoic passivity; and a penchant for disciplined work. And while the VVV families certainly exhibited some of these characteristics, these traits were not necessarily controlling ones nor were they alone in contributing to ethnic mobility.

The latter chapters explore some of the major ways in which change affected Japanese Americans in particular and race relations in general during World War II. By the mid-1950s, when this account of the VVV ends, Hawai`i had been thrust into a new international setting and was caught in a vastly different web of global economic development. The most critical change was the emergence of the United States and U.S. capitalism as preeminent through most of the world. The nations and peoples on the rim of the Pacific Ocean, as well as within what was sometimes called the "American Lake," were inexorably drawn into an increasingly contentious setting. One striking result was an unprecedented economic boom in the United States. Another was the rapid growth of nationalist, sometimes communist-led, movements that would eventually lead to diplomatic, military, and ideological confrontations in many areas and to major wars in China, Korea, and Southeast Asia. As the stories hinted at by the recollections of men like Yugo Okubo suggest, economic growth and the cold war became the larger contexts for the VVV and the rest of Hawai`i.

Where the previous century had featured tight control by a handful of haole families, the post–World War II era revealed several serious challengers to that older hegemony. First, the military, in itself and as part of the federal government, emerged as a major player in the islands, far more influential than in the prewar years. Given Hawaii's central position in the Pacific/Asia context, the growing power of the military was a foregone conclusion; in any case, that power was an integral part of what has been termed the militarizing of U.S. society.[3] Second, national and transnational corporations began moving into Hawai`i, using large cash reserves to purchase land and build resorts for a booming middle-class tourism. Third, the International Longshoremen's and Warehousemen's Union waged a series of successful strikes against the Big Five, leading to the growth of a solid middle-class anchored by workers in the fields and on the docks.[4] Fourth, and partly as a result of all the other changes, the Democratic Party emerged as a formidable challenger to the old Republican order. In 1954, voters ushered in what is sometimes called the "bloodless revolution." Organized labor, new voters, inmigrants from the mainland, and, perhaps most visibly, the returning Japanese American veterans propelled the Democratic Party to the pre-eminent position it maintained to the end of the twentieth century.

The VVV stories shed valuable light on questions of immigration and cultural retention. The men who told them grew up in multicultural Hawai`i and became the key part of a racial experiment to keep the peace and to forge a new racial politics in wartime. Through them, U.S. society negotiated the initial stages of a process that nearly made the nisei haole. Exploring the VVV experience informs us in four basic areas: First, the textured lives of Hawaii's nisei men offer concrete detail that should help us avoid facile stereotyping or caricaturing of this group; second, the VVV and events around its formation illustrate ways in which a vulnerable minority group devised strategies for advancement; third, these stories demonstrate the complex nature of race relations in Hawai`i prior to and after Pearl Harbor and the deliberate planning required to deal with the immediate crisis and the future of race relations; fourth, the VVV is a case study of racial formation or re-formation.

The lives of the men, together with those of their parents, provide an unusual ethnographic glimpse into Japanese American family life of the 1920s and 1930s. We sense the disconnect between the nisei and the issei, as well as that between the nisei and things associated with their grandparents and their cultural heritage. At the same time, and perhaps somewhat paradoxically, there is strong evidence that Japanese-language learning was more effective and more appreciated than other studies have reported. Perhaps its effectiveness helps account for the fact that the Military Intelligence Service, with about three thousand nisei, was extremely effective.

We now have a better sense of Japanese American experiences and perceptions of public and private schools, including the fact that very few of the men expected to advance far in prewar Hawai`i. No VVV member interviewed was enrolled at an elite private institution, but several felt they had received fine secondary schooling, especially those who had good experiences at Miles Carey's McKinley High School. There was little dating—indeed, the language-school schedule precluded a fuller social life, including sports. For the latter, judo and kendo at Japanese schools and unofficial games had to suffice. Nonetheless, there were gifted athletes who went on to compete at high levels in college and the military, and as professionals. The degree to which boxing was popular will surprise those unaware of the tough working-class backgrounds of so many nisei.

Racial attitudes among the VVV families probably reflected the larger Japanese American community's. There was no questioning haole superiority—until the wartime experiences dismantled many assumptions. Native Hawaiians occupied an ambiguous position, but there was a clear sense of Japanese superiority to others, especially Filipinos and Okinawans, largely because the issei asserted claims of homeland political and military power. Those from weaker nations were *yabanjin*, barbarians.

The men had favorable recollections of the year spent working at Schofield Barracks. The six weeks most had spent in the Hawai`i Territorial Guard were stressful but rewarding, so their rejection in January was difficult for them. The formation of the VVV itself was thus seen as a form of "redemption" and most worked seriously at their manual labor assignments before moving on in January 1943.

The ways in which the vulnerable Japanese American minority group devised strategies for survival and advancement during the war—the second area in which the VVV experience informs us—point up the major differences between Hawai`i and the mainland. The material conditions created vastly different parameters for belief and action, since the Japanese made up nearly 40 percent of the islands' population and over one-half of the labor force. They raised much of the food, serviced the sugar, pineapple, and longshore industries, and were the barbers, launderers, masons, electricians, carpenters, and bookkeepers of the society. They built defense installations and maintained barracks. Nonetheless, there was enormous pressure to imprison them all, remove most to mainland concentration camps, or create one large site on the island of Molokai for 160,000 Japanese Americans.

The ethnic community was successfully prodded into giving blood, buying war bonds, declaring their loyalty, and volunteering for defense jobs. Nisei elected officials were pressured to resign their positions, while others signed on with the Hawai`i Territorial Guard. Shigeo Yoshida became their de facto leader as one of three members of the Military Governor's Morale Section. Along with haole Charles Loomis and Chinese American Hung Wai Ching, Yoshida played a crucial role in defining and advancing the cause of Japanese Americans. Indeed, it is remarkable to recall that he wrote some of the important statements for the military governor that outlined official policies toward his own community.

The Emergency Service Committees on major islands enlisted influential nisei leaders to serve as an interface between the Morale Section and the Japanese American community. These leaders did much to interpret official policies to their issei parents and reduced anxiety considerably, although there continued to be significant suffering, especially among those whose livelihoods had depended on trade with Japan.

The office of the Swedish Consul sheltered the efforts of Shimeji Kanazawa, who provided an international stage from which to advocate for the rights of both Japanese subjects and Japanese Americans during the war. Perhaps most remarkable, there were even successful efforts to maintain control over Japanese-language schools in Hawai`i, among the most targeted of the institutions suspected of fostering disloyalty to the United States.

The third area on which the VVV experience sheds light involves the complex, fluid, and dangerous nature of race relations prior to and immediately following the attack on Pearl Harbor, especially in 1942 when official U.S. policy toward the nisei dramatically shifted. The Japanese attack on Pearl Harbor was a brutal assault not only on America's critical Pacific military outpost but on cherished notions of white superiority and invulnerability. In Hawai`i, in ways that could not have been replicated on the continent, the need to pursue an effective wartime strategy dictated an active policy of racial tolerance and inclusion. That policy overshadowed older traditions of haole supremacy. After all, in the eyes of the military, the potential for racial disorder, perhaps even the specter of race riots, was not unthinkable.

As Captain I. H. Mayfield reported to the Office of Naval Intelligence in spring 1945, the war "necessitated many disruptures and readjustments in this community." There was particular fear that "riots and wholesale dismissal of essential workers because of racial considerations" as well as the "creation of unnecessary fears and dissatisfactions among the various groups" would have "retarded the war effort and given our armed forces additional police duties." Mayfield noted that, "so far as the relationship between the various races is concerned, Hawai`i is more than a melting pot. It had, and still has, potentialities for a first class racial clash which can seriously hamper the prosecution of the war in this theater."[5] The situation was highly volatile and successful prosecution of the war turned on judicious treatment of the Japanese American community.

To emphasize the unsettling impact of the new racial order, Kendall Fielder, head of Army Intelligence, warned the nisei, at about the same time as Mayfield's report, not to let down their racial guard. Savage battles in the Pacific produced casualties by the thousands, many of whom were shipped to Hawai`i to recover from close and vicious encounters with the Japanese. In this context, it would be imperative that the nisei understand that "your Number One mission is to influence and control the conduct of the Japanese element of Hawaii's population. Do everything you can to keep them from bringing suspicion and criticism on themselves. . . . You must try to retain the confidence of the authorities and of the prominent haoles, some of whom holler like stuck pigs."[6]

Finally, consider the actions of the ESC when it wrote to Fielder on February 27, 1945, requesting that the army rescind anti-Japanese regulations. Dr. Ernest Murai explained that the territorial legislature was considering resolutions "calling for the modification of the regulations pertaining to air travel and the purchase of liquor by enemy aliens." Murai had reason to believe that other resolutions would seek to remove even more anti-Japanese regulations. These actions did not, in his mind, accurately reflect the anti-Japanese sentiment among these legislators and reflected only the mindset of political opportunists. Murai and his nisei colleagues did not intend to sit idly by and have history distorted: "We do not wish to see certain legislators claiming all the credit later and even boasting that they were the ones which brought about the changes. If the Army can 'beat them to the punch,' so to speak, and change or rescind those which are no longer necessary, we believe it will be to the Army's credit."[7]

It is striking to reflect on the self-conscious and deliberate planning on the part of civilian and military leaders in Hawai`i throughout the war. They were surely correct in anticipating racial problems of many varieties, ranging from the outcries of wounded haole supremacists to the demands for vengeance from Filipinos, Koreans, and Chinese who continually learned more of Japan's brutalities and to the potential of back-lash from chauvinist issei or *kibei*.

Fourth, the experiences of the VVV illuminate a curious case of racial formation—an initial step in the re-formation and rehabilitation of Japanese Americans into "honorary" whites. I believe it was this evolu-tion of the image of Japanese Americans that so depressed Yugo Okubo and fueled resentment toward his former VVV comrades. Mari Mat-suda, critical legal scholar, has insisted that this interpretation is a highly charged ideological attempt to punish activist movements that challenge racism, sexism, and class injustice by positing a "reasonable" alternative to radical theory and action.[8] "We Shall Not Be Used" became Matsuda's rallying cry for Asian Americans to take a principled stand against the attempt to co-opt the movement. Her position was anticipated as early as 1970 by Asian American studies specialists at UCLA. In *Roots: An Asian American Reader*, Alan Nishio warned of the dangers of being ma-nipulated as a "middleman minority," and Amy Tachiki advocated a "yel-low power" counterpart to the black, brown, and red movements.[9]

Earlier radical left politics had convinced Okubo and men like him that the VVV and Japanese American successes should have led to more basic social change. In Okubo's view: "It is the systematic turning the pile over to give somebody else a chance, . . . but not anything different. Did we have a special role? You know what I mean? If we didn't have, fine, forget it, you know what I mean? But if you say that we had a special role, then we failed. . . . Isn't that some defect in the people who were in the Triple V? I hate to pick on them. What is your role? What is your reason? To do some chickenshit road project during the war?" (52).

Perhaps the most liberal of them disappointed Okubo most: "Some-times I used to get people like Edwin Honda and Ed Nakamura here. I'd talk. I remember one time, 'Let's take a stand on rent control!'" In Hawai`i, where the nisei were buying their own homes in droves and building small apartment units as investments, rent control was not likely to generate much support. When Okubo suggested the vets protest the anticommunist John Wayne film, "Big Jim McLane," to be shot in Hawai`i, "everybody turned against me" (54–55). He concluded:

> If we are to be credited with the shaping of society, let us be credited
> for our silence while living in the country Anthony Lewis calls the
> most dangerous and destructive in the world.
>   If we are to be credited let it be for what once was a noble cause 40
> years ago. Let us be credited today for our unquestioning of the status

quo, our blindness to injustice, and our ignoring of the victims of society.

Let us be credited for being able to play golf and listen to EF
Hutton.

Let us be credited for our grandchildren who might get angry and
fight for justice at home and abroad.[10]

Yugo Okubo did not live to see this book; if he had, perhaps he might
have reconsidered the possibility that he and his comrades had made a
difference and had left a considerable legacy, in the expansion of opportunities for more people in Hawai'i and certainly not least in the potential of their children and grandchildren to "get angry and fight for
justice."

At the VVV's twentieth-anniversary reunion in 1962, George Tokuyama recalled his sense of the old mission and seemed in his prayer to
be warning the group about the serious trials the entire nation would
soon face as a result of continuing social injustice and escalating combat in Southeast Asia: "O God before whose face empires rise and pass
away, establish our nation in righteousness. . . . Deliver us from race
prejudice and from such inequalities of wealth as beget ill-will and spoil
fraternity. . . . Keep us from national pride and boasting. Save our loyalty to our country from narrowness, and our flag from selfish shame.
By our love for our land may we measure the love of others for their
lands, honoring their devotion as we honor our own."[11]

In the end, for the nisei themselves, Yuriko Tsunehiro, a coed class-
mate at the time of the VVV, might have said it best: "More important
than anything else, however, was the pride they restored in us after the
shame we were forced to endure. They gave us our first step in our claim
to first class citizenship that had been denied us, and now we could hold
our heads up high."[12]

Shigeo Yoshida thought the VVV story was critical. It was forcefully
conveyed to Assistant Secretary of War John McCloy and both the Roo-
sevelts and "definitely had a part in convincing the War Department to
open up things [for the 442]" (25). In his 1946 memorial service message that commemorated the fallen members of the VVV, Yoshida said:

It was the VVV which marked the turning point in the treatment of the people of Japanese ancestry in this Territory and their acceptance by the rest of
the community. What followed afterward—the record of the 100th, the formation of the 442d and its history of hard-won battles, the less-publicized
but equally important and impressive record of the interpreter groups, and

work of the civilians on the home front—was the natural result of the trend which was started in the early months of the war when a group of you men, who numbered at no time more than 170, demonstrated to a suspicious and skeptical community that the Americans of Japanese ancestry were every bit as American and every bit as loyal to this country and to her ideals as any other group of Americans. (SYC)

By the end of the war, the VVV initiative and the entire Japanese American project were hailed as major successes. No serious racial conflicts had been recorded, and Hawaii's contributions to the war effort, especially from the large and important Japanese American population, had been outstanding. Most important, the formula developed to incorporate minority races into a smooth pattern of accommodation had been fine-tuned. Shigeo Yoshida, toward the end of his life, reflected on the significance of the VVV and World War II: "Someday, I hope some competent historian will record the full story of this period with proper documentation, and with full credit to those I have mentioned and to others who helped to steer the course of the war in Hawai`i so far as the civilians were concerned."[13]

Shigeo Yoshida would have disagreed with some of the interpretations I have imposed on his and the VVV stories. But we would have agreed that he and the VVV were important elements in the remaking of Hawai`i during and after World War II. Certainly it became a more equitable place for all Japanese Americans. Race relations changed forever, and that powerful model has been in effect for more than half a century. In the third millenium, and in the process of rethinking the social order, this model may require serious reconsideration. Understanding its origins and utility will be essential to that undertaking.

Appendix

Roster of Varsity Victory Volunteers

Akimoto, Tamotsu
Amioka, Shiro
Amioka, Ted T.
Aoki, Tsugio
Asano, Fred N.
Betsui, Daniel D.
Buto, Junichi
Chinen, Jenhatsu
Chinen, Masahide
Chinen, Richard K.
Doi, Masato
Doi, Wallace T.
Emura, Edward T.
Fujioka, Shigeo
Fujita, David
Fujita, Yasuhiro
Fujitani, Atsushi
Fujitani, Yoshiaki
Furukawa, Sumu
Goto, Walter R.
Hamaguchi, Akira
Hamaishi, Clarence Y.
Harunaga, Toshio
Hashimoto, Akira
Hashizume, Shuichi
Hayashi, Yoshimi
Hedani, Takao
Higa, Warren T.
Higashino, Edwin T.
Himeda, Kikuji

Himoto, Teruo
Hirai, Seichi
Hirano, Yoshiyuki
Hirono, Howard M.
Hirota, Jyun
Honda, Edwin H.
Honma, Tsuneo
Hoshijo, Anki
Iha, Edward S.
Ikeda, Chiyoki
Ikeda, Tadashi
Ikehara, Minoru
Ishihara, Stanley S.
Ishii, Shigeru
Isonaga, Herbert S.
Iwasa, Walter M.
Kadowaki, Robert N.
Kagawa, Shoso
Kagihara, Allen
Kajihara, Takashi
Kashiwada, James T.
Kato, Hiroshi
Kawabata, Taketo
Kawabe, Toshiro
Kawate, Kenneth K.
Kikawa, Robert S.
Kimura, Kongo
Kimura, Stanley T.
Kitagawa, Isamu
Kobayashi, Roy T.

Kogami, Toshiyuki
Komesu, Phillip
Komoto, Iro
Kono, Kiyoshi
Kuniyoshi, Hideo
Kushi, Sukeyoshi
Makino, Hideo
Manabe, Benjamin M.
Matsumoto, Ranceford Y.
Matsunaga, Joseph J.
Mayeda, Thomas
Mikami, Yoshiharu
Minami, Hiroshi
Mita, Wilfred M.
Miura, David M.
Miyake, James S.
Miyake, Walter S.
Miyasaka, George
Miyashiro, Yeiyu
Morisako, Henry H.
Morisawa, Jackson Soji
Morita, Tom T.
Murata, Robert S.
Nagahisa, Henry S.
Nagaji, Grover K.
Nagao, Wallace T.
Nagasako, Melvyn M.
Nagata, Shogo
Nakagawa, Patrick Y.
Nakahata, Yutaka

Nakama, Henry S.
Nakamine, Roy K.
Nakamura, Allan I.
Nakamura, Edward H.
Nakashima, Shigemitsu
Namba, Ryoji
Narusaki, Mamoru
Nikaido, Thomas T.
Nishikawa, Akio
Nishimura, James S.
Nogawa, Raymond K.
Nosaka, Seichi
Oka, George K.
Oka, James I.
Okazaki, Edward Y.
Okubo, Yoshio
Okubo, Yugo
Okuda, James T.
Okumoto, Walter T.
Onaga, Mitsuru
Ono, Masao
Ono, Morimasa
Ono, Seichi
Ono, Tamotsu
Onodera, John T.
Otani, Akira
Oyasato, Henry C.
Sagawa, Masaichi
Saito, Herbert T.

Sakamoto, Ronald Y.
Saruwatari, Kenneth K.
Sato, Harry N.
Serikawa, Fumio
Shikuma, Henry T.
Shintani, Thomas T.
Suzuki, Terry T.
Takara, John H.
Takekawa, Claude Y.
Takemoto, Kaname
Takemura, Tadashi
Taketa, Morris
Takizawa, Garret T.
Tanaka, Harry T.
Terada, Herbert M.
Tokuyama, George H.
Tomita, Hiroichi
Tomita, Katsumasa
Tottori, Calvin A.
Toyota, Ralph H.
Tsuji, Ernest Y.
Tsukazaki, Norman T.
Tsukiyama, Ted T.
Uchima, Unkei
Ueki, Wilfred O.
Urabe, Howard M.
Uyeda, Kenichi
Uyeda, Kenso
Uyehara, Harry K.

Uyemura, Richard S.
Uyetake, Joso
Watanabe, Stanley M.
Watase, Edward K., Jr.
Yabusaki, George H.
Yamada, Allen H.
Yamada, Edward Y.
Yamaguchi, Tokio
Yamamoto, George K.
Yamamoto, Joji
Yamamoto, Richard S.
Yamamoto, Satoki
Yamaoka, Noboru
Yanagi, Glenn
Yasuda, Joseph K.
Yempuku, Ralph T.
Yokoyama, Kenneth K.
Yoshimasu, Lincoln M.
Yoshimoto, Tsugio
Zakimi, Saiji
Zukemura, Richard H.

*U.S. Army Liaison
Personnel:*

Capt. Richard T.F. Lum
Lt. Frank Judd
Lt. Thomas Kaulukukui
M/Sgt. William K. Jarrett
M/Sgt. George P. Aikau

Notes

Note on Sources

The most valuable sources for this book were the personal accounts of former members of the Varsity Victory Volunteers and the people intimately associated with them. More than thirty interviews and taped discussions were transcribed verbatim, edited, reviewed by the interviewees, and bound. They are in the VVV Collection of the University of Hawaii's Hamilton Research Library's Special Collections. Unless otherwise noted, all quotes in this book are from these interviews, and the page numbers refer to the transcribed versions. See the Bibliography for more information about these interviews.

Some of the VVV members kept personal papers and records. Especially significant were the personal collections of Hung Wai Ching (HWCC), Ted Tsukiyama (TTC), Ralph Yempuku (RYC), and Shiro Amioka (SAC). Tsukiyama, fortunately, shot many rolls of film documenting the VVV experience. The negatives, stored for four decades in an old Best Pal candy box, proved to be in good condition and provided most of the photos in this book. They are also in the University of Hawaii's Hamilton Library. Shigeo Yoshida's papers (SYC) included a number of important items. Dr. Ernest Murai's voluminous collection has crucial documents from his work on the Emergency Service Committee. That collection was secured from Murai's widow by Professor Shigehiko Shiramizu of Musashi University in Tokyo, who was researching Japanese American participation in WWII Hawai`i. Portions of that collection were photocopied and are in the possession of the author.

Introduction

1. Akira Otani, interview by the author, VVV Collection, Special Collections, Hamilton Research Library, University of Hawaii, Honolulu, 16.

2. See John Dower, *War Without Mercy* (New York: Pantheon Books, 1986).

3. On Japanese Americans' World War II experiences see, esp., Andrew Lind, *Hawaii's Japanese: An Experiment in Democracy* (Princeton: Princeton University Press, 1946).

4. My forays into the historical context of the VVV are based on Michael Frisch's suggestion that the most important questions in oral history deal with issues that re-

quire examination in and through particular examples, "because they require pre-cise location in cultural space and historical time" (see Frisch, *A Shared Authority: Essays on the Craft and Meaning of Oral and Public History* [Albany: SUNY Press, 1990], xvi). These details should contribute to an ethnography of nisei males grow-ing up in Hawai`i in that period comparable to the richer, more sensitive literature already available on Japanese Americans on the "mainland."

5. Stanley Aronowitz properly warns that "there can be no 'essential' identity. What in one context appears clear, say, that oppression is firmly situated in skin color, sexual practices, national origins—in which cases identity appears anchored in the human condition—may, in other contexts, be entirely different" (see Aronowitz, *Dead Artists, Live Theories, and Other Cultural Problems* [New York: Rout-ledge, 1994], 197).

6. Robert Westbrook, "Christopher Lasch, Historian and Social Critic," *Perspectives* 32, 4 (April 1994): 27.

7. Alejandro Portes and Min Zhou in "The New Second Generation: Segmented Assimilation and Its Variants," *The Annals of the American Academy of Political and Social Science* 530 (November 1993), 82 argue that assumptions based on European immigration in the early twentieth century are misleading when applied to post-1965 groups. I think this may also be true for some earlier non-European immigrants like the Japanese.

8. This book is part of a long-term effort to examine one ethnic group in one location over several generations. Some immigrant experiences were discussed in Franklin Odo and Kazuko Sinoto, *A Pictorial History of the Japanese in Hawai`i, 1885–1924* (Honolulu: Bishop Museum Press, 1985), and in Odo and Harry Urata, "Hole Hole Bushi: Songs of Hawaii's Japanese Immigrants," *Mana* 6, 1 (1981), 69–75.

9. Dennis Ogawa, *Kodomo no tame ni: For the sake of the children* (Honolulu: University Press of Hawaii, 1978), xxii. See also Gavan Daws, *A Shoal of Time* (New York: Macmillan, 1968); Lawrence Fuchs, *Hawaii Pono: A Social History* (New York: Harcourt, Brace and World, 1961).

10. One unorthodox view of the nisei as a success story is Eileen Tamura, *Americanization, Acculturation, and Ethnic Identity: The Nisei Generation in Hawaii* (Urbana: University of Illinois Press, 1994). On the nisei as rather ordinary children of im-migrants, see Franklin Odo, "The Rise and Fall of the Nisei" (*Hawaii Herald*, Au-gust–November 1984).

11. I am indebted to Jeff Chang for observing that a common element of un-problematic "celebration" of Hawaii's contemporary multiracial, multicultural so-ciety occurs even in Gary Okihiro, *Cane Fires: The Anti-Japanese Movement in Hawaii, 1865–1945* (Philadelphia: Temple University Press, 1991); Ron Takaki, *Pau Hana* (Honolulu: University of Hawaii Press, 1983); and Stephen Sumida, *And the View from the Shore: Literary Traditions of Hawai`i* (Seattle: University of Washington Press, 1991).

12. See, for example, Nicholas B. Dirks, Geoff Eley, and Sherry B. Ortner, *Culture/Power/History: A Reader In Contemporary Social Theory* (Princeton: Princeton University Press, 1994). On U.S. race relations, see Michael Omi and Howard Winant, *Racial Formation in the United States: From the 1960s to the 1990s* (New York:

Routledge, 1994); I agree with Omi and Winant that Antonio Gramsci's concept of hegemony is most helpful in relating race formation to other "axes of oppression and difference—most importantly class and gender" (66–67). For Asian Americans, see E. San Juan Jr., *Racial Formations/Critical Transformations: Articulations of Power in Ethnic and Racial Studies in the United States* (New Jersey: Humanities Press, 1992).

13. As cited in Stephen Gill, "Epistemology, Ontology, and the 'Italian School,'" in *Gramsci, Historical Materialism, and International Relations*, ed. Gill (Cambridge: Cambridge University Press, 1993), 42.

14. Perhaps the very ferocity of the historical condemnation of the pre–World War II plantation society helps explain the tendency to romanticize the accomplishments of post-1954 contemporary society. Noel Kent's *Hawaii: Islands Under the Influence* (Honolulu: University of Hawaii Press, 1993) is more nuanced and mindful of the problems inhering in the post–World War II society.

15. The National Museum of American History of the Smithsonian Institution in Washington, D.C., and the Japanese American National Museum in Los Angeles have significant exhibitions on this topic. Within a year after the end of World War II, the nisei wartime record was being heralded; see Lawrence H. Sakamoto, *Hawaii's Own: Picture Story of 442nd Regiment, 100th Battalion and Interpreters* (Honolulu: Privately printed, c. 1946). See also George Cooper and Gavan Daws, *Land and Power in Hawai`i* (Honolulu: University of Hawaii Press, 1990), who suggest: "It would be historically valuable, and humanly good, to hear about the experiences of those [Japanese Americans] in the first generation of Democratic politics in Hawaii spelled out firsthand and from the inside" (455).

16. For vigorous and unstereotyped portrayals, see Milton Murayama, *All I Asking for Is My Body* (Honolulu: University of Hawaii Press, 1988); Edward Sakamoto, *Hawaii No Ka Oi: The Kamiya Family Trilogy* (University of Hawaii Press, 1995); and Jon Shirota, *Lucky Come Hawaii* (New York: Bantam Books, 1965; reprint, Honolulu: Bess Press, 1988)) and *Pineapple White* (Los Angeles: Ohara Publications, 1972).

Chapter 1

1. Groups of nisei and sansei are today actively pursuing family histories. The Hawaii Hiroshima Heritage Study Group, formed by nisei soon after the 1985 celebration of the centennial of Hawaii's *kanyaku imin* (contract labor) arrival, continues to meet monthly.

2. This is a classic example of the "post hoc ergo propter hoc" mode of ahistorical explanation; that is, assuming the explanatory power of variables as causative agents simply because they may be discerned before the event.

3. See Sucheng Chan, *Asian Americans: An Interpretive History* (Boston: Twayne, 1991).

4. For a classic example, see Anthony Marsella, "Counseling and Psychotherapy with Japanese Americans: Cross-Cultural Considerations," *American Journal of Orthopsychiatry* 63, 2 (April 1993), 200–208.

5. "Orthodoxy—emperor, loyalty, village, family-state—occupied but a portion of the wider ideological landscape as Meiji turned to Taisho [1912–1926]; . . . it often

seems as if orthodoxy wholly dominated the public landscape in the late Meiji period. In fact, however, the imperial orthodoxy coexisted with rival formulations, of which only socialism was emphatically excluded from the realm of permissible civic discourse. And ideologically even socialism survived in the following decades" (Carol Gluck, *Japan's Modern Myths: Ideology in the Late Meiji Period* [Princeton: Princeton University Press, 1985], 276–277).

6. Japanese vernacular newspapers were established in 1892 in Hawai`i and even earlier on the mainland. See Tamura Norio and Shiramizu Shigehiko, eds., *Beikoku shoki no Nihongo shinbun* [Japanese-language newspapers in the United States in the immigration era] (Tokyo: Keiso Shobo, 1986).

7. The classic exposition of the original paradigm remains Edward Said, *Orientalism* (New York: Vintage Books, 1979).

8. Ogawa, *Kodomo no tame ni*, 55. See also Linda Tamura, *The Hood River Issei: An Oral History of Japanese Settlers in Oregon's Hood River Valley* (Urbana: University of Illinois Press, 1993).

9. Buddhism was actually the object of persecution during the early years of the Meiji era, and Bushido was being displaced by a fierce brand of capitalism. See Irokawa Daikichi, *The Culture of the Meiji Period*, ed. and trans. Marius Jansen (Princeton: Princeton University Press, 1985).

10. Masakazu Iwata, *Planted in Good Soil: A History of the Issei in United States Agriculture* (New York: Peter Lang, 1992), vol. 1, 92.

11. See Kenneth Pyle, *The New Generation in Meiji Japan: Problems of Cultural Identity, 1885–1895* (Stanford: Stanford University Press, 1969); Mikiso Hane, *Peasants, Rebels, and Outcastes: The Underside of Modern Japan* (New York: Pantheon, 1982).

12. See Anne Walthall, *Peasant Uprisings in Japan: A Critical Anthology of Peasant Histories* (Chicago: University of Chicago Press, 1991); Herbert Bix, *Peasant Protest in Japan, 1590–1884* (New Haven: Yale University Press, 1986); William Kelly, *Deference and Defiance in Nineteenth-Century Japan* (Princeton: Princeton University Press, 1985).

13. Daikichi, *Culture of the Meiji Period*, 16–17.

14. On the emigration process, see especially Kodama Masaaki, *Nihon iminshi kenkyu josetsu* [Introduction to research on Japanese emigrants] (Hiroshima: Keisui Sha, 1991). Today's decreased emphasis on poverty as a factor in driving the Japanese to emigrate reflects a recognition that it took at least modest capital and hope, more than abject poverty and desperation, to make such a drastic move. The dramatic rise in tenantry rates was one indication of downward mobility as a factor, as we will see in the case of VVV member Akira Otani's father, Matsujiro Otani.

15. The *jiyu minken undo*, or popular rights movement, was especially important. Socialist and anarchist groups were organized with important connections involving issei communities on the mainland and in Hawai`i. See, for example, Yuji Ichioka, *The Issei: The World of the First Generation Japanese Immigrants, 1885–1924* (New York: Free Press, 1988), 102–13.

16. Hane, *Peasants, Rebels, and Outcastes*, 17.

17. Odo and Sinoto, *A Pictorial History*, 17–22.

18. Ibid., 43.

19. "The Sansei Experience," *Nichibei josei jyanaru: US-Japan Women's Journal*, no. 2 (1992): 91.

20. Tamura, *Americanization*, 33–34.

21. Suzuki Toshiaki, "Mauishima no koko to nihonjin," in *Hawai Nikkeishakai no bunka to sono henyo* [Culture change in Hawaii's Japanese American society], ed. Okita Yukuji (Kyoto: Nakamichiya, 1998), 187.

22. Mark Lincicome, *Principle, Praxis, and the Politics of Educational Reform in Meiji Japan* (Honolulu: University of Hawaii Press, 1995), 238–246.

23. Michio Nagai, "Westernization and Japanization: The Early Meiji Transformation of Education," in *Tradition and Modernization in Japanese Culture*, ed. Donald Shively (Princeton: Princeton University Press, 1971), 58, quoted in Lincicome, *Principle*, 36.

24. Tamura, *Americanization*, 123, fig. 7.

25. There has always been a powerfully utilitarian cast to the traditional Japanese value placed on education; in general, education reproduces the existing social order rendered as a meritocracy. See Ronald Dore, *The Diploma Disease: Education, Qualification, and Development* (Berkeley: University of California Press, 1976); Barbara Finkelstein, Anne Imamura, and Joseph Tobin, eds., *Transcending Stereotypes: Japanese Culture and Education* (Yarmouth, Maine: Intercultural Press, 1991).

26. Ronald Dore, *Education in Tokugawa Japan* (Berkeley: University of California Press, 1965); Herbert Passin, *Society and Education in Japan* (New York: Teachers College Press, 1965).

27. Charles Ryu, "1.5 Generation," in *Asian Americans*, ed. Joann Lee (New York: New Press, 1991), 50.

28. This follows major interest in the Jewish and African diasporas. Asian American versions are not as likely to center on the homeland—that is, an "Asia-centric" ideology.

29. Robert E. Park, *Race and Culture* (New York: Free Press, 1950).

30. Luis V. Teodoro Jr., *Out of the Struggle: The Filipino in Hawaii* (Honolulu: University Press of Hawaii, 1981).

31. Odo and Sinoto, *A Pictorial History*, 40.

32. Ibid., 22, 75.

33. Ibid., 75–77, 81; for the mainland, see Ichioka, *Issei*, 28–39.

34. On picture brides, see Barbara Kawakami, *Japanese Immigrant Clothing* (Honolulu: University of Hawaii Press, 1993), esp. 9–14; Odo and Sinoto, *A Pictorial History*, 80–126; and Yukiko Kimura, *Issei: Japanese Immigrants in Hawaii* (Honolulu: University of Hawaii Press, 1988),142–46.

35. Odo and Sinoto, *A Pictorial History*, 75–76.

36. The information in table 1 and the data that follow are compiled from the VVV Project, 1984, author's papers.

37. By 1920, for example, two-thirds of the carpenters in Hawai`i were Japanese. The range of economic activity was impressive as early as the 1890s (Odo and Sinoto, *A Pictorial History*, 152–58); Tamura notes that "Japanese men in the territory reached a normal proportion in the professions by 1930" (*Americanization*, 221).

38. Barney Ono, interview by the author, VVV Collection, Special Collections, Hamilton Research Library, University of Hawaii, Honolulu, 3–4. Hereafter, quotes

from my oral history interviews of VVV members and organizers will be identified by page number in the text, not footnoted.

39. See Notes on Sources for further explanation of this and all subsequent quotes taken from interviews with Varsity Victory Volunteer members.

40. At least 838 Japanese, issei and nisei, were drafted in Hawai'i during World War 1. Some of them applied for naturalization—a privilege accorded aliens who served in the armed forces—but it was ultimately denied to veterans of Japanese nationality, who were insulted by the discrimination (Odo and Sinoto, *A Pictorial History*, 208–209).

41. Yukiko Kimura used this slender volume in an essay on the fishing industry in Hawaii (Issei, 112–121). My translation differs from her version. Matsujiro Otani, Waga hito to narishi ashiato—hachijunen no kaiko[Becoming a man—memoirs of my eighty years] [Honolulu: M. Otani, 1971].

42. Ibid., 1–3. Richard Mitchell finds "bribery" common in all societies; in Japan, elaborate systems of gift giving complicate the line between acceptable exchange and illegal or immoral behavior (*Political Bribery in Japan* [Honolulu: University of Hawaii Press, 1996]).

43. Non-Okinawan historians rarely note the critical nature of the relationships between *naichi* and *Uchinanchu* (Okinawan term for themselves), although this relationship is addressed to some degree in Ethnic Studies Oral History Project and United Okinawan Association, *Uchinanchu: A History of Okinawans in Hawaii* (Honolulu: Ethnic Studies Oral History Project and United Okinawan Association, 1981).

44. Jiro Nakano, *Kona Echo: A Biography of Dr. Harvey Saburo Hayashi* (Kona, Hawai'i: Kona Historical Society, 1990), 45.

Chapter 2

1. See Roger Daniels, *The Politics of Prejudice: The Anti-Japanese Movement in California and the Struggle for Japanese Exclusion* (Berkeley and Los Angeles: University of California Press, 1962); for a more recent treatment, see Sucheng Chan, *Asian Americans: An Interpretive History* (Boston: Twayne, 1991).

2. For the Japanese workers, at least, one major lesson was that they could not count on the other ethnic groups. Hence, the 1924 Kauai and 1937 Maui all-Filipino strikes generated very little Japanese support. On the 1920 strike, see Takaki, *Pau Hana*, and Edward Beechert, *Working in Hawaii: A Labor History* (Honolulu: University of Hawaii Press, 1985).

3. "A racial project is simultaneously an interpretation, representation, or explanation of racial dynamics, and an effort to reorganize and redistribute resources along particular racial lines," according to Omi and Winant, *Racial Formation*, 56.

4. Harry Maxwell Naka, "The Naturalization of the Japanese Veterans of the American World War Forces" (master's thesis, University of California, Berkeley, 1939).

5. Kihara Ryukichi, *Hawai Nipponjinshi* [A history of the Japanese in Hawaii] (Tokyo: Anseisha, 1936), 658.

6. Quoted in Tamura, *Americanization*, 78–79.

7. Gill, "Epistemology," 41.

8. Lind, *Hawaii's Japanese*, 14.

9. Odo and Sinoto, *A Pictorial History*, 127.

10. Tamura, *Americanization*, 107–109, figs. 2, 3, 4. Japanese elementary school children made it into high school at far lower rates than did haoles, Koreans, or Chinese and slightly lower than Hawaiians.

11. Gary Okihiro summed up the looming confrontation: "By 1919, the 'Japanese problem,' in the eyes of military intelligence, had taken on epic proportions: a battle for the control of Hawaii. The problem was rooted in the growing and permanent Japanese population of the territory: their birthrate, the number of men of military age, the number of eligible voters, and the loyalties of aliens and citizens" (*Cane Fires*, 108, 112).

12. For more on Japanese-language schools, see Odo and Sinoto, *A Pictorial History*, 127–143; Ozawa Gijo, ed., *Hawai Nihongo Gakko Kyoikushi* [History of Japanese language school education in Hawaii] (Honolulu: Hawaii Kyoiku Kai, 1972); Takagi Mariko, "Moral Education in Pre-war Japanese Language Schools in Hawaii" (MA thesis. University of Hawai'i at Manoa, 1987).

13. Odo and Sinoto, *A Pictorial History*, 128.

14. The Japanese Educational Association, a territorywide organization, met for the first time in 1915. It hired Professor Yaichi Haga of Tokyo Imperial University to revise the textbooks in order "make them more consistent with the history, mores, and values of Hawai'i and America" (Odo and Sinoto, *A Pictorial History*, 129).

15. See especially Gijo, *Hawaii Nihongo gakko kyoikushi*, 77–138; Kihara, *Hawai Nipponjinshi*, 225–234.

16. Roland Kotani, *A Century of Struggle: The Japanese in Hawaii* (Honolulu: Hawaii Hochi, 1985), 51.

17. Yasutaro Soga, editorial, *Nippu Jiji*, August 11, 1922, quoted in Tamura, *Americanization*, 150–151.

18. For the most important of Makino's contributions, see Makino Biography Committee, *Life of Kinzaburo Makino* (Honolulu: Michie Makino, 1965), 15–16.

19. Ibid., 65–66.

20. Quoted in Tamura, *Americanization*, 60.

21. Sato has argued that HCE be treated as a separate language, living, evolving, worthy of serious study (*The Syntax of Conversation in Interlanguage Development* [Tubingen: G. Marr, 1990]).

22. Marielouise Morley, "A Study of the 1924 Graduates of Punahou" (master's thesis, University of Hawaii, 1936), 4. When John Fox arrived to assume the presidency in 1944, he found that Punahou was "about an eighty percent *haole* school. Orientals—children of Japanese, Chinese, and Filipino extraction—were limited by a fixed ten percent quota. Although there was no limit on children with Hawaiian blood, they comprised only about ten percent of the student body. . . . From the outset, Fox says, he was determined to abolish the quota but 'tried to keep it quiet because I was ashamed of it'" (Nelson Foster, ed., *Punahou: The History and Promise of a School of the Islands* [Honolulu: Punahou School, 1991], 119–120).

23. Judith Hughes, "The Demise of the English Standard School System in Hawai'i," *Hawaiian Journal of History* 27 (1993): 71.

24. Quoted in Tamura, *Americanization*, 112.

25. Yoshida penned a famous essay, "Speak American," in 1942, to persuade fellow Japanese Americans to speak Standard English, avoiding the use of pidgin and Japanese (*Hawaii Educational Review* 31 (1942): 106; reprinted in Ogawa, *Kodomo no tame ni*, 329–331).

26. Tamura, *Americanization*, 23; for women in the workforce, see Tamura, "The Americanization Campaign and the Assimilation of the Nisei in Hawaii, 1920 to 1940," Ph.D. dissertation (Honolulu: University of Hawaii, 1990), 46, table 21.

27. See interviews in "Remembering Kakaako, 1910–1950" (Honolulu: University of Hawaii Ethnic Studies Oral History Project, 1978).

28. In the 1990s, there are Okinawans—Uchinanchu, in the Okinawan language —who insist on the distinction between them and the "Japanese." See also Philip Ige, "An Okinawan Nisei in Hawaii," in *Uchinanchu: A History of Okinawans in Hawaii*, (Honolulu: University of Hawaii Ethnic Studies Program and United Okinawan Association, 1981), 149–160. On the modern Okinawan community in Hawai'i, see Wesley Ueunten, "Maintenance of the Okinawan Community in Hawaii" (master's thesis, University of Hawai'i, 1989).

29. Odo and Sinoto, *A Pictorial History*, 158.

30. Transcript of Yoshimi Hayashi lecture, Buddhist Study Center Oral History Project, Honolulu, December 5, 1991.

31. It was clear that Namba, by the 1980s, had come to respect Okinawans for their ability to organize and flourish; this was not the case, he thought, of other groups. "Like your blacks. Why can't they get above that?" (13). For more on Okinawans, see Okinawa Club of America, *History of the Okinawans in North America* (Los Angeles: Asian American Studies Center, UCLA, and the Okinawan Club of America, 1988), and Ige, *Uchinanchu*.

32. On Japanese Christians on the West Coast, see Brian Hayashi, *"For the Sake of Our Japanese Brethren": Assimilation, Nationalism, and Protestantism Among the Japanese of Los Angeles, 1895–1942* (Stanford: Stanford University Press, 1995), and Yoshida Ryo, "Kirisutokyoka to Hawai Nikkeijin no Amerikaka" [Christianization and Americanization of Hawaii's Japanese Americans], *Shukyo kenkyu*, no. 296 (June 1993), 79–103.

33. Shigeo Yoshida, a generation older, recalled: "My parents always [said] I will need it some day. Well, they were right." He laughed. "I wish I had gone to language school. But at that time my answer was 'I'm American.' . . . And we could also see, young as we were, what influence Japan could have on us through the language school. We celebrated the emperor's birthday, for instance." More laughter. "Even at that age, I was sensitive to the idea that the language school may contribute to our [not] being accepted as full Americans" (14–15).

34. Hayashi, Buddhist Studies Center oral history.

35. In a detailed chapter, "Japanese Language Schools," Tamura devotes one brief paragraph to two nisei who enjoyed and benefited from the experience (*Americanization*, 158). For MIS achievements, see Military Intelligence Service Veterans of Honolulu, *Secret Valor: M.I.S. Personnel, World War II Pacific Theater, Pre-Pearl Harbor to Sept. 8, 1951* (Honolulu: MIS Veterans Club of Hawaii, 1993).

36. For this issue in starkly confrontational perspective, see Okihiro, *Cane Fires*, 129–162.

37. See Kotani, *A Century of Struggle*, 135–141. Also, John Reinecke, *A Man Must Stand Up: The Autobiography of a Gentle Activist*, ed. Alice Beechert and Edward Beechert (Honolulu: Biographical Research Center, 1993).

38. Teruo Himoto interview by Greg Beuthin, September 24, 1992 (author's papers).

39. I think Tamura understates the severity and number of tragedies exacted by this policy: "In attending school regularly, obeying school rules, and minding their teachers, the Nisei behaved as Americanizers hoped they would. But the Nisei pursued schooling with a seriousness that went beyond the wishes of Americanizers, who . . . learned that they were ineffective in curbing Nisei aspirations, and therefore, Nisei achievement" (*Americanization*, 124). Many nisei and sansei teachers today behave as if this had been the sole trajectory assumed by their entire ethnic group and that the lack of such values explains, in the educational "deficit" model, the failure of other groups, including Native Hawaiians, Filipinos, and Puerto Ricans, in more contemporary school settings in Hawai`i. The result is a view of the problems that, however unintended, results in a denigration of other cultures in contemporary Hawai`i.

40. Tamura, "Americanization Campaign," 449–450, tables 13–14.

41. On the Fukunaga tragedy, see Daws, *A Shoal of Time*, 317–327; Kotani, *A Century of Struggle*, 59–65; Gijo, *Hawai Nihongo gakko kyoikushi*, 153–154.

Chapter 3

1. For data on schooling of the nisei, see Tamura, *Americanization*, esp. chap. 5.

2. Michael Slackman, "The Orange Race: George S. Patton, Jr.'s Japanese-American Hostage Plan," *Biography* 7, 1 (1984): 1–49, and *Target Pearl Harbor* (Honolulu: University of Hawaii Press, 1990); Okihiro, *Cane Fires*. See also Daws, *A Shoal of Time*, and Fuchs, *Hawaii Pono*.

3. Eleanor Nordyke, *The Peopling of Hawai`i*, 2d ed. (Honolulu: University of Hawai`i Press, 1989), 178–181, table 3-1.

4. Kihara, *Hawai Nipponjinshi*, 277. For 1925, 70,860 nisei and 57,208 *issei*, a total of 128,068; for 1933, 103,467 nisei and 43,523 *issei*, a total of 146,990.

5. For a history of labor in Hawai`i, see Beechert, *Working in Hawaii*. On organizing the ILWU, see Sanford Zalburg, *A Spark is Struck! Jack Hall and the ILWU in Hawaii* (Honolulu: University Press of Hawaii, 1979). On public education, see Ralph Stueber, "Hawaii: A Case Study in Development Education, 1778–1960" (Ph.D. diss., University of Wisconsin, 1964); Alan Shoho, "Americanization Through Public Education of Japanese-Americans in Hawaii, 1930–1941" (Ph.D. diss., Arizona State University, 1990).

6. The ILWU produced a racial variant of its own by alienating several important nisei labor leaders who felt that the policy simply affirmed mainland haole leadership at the expense of homegrown Japanese American talent. See Kotani, *A Century of Struggle*, 125–141.

7. Chan, *Asian Americans*, 55–56.

8. For Filipinos in Hawai`i, see Teodoro, *Out of the Struggle*. On efforts to convince the nisei that careers as sugar workers would be rewarding, see Gail Nomura,

"The Debate over the Role of Nisei in Prewar Hawaii, 1927–1941," *Journal of Ethnic Studies* 15, 1 (spring 1987): 95–115; and Okihiro, *Cane Fires*, 129–162.

9. On the internment of Japanese Americans, see Brian Niiya, ed., *Japanese American History: An A-to-Z Reference from 1868 to the Present* (Los Angeles: Japanese American National Museum, 1993).

10. Sixth Annual Conference of New Americans (1932), *Proceedings*, 7–10 (Stirling denounced the original Massie-Kahahawai verdict as "having lessened the prestige of white peoples"), and Seventh Annual Conference of New Americans (1933), *Proceedings*, 8–9, both quoted in Okihiro, *Cane Fires*, 143, 148.

11. For a comparative analysis of the Fukunaga and Massie cases, see Kotani, *A Century of Struggle*, 71–84.

12. The director of the Honolulu Symphony Orchestra during the 1930s, Fritz Hart, routinely recruited from most of Hawaii's ethnic groups. One Hawai`i resident, Ted Trent, reacting to the negative national press precipitated by the Massie case, wrote to the *Star Bulletin* on March 14, 1932, that the sixty-two-member symphony orchestra was "made up of seven Filipinos, two Japanese, one Hawaiian, two Chinese, two Portuguese, one Porto Rican, two Italians, and 45 Anglo-Saxons." Not everyone approved of this degree of inclusion. One of the violinists, Charles Weeber, was also Honolulu's first chief of police. In 1937 the national leadership of the American Federation of Musicians (AFM) withheld permission for the use of military players in the Honolulu Symphony, a move that would have severely limited the numbers of "Anglo-Saxons." Weeber, then president of the Honolulu Symphony Society, wrote to the AFM, explaining that there was a dire need for military performers, since although Honolulu had a population of about 200,000, "all but about 25,000 of these are Orientals with no musical background and very little musical ability, if any." In the end, money and power in the form of Walter Dillingham prevailed; after his direct appeal to the AFM leadership, the military was allowed to participate for another quarter-century (Dale Hall, "Fritz Hart and the Honolulu Symphony" *[Hawaiian Journal of History* 29 (1995): 167–169]). Hung Wai Ching remembered several individuals in California who supported Japanese Americans during the World War II internment period, including Ray Lyman Wilbur, president of Stanford University. But the number was small—they met privately to work on behalf of the Japanese Americans. "And I reported to them twice. I went to San Francisco, talked to them [about] how we're handling our situation here in Hawai`i; . . . they remember that in America there were rights . . . not all haoles were bad" (13).

13. Frederick Kinzaburo Makino claimed Lightfoot as a personal friend and was responsible, it appears, for convincing him to represent Japanese plaintiffs in these cases (Makino Biography Committee, *Life of Kinzaburo Makino*, 28–30, 48–62).

14. See Gwenfread Allen, *The Y.M.C.A. in Hawaii: 1869–1969* (Honolulu: YMCA, 1969).

15. A national survey by the Russell Sage Foundation in 1920 ranked Hawaii's school system twenty-third among fifty-three states and territories. This report noted that one of Hawaii's "strengths" was that "educational opportunities were more equitably distributed throughout the entire area; . . . in this respect Hawaii was [more democratic]." Hawaii Territory, Department of Public Instruction, Biennial Report, 1920, cited in Tamura, *Americanization*, 93, 96–97.

16. See Shirley JoAnn Williams, "The Educational Theory and Philosophy of Miles Elwood Cary: Implications for Democracy in a Global Civic Culture" (Ph.D. diss, Northern Illinois University, 1991).

17. "Our Growing Democracy," personal collection of Shiro Amioka. Amioka's voluminous papers also include poems he copied out that influenced him; one, the "Oath of the Athenian Young Man," ends: "Thus in all these ways we will transmit this city, not less, but greater, better, and more beautiful than it was transmitted to us."

18. Note from Arthur Harris to author, Honolulu, November 16, 1994. Harris joined Cary at the Poston Concentration Camp during World War II, succeeding him as director of education when Cary returned to McKinley.

19. SAC (author's papers).

20. Claude Takekawa interview, Buddhist Study Center Oral History Project, Honolulu, January 16, 1992 (author's papers).

21. Harry Tanaka interview, Buddhist Study Center Oral History Project, Honolulu, February 13, 1992 (author's papers).

22. Okihiro paints a much bleaker picture of the role of the public schools in *Cane Fires*.

23. Himoto interview by Beuthein, 2.

24. Milton Murayama put the issue dramatically in *All I Asking for Is My Body*: "Whenever anybody spoke goody-good English outside of school, we razzed them, 'You think you *haole*, eh?' 'Maybe you think you shit ice cream, eh?' 'How come you talk through your nose all the time.' Lots of them talked nasally to hide the pidgin accent" (63).

25. See essays by former governor George Ariyoshi or Bernice Hirai, for example, on the value placed on education for these nisei in Dorothy Hazama and Jane Komeiji, *Okage Sama De: The Japanese in Hawai`i, 1885–1985* (Honolulu: Bess Press, 1986), 57, 59, 102–103). The book ends with a "letter to youths of Japanese descent" in which the Hazama and Komeiji hope young people will "retain those values that have proven to be the strengths in the legacy from your grandparents and your parents, some of which are the belief in strong family ties, hard work, and perseverance (*ganbari*), education, and sensitivity and humility in relating to others" (255).

26. Tamura notes that some issei parents took their children to probation officers if they defied parental rules against "dances, football games, and American movies" (*Americanization*, 173).

27. As Irokawa Daikichi points out, this story and its message do not become fixed in Japan until the Russo-Japanese War in 1904–5, indicating that at least some of the recent Meiji chauvinism was reaching beyond Japan (*The Culture of the Meiji Period*, trans. and ed. Marius Jansen [Princeton: Princeton University Press, 1985], 299–301). For the story itself, see Paul Varley, *Warriors of Japan: As Portrayed in the War Tales* (Honolulu: University of Hawaii Press, 1994), 179–199.

28. Inouye, with Lawrence Elliott, *Journey to Washington* (Englewood Cliffs, NJ: Prentice-Hall, 1969), 36. See also Eiichiro Azuma, "Interethnic Conflict Under Racial Subordination: Japanese Immigrants and Their Asian Neighbors in Walnut Grove, California, 1908–1941," *Amerasia Journal* 20, 2 (1994): 47.

29. Tamura, *Americanization*, is an exception to the tendency to ignore the schools' significance. See, for example, Stephen Fugita and David O'Brien, *Japanese*

American Ethnicity: The Persistence of Community (Seattle: University of Washington Press, 1991).

30. Not one basic work on Hawaii's history or the Japanese experience in Hawai`i treats this topic, although it was of enormous psychological consequence to the victims. This ability to capture perceptions and experiences ignored in established historical accounts or identified documentary sources is, it seems to me, one of the most important virtues of oral history. For a poignant story, see "Masaji Marumoto: A Personal History, Part 1: The Formative Years," *East-West Photo Journal*, winter 1980, 26–27.

31. New Americans Conference (1933), 44, quoted in Tamura, *Americanization*, 84.

32. Quoted in Tamura, *Americanization*, 85.

33. Ibid.

34. Mimeographed letter to supporters of the campaign (author's papers); the petition was delivered to Secretary of State Cordell Hull. The committee was chaired by Masatoshi Katagiri and included Shunzo Sakamaki, Shigeo Yoshida, Arthur Akinaka, Katsuro Miho, and Wilfred Tsukiyama. Personal collection of Shigeo Yoshida (hereafter, in notes and in the text, SYC).

35. Center for Oral History, *An Era of Change: Oral Histories of Civilians in World War II Hawai`i* (Honolulu: Center for Oral History, 1994), 5:1621, 1659–1660.

36. Ichioka, *Issei*, 210–226. On the mainland, the issue of naturalization rights was much more critical than in Hawai`i. For example, many states, following California's lead in 1913, had prohibited *issei* from buying land on the basis of their ineligibility for naturalization.

37. See Jiro Nakano, *Kona Echo: A Biography of Dr. Harvey Saburo Hayashi* (Kona, Hawai`i: Kona Historical Society, 1990), and *Samurai Missionary: The Reverend Shiro Sokabe* (Honolulu: Hawaii Conference of the United Church of Christ, 1984).

38. See Ichioka, *The Issei*, on efforts to convince issei to assimilate into America in a more thoroughgoing (*naimenteki*) fashion, partly by accepting Christianity (180–189); also see Hayashi, '*For the Sake of Our Japanese Brethren*'; and Yoshida Ryo, "Kaishushugi to Hawai Nihonjin shakai [Hawaii's JapaneseSociety and Christian Missions]," *Kirisutokyo shakai mondai kenkyu* [Christianity and social issues research] 36 (1986): 36–63.

39. On the Buddhist leadership's initiatives, see Louise H. Hunter, *Buddhism in Hawaii: Its Impact on a Yankee Community* (Honolulu: University of Hawaii Press, 1971). Bishop Yemyo Imamura of the Nishi Hongwanji, a particularly important figure, relied on a haole convert, Ernest Hunt, to lead efforts to "Americanize" Buddhism.

Chapter 4

1. The epigraph is from the Yempuku interview, 24–25.

2. See Dower, *War Without Mercy*, esp. 147–180. Okihiro, *Cane Fires*, deals with the U.S. government's responses from the turn of the century into the 1940s as the Japanese in Hawai`i became increasingly victimized.

3. The litany of examples of this type prompted Thurston Clarke to suggest that, rather than overconfidence, the official U.S. attitude should be considered "de-

luded or arrogant" (*Pearl Harbor Ghosts: A Journey to Hawaii, Then and Now* [New York: Morrow, 1991], 111–119).

4. Ibid.

5. On the movement to control the Chinese, see William Wu, *The Yellow Peril: Chinese Americans in American Fiction, 1850–1940* (Hamden, Conn.: Archon Books, 1982). For the Japanese, see Daniels, *Politics of Prejudice*, and *Asian America: Chinese and Japanese in the United States since 1850* (Seattle: University of Washington Press, 1988).

6. Quoted in Daniels, *Asian America*, 199–200. Also see Martin Grodzin, *Americans Betrayed: Politics and the Japanese Evacuation* (Chicago: University of Chicago Press, 1949).

7. See esp. the detailed indictment of the government's actions justifying the curfew and exclusion regulations following Roosevelt's Executive Order 9066 in Peter Irons, *Justice at War: The Story of the Japanese American Internment Cases* (New York: Oxford University Press, 1983); also see Jacobus tenBroek, Edward Barnhart, and Floyd Matson, *Prejudice, War, and the Constitution: Causes and Consequences of the Evacuation of the Japanese Americans in World War II* (Berkeley: University of California Press, 1970), esp. 68–96.

8. For a fictional treatment of this attitude, see Frank Deford, *Love and Infamy* (New York: Viking, 1993).

9. Center for Oral History, *An Era of Change*, 1:79.

10. One of the unintended consequences of imposing martial law was the drastic erosion of the power held by the Big Five. Several habeas corpus cases provided the basis for arguably the most serious conflict involving military-civilian power relations in U.S. history. See J. Garner Anthony, *Hawaii Under Army Rule* (Stanford: Stanford University Press, 1955); also Fred Israel, "Military Justice in Hawaii, 1941–1944," *Pacific Historical Review* 36, 3 (1967): 243–267; Harry Scheiber and Jane Scheiber, "Constitutional Liberty in World War II: Army Rule and Martial Law in Hawaii, 1941–1946," *Western Legal History*, 3, 2 (1990): 340–378; and Douglas Smith, "Martial Law in Hawaii Revisited: A Battle Against an Abuse of Military Discretion" (Ph.D. dissertation, University of Hawaii, 1989).

11. Gwenfread Allen, *Hawaii's War Years, 1941–1945* (Honolulu: University of Hawai`i Press, 1950); Desoto Brown, *Hawaii Goes to War* (Honolulu: Editions Limited, 1989).

12. Shirley Geok-lin Lim and Amy Ling, *Reading the Literatures of Asian America* (Philadelphia: Temple University Press, 1992), 23.

13. Allen, *Hawaii's War Years*, 265.

14. Personal conversations, 1991–93. Tamashiro and his wife, Gloria, regularly lectured on the World War II experience.

15. Allen, *Hawaii's War Years*, 6.

16. Thomas Kaulukukui, "I Am a Volunteer" (mimeo), author's papers, 3.

17. Allen, *Hawaii's War Years*, 141–142.

18. Leonard Hoshijo, personal communication, Honolulu, October 31, 1994, from remarks prepared for Anki Hoshijo's memorial. Anki was one of the VVV members who never agreed to an interview. His view, according to his sons, Leonard and Bill, was that too much had already been made of the war and he did not want to contribute to any further "glorification" of it. Both his sons understood that this

book was not intended to glorify the war but were unable to persuade their father to cooperate.

19. Early in the morning, on about their third day in the immigration center, Otani was awakened by the drip of some sticky fluid on his left arm. It was coming from the bunk bed above his own and smelled of blood. He yelled for one of the other internees, a doctor, who ran over with a flashlight and discovered that the man in the upper bunk had slit his wrist. The man survived (Otani, *Waga hito to narishi ashiato*, 63).

Chapter 5

1. A fine example of the oral histories compiled about Japanese Americans during World War II is the Densho Project, Seattle, Washington. See also Leslie A. Ito, ed., *Japanese Americans during World War II: A Selected, Annotated Bibliography of Materials Available at UCLA*, 2d ed., revised and expanded (Los Angeles: UCLA Asian American Studies Center Reading Room/Library, 1997); Civil Liberties Public Education Fund Grant Program, "Personal Justice Denied: The Legacy Continues," national conference project summaries (San Francisco and Berkeley: Civil Liberties Public Education Fund and Asian American Studies Program, UC Berkeley, 1998).

2. William Puette, *The Hilo Massacre* (Honolulu: University of Hawai'i Center for Labor Education and Research, 1988).

3. Capt. I. H. Mayfield, Office of Naval Intelligence, "Report on the Morale Section (December, 1941–February, 1945)," 8, SYC (hereafter, Mayfield Report).

4. Hemenway to Frederick Simpich, G2, Territorial Office of Civilian Defense, Honolulu, December 15, 1941 (personal collection of Ted Tsukiyama, hereafter, TTC).

5. Mayfield Report, 2. The account that follows relies primarily on this report, with support from the Hung Wai Ching and Shigeo Yoshida interviews and Allen, *Hawaii's War Years*.

6. Mayfield Report, 2–3.

7. Ibid., 6–7.

8. Poindexter to Smoot, in General Files of Joseph Boyd Poindexter, War File, Hawaii Territorial Guard, Hawai'i State Archives.

9. Ibid.

10. Smoot memo to Office of Military Governor, RG 338, Box 1, National Archives, College Park, Md.

11. Ibid.

12. This account is based on a paper by William Kaneko, "Japanese Americans Evicted in World War II Hawai'i," (Washington, D.C.: Columbus School of Law, Catholic University, typescript, fall 1995, 32–33), which cites the list in a memorandum from Major R. Penhallow to Commanding Officer [Smoot], Hawaii Territorial Guard. In 1990, the removed residents received letters of apology from President George H. W. Bush and checks for $20,000.

13. Ted Tsukiyama, speech at a Pearl Harbor Day retreat at the U.S. War Museum, Ft. DeRussy, 1977, adapted for "Varsity Victory Volunteers: Pearl Harbor Tragedy and Triumph," *Honolulu Star-Bulletin*, December 7, 1978.

14. Censorship was a huge industry in wartime Hawai`i. Censors listened in on radio, cable, and telephone communication and approved film for photographs, but the most arduous task was reviewing the vast mail traffic entering and leaving the islands. In all, several hundred censors read mail in about fifty languages, plus Braille and shorthand. See Allen, *Hawaii's War Years*, 146–148; Tsukiyama letter in TTC.

15. Hung Wai Ching, interview by Shigehiko Shiramizu and Franklin Odo, Honolulu, November 1992. See, also, for treatment of blacks in Hawai`i, Beth Bailey and David Farber, *The First Strange Place: The Alchemy of Race and Sex in World War II in Hawaii* (New York: Free Press, 1992).

16. Emmons assumed that, in the event of an invasion, "a Jap in uniform is a Jap." He also suggested that the nisei might be used in North Africa to fight "black Axis colonials," or for "guard duty, or as labor battalions." In this way they would be good propaganda but would also be "hostages" and "discourage fifth column work and sabotage by the Japanese remaining on these islands" (Harold Jones to Donovan, 11 May 1942, Office of Strategic Services, RG 226, Field Station Files 190, "OSS Washington, Director's Office, Operational Files, Series 21," Box 569, Folder 324, National Archives, College Park, Md.). Thanks to Lawrence McDonald, NARA, for locating this document.

17. Kendall Fielder, interview by A. A. "Bud" Smyser and Ted Tsukiyama, Honolulu, August 17, 1979; interview notes in TTC. Fielder felt Hawai`i was really "lucky" that Shivers was in charge, that California fared badly, and that General John DeWitt, in charge of the Western Defense Command, had "gone off the deep end."

18. SYC; quotations in the paragraphs that follow are also from this memo of December 16, 1941.

19. Office of the Territorial Director of Civilian Defense, December 18, 1941, SYC.

20. SYC; quotations in the paragraphs that follow are also from this report. Like other key Morale Section documents, this one might well have been written by Shigeo Yoshida, an assumption supported by information gleaned from Alberta Tarr in interviews by Yoshida and Loomis.

21. Alberta Tarr, interview by Shigeo Yoshida, January 15, 1942, Honolulu, Hawai`i, SYC. All quotes from Tarr that follow are from this interview. Yoshida may have relied, I believe, on notes from the interviews to compile the Morale Section document.

22. In New York City before Pearl Harbor, Grace Iijima and her issei mother knitted wool scarves for British pilots for the Canadian Red Cross. After Pearl Harbor, the American Red Cross took over and told Grace: "She's not a citizen, don't let her touch the wool!" According to Grace, her mom was a much better knitter. "The American Red Cross, I think, is a very jingoistic group, really, . . . really narrow-minded" (interview by Franklin Odo and Ron Uba, Japanese American Citizens League and Columbia University Oral History Research Center Oral History Project, May 25, 1997, New York City).

23. Some observers failed to note this point. Some nisei women could assert that insensitive or racist remarks were more damaging to them than to their issei mothers because the immigrants could not understand English well. See Mei Nakano,

Japanese American Women: Three Generations, 1890–1990 (Berkeley: Mina Press, 1990}, and Evelyn Nakano Glenn, *Issei, Nisei, Warbride: Three Generations of Japanese American Women in Domestic Service* (Philadelphia: Temple University Press, 1986).

24. See Odo and Sinoto, *A Pictorial History*, 207; also, Masayo Duus, *Nihon no Imbo* [Japan's conspiracy] (Tokyo: Bungei Shunju, 1991), 101.

25. Center for Oral History, *An Era of Change*, 1:77.

26. Ronald Takaki is incorrect in asserting that "the press in Hawaii behaved responsibly" (*Strangers from a Different Shore: A History of Asian Americans* [Boston: Little, Brown, 1989], 383).

27. See Michi Weglyn, *Years of Infamy: The Untold Story of America's Concentration Camps* (New York: Morrow, 1976).

28. Bourland memo of January 16, 1942, to Emmons, Military Government of Hawaii, RG 338, General Emmons Reading File, Box 15, National Archives, College Park, Md.

29. Allen, *Hawaii's War Years*, 96–97 (emphasis in original).

30. Edgar Rice Burroughs to Emmons, Military Government of Hawaii, RG 338, General Emmons Reading File, Box 15, National Archives, College Park, Md. Burroughs would maintain his hostile attitude toward the resident Japanese American community, and in August 1944, Shigeo Yoshida, acting on behalf of the nisei Emergency Service Committee, arranged a meeting with the writer. The committee met with Burroughs at Dr. Ernest Murai's home, where they specifically criticized the writer's June 30, 1944 article, "Our Japanese Problem," in *Hawai`i* magazine. There did not appear to be any resolution, since subsequent ESC minutes disclose no further discussions with or about Burroughs (Emergency Service Committee [ESC] minutes, August 4 and 18, 1944, SYC).

31. See tenBroek et al., *Prejudice*.

32. Cited in Clarke, *Pearl Harbor Ghosts*, 235–236.

33. Order from Green, Military Government of Hawaii, RG 338, General Emmons Reading File, Box 15, National Archives, Suitland, Md.

34. Report from Green to Poindexter, in General Files of Joseph Boyd Poindexter, War File, Hawaii Territorial Guard, Hawai`i State Archives.

Chapter 6

1. Kotani, *A Century of Struggle*, 88.

2. One of the earliest significant works on the World War II internment of nearly 120,000 people of Japanese descent, two-thirds of whom were U.S. citizens, is still the most authoritative and provocative: Weglyn, *Years of Infamy*.

3. Audrie Girdner and Anne Loftis, *The Great Betrayal* (London: Macmillan, 1969), 24.

4. See, for example, tenBroek et al., *Prejudice*.

5. Reinecke, *A Man Must Stand Up*, 37.

6. Andrew Lind reports that some nisei demanded that their own issei parents refrain from wearing Japanese clothing, including treasured kimono and cherished

tabi (cloth footwear); in extreme cases, nisei children cruelly taunted their mothers: "They curse the Japanese emperor in her presence and when she forecasts evil will befall them, they dare the mighty son of heaven to try it" (*Hawaii's Japanese*, 117).

7. John Tsukano, *Bridge of Love* (Honolulu: Hawaii Hosts, 1985), 151.

8. My thanks to Bud Smyser, who had this undated petition in his possession and generously sent it to me on June 4, 1992. In an oversized, magazine-format publication on the first year of the war in the Pacific, however, Allen did authorize the use of "Japs" (*Hawaii at War: On Guard in the Pacific* [Honolulu: Honolulu Star-Bulletin, n.d]).

9. Green to H. E. Gregory, Chairman of Regents, University of Hawaii, January 26, 1942, Military Government of Hawaii, RG 338, General Emmons Reading File, Box 15, National Archives, College Park, Md.

10. This part of the story has become as much mythology as history; an early version appeared in 1946: "Disillusioned and humiliated because HTG members of other races had not been inactivated also, they sent a petition to the military governor offering themselves 'for whatever services you may see fit to use us'" (Sakamoto, *Hawaii's Own*, 63).

11. TTC; Tsukiyama retained the original notes and text of this petition.

12. From Ralph Yempuku, author's papers.

13. ESC, "Progress Report I," March 6, 1942, SYC.

14. Tsukano, *Bridge of Love*, 78.

15. Ibid., 80.

16. Lind, *Hawaii's Japanese*, 88. The Paulette paper is in SYC.

17. B. H. Wells, Executive Vice-President and Secretary of the HSPA to Lt. General Delos Emmons, Governor General of Hawaii, January 31, 1942, RG 338, General Emmons Reading File, Box 15, National Archives, College Park, Md.

18. Ibid.

19. Mrs. H. Inouye to John Young, November 20, 1944. She added: "P.S. I hope you would excuse my not too well expressed letter. I am so happy that my English don't come out." She was so delighted, that is, that she had trouble adequately expressing her thoughts. Letter enclosed in communication, John Young to author, August 1, 1984.

20. Young to author, 8–9.

21. Barney Ono remembers being among that first small group of "five or six": "See, when the first group met, it was in a big hall; then we met in the back room and Shigeo wrote the letter" (9). Ryoji Namba recalled attending the meeting with Ted Tsukiyama and Dick Uyemura as well and thought there might have been one or two more (27–28).

22. Takekawa interview, Buddhist Study Center.

23. Himoto interview by Beuthin, 4.

24. Hung Wai Ching, interview on KHET, Honolulu, September 23, 1987.

25. Lind, *Hawaii's Japanese*, 146–147.

26. Contact Group papers and correspondence in the Murai collection, acquired from Dr. Ernest Murai's widow by Shigehiko Shiramizu of Musashi University in Tokyo; author's papers.

Chapter 7

1. On the structure of the VVV, I draw on Yutaka Nakahata, ed., *The Varsity Victory Volunteers* (n.p., n.d.; c. January–March 1943), pamphlet, author's papers; VVV interviews; and the Shigeo Yoshida, Ted Tsukiyama, and Shiro Amioka personal papers.

2. On Chun, see Linda Menton, "World War II and the Civilian Community," *Oral History Recorder* 11, 2 (summer 1994): 4. Mary Samson Hendrickson interview, Center for Oral History, *An Era of Change*, 1:210.

3. See T. Michael Holmes, *The Specter of Communism in Hawaii* (Honolulu: University of Hawaii Press, 1994), 32–34, which suggests that "the issue of communism was quiescent during the war" primarily because the Soviet Union had become an ally after Nazi Germany's invasion on June 21, 1941, and because a number of Japanese Americans in Hawai'i were Communist Party members or leaders.

4. In the notorious 1931 Massie-Kahahawai case, then Governor Lawrence Judd commuted the sentences of the four convicted murderers from ten years to one hour, served in his office (Daws, *A Shoal of Time*, 319–327).

5. Kaulukukui, "I Am a Volunteer," 6.

6. Ibid.

7. Center for Oral History, *An Era of Change*, 1:xlviii.

8. Himoto interview by Beuthein, 4–5.

9. By May 1942, John McCloy was wondering whether "it might be well to use our American citizen Japanese soldiers in an area where they could be employed against the Germans" (memo, John J. McCloy to Dwight D. Eisenhower, May 20, 1942, enclosing letter, Milton Eisenhower to McCloy, May 18, 1942 [both quoted in Daniels, *Concentration Camps USA*, 145]). John Tsukano thought that Hung Wai Ching saw McCloy's visit as paving the way for Japanese Americans to be accepted for combat (*Bridge of Love*, 60).

10. Nakahata, *Varsity Victory Volunteers*, 16.

11. "Ex-Sergeant Recalls 1942," *Honolulu Star-Bulletin*, August 31, 1967, C-1, C-3.

12. Nakahata, *Varsity Victory Volunteers*, 16.

13. Even in this 1985 interview, Nakahata seemed apprehensive about voicing criticism. "Oh, Richard Chinen will take offense." He laughed. "But sardines—they open the can, heat it up and just serve it on rice. That I didn't care for very much" (49).

14. Leonard Hoshijo, personal communication.

15. Ralph Yempuku, interview on KHET, Honolulu, September 23, 1987, 24.

16. Okubo thought that Chinen had received a warm welcome when he joined the VVV shortly after the group was formed; the problems arose with the arrival of later contingents of recruits. Chinen was extremely loyal to his friends and "very protective." Later, when the 442d was training at Camp Shelby in Mississippi, Chinen discovered that a mainland Japanese American cook—"small, meek looking"—was having trouble with a landlord. Richard simply "went out and straightened the landlord out," Okubo said (32). Years later, Chinen and Anki Hoshijo reared their families together in Honolulu. Hoshijo's son Bill remembered "Uncle Richard" well since the kids played with one another and had overnight stays—"Richard was the

type to give you the shirt off his back, completely generous," he told me in the late 1980s. Personal communication.

17. Nakahata, *Varsity Victory Volunteers*, 16.

18. Ibid., 20.

19. Newcomers to Hawai`i are invariably astonished at the popularity of Spam as a food item there; Isonaga's description of its alternative may be one explanation.

20. Ralph Yempuku, Ted Tsukiyama, Ralph Toyota, interview on KHET, Honolulu, September 23, 1987.

21. "A Boys Victory Brigade," May 6, 1942, SYC; "Junior Victory Brigade: Summer Work Camp at Central Intermediate School," n.d., SYC. The boys were not paid and were allowed to return home from Saturday afternoons until 7:30 A.M. on Mondays. While not officially articulated, it seems clear that this project was based on the successful VVV model. The records do not mention the ethnic backgrounds of the boys.

22. *Varsity Victory Volunteers* (newsletter, hereafter referred to as *The VVV* and cited by date or number of issue) 1, 9 (July 11, 1942); Doi interview, 27–28; Ono, interview on KHET, Honolulu, September 23, 1987, 30.

23. Jane Albritton, letter to author, March 4, 1992, emphasis in original (author's papers). Pearl's son, Bruce Yamashita, enrolled in the Marine Corps Officers Candidates training program in the 1980s but was unfairly dropped days before graduation; later, a major protest movement ensured that Yamashita was ultimately reinstated and awarded the rank of captain.

24. *The VVV* (newsletter) 1, 31 (December 12, 1942); hereafter cited by date in the text.

25. Nakahata, *Varsity Victory Volunteers*, 27.

26. TTC.

27. Allen, *Hawaii's War Years*, 112–113.

28. Yuriko Tsunehiro, "My Search for America," student paper, University of Hawai`i at Manoa, 1983; when I asked Yuri to flesh out some details in the original, she dashed off several more pages of material (author's papers). Yuri's quotes in the paragraphs that follow in the text are from this paper.

29. Yuri learned later that this policy "was practiced on all the islands, . . . no wonder the Japanese elderlies were seen trembling at the counter." Like many others, Yuri welcomed the postwar formation of Trans Pacific Airlines, now Aloha Airlines, by a group of Chinese executives. "The Japanese flocked to Aloha Airlines from the very beginning and its apparent stability can be partly attributed to the faithful following of Japanese who never forgot" (ibid.).

30. The reference to the bowl alludes to a widely held image of young Japanese American boys with homestyle haircuts trimmed neatly and precisely around a rice bowl.

31. Nakahata, *Varsity Victory Volunteers*, 16–21.

32. Allen, *Hawaii's War Years*, 247, 353–354. Sex was not a topic easily approached in these interviews; I did not push it.

33. Bailey and Farber, *First Strange Place*, 95–132. This work manages, almost completely, to ignore the presence of Japanese Americans in Hawai`i; their chapter on prostitution is a case in point.

34. ESC, "Progress Report II," April 24, 1942, SYC.

35. Ono, KHET interview, 13–14.

36. Yempuku, Toyota, and Tsukiyama, KHET interview, 20.

37. Kaulukukui, "I Am a Volunteer," 8–9.

38. Ibid., 9.

39. Yutaka Nakahata and Ralph Toyota, "Varsity Victory Volunteers: A Social Movement," *Social Process in Hawaii* 8 (1943): 34.

40. Nakahata, *Varsity Victory Volunteers*, 21. Ono, KHET interview, 11.

41. Masato Doi, "Frankie," microfilm S51087, Special Collections, Hamilton Library, University of Hawai`i at Manoa. Doi had at least two very close haole friends: David Morrison, a boyhood classmate through early school years on the Big Island; and the high school teacher at Mid-Pacific Institute who was like a "blood brother" to Doi (6, 16).

42. Nakahata, *Varsity Victory Volunteers*, 27–28.

43. Ibid., 18.

44. Allen, *Hawaii's War Years*, 250.

45. Members of the 1399th, a segregated engineering unit of the 370th Engineer Battalion established on October 1, 1942, still bristle at being "disrespected" when World War II contributions by Japanese American units are acknowledged; they completed fifty-four major projects on Oahu, including construction of numerous buildings and jungle-training facilities (*Chowhounds: 1399th Engineer Construction Battalion, 1944–1994*, fiftieth-anniversary-celebration pamphlet [Honolulu: N.p., n.d.]).

46. The finals included: 112 pounds: Takashi Kajihara over Soji (Jackson) Morisawa; 118 pounds: Wallace Nagao over Stanley Watanabe; 126 pounds: Akira Hamaguchi over Herbert Terada; 135 pounds: Eddie Watase over Shiro Amioka; 145 pounds: Kenneth Kawate over Teruo Himoto; 160 pounds: Hiroshi Kato over Howard Hirono. The wrestling results: 112: Garrett Takizawa over Masato Doi; 118: Stanley Watanabe over Hiroichi Tomita; 126: Toshiro Kawabe over Akira Hamaguchi; 135: Masao Ono over Claude Takekawa; 145: Kenneth Kawate over Hiroshi Minami; 155: Ryoji Namba over Jyun Hirota; heavyweight: Tsuneo Honma over Richard Uyemura; unlimited: Unkei Uchima (*The VVV,* August 22, 1942).

47. Beuthein interview of Himoto, 5.

48. Namba also noted: "Even right now [Oka] doesn't show up for all kind of events. You know we have these annual banquets or whatever. But when he shows up everybody feel so good. They love that guy . . . even Ralph [Yempuku]. Ralph gets the biggest kick when he sees him" (46).

49. Hemenway was genuinely committed to the VVVs, to whom he had dedicated his poem "With Apologies to Rudyard Kipling":

Aloha to the VVV's
When the last dictator is vanquished
And the guns are quiet and still,
And victory rides on our banners,
And justice and tolerance rule,
You may rest
And you'll surely have earned it

For the work you've so cheerfully done;
But your country'll again call you to service
In the peace which we hope will come soon.
For the help of all men will be needed;
All lovers of freedom must share
In building the world of the future
Where peace and goodwill shall endure.
A world where all men shall be equal
Tho' they come from the East or the West.
Where race lines shall not foil endeavor,
And character shall be the test.
Where friendliness, honor and kindness
Shall guide in the lives of us all.
Such a world is worth all the struggle,
     the heartbreaks, the sorrow and toil.
For liberty's not given for nothing—
Liberty has to be won. (*The VVV*, June 13)

50. Native Hawaiians in urban areas may have been forced into more direct and dependent relationships; many were elected or appointed politicians or employed in public-sector patronage positions. For rural conditions, see Davianna McGregor, "Kupa`a I Ka `Aina: Persistence on the Land" (Ph.D. dissertation, University of Hawai`i, 1989).

51. Nakahata, *Varsity Victory Volunteers*, 33.

52. Allen, *Hawaii's War Years*, 40, 60, 173.

53. Shigeo Yoshida, notes for lecture to Punahou Academy, SYC.

54. Allen, *Hawaii's War Years*, 274–276.

55. Ono, KHET interview, 28–29. The pressure to buy war bonds was pervasive. Mitsuru Yamada, deprived of his fishing boat as a result of the war, was forced to take an "unskilled labor" position with the army. He was paid only "fifty cents an hour. . . . And then on top that we gotta buy savings bond; . . . you gotta eat and support your family. . . . You gotta put only about four or five dollar one payday. . . . Oh, they [the army] tell you to buy. Well, [cannot] help, you gotta buy" (Center for Oral History, *An Era of Change*, 2:660).

56. "*The VVV*", an outline for a speech by Ted Tsukiyama, TTC. Captain Lum wrote "Approved" and signed the document, dated May 14, 1942.

57. Weglyn, *Years of Infamy*, 143–144.

58. Ralph Yempuku Collection (RYC). Author's papers.

59. Lyn Crost, *Honor by Fire: Japanese Americans at War in Europe and the Pacific* (Novato, Calif.: Presidio Press, 1994), 60–63.

Chapter 8

1. Paul Kennedy, *The Rise and Fall of the Great Powers: Economic Change and Military Conflict from 1500 to 2000* (London: Fontana Press, 1989), 447–450.

2. Chan, *Asian Americans*, 122.

3. Lind, *Hawaii's Japanese*, 83–84.

4. Author's papers, courtesy of Yasuhiro Fujita, a VVV member.

5. Tanaka talk, Buddhist Study Center, Honolulu, February 13, 1992, draft transcript, 14–15 (author's papers).

6. Takekawa talk, Buddhist Study Center, January 16, 1992, Honolulu, Hawai'i.

7. Reverend Fujitani felt this was an important point, partly, it seems, to put a less "heroic" face on the image of nisei clamoring for combat duty. Today his claim to a "Hawaiian heritage," meaning a legacy belonging to all residents of Hawai'i, would be problematic, because "Hawaiian" has become so definitively associated with the islands' native people.

8. Matsuo, *Boyhood to War*, 48–49.

9. Daniel Inouye, *Journey to Washington* (Englewood Cliffs, N.J.: Prentice-Hall, 1967), 34.

10. McCloy to Roosevelt, May 31, 1943, HWCC, author's papers. (Mrs. Roosevelt forwarded a copy for Hung Wai's information.) Quotes in the paragraphs that follow are from this letter.

11. That the Japanese became an "enemy race" is precisely the argument of John Dower's *War Without Mercy*.

12. *Honolulu Star-Bulletin*, May 7, 1943.

13. On the training at Shelby and battlefront stories, see, for example, Chester Tanaka, *Go for Broke: A Pictorial History of the Japanese American 100th Infantry Battalion and the 442nd Regimental Combat Team* (Richmond, Calif.: Go For Broke, 1982); Duus, *Nihon no Imbo*; Tsukano, *Bridge of Love*; Thelma Chang, *I Can Never Forget: Men of the 100th/442d* (Honolulu: Sigi Productions, 1991); and Matsuo, *Boyhood to War*.

14. John Terry, *With Hawaii's AJA Boys at Camp Shelby, Mississippi* (Honolulu: Honolulu Star-Bulletin, n.d.), pamphlet, 20.

15. Tsukano, *Bridge of Love*, 152. Among the best were Anki Hoshijo, Joe Matsunaga, Roy Nakamine, Wallace Nagao, and Richard Kato, all former VVV boxers.

16. Takekawa talk.

17. Quoted in Terry, *With Hawaii's AJA Boys*, 17–18.

18. Ibid.

19. Hemenway to Uchima, May 18, 1943, quoted in Tsukano, *Bridge of Love*, 139.

20. Tsukano, *Bridge of Love*, 140.

21. Ibid.

22. Hemenway to Yempuku, June 26, 1943, and Kometani to Hemenway, June 1943, quoted in Tsukano, *Bridge of Love*, 175, 174.

23. Ibid., 149.

24. "Report Submitted upon Governor's Request," August 19, 1944, SYC.

25. Matsuo, *Boyhood to War*, 134; the 442nd Historical Archival Center in Honolulu, fact sheet (n.p, n.d.), lists 788 total killed in action and died of wounds.

26. This account of VVVs killed in action follows Bill Thompson, "A Country Stolen: The Story of the VVV," *Hawaii Herald*, March 17, 1995.

27. Quoted in Matsuo, *Boyhood to War*, 164.

28. Matsuo, *Boyhood to War*, 218.

29. Leonard Hoshijo, personal communication.

30. See, for one account, Chang, *I Can Never Forget*, 164–174.

31. Matsuo, *Boyhood to War*, 205.

32. See Lyn Crost, *Honor by Fire*; also forthcoming volume on MIS by military historian Jim McNaughton. McNaughton notes that the Air Force and Navy were much slower to acknowledge the value of these nisei linguists.

33. For Merrill's Marauders, see Roy Matsumoto's account in *American Patriots*, ed. Stanley Falk and Warren Tsuneishi (Washington, D.C.: Japanese American Veterans Association of Washington, D.C., 1995), 62–64.

34. Tanaka talk.

35. Hayashi talk, Buddhist Studies Center oral history.

36. Tsukano, *Bridge of Love*; and Duus, *Nihon no Imbo*.

37. Also based on a personal communication, Tsukiyama to the author, October 9, 1997, TTC, author's papers.

38. ESC minutes, February 9, 1945, SYC.

39. Takekawa talk.

40. Ibid.

41. See Tomi Kaizawa Knaefler, *Our House Divided: Seven Japanese American Families in World War II* (Honolulu: University of Hawaii Press, 1991).

42. See especially Lind, *Hawaii's Japanese*; Fuchs, *Hawaii Pono*; Daws, *A Shoal of Time*; and Ogawa, *Kodomo no tame ni*.

43. See Allen, *Hawaii's War Years*, 305–326.

44. Steve Lum, "Herbert Isonaga: Portrait of a VVV 'Gang' Member," *Hawaii Herald*, February 21, 1992.

45. Thomas Maretzki and John McDermott, "The Caucasians," in *People and Cultures of Hawaii: A Psychocultural Profile*, ed. John McDermott, Wen-Shing Tseng, and Thomas Maretzki (Honolulu: John Burns School of Medicine and University of Hawaii Press, 1980), 31.

46. ESC minutes, July 20, 1945. SYC.

47. Ibid., May 12, 1944, SYC.

48. Green to McCloy, June 2, 1942, Military Government of Hawaii, Office of Internal Security, RG 338, "Correspondence, Reports, etc. Re: History of OMG (Office of Military Governor), 1942–45," Box 839, National Archives. In February 1946, the U.S. Supreme Court finally ruled that Congress had not intended "to authorize the supplanting of courts by military tribunals" (Allen, *Hawaii's War Years*, 182).

49. ESC minutes, May 12, 1944, SYC.

50. Green to McCloy, June 2, 1942.

51. No author, no date. SYC.

52. Matsuo, *Boyhood to War*, 26–27.

53. Richard Oguro, *Sempai Gumi: Story of the First Group of AJAs From Hawaii and American Concentration Camps to Attend Army Language School at Camp Savage, Minnesota* (Honolulu: Privately published, 1982), 70.

54. This was true throughout the West Coast fishing communities like Terminal Island in San Pedro, California. Issei fishermen pioneered long-range tuna expeditions and introduced large-scale use of ice, depth charts, and shortwave radio—

the latter two innovations easily translated into the language of espionage and sabotage.

55. Morale Section, "Third Progress Report," March 5, 1942, SYC.

56. Open letter from Shigeo Yoshida to "Members of the Emergency Service Committee," Honolulu, July 13, 1943, SYC.

57. Helen Chapin, "From Makaweli to Kohala: The Plantation Newspapers of Hawai`i," *Hawaiian Journal of History* 23 (1989): 179.

58. See Robert W. O'Brien, *The College Nisei* (Palo Alto, Calif.: Pacific Books, 1949); and Thomas James, *Exile Within: The Schooling of Japanese Americans, 1942–1945* (Cambridge: Harvard University Press, 1987).

59. Betty Hemphill with Robert Hemphill, *The Crossroads Witness* (Honolulu: Church of the Crossroads, 1988), 60.

Chapter 9

1. Takekawa talk.

2. Leonard Hoshijo, personal communication.

3. *Ka Leo O Hawaii*, April 25, 1946, 3. The front page of this issue featured the three women who were selected to head the campus's major publications. Among them was Helen Geracimos (now Chapin), who told me over the phone on November 22, 1994, that the veterans virtually controlled student activities because of their maturity and experiences.

4. Tanaka talk.

5. Hoshijo, personal communication.

6. Okubo to Odo, October 1, 1985, author's papers.

7. Kotani reinforces this interpretation in *A Century of Struggle*, chap. 8.

8. Amioka retirement speech, Honolulu, 1985, SAC.

9. Amioka, lecture to Kapiolani Community College class, September 17, 1974, SAC.

Conclusion

1. See, for example, Eric Foner, *The Story of American Freedom* (New York: Norton, 1998), 236–247.

2. This appeared to be the rationale for the subtitle of Hosokawa's 1969 *Nisei: The Quiet Americans*.

3. See John Gillis's introduction and Paul Koistinen, "Toward a Warfare State: Militarization in America during the Period of the World Wars," in *The Militarization of the Western World*, ed. Gillis (New Brunswick: Rutgers University Press, 1989).

4. See Beechert, *Working in Hawaii*.

5. Mayfield Report.

6. Ibid.

7. Ernest Murai, "Security Regulations Pertaining to Enemy Aliens and the Americans of Japanese Ancestry," SYC. The memo concludes with a plea for removal of all regulations implying suspicion.

8. See John Hayakawa Torok, "Finding the Me in LitCrit Theory: Thoughts on Language Acquisition and Loss," *University of Miami Law Review* 53, 4 (July 1999): 1019–1036.

9. Tachiki, "Emergence of Yellow Power." Even earlier, a few voices from the Left criticized Japanese and Asian American opportunism, but these tended to target individuals rather than ethnic groups.

10. Okubo to Odo, August 9, 1985, author's papers.

11. Twentieth-anniversary memorial program, author's papers.

12. Tsunehiro, "My Search for America," 9, author's papers.

13. Quoted in Tsukano, *Bridge of Love*, 47–48.

Bibliography

Audiotaped Interviews

The audiotapes and complete transcriptions are at the University of Hawaii at Manoa, in the Hamilton Library Special Collections. All interviews were conducted by Franklin Odo in Honolulu, Hawai`i, unless otherwise noted.

Amioka, Shiro:
  1. August 27, 1985, 49 pages.
  2. Ca. September 1985, 48 pages.
Ching, Hung Wai. By Franklin Odo and Ted Tsukiyama, October 1, 1984, 88 pages.
Doi, Masato. July 20, 1989, 47 pages.
Isonaga, Herbert:
  1. May 30, 1985.
  2. June 14, 1985, total: 51 pages.
Kaulukukui, Thomas, Sr. January 8, 1985, 38 pages.
Lum, Richard. By Franklin Odo and Ted Tsukiyama, February 19, 1985, 32 pages.
Nakahata, Yutaka. July 16, 1985, 63 pages.
Namba, Ryoji:
  1. August 26, 1985, 32 pages.
  2. September 25, 1985, 30 pages.
Okubo, Yugo. Hilo, Hawai`i. October 5, 1985, 62 pages.
Tsukiyama, Ted. February 13, 1985, 45 pages.
Yamamoto, George:
  1. March 13, 1985.
  2. July 2, 1985, total: 47 pages.
Yempuku, Ralph. March 28, 1985, 59 pages.
Yoshida, Shigeo. By Franklin Odo, Ted Tsukiyama, Thelma Yoshida, August 8, 1984, 31 pages.
Young, John. By Franklin Odo and Ted Tsukiyama, June 29, 1984, 31 pages.
Zukemura, Richard. July 19, 1989, 37 pages.

Videotaped Interviews

Videotapes and complete transcriptions produced by Chris Conybeare and Joy Chong, KHET Television, Honolulu, Hawai`i. Interviews in Honolulu and by Franklin Odo unless otherwise noted.

Ching, Hung Wai. September 23, 1987, 62 pages.
Fujitani, Yoshiaki. By Franklin Odo and Chris Conybeare, March 4, 1988, 31 pages.
Morisawa, Jackson. March 4, 1989, 39 pages.
Nakamura, Edward. By Franklin Odo and Chris Conybeare, March 7, 1989, 26 pages.
Ono, Barney. June 9, 1988, 48 pages.
Otani, Akira. April 5, 1988, 42 pages.
Toyota, Ralph, Ted Tsukiyama, and Ralph Yempuku. Ca. 1987, 33 pages.

Talks at the Honolulu Buddhist Study Center

These talks were hosted by Bishop Yoshiaki Fujitani.

Hayashi, Yoshimi. December 5, 1991, 8 pages.
Takekawa, Claude. January 16, 1992, 20 pages.
Tanaka, Harry. February 13, 1992, 32 pages.

Other Interviews

Himoto, Teruo. By Greg Beuthin, Honolulu, Hawai`i, September 24, 1992, 6 pages. Used with permission of Greg Beuthin.
Iijima, Grace. By Franklin Odo and Ron Uba, New York, May 25, 1997. Japanese American Citizens League and Columbia University Oral History Research Center Oral History Project.

Print Sources

Allen, Gwenfread. *Hawaii's War Years, 1941–1945*. Honolulu: University of Hawaii Press, 1950.
Allen, Riley, ed. *Hawaii at War: On Guard in the Pacific*. Honolulu: Honolulu Star-Bulletin, n.d.
Anderson, Benedict. *Imagined Communities: Reflections on the Origin and Spread of Nationalism*. Rev. ed. London: Verso, 1991.
Anthony, J. Garner. *Hawaii Under Army Rule*. Stanford: Stanford University Press, 1955.
Army Historical Series Advisory Committee. *American Military History*. Washington, D.C.: U.S. Army Center of Military History, 1969.
Aronowitz, Stanley. *Dead Artists, Live Theories, and Other Cultural Problems*. New York: Routledge, 1994.
Azuma, Eiichiro. "Interethnic Conflict Under Racial Subordination: Japanese Immigrants and Their Asian Neighbors in Walnut Grove, California, 1908–1941." *Amerasia Journal* 20, 2 (1994).

Bailey, Beth, and David Farber. *The First Strange Place: The Alchemy of Race and Sex in World War II in Hawaii*. New York: Free Press, 1992.

Balch, J. A. *Shall the Japanese Be Allowed to Dominate Hawaii?* Honolulu: Privately printed, 1942.

Beechert, Edward. *Working in Hawaii: A Labor History*. Honolulu: University of Hawaii Press, 1985.

Bix, Herbert. *Peasant Uprisings in Japan, 1590–1884*. New Haven: Yale University Press, 1986.

Brown, Desoto. *Hawaii Goes to War*. Honolulu: Editions Limited, 1989.

Burrows, Edwin. *Hawaiian Americans: An Account of the Mingling of Japanese, Chinese, Polynesian, and American Cultures*. New Haven: Yale University Press, 1947.

Center for Oral History. *An Era of Change: Oral Histories of Civilians in World War II Hawai`i*. Honolulu: Center for Oral History, 1994.

Chan, Sucheng. *Asian Americans: An Interpretive History*. Boston: Twayne, 1991.

Chang, Thelma. *I Can Never Forget: Men of the 100th/442d*. Honolulu: Sigi Productions, 1991.

Chapin, Helen. "From Makaweli to Kohala: The Plantation Newspapers of Hawai`i." *Hawaiian Journal of History* 23 (1989).

Clarke, Thurston. *Pearl Harbor Ghosts: A Journey to Hawaii, Then and Now*. New York: Morrow, 1991.

Coggins, Cecil Henry. "The Japanese Americans in Hawaii." *Harper's*, June 7, 1943, 75–82.

Cooper, George, and Gavan Daws. *Land and Power in Hawai`i*. Honolulu: University of Hawaii Press, 1990.

Crost, Lyn. *Honor by Fire: Japanese Americans at War in Europe and the Pacific*. Novato, Calif.: Presidio Press, 1994.

Daniels, Roger. *Asian America: Chinese and Japanese in the United States since 1850*. Seattle: University of Washington Press, 1988.

———. *Concentration Camps USA: Japanese Americans and World War II*. New York: Henry Holt, 1972.

———. *The Politics of Prejudice: The Anti-Japanese Movement in California and the Struggle for Japanese Exclusion*. Berkeley and Los Angeles: University of California Press, 1962.

Daws, Gavan. *A Shoal of Time*. New York: Macmillan, 1968.

Deford, Frank. *Love and Infamy*. New York: Viking, 1993.

Dirks, Nicholas, Geoff Eley, and Sherry Ortner. *Culture/Power/History: A Reader in Contemporary Social Theory*. Princeton: Princeton University Press, 1994.

Dore, Ronald. *The Diploma Disease: Education, Qualification, and Development*. Berkeley: University of California Press, 1976.

———. *Education in Tokugawa Japan*. Berkeley: University of California Press, 1965.

Doshisha University Jinbun Kagaku Kenkyujo. "1920 nendai no Hawai ni okeru Nikkeijin no Amerikaka" [Americanization of Japanese Americans in Hawai`i during the 1920s]. Kyoto: Doshisha University, 1993.

Dower, John. *War Without Mercy*. New York: Pantheon, 1986.

Duus, Masayo. *Nihon no inbo* [Japan's conspiracy]. Tokyo: Bungei Shunju, 1991.

———. *Unlikely Liberators: The Men of the 100th and 442nd.* Translated by Peter Duus. Honolulu: University of Hawaii Press, 1987.

Ethnic Studies Oral History Project and United Okinawan Association. *Uchinanchu: A History of Okinawans in Hawaii.* Honolulu: Ethnic Studies Oral History Project and United Okinawan Association, 1981.

Falk, Stanley, and Warren Tsuneishi. *American Patriots.* Washington, DC: Japanese American Veterans Association of Washington, D.C., 1995.

"Fifteenth New Americans Conference, July 15–21, 1941." Program. Honolulu, 1941.

Finkelstein, Barbara, Anne Imamura, and Joseph Tobin, eds. *Transcending Stereotypes: Japanese Culture and Education.* Yarmouth, Maine: Intercultural Press, 1991.

Foner, Eric. *The Story of American Freedom.* New York: Norton, 1998.

Foster, Nelson, ed. *Punahou: The History and Promise of a School of the Islands.* Honolulu: Punahou School, 1991.

Frisch, Michael. *A Shared Authority: Essays on the Craft and Meaning of Oral and Public History.* Albany: State University of New York Press, 1990.

Fuchs, Lawrence H. *Hawaii Pono: A Social History.* New York: Harcourt, Brace and World, 1961.

Fugita, Stephen, and David O'Brien. *Japanese American Ethnicity: The Persistence of Community.* Seattle: University of Washington Press, 1991.

Gill, Stephen. "Epistemology, Ontology, and the 'Italian School,'" in *Gramsci, Historical Materialism, and International Relations,* ed. Stephen Gill. Cambridge: Cambridge University Press, 1993.

Girdner, Audrie, and Anne Loftis. *The Great Betrayal.* London: Macmillan, 1969.

Glenn, Evelyn Nakano. *Issei, Nisei, Warbride: Three Generations of Japanese American Women in Domestic Service.* Philadelphia: Temple University Press, 1986.

Gluck, Carol. *Japan's Modern Myths: Ideology in the Late Meiji Period.* Princeton: Princeton University Press, 1985.

Gordon, Michael. "Suspects in Paradise: Looking for Japanese 'Subversives' in the Territory of Hawaii, 1939–1945." MA thesis, University of Iowa, 1983.

Grodzin, Martin. *Americans Betrayed: Politics and the Japanese Evacuation.* Chicago: University of Chicago Press, 1949.

Hall, Dale. "Fritz Hart and the Honolulu Symphony." *Hawaiian Journal of History* 29 (1995).

Hane, Mikiso. *Peasants, Rebels, and Outcastes: The Underside of Modern Japan.* New York: Pantheon, 1982.

Harrington, Joseph. *Yankee Samurai: The Secret Role of Nisei in America's Pacific Victory.* Detroit: Pettigrew Enterprises, 1979.

Hayashi, Brian. *"For the Sake of Our Japanese Brethren": Assimilation, Nationalism, and Protestantism Among the Japanese of Los Angeles, 1895–1942.* Stanford: Stanford University Press, 1995.

Hazama, Dorothy, and Jane Komeiji. *Okage Sama De: The Japanese in Hawai`i, 1885–1985.* Honolulu: Bess Press, 1986.

Hemphill, Betty, with Robert Hemphill. *The Crossroads Witness.* Honolulu: Church of the Crossroads, 1988.

Hirano, Yukie, and Yasunobu Kesaji. "Notes on Juvenile Delinquency in War-time Honolulu." *Social Process in Hawaii* 8 (November 1943), 77–81.

Holmes, T. Michael. *The Specter of Communism in Hawaii.* Honolulu: University of Hawaii Press, 1994.

Hosokawa, Bill. *JACL in Quest of Justice: The History of the Japanese American Citizens League.* New York: Morrow, 1982.

———. *Nisei: The Quiet Americans.* New York: Morrow, 1969.

Hughes, Judith. "The Demise of the English Standard School System in Hawai`i." *Hawaiian Journal of History* 27 (1993).

Hunter, Louise H. *Buddhism in Hawaii: Its Impact on a Yankee Community.* Honolulu: University of Hawaii Press, 1971.

Ichihashi, Yamato. *Japanese in the United States.* Stanford: Stanford University Press, 1932. Reprint, New York: Arno Press and New York Times, 1969.

Ichioka, Yuji. *The Issei: The World of the First Generation Japanese Immigrants, 1885–1924.* New York: Free Press, 1988.

———. "Japanese Immigrant Nationalism: The Issei and the Sino-Japanese War, 1937–1941." *California History* 69, 3 (fall 1990): 260–275, 310–311.

Ige, Philip. "An Okinawan Nisei in Hawaii," in *Uchinanchu: A History of Okinawans in Hawaii.* Honolulu: University of Hawaii Ethnic Studies Program and United Okinawan Association, 1981, 149–160.

Inouye, Daniel. *Journey to Washington.* Englewood Cliffs, N.J.: Prentice-Hall, 1967.

Irokawa Daikichi. *The Culture of the Meiji Period.* Translated and edited by Marius Jansen. Princeton: Princeton University Press, 1985.

Irons, Peter. *Justice at War: The Story of the Japanese American Internment Cases.* New York: Oxford University Press, 1983.

Israel, Fred. "Military Justice in Hawaii, 1941–1946." *Pacific Historical Review* 36, 3 (1967).

Ito, Kazuo. *Issei: A History of Japanese Immigrants in North America.* Translated by Shinichiro Nakamura and Jean Gerard. Seattle: Executive Committee for Publication of *Issei*, 1973.

Ito, Leslie, ed. *Japanese Americans During World War II: A Selected, Annotated Bibliography of Materials Available at UCLA.* 2d ed., rev. and expanded. Los Angeles: UCLA Asian American Studies Center Reading Room/Library, 1997.

Iwata, Masakazu. *Planted in Good Soil: A History of the Issei in United States Agriculture.* 2 vols. New York: Peter Lang, 1992.

James, Thomas. *Exile Within: The Schooling of Japanese Americans, 1942–1945.* Cambridge, Mass.: Harvard University Press, 1987.

Jim, Dorothy, and Takiko Takiguchi. "Attitudes on Dating of Oriental Girls with Service Men." *Social Process in Hawaii* 8 (November 1943), 66–76.

Ka Leo O Hawaii [The voice of Hawai`i]. University of Hawaii student newspaper, April 25, 1946.

Kaneko, William. "Japanese Americans Evicted in World War II Hawai`i." Unpublished paper, Columbus School of Law, Catholic University, 1995.

Kashima, Tetsuden, ed. *Personal Justice Denied: The Legacy Continues.* San Francisco and Los Angeles: Civil Liberties Public Education Fund, 1998.

Kaulukukui, Thomas. "I Am a Volunteer." Fiction, privately printed. N.p., n.d. Author's possession.

Kawahara, Kimie, and Yuriko Hatanaka. "The Impact of War on an Immigrant Culture." *Social Process in Hawaii* 8 (November 1943), 36–44.

Kawakami, Barbara. *Japanese Immigrant Clothing*. Honolulu: University of Hawaii Press, 1993.

Kelly, William. *Deference and Defiance in Nineteenth-Century Japan*. Princeton: Princeton University Press, 1985.

Kendis, Kaoru Oguri. *A Matter of Comfort: Ethnic Maintenance and Ethnic Style Among Third-Generation Japanese Americans*. New York: AMS Press, 1989.

Kennedy, Paul. *The Rise and Fall of the Great Powers: Economic Change and Military Conflict from 1500 to 2000*. London: Fontana Press, 1989.

Kent, Noel. *Hawaii: Islands Under the Influence*. Honolulu: University of Hawaii Press, 1993.

Ketelaar, James. *Of Heretics and Martyrs in Meiji Japan: Buddhism and Its Persecution*. Princeton: Princeton University Press, 1990.

Kihara, Ryukichi. *Hawai Nipponjinshi* [A history of the Japanese in Hawaii]. Tokyo: Anseisha, 1936.

Kimura, Yukiko. *Issei: Japanese Immigrants in Hawaii*. Honolulu: University of Hawaii Press, 1988.

———. "Rumor Among the Japanese." *Social Process in Hawaii* 9 (May 1947), 84–92.

———. "Some Effects of the War Situation upon the Alien Japanese in Hawaii." *Social Process in Hawaii* 8 (November 1943), 18–28.

Kitagawa, Daisuke. *Issei and Nisei: The Internment Years*. New York: Seabury Press, 1967.

Kitano, Harry. *Generations and Identity: The Japanese Americans*. Needham Heights, Mass.: Ginn Press, 1993.

Knaefler, Tomi Kaizawa. *Our House Divided: Seven Japanese American Families in World War II*. Honolulu: University of Hawaii Press, 1991.

Kodama Masaaki. *Nihon iminshi kenkyu josetsu* [Introduction to research on Japanese emigrants]. Hiroshima: Keisui Sha, 1991.

Koistinen, Paul. "Toward a Warfare State: Militarization in America During the Period of the World Wars," in *The Militarization of the Western World*, ed. John Gillis. New Brunswick, N.J.: Rutgers University Press, 1989.

Kojo Munesaka, ed. *Jyapanizu-Amerikan* [Japanese Americans]. Kyoto: Minerva Press, 1985.

Kotani, Roland. *The Japanese in Hawaii: A Century of Struggle*. Honolulu: Hawaii Hochi, 1985.

LaViolette, Forrest. *Americans of Japanese Ancestry: A Study of Assimilation in the American Community*. Toronto: Canadian Institute of International Affairs, 1946.

Lee, Joann. *Asian Americans*. New York: New Press, 1991.

Lim, Shirley Geok-lin, and Amy Ling. *Reading the Literatures of Asian America*. Philadelphia: Temple University Press, 1992.

Lincicome, Mark. *Principle, Praxis, and the Politics of Educational Reform in Meiji Japan*. Honolulu: University of Hawaii Press, 1995.

Lind, Andrew. *Hawaii's Japanese: An Experiment in Democracy*. Princeton: Princeton University Press, 1946.

———. *The Japanese in Hawaii Under War Conditions*. Honolulu: American Council, Institute of Pacific Relations, 1943.

———. "A Preliminary Study of Civilian Morale." *Social Process in Hawaii* 8 (November 1943), 5–17.

Lum, Steve. "Herbert Isonaga: Portrait of a VVV 'Gang' Member." *Hawaii Herald* 13, 4 (February 21, 1992).

Makino Biography Committee. *Life of Kinzaburo Makino*. Honolulu: Michie Makino, 1965.

Maretzki, Thomas, and John McDermott. "The Caucasians," in *People and Cultures of Hawaii: A Psychocultural Profile*, ed. John McDermott, Wen-Shing Tseng, and Thomas Maretzki. Honolulu: John Burns School of Medicine and University of Hawaii Press, 1980.

Marsella, Anthony. "Counseling and Psychotherapy with Japanese Americans: Cross-Cultural Considerations." *American Journal of Orthopsychiatry* 63, 2 (April 1993).

Marumoto, Masaji. "Masaji Marumoto: A Personal History, Part 1: The Formative Years." *East-West Photo Journal* (Winter 1980).

Matsuo, Dorothy. *Boyhood to War: History and Anecdotes of the 442nd Regimental Combat Team*. Honolulu: Mutual, 1992.

Mayfield, Captain I. H., Office of Naval Intelligence. "Report on the Morale Section." Unpublished report. N.p., n.d., Shigeo Yoshida Collection. Author's possession.

McGregor, Davianna. "Kupa`a I Ka `Aina: Persistence on the Land." Ph.D. diss., University of Hawaii, 1989.

Menton, Linda. "World War II and the Civilian Community." *Oral History Recorder* 11, 2 (summer 1994).

Military Intelligence Service Veterans of Honolulu. *Secret Valor: M.I.S. Personnel, World War II Pacific Theater, Pre-Pearl Harbor to Sept. 8, 1951*. Honolulu: MIS Veterans Club of Hawaii, 1993.

Mitchell, Richard. *Political Bribery in Japan*. Honolulu: University of Hawaii Press, 1996.

Montero, Darrell. *Japanese Americans: Changing Patterns of Ethnic Affiliation over Three Generations*. Boulder, Colo.: Westview Press, 1980.

Morley, Marielouise. "A Study of the 1924 Graduates of Punahou." M.A. thesis, University of Hawaii, 1936.

Moskos, Charles C., Jr. *The American Enlisted Man: The Rank and File in Today's Military*. New York: Russell Sage Foundation, 1970.

Murakami Yumiko. *Yero Fuesu* [Yellow Face: Images of Asians in Hollywood]. Tokyo: Asahi Shimbun Sha, 1993.

Murayama, Milton. *All I Asking for Is My Body*. Honolulu: University of Hawaii Press, 1988.

Murphy, Thomas. *Ambassadors in Arms: The Story of Hawaii's 100th Battalion*. Honolulu: University of Hawaii Press, 1954.

Nagai, Michio. "Westernization and Japanization: The Early Meiji Transformation of Education," in *Tradition and Modernization in Japanese Culture*, ed. Donald Shively. Princeton: Princeton University Press, 1971.

Nagata, Donna. *Legacy of Injustice: Exploring the Cross-generational Impact of the Japanese-American Internment.* New York: Plenum Press, 1993.

Naka, Harry Maxwell. "The Naturalization of the Japanese Veterans of the American World War Forces." M.A. thesis, University of California, Berkeley, 1939.

Nakahata, Yutaka. *The Varsity Victory Volunteers.* Pamphlet. Honolulu: Tongg, 1943.

Nakahata, Yutaka, and Ralph Toyota. "Varsity Victory Volunteers: A Social Movement." *Social Process in Hawaii* 8 (November 1943), 29–35.

Nakano, Jiro. *Kona Echo: A Biography of Dr. Harvey Saburo Hayashi.* Kona, Hawaii: Kona Historical Society, 1990.

―――. *Samurai Missionary: The Reverend Shiro Sokabe.* Honolulu: Hawaii Conference of the United Church of Christ, 1984.

Nakano, Mei. *Japanese American Women: Three Generations, 1890–1990.* Berkeley, Calif.: Mina Press, 1990.

Nihon imin hachijunensai saiten iinkai. *Burajiru Nihon imin hachijunenshi* [Eighty years of Japanese immigrants in Brazil].San Paolo: Brazil Japan Culture Association, 1991.

Niiya, Brian, ed. *Japanese American History: An A-to-Z Reference from 1868 to the Present.* Los Angeles: Japanese American National Museum, 1993.

Nomura, Gail. "The Debate over the Role of Nisei in Prewar Hawaii: The New Americans Conference, 1927–1941." *Journal of Ethnic Studies* 15, 1 (spring 1987), 95–116.

Nordyke, Eleanor. *The Peopling of Hawai`i*, 2d ed. Honolulu: University of Hawaii, 1989.

Oba, Ronald, ed. *The Men of Company F, 442nd RCT.* Honolulu: Privately printed, 1989.

O'Brien, Robert W. *The College Nisei.* Palo Alto, Calif.: Pacific Books, 1949.

Odo, Franklin. "The Rise and Fall of the Nisei." *Hawaii Herald*, six parts (August–November 1984).

Odo, Franklin, and Kazuko Sinoto. *A Pictorial History of the Japanese in Hawai`i, 1885–1924.* Honolulu: Bishop Museum Press, 1985.

Odo, Franklin, and Harry Urata. "Hole Hole Bushi: Songs of Hawaii's Japanese Immigrants." *Mana* 6, 1 (1981).

Ogawa, Dennis. *Kodomo no tame ni: For the Sake of the Children.* Honolulu: University of Hawaii Press, 1978.

Oguro, Richard S. *Senpai Gumi: Story of the First Group of AJAs from Hawaii and American Concentration Camps to Attend Army Language School at Camp Savage, Minnesota.* Honolulu: privately printed, 1982.

Okihiro, Gary. *Cane Fires: The Anti-Japanese Movement in Hawaii, 1865–1945.* Philadelphia: Temple University Press, 1991.

Okinawa Club of America. *History of the Okinawans in North America.* Los Angeles: UCLA Asian American Studies Center and the Okinawa Club of America, 1988.

Omi, Michael, and Howard Winant. *Racial Formation in the United States: From the 1960s to the 1990s.* New York: Routledge, 1994.

100th Infantry Battalion Publication Committee. *Remembrances*. Honolulu: Privately printed, 1992.

Otani, Matsujiro. *Waga hito to narishi ashiato—hachijunen no kaiko* [Becoming a man—memoirs of my eighty years]. Honolulu: M. Otani, 1971.

Ozawa, Gijo, ed. *Hawai Nihongo Gakko Kyoikushi* [History of Japanese language school education in Hawaii]. Honolulu: Hawaii Kyoiku Kai, 1972.

Park, Robert. *Race and Culture*. New York: Free Press, 1950.

Passin, Herbert. *Society and Education in Japan*. New York: Teachers College Press, 1965.

Portes, Alejandro, and Min Zhou. "The New Second Generation: Segmented Assimilation and Its Variants." *The Annals of the American Academy of Political and Social Science* 530 (November 1993).

Puette, William. *The Hilo Massacre*. Honolulu: University of Hawaii Center for Labor Education and Research, 1988.

Pyle, Kenneth. *The New Generation in Meiji Japan: Problems of Cultural Identity, 1885–1895*. Stanford: Stanford University Press, 1969.

Rademaker, John A. *These Are Americans: The Japanese Americans in Hawaii in World War II*. Palo Alto, Calif.: Pacific Books, 1951.

Reinecke, John. *A Man Must Stand Up: The Autobiography of a Gentle Activist*, ed. Alice Beechert and Edward Beechert. Honolulu: Biographical Research Center, 1993.

"Report of the President." *University of Hawai`i Ka Leo*, June 30, 1942.

Robinson, Greg. *By Order of the President: FDR and the Internment of Japanese Americans*. Cambridge: Harvard University Press, 2001.

Ryu, Charles. "1.5 Generation," in *Asian Americans*, ed. Joanne Lee. New York: New Press, 1991.

Said, Edward. *Orientalism*. New York: Vintage Books, 1979.

Saiki, Patsy Sumie. *Ganbare!: An Example of Japanese Spirit*. Honolulu, Kisaku, 1983.

———. *Japanese Women in Hawaii*. Honolulu: Kisaku, 1985.

Sakamoto, Edward. *Hawaii No Ka Oi: The Kamiya Family Trilogy*. Honolulu: University of Hawaii Press, 1995.

Sakamoto, Lawrence. *Hawaii's Own: Picture Story of 442nd Regiment, 100th Battalion and Interpreters*. Honolulu: Privately printed, n.d. (c. 1946).

San Juan, E., Jr. *Racial Formations/Critical Transformations: Articulations of Power in Ethnic and Racial Studies in the United States*. Atlantic Highlands, N.J.: Humanities Press, 1992.

Sato, Charlene. *The Syntax of Conversation in Interlanguage Development*. Tubingen: G. Marr, 1990.

Scheiber, Harry, and Jane Scheiber. "Constitutional Liberty in World War II: Army Rule and Martial Law in Hawaii, 1941–1946." *Western Legal History* 3 (1990).

Shibutani, Tamotsu. *The Derelicts of Company K: A Sociological Study of Demoralization*. Berkeley: University of California Press, 1978.

Shirey, Orville. *Americans: The Story of the 442nd Combat Team*. Washington, D.C.: Infantry Journal Press, 1946.

Shirota, Jon. *Lucky Come Hawaii*. New York: Bantam Books, 1965; reprint, Honolulu: Bess Press, 1988.

———. *Pineapple White*. Los Angeles: Ohara Publications, 1972.

Shivers, Robert. "Cooperation of the Various Racial Groups with Each Other and with the Constituted Authorities Before and After December 7, 1941." Honolulu: Emergency Service Committee, 1946.

Shoho, Alan. "Americanization Through Public Education of Japanese-Americans in Hawaii, 1930–1941." Ph.D. diss., Arizona State University, 1990.

Slackman, Michael. "The Orange Race: George S. Patton, Jr.'s Japanese-American Hostage Plan." *Biography* 7, 1 (1984).

———. *Target: Pearl Harbor*. Honolulu: University of Hawaii Press, 1990.

Smith, Bradford. *Americans from Japan*. Philadelphia: Lippincott, 1948.

Smith, Douglas. "Martial Law in Hawaii Revisited: A Battle Against an Abuse of Military Discretion." Ph.D. diss., University of Hawaii, 1989.

Soga, Yasutaro. *Gojunenkan no Hawai kaiko* [My fifty years in Hawaii]. Honolulu: Gojunenkan no Hawai Kaiko Publication Committee, 1953.

Stephan, John. *Hawaii Under the Rising Sun: Japan's Plans for Conquest After Pearl Harbor*. Honolulu: University of Hawaii Press, 1984.

Stueber, Ralph. "Hawaii: A Case Study in Development Education, 1778–1960." Ph.D. diss., University of Wisconsin, 1964.

Sumida, Stephen. *And the View from the Shore: Literary Traditions of Hawai`i*. Seattle: University of Washington Press, 1991.

Suzuki, Toshiaki. "Mauishima no koko to nihonjin" [Maui's high schools and the Japanese], in *Hawai Nikkeishakai no bunka to sono henyo* [Culture change in Hawaii's Japanese American society], ed. Okita Yukuji. Kyoto: Nakamichiya, 1998.

Tachiki, Amy. "The Emergence of Yellow Power in America," in *Roots: An Asian American Reader*, ed. Amy Tachiki, Eddie Wong, and Franklin Odo, with Buck Wong. Los Angeles: UCLA Asian American Studies Center, 1971.

Takagi-Kitayama, Mariko. "Moral Education in Pre-war Japanese Language Schools in Hawaii." M.A. thesis, University of Hawaii, 1987.

———. *Nikkei Amerikajin no Nihonkan* [Japan as viewed by Japanese Americans]. Tokyo: Tankosha, 1992.

Takaki, Ron. *Pau Hana: Plantation Life and Labor in Hawaii, 1835–1920*. Honolulu: University of Hawaii Press, 1983.

———. *Strangers from a Different Shore: A History of Asian Americans*. Boston: Little, Brown, 1989.

Takehashi, Jen. *Nisei/Sansei: Shifting Japanese American Identities and Politics*. Philadelphia: Temple University Press, 1997

Tamashiro, John Gerald. "The Japanese in Hawaii and on the Mainland During World War II as Discussed in the Editorial Pages of the *Honolulu Advertiser* and the *Honolulu Star Bulletin*." MA thesis, University of Hawai`i at Manoa, 1972.

Tamura, Eileen. *Americanization, Acculturation, and Ethnic Identity: The Nisei Generation in Hawaii*. Urbana: University of Illinois Press, 1994.

———. "The Americanization Campaign and the Assimilation of the Nisei in Hawaii, 1920 to 1940." Ph.D. diss., University of Hawaii, 1990.

Tamura, Linda. *The Hood River Issei: An Oral History of Japanese Settlers in Oregon's Hood River Valley*. Urbana: University of Illinois Press, 1993.

Tamura Norio and Shigehiko Shiramizu, eds. *Beikoku shoki no Nihongo shinbun* [Japanese-language newspapers in the United States in the immigration era]. Tokyo: Keiso shobo, 1986.

Tanaka, Chester. *Go for Broke: A Pictorial History of the Japanese American 100th Infantry Battalion and the 442nd Regimental Combat Team.* Richmond, Calif.: Go For Broke, 1982.

tenBroek, Jacobus, Edward Barnhart, and Floyd Matson. *Prejudice, War, and the Constitution: Causes and Consequences of the Evacuation of the Japanese Americans in World War II.* Berkeley: University of California Press, 1970.

Teodoro, Luis V., Jr. *Out of the Struggle: The Filipino in Hawaii.* Honolulu: University Press of Hawaii, 1981.

Terry, John. *With Hawaii's AJA Boys at Camp Shelby, Mississippi.* Honolulu: Honolulu Star-Bulletin, n.d.

Torigoe Hiroyuki. *Okinawa Hawai imin: issei no kiroku* [Hawaii's Okinawan immigrants: Recollections from the immigrants]. Tokyo: Chuo Koron Sha, 1988.

Torok, John Hayakawa. "Finding the Me in LitCrit Theory: Thoughts on Language Acquisition and Loss." *University of Miami Law Review* 53, 4 (July 1999).

"Tripuru-V gojisshunen: jumbi ni tabo no Takekawa-san" [50th anniversary of the Triple V: Mr. Takekawa busy with preparations]. No author. *The Hawaii Hochi,* February 6, 1992, 5.

Tsukano, John. *Bridge of Love.* Honolulu: Hawaii Hosts, 1985.

Ueunten, Wesley. "Maintenance of the Okinawan Community in Hawaii." M.A. thesis, University of Hawaii, 1989.

U.S. Army. MTOUSA. I and E Section. *The Story of the 442nd Combat Team.* Pamphlet. N.p., n.d.

Varley, Paul. *Warriors of Japan: As Portrayed in the War Tales.* Honolulu: University of Hawaii Press, 1994.

Wakukawa, Ernest. *A History of the Japanese People in Hawaii.* Honolulu: Toyo Shoin, 1938.

Walls, Thomas. *The Japanese Texans.* San Antonio: University of Texas Institute of Texan Cultures, 1987.

Walthall, Anne. *Peasant Uprisings in Japan: A Critical Anthology of Peasant Histories.* Chicago: University of Chicago Press, 1991.

Weglyn, Michi. *Years of Infamy: The Untold Story of America's Concentration Camps.* New York: Morrow, 1976.

Westbrook, Robert. "Christopher Lasch, Historian and Social Critic." *Perspectives* 32, 4 (April 1994).

Williams, Shirley JoAnn. "The Educational Theory and Philosophy of Miles Edwood Cary: Implications for Democracy in a Global Civic Culture." Ph.D. diss., Northern Illinois University, 1991.

Wilson, Robert, and Hosokawa, Bill. *East to America: A History of the Japanese in the United States.* New York: Morrow, 1980.

Wu, William. *The Yellow Peril: Chinese Americans in American Fiction, 1850–1940.* Hamden, Colo.: Archon Books, 1982.

Yoneda, Karl. *Ganbatte: Sixty-Year Struggle of a Kibei Worker.* Los Angeles: UCLA Asian American Studies Center, 1983.

Yoo, David. *Growing Up Nisei: Race, Generation, and Culture Among Japanese Americans of California, 1924–49*. Urbana: University of Illinois Press, 2000.

Yoshida, Ryo. "Kaishushugi to Hawai Nihonjin shakai [Hawaii's Japanese Society and Christian Missions]." *Kirisutokyo shakai mondai kenkyu* [Christianity and social issues research] 36 (1986).

———. "Kirisutokyo to Hawai Nikkeijin no Amerikaka [Christianization and Americanization of Hawaii's Japanese Americans]." *Shukyo kenkyu* [Research on religions] 296 (June 1993).

Yoshii, Michael. "The Sansei Experience." *Nichibei josei jyanaru: US-Japan Women's Journal* 2 (1992).

Zalburg, Sanford. *A Spark Is Struck! Jack Hall and the ILWU in Hawaii*. Honolulu: University of Hawaii Press, 1979.

Acknowledgments

This book would not have been possible without the support and assistance of many individuals, including archivists and librarians at the University of Hawaii's Hamilton Library, the Hawaii State Archives, and the National Archives and Records Administration. In the beginning, support was provided by former members of the Varsity Victory Volunteers, led by Ralph Yempuku. The inspiration, however, came from Hung Wai Ching, who practically bullied them into creating a modest oral history project, for which I was retained. Many VVV members responded to an initial written survey and nearly thirty graciously agreed to several hours each of audio or video taping. Chris Conybeare and Joy Chong, then of KHET-TV in Honolulu, provided crews and equipment for the video sessions. I am happy to acknowledge the special contributions of one VVV member, Ted Tsukiyama, whose own research initiatives and persistence were significant. And I am especially grateful for the group's willingness to wait nearly two decades for publication, providing me with complete access to their resources while imposing no intellectual or interpretive restrictions, even when they reviewed sections with which they certainly disagreed. In this project, a number of individuals, including many volunteers, assisted with thousands of hours spent searching for documents and tediously transcribing oral history tapes. Among the most helpful: Pam Funai, Roland Kotani, Tracy Kubota, Dean Minakami, Jennifer Kim Mikami, Mark Santoki, Rachel Odo, Jonathan Odo, David Odo, Enid Odo, Noriko Sanefuji, Joseph Yi, and Tom Nakanishi. However, Rene Yoshida was uniquely helpful and I am especially grateful to her for her unflagging spirit and enormous contributions.

Finally, Temple University Press's editor-in-chief, Janet Francendese, deserves commendation for her professional shepherding of a bulky manuscript into a publishable book. In the process, comments by Michael Omi and Lane Hirabayashi were invaluable. I am grateful to the Smithsonian Institution's leadership, including former provost Dennis O'Connor, Secretary Lawrence Small, and Undersecretary for American Museums and National Programs Sheila Burke, for supporting my writing efforts.

Index